Coughlin is one of the principal contributors to the rapidly developing probabilistic voting literature, which is at the leading edge of public-choice theory. In this book, he both reviews the existing literature and presents new results that unify and extend his own contributions and other developments in the literature. The book will be important reading for scholars and students of public-choice theory in economics, political science, and other fields.

Probabilistic voting theory

Probabilistic voting theory

PETER J. COUGHLIN
University of Maryland at College Park

CAMBRIDGE UNIVERSITY PRESS
Cambridge, New York, Melbourne, Madrid, Cape Town, Singapore, São Paulo

Cambridge University Press
The Edinburgh Building, Cambridge CB2 8RU, UK

Published in the United States of America by Cambridge University Press, New York

www.cambridge.org
Information on this title: www.cambridge.org/9780521360524

© Cambridge University Press 1992

First published 1992
This digitally printed version 2008

A catalogue record for this publication is available from the British Library

Library of Congress Cataloguing in Publication data
Coughlin, Peter J.
Probabilistic voting theory / Peter J. Coughlin.
    p.   cm.
Includes bibliographical references and index.
ISBN 0–521–36052–8
1. Social choice – Mathematical models.   2. Voting – Mathematical
    models.   I. Title.
    HB846.8.C68   1991
    324′.01–dc20   91–14319
                                                        CIP

ISBN 978-0-521-36052-4 hardback
ISBN 978-0-521-06329-6 paperback

to
Kathy and Charlie

Contents

Contents

Acknowledgments

The material in this book was developed over the last decade and has, during that period, been greatly improved by helpful comments and suggestions provided by Kenneth Arrow, Otto Davis, Arthur Denzau, James Enelow, Allan Feldman, Jerry Green, Melvin Hinich, Anne Krueger, John Ledyard, R. Duncan Luce, Steven Matthews, Martin McGuire, Dennis Mueller, Peter Murrell, Shmuel Nitzan, Wallace Oates, Mancur Olson, Peter Ordeshook, Thomas Palfrey, Thomas Romer, Howard Rosenthal, Amartya Sen, Steven Slutsky, and anonymous referees. This book has also been greatly improved by the editorial guidance provided by Colin Day and Emily Loose.

I gratefully acknowledge the financial assistance provided by National Science Foundation Grant No. SES–8409352 and the College of Behavioral and Social Sciences at the University of Maryland, which made it possible for me to prepare a draft version of this book. A second version was prepared during 1987–8 while I was a Fellow at the Center for Advanced Study in the Behavioral Sciences at Stanford University. I gratefully acknowledge the financial assistance provided by the Center (with support from National Science Foundation Grant No. BNS–8700864 and the Alfred P. Sloan Foundation) and the Graduate Research Board at the University of Maryland during that period. Last, but not least, I also gratefully acknowledge the financial assistance provided by a University of Maryland Sabbatical for the Fall 1989 semester, which made it possible for me to prepare the final version of this book.

CHAPTER 1

Majority rule and models of elections

Democratic nations settle the question of who should hold various public offices by holding elections. The answers provided by the electoral process strongly influence the public policies that the people in these countries end up living with. As a consequence, public-choice scholars are interested in the *implications* of the choices that voters can be expected to make *for* the choices made by elected public officials and by politicians who would like to get elected. Among the most important choices of elected officials and office-seeking politicians that are affected by what they believe about the voters' choice behavior are the positions that they choose on the leading policy questions of the day and the way in which they allocate their campaign resources. The first includes their positions on taxes and budget deficits, the appropriate levels of government expenditure on alternative programs, various possible pieces of social legislation, and many other matters. The second includes how they spend their campaign funds[1] and how they spend their time during the campaign.[2] As a consequence, various public-choice scholars have developed and analyzed models of the relation between the choices that public officials and office-seeking politicians make and the choices that they expect the voters to make.

Because of the nature of the institutions that are being studied and the variety of problems that have been addressed, the research on these models has (not surprisingly) been multidisciplinary, drawing on concepts and methods from economics, mathematics, political science, psychology, statistics, and other fields. The models of elections that have been developed in the resulting literature can be used (along with other models, methods, and approaches) to learn both about elections themselves and about phenomena that are affected by elections. For instance, these models can potentially be used to address such questions as: In a

---

[1] For example, how much money should be spent on various media alternatives, how much on travel, and how much on opinion polls.

[2] For example, how much time should be spent in various locations and on alternative ways of potentially communicating with the voters.

situation for which campaign resources have already been allocated, are there "best" policy positions that can be taken? If so, what are they? In a situation for which policy positions have already been selected, is there a best allocation of campaign resources? If so, what is it? More broadly, the models can also be used to answer questions about the nature of the public policies we can expect in a society that uses elections to select its leading public officials. The answers are especially useful for economists, political scientists, and other scholars who want to know what policy positions and campaign resource allocations can be expected from rational public officials and office seekers. The answers may also be useful to campaign strategists. Even more broadly, knowledge about elections is important in understanding any phenomenon that is affected by government policies, because such knowledge makes it possible for us to understand what policies can be expected to occur.

Existing research on majority-rule and election models has provided researchers from various disciplines with insights into concerns in their separate fields. In addition, this research has also been used to address questions that transcend traditional disciplinary lines. Because so many government decisions are affected by the outcomes of elections (as has been dramatically illustrated recently by the changes in policies that followed the elections of President Reagan in the United States, Prime Minister Thatcher in the United Kingdom, and President Mitterrand in France), research on election models is clearly of great importance.

The bulk of this chapter is devoted to surveying the work that has been done on majority rule in general and on elections in particular. Section 1.1 reviews the most important results about majority rule that have been turned up so far. Section 1.2 identifies some alternative inferences that can be drawn from what has been learned about the so-called majority-rule relation (i.e., the binary relation, "beats or ties," on the set of possible alternatives which is such that, for any pair of alternatives, one alternative beats or ties the other if and only if at least as many voters prefer it as prefer the other).

Section 1.3 reviews some of the models public-choice scholars have developed that move beyond the majority-rule relation, in particular by incorporating additional features that are present in political institutions that use majority rule. The primary focus is on the initial public-choice models of elections that went beyond the majority-rule relation and what has been learned about the possibility of having a pure strategy equilibrium for the two candidates in the models. Section 1.4 covers work on alternative election models that have varying voter perceptions of candidate positions, and/or more than two candidates, and also discusses some alternative equilibrium concepts for election models that have been studied.

Section 1.5 concentrates on important studies that have incorporated abstentions and/or candidate uncertainty about voter behavior into election models. Section 1.6 discusses the distinction that this literature has drawn between "deterministic" and "probabilistic" voting models, that is, between models in which candidates are certain about what the voters' choices will be (and, hence, have deterministic expectations about these choices) and those models in which they are uncertain about what the voters' choices will be (and, hence, have probabilistic expectations).

The broad foundations developed in this and the next six sections – based on Coughlin (1990b) – serve to place the ensuing chapters in the context of related work. The discussion in these sections also provides a rationale for studying models in which candidates are uncertain about voters' choices. In addition, this survey of the existing literature on majority rule and election models makes it easier for me to compare and contrast the material in Chapters 2–6 with related research at the appropriate points in those chapters. Section 1.7 provides a preview of subsequent chapters.

1.1 Majority rule

Majority rule is used to determine who will hold certain public offices and for other purposes such as to determine which of the propositions that appear on a ballot will become law, to decide which bills will receive the approval of a legislative body, and to provide the basis for committee decisions. The properties of majority rule (as an abstract decision rule) have been carefully studied by a number of public-choice scholars. From their results, various inferences have been drawn about the public policies that can be expected when government officials are selected by elections, the propositions that will become law through referenda, the bills that will be passed by legislatures, the decisions that will emerge from committees, and a variety of other outcomes of (borrowing the catch-all phrase used by Inman, 1987) "majority-rule processes."

One of the best-known properties of majority rule is the fact that there may be no alternative that is unbeaten under the rule, implying that no matter what alternative may be selected, it is possible to replace it with a different alternative by a majority vote. Thus, it may very well be the case that any alternative that is initially chosen can be beaten by some other alternative, that the replacement selected can (in turn) be replaced by another, and so on ad infinitum. Under some circumstances, the sequence generated in this way can be (using a term from Pattanaik, 1971, p. 11) an "infinitely descending chain" with distinct alternatives (i.e., is such that no two elements in the infinitely descending chain are the same). For instance, consider the amount that the government is going to spend on a publicly produced good and assume that each voter always prefers a larger to a smaller amount. Then any infinite sequence of increasing amounts has the property described. It is also well known that a sequence of alternatives in which each alternative is preferred (by a majority of voters) to the one that immediately precedes it can, alternatively, be an infinitely descending chain that contains a cycle; that is, it contains a subsequence that returns us to an earlier alternative. As a consequence, the absence of an unbeaten alternative need not involve an infinite chain of distinct alternatives. What's more, when this is the case, majority voting can potentially lead us through the same subsequence of alternatives over and over again. Thus, the set of alternatives does not have to be infinite for majority rule to generate an infinitely descending chain. Indeed, as is widely known, whenever there are three or more alternatives, voter preferences can be specified that lead to a "voting cycle" under majority rule. The fact that such voting cycles can occur with majority rule was first recognized by de Condorcet (1785). The pervasiveness of the possibility of voting cycles was first recognized by Arrow (1950, 1951, 1952, 1963, 1967), who established that the possibility of a voting cycle is, in fact, endemic to all social-choice rules that have the key axiomatic features possessed by majority rule.[3]

The best-known result about the conditions under which there will be an unbeaten alternative under majority rule is, unquestionably, the *median-voter theorem*. This result is for models in which the set of possible alternatives can be meaningfully lined up from left to right (e.g., only one policy variable is being considered, and that policy variable is unidimensional). It specifically applies when the voters have *single-peaked* preferences on the set of possible alternatives – that is, every

---

[3] For further information about Arrow's theorem and discussions of more recent work on abstract collective choice rules, the reader is referred to Sen (1970, 1977a,b, 1986, 1987), Pattanaik (1971), Plott (1971, 1976), Taylor (1971, 1975), Von Weizsacker (1972), Arrow (1973a,b, 1977a,b, 1987), Fishburn (1973, 1983, 1987), Riker and Ordeshook (1973), Mayston (1974), Shepsle (1974), Brams (1975, 1985), Kramer and Hertzberg (1975), Mueller (1976, 1979, 1989a), Frey (1978), Frohlich and Oppenheimer (1978), Kelly (1978, 1988), van den Doel (1978), Abrams (1980), Feldman (1980, 1987), Aranson (1981), Riker (1982a,b), Moulin (1983, 1988), Lockwood (1984), d'Aspremont (1985), Schofield (1985), Arrow and Raynaud (1986), Ordeshook (1986), Schwartz (1986), Inman (1987), Storcken (1987), Ingberman and Inman (1988), and Laffont (1988).

voter has a best possible alternative, and as one moves away from this alternative (either to the left or to the right) the voter is less and less pleased about the options encountered. This condition can be stated in the terminology of microeconomics: "Each voter is assumed to have a strictly convex preference ordering ... over [a continuum of] alternatives (strict convexity and unidimensionality are equivalent to [the] single-peakedness condition)" (Kramer, 1977a, p. 691). The median-voter theorem says that when the circumstances just described hold, an alternative cannot be beaten by any other alternative (under majority rule) if and only if it is the most preferred choice for the (or a) so-called median voter – a voter whose most preferred alternative is such that half or more of (all of) the voters' most preferred points are the same as or to the left of it and half or more of (all of) the voters' ideal points are the same as or to the right of it.

Under the premise of the median-voter theorem, a median voter necessarily exists. Therefore, the theorem implies the existence of an unbeaten alternative and simultaneously identifies its location. The fact that the median-voter theorem holds in simple models of elections was first recognized by Hotelling (1929). Black (1948, 1958) subsequently established that it is a general property of majority rule. Arrow (1951, 1963) contributed to this line of research by providing a more general formulation of single-peakedness (as a property on "triples," i.e., on the three-element subsets of the set of alternatives). Later work by Downs (1957a,b) provided the first detailed application of the median-voter result to an explicit election model. Barr and Davis (1966) and Davis and Haines (1966) carried out the first significant applications of the resulting election model to policy issues (viz., the expenditures of municipalities and other local governments).[4]

Subsequent work by Inada (1964, 1969), Ward (1965), Sen (1966, 1969a), Sen and Pattanaik (1969), Pattanaik (1968, 1970a,b), Pattanaik and Sengupta (1974), and others succeeded in identifying conditions other than single-peakedness that are sufficient to ensure that there is

---

[4] For further discussion of single-peakedness and/or the median voter theorem, see Davis, Hinich, and Ordeshook (1970), Sen (1970, 1986, 1987), Ostrom and Ostrom (1971), Taylor (1971, 1975), Fishburn (1973), Mayston (1974), Shepsle (1974), Kramer and Hertzberg (1975), Mueller (1976, 1979, 1989a), Kramer (1977a), Frey (1978), Frohlich and Oppenheimer (1978), Brams (1978, 1985), Kelly (1978, 1988), van den Doel (1978), Abrams (1980), Feldman (1980), Riker (1982a,b), Austen-Smith (1983), Moulin (1983, 1988), Enelow and Hinich (1984a), Romer and Rosenthal (1984), Oates (1985), Arrow and Raynaud (1986), Blumel, Pethig, and von dem Hagen (1986), Calvert (1986), Ordeshook (1986), Schwartz (1986), Inman (1987), Miller (1987), Coughlin (1988), Ingberman and Inman (1988), and Laffont (1988).

an unbeaten alternative under majority rule in each possible finite set of feasible alternatives. Mueller (1979) described this research as follows: "[This] stream of literature has attempted to establish equilibrium conditions by placing restrictions on the preferences of the individuals voting as the single-peakedness condition does (pp. 42–3)." Mueller then observed that the reason these conditions have not been widely applied in policy analyses is because "the conditions proposed often do not lend themselves to straightforward interpretations, as single-peakedness does, nor is it clear that they can be plausibly assumed to exist in reality" (p. 43).

It has been shown that for finite sets of alternatives the likelihood of there being no unbeaten alternative under majority rule "increases rapidly as the number of alternatives voted upon increases" (Berg, 1988, p. 508). (For a detailed list of the references in which this result has been established, see Gehrlein, 1983.) Related work has also established that when the set of alternatives is infinite and has two or more dimensions (because, for instance, two or more policy variables are being considered) and when it is assumed that individuals have strictly quasiconcave utility functions, the conditions for the existence of unbeaten alternatives derived by Inada and others almost always fail to be satisfied and, what is more, there is almost never an unbeaten alternative (under majority rule). The fact that there may be no equilibrium alternative under these circumstances was illustrated by suggestive examples in Black and Newing (1951) and Black (1958). The fact that the absence of a majority-rule equilibrium is pervasive when the alternative set is multidimensional was subsequently established (at various levels of generality and with various assumptions about voters' preferences) by Plott (1967), Kramer (1973), Sloss (1973), Rubenstein (1979), Schofield (1978a,b, 1980, 1983a,b, 1984a,b, 1986, 1989), and Cox (1984a).

The only models with multidimensional alternative sets in which majority-rule equilibria have been shown to exist are those for which one of the following holds: (i) the distribution of voters' preferences satisfies stringent symmetry assumptions (see the analyses, at varying levels of generality and with differing assumptions about voters' preferences, in Plott 1967; Tullock, 1967a,b; Davis, DeGroot, and Hinich, 1972; Wendell and Thorson, 1974; Hoyer and Mayer, 1975; McKelvey and Wendell, 1976; Grandmont, 1978; Matthews, 1979, 1980; McKelvey, Ordeshook, and Ungar, 1980; and Enelow and Hinich, 1983a); (ii) a closely related convexity assumption is satisfied (see Arrow, 1969; Greenberg, 1979, p. 633; or Schofield, 1985, sect. 7.3); or (iii) the majority-rule comparisons are restricted to pairs of alternatives that differ in only one dimension, and for which suitable assumptions about the voters' preferences are made (see Black and Newing, 1951, sect. III; Kadane, 1972; and Slutsky, 1977).[5]

A number of authors have analyzed the continuity properties of functions from n-tuples of voters' preferences to social preferences that are defined by majority rule and related decision rules. Denzau and Parks (1975) established that the voters' preferences being single-peaked can assure continuity. In Denzau and Parks (1983), they showed how this conclusion can be used to derive the existence of a voting-market equilibrium when there is one public dimension. Slutsky (1977) showed that majority rule has continuity properties when comparisons are restricted to pairs that differ in only one dimension and used this to prove an equilibrium-existence result for a voting-market model with many public goods. Coughlin and Lin (1981) established that majority rule also has continuity properties when, alternatively, Grandmont's (1978) conditions are satisfied. Chichilnisky (1982) and Ferejohn and Packel (1983) demonstrated that majority rule and many related rules do not assure continuity when the alternatives and the voters' preferences are unrestricted. Ferejohn and Packel (1983) also established that there are, nonetheless, still some (other) decision procedures that are continuous and "also satisfy a variety of attractive properties" (p. 72). Chichilnisky and Heal (1983) subsequently found "conditions [that] are necessary for the existence of satisfactory majority rules" (p. 70). As they pointed out, the conditions can be thought of as being "a generalization of conditions such as single peakedness . . . which were earlier shown to be sufficient for majority voting to be an acceptable rule" (p. 68).

One final (very significant) property of majority rule that arises when cycles exist is that for any pair of alternatives, it is (usually) possible to find a sequence (in which each alternative in the sequence is preferred, by a majority of voters, to the one that immediately precedes it) that starts at the first alternative in the pair and ends at the second. This tells us that when cycles exist, it is (usually) possible for majority-rule sequences to wander all over the set of alternatives. This particular result has been developed (again, at various levels of generality and with

---

[5] For further discussion of the topics discussed in this and the two preceding paragraphs, see Sen (1970, 1986, 1987), Pattanaik (1971), Plott (1971; 1976, p. 531), Taylor (1971, 1975), Arrow (1973b), Fishburn (1973), Riker and Ordeshook (1973), Mayston (1974), Shepsle (1974), Mueller (1976, 1979, 1989a), Kramer (1977a), Frey (1978), Frohlich and Oppenheimer (1978), Kelly (1978), van den Doel (1978), Abrams (1980), Feldman (1980), Riker (1982a,b), Austen-Smith (1983), Moulin (1983), Enelow and Hinich (1984a), Schofield (1985), Arrow and Raynaud (1986), Blumel, Pethig, and von dem Hagen (1986), Calvert (1986), Schwartz (1986), Shepsle (1986a), Inman (1987), Miller (1987), Storcken (1987), and Ingberman and Inman (1988).

various assumptions about voters' preferences) by McKelvey (1976, 1979), Bell (1978, 1981), Schofield (1978a,b, 1980, 1983a,b, 1984a, 1986, 1989), Cohen (1979), and Cohen and Matthews (1980).[6]

1.2   Inferences from the properties of the majority-rule relation

The results described so far have led some public-choice scholars to conclude that, except in (empirically) rare cases, no matter what policies are initially selected, they are (almost always) replaced by alternative policies in the next election or the next time the deciding legislature or committee considers them. This broad inference has been best summarized by Riker (1982a, p. 19) in his assertion that "what we have learned is simply this: Disequilibrium, or the potential that the status quo be upset, is the characteristic feature of politics."

A natural next step from this broad inference is to conclude that the political institutions currently used in the world's democratic nations lead to outcomes that are a "muck," and we should, therefore, replace them with institutions in which there are more stability and more reason to believe that we have desirable public policies (rather than fleeting policies that happen to have risen to the top of the heap for the moment). People who have a predisposition for socialism can see this conclusion as a rationale for reducing the role of elected officials in favor of (appointed) central-planning boards. Others with a libertarian bent can see this conclusion as an argument for drastically restricting the scope of decisions made by government, and still others can see this conclusion as a justification for tossing out democratic institutions altogether and replacing them with dictators. Nevertheless, though it is tempting to jump from results about the majority-rule relation to the conclusion that existing political institutions should be scrapped, that leap may be rather heroic. Specifically, for reasons that are given later, the inference that disequilibrium is the characteristic feature of politics may be unjustified.

The basis for using results about majority rule to make broad inferences about the policies that are adopted in democratic nations is the view that committees and elections (and other related institutions) can be studied with one model – in particular, that they can be studied

---

[6] For further discussion of this particular property of majority rule, see Mueller (1979, 1989a), Riker (1982a,b), Austen-Smith (1983), Enelow and Hinich (1984a), Romer and Rosenthal (1984), Schofield (1985), Calvert (1986), Ordeshook (1986), Shepsle (1986a), Inman (1987), Miller (1987), Ingberman and Inman (1988), and Kelly (1988).

simultaneously by studying the majority-rule relation. This view can be traced back to Black (1948, 1958) and Arrow (1950, 1951, 1963). In fact, expressed in a succinct form, it provided the title for Black's classic volume *The Theory of Committees and Elections*. This approach has the advantage that, quoting Arrow (1951, p. 87), "the same system may be given several different interpretations, permitting a considerable saving of time." However, it also has a serious disadvantage: The model that has been the focus of study has abstracted most of the details of committees, elections, legislatures, referenda, and the other institutions that use majority rule.

The widespread acceptance of the approach of concentrating on a highly abstract model of majority rule resulted, no doubt, from two things. The first is the fact that many details vary as we move from any single majority-rule institution to any other. The second is the widespread recognition that because of these differences the addition (to the basic model of majority rule that has been used) of some of the other important features of any one of the institutions that involve majority rule would make the resulting model more relevant for analyses of that particular institution but also would (simultaneously) tend to make the resulting model less relevant for the other institutions that involve majority rule. Of course, using a highly abstract model of majority rule would be advantageous if the theorems that had been derived using just the majority-rule relation matched the empirical observations that have been made about institutions in which majority rule plays a role. Indeed, if this occurred, Occam's razor would be an arguement for not considering any additional institutional details because they would make the resulting analyses unnecessarily complicated.

Such circumstances, however, have not arisen. Rather, as Tullock (1981a) has argued, in contrast to what has been shown to be true about the majority-rule relation, government policies do not tend to change quickly or to wander all over the set of possible policies. As a consequence, it is hard to resist the alternative inference that the primary contribution of recent work on the majority-rule relation is as a reductio ad absurdum that tells us to reconsider the basic model to see how it should be modified so that theory and empirical observations match up. As Romer and Rosenthal (1984) put it: "The public policies of most mature democracies, however, do not reflect the kind of indeterminate cycling that this instability suggests. Instead, we see that public policies and the composition of governments are fairly stable. . . . This . . . suggests that research on voting models should focus on the aspects of the political process . . . that somehow 'solve' the instability problem" (p. 466).

1.3   Beyond the majority-rule relation

Some public-choice scholars have responded to the negative (or pessimistic) results that have been derived about the majority-rule relation by turning their attention to variations on majority rule. A good example of this response is the work that has been done on voting rules that require a "special majority" (exceeding $\frac{1}{2}$), which can be a function of the number of voters in a society, and of either the number of alternatives or the dimensionality of the policy space, and which can assure the existence of an equilibrium.[7] Greenberg (1979), in particular, has made it clear that this line of research has been (at least partially) stimulated by the negative results that have been established about majority rule, describing it as "work to forward our knowledge of what majority rules do give rise to an equilibrium" (p. 627). Another example of a variation on majority rule is using lotteries to make pairwise choices, basing the probabilities on the votes for the alternatives under consideration (e.g., see Coleman, 1973; Fishburn and Gehrlein, 1977; and Mueller, 1989b, 1990). Mueller (1989b) has emphasized that this second line of research is also (at least partially) stimulated by the negative results in the literature on majority rule, arguing that "when cycles exist under the simple majority rule, the probabilistic majority rule provides a fair mechanism for ending the cycle" (p. 165).

Those scholars who have not focused on variations on majority rule have modified the underlying model, modified the equilibrium concept, or both. Because these approaches allow majority rule to be kept intact, they seem to have the most potential for giving us insights about existing democratic institutions (rather than insights about the world that we might live in if our political institutions were changed).

Some steps have already been taken toward the development of separate analyses for the separate institutions that involve majority rule. Significantly, some of these analyses have both more empirically relevant details and implications that are more compatible with empirical observations. Important research in this vein is the work on referenda and legislative decision making (with more institutional details than are contained in the majority-rule relation) by Romer and Rosenthal (1978, 1979), Shepsle (1979a,b), Denzau and Mackay (1981, 1983), Shepsle and Weingast (1981a,b, 1984, 1987), Enelow and Hinich (1983b,c),

---

[7] For example, see Ferejohn and Grether (1974), Kramer (1977b, pt. 6), Schofield (1978a,b, 1980, 1983a,b, 1984a,b, 1985, 1986, 1989), Blair (1979), Greenberg (1979), Nakamura (1979), Slutsky (1979), Matthews (1980, 1982), Coughlin (1981, 1986a), Greenberg and Weber (1985a), Strnad (1985), McKelvey and Schofield (1986, 1987), Schwartz (1986), and Caplin and Nalebuff (1988; 1991).

Ingberman (1985), Riker (1986), Austen-Smith and Riker (1987), Baron and Ferejohn (1987), Calvert (1987), Austen-Smith and Banks (1988, 1989), Austen-Smith (1989), Matthews (1989), Weingast (1989), and Harrington (in press). Saliently, some of these models have "legislative equilibria" even when policy spaces are multidimensional. This work has already provided a number of new insights into the nature of the outcomes from referenda and legislative processes and has been applied to public school budgets (Romer and Rosenthal, 1978, 1979), congressional oversight of federal agencies (Weingast and Moran, 1983), pork barrel legislation (Shepsle and Weingast, 1981b; Weingast, Shepsle, and Johnsen, 1981), the gatekeeping and monopoly power of committees (Denzau and Mackay, 1983), public projects that can potentially fill a gap that is due to a market failure (Shepsle and Weingast, 1984), the power of legislative committees (Shepsle and Weingast, 1987), and other matters.[8]

The remaining material in this survey concentrates on the research on models of elections that go beyond the majority-rule relation. Before launching into a discussion of what has been done, I want to make it clear that the public-choice literature on elections has primarily been concerned with the decisions that are made by political candidates (i.e., elected officials and potential elected officials who are concerned about the impact of their decisions on the next election). What is more, the primary focus in this literature has been on elections with two candidates (e.g., a current office holder and a challenger, or two nominees for an office that is being vacated by someone else).

Throughout the public-choice literature on elections, two basic assumptions about the decisions by candidates are usually included. The first is that decisions made by political candidates are chosen carefully and strategically (for the purpose of accomplishing a particular objective), that is, the candidates' behavior is "purposive." The second assumption is that the goals that political candidates have in mind when making decisions are usually to maximize the amount they expect to win by, to minimize the amount they expect to lose by, or to maximize the probability of winning. The first two of these objectives are directly captured by the assumption that candidates want to maximize their expected plurality. Stigler (1972, pp. 98–100), Kramer (1977b, p. 317), and others have argued that this objective will be adopted because the

---

[8] For further discussion of this line of research, see Enelow and Hinich (1984a), Romer and Rosenthal (1984), Ordeshook (1986), Shepsle (1986a,b), Inman (1987), Ingberman and Inman (1988), Mueller (1989a), Riker (1990), and Rosenthal (1990). For a discussion of how this literature is related to other studies of institutions in public choice, see Ostrom (1986).

effectiveness of a party (or candidates) in office will be an increasing function of its (or their) margin of victory. For a discussion of other goals for candidates that can also potentially lead to expected plurality maximization, see Kingdon (1966, p. 112).

The third objective of condidates can easily differ from maximizing their expected plurality when the electorate is small (e.g., see the examples in Kramer, 1966, pp. 140–1; Wittman, 1975, pp. 47–8; or Denzau and Kats, 1977, p. 233). However, when the electorate is large enough to be thought of as a random sample or when suitable symmetry assumptions are satisfied, the objectives of maximizing the probability of winning and maximizing expected plurality are equivalent.[9] Hence, in most of the public-choice literature, it is assumed that each candidate wants to maximize his expected plurality.

It should be noted that some of the references in the public-choice literature are concerned with the relation between candidate (or party) positions and the amount of support within political parties (see Coleman, 1971, 1972; Aranson and Ordeshook, 1972; Aldrich, 1983a,b,c; Hinich, 1983; and Aldrich and McGinnis, 1989). An alternative concern worth mention (viz., because it is useful for understanding the behavior of strongly ideological candidates) is with candidates who maximize a utility function that captures tradeoffs between the candidate's policy preferences and either the probability of winning or the expected plurality (see Wittman, 1973, 1975, 1977, 1983, 1990; Brams, 1978, sects. 4.3–4.5, and 1985, sects. 8.3–8.5; Cox, 1984b; Hansson and Stuart, 1984; Calvert, 1985; Ginsburgh, Pestieau, and Thisse, 1987; Mitchell, 1987; Enelow, 1990; and Lindbeck and Weibull, 1990).[10]

Because the outcome of an election almost always depends on the policy proposals and/or the campaign resource allocations of both candidates – rather than, say, just on the policy proposals and/or campaign resource allocation of just one of them – the two basic assumptions mentioned earlier lead to the conclusion that the decisions of two candidates should be studied simultaneously. As a consequence, when the decision of one particular candidate is analyzed, the comparable

---

[9] For the specific assumptions that lead to this conclusion, see (i) Hinich (1977, pp. 212–13), where an argument based on a central limit theorem is used; (ii) Ledyard (1984, pp. 20–1) and Calvert (1986, pp. 39–40), where arguments based on a law of large numbers are used; (iii) Ordeshook (1986, sect. 4.5), where the assumption that the distribution of plurality is symmetric around its mean is used; and (iv) Aranson, Hinich, and Ordeshook (1973, 1974), Samuelson (1984), and Lindbeck and Weibull (1987), where variations on these approaches have been used.

[10] For discussions of still other objectives that political candidates may have, see Aranson, Hinich, and Ordeshook (1973, 1974), Fenno (1973, chap. 1), and Fiorina (1974, especially pp. 31–8). For an analysis of election goals in two-party competitions for legislative seats, see Snyder (1989).

decision of the other candidate in the race is also usually taken into account. This is generally done by modeling their decisions as a two-person noncooperative game.

The first significant election models in the public-choice literature were the unidimensional model suggested by Hotelling (1929) and developed by Downs (1957a,b) and the multidimensional models developed by Davis and Hinich (1966, 1967, 1968, 1971, 1972). These models include the key institutional features mentioned earlier and retain (directly analogous) versions of the following four assumptions, which have been of central importance in analyses of the majority-rule relation: (i) each voter has a preference ordering on the set of alternatives, (ii) each voter casts a ballot for a particular alternative with probability 1 unless this voter is indifferent between the two alternatives that are available, (iii) each person who votes for a particular alternative with probability 1 does so for the alternative (in the set of two available alternatives) that this person prefers, and (iv) the preferences of the voters are common knowledge. In particular, in the election models referred to earlier, only two (superficial) alterations are made: In (ii), the "two alternatives that are available" becomes the "two alternatives proposed by the candidates"; in (iii), "alternative (in the set of two available alternatives)" becomes "candidate who has proposed the alternative." As a consequence, the substance of the four assumptions remains the same.

Because the assumptions in the first election models are essentially the same as the assumptions used in specifying the majority-rule relation, "the results concerning the instability of majority rule equilibria in a multidimensional world carry over directly for [this] literature on representative democracy. The problem a candidate faces in choosing a multidimensional platform ... is ... the same as finding an issue, in multidimensional space, which defeats all other issues" (Mueller, 1979, p. 102). Hence, there are still almost always no "electoral equilibria," the exceptions being (again) the cases covered by the special symmetry conditions, convexity assumptions, or feasibility restrictions mentioned in the discussion of majority-rule equilibria in Section 1.1.[11]

---

[11] For further discussions of (i) the unidimensional Hotelling–Downs model and (ii) the multidimensional Davis–Hinich models and the restrictive conditions on the distribution of voters preferences that imply that these multidimensional models have electoral equilibria, the reader is referred to Davis et al. (1970), Plott (1971), Taylor (1971, 1975), Riker and Ordeshook (1973), Mayston (1974), Shepsle (1974), Kramer and Hertzberg (1975), Mueller (1976, 1979, 1989a), Ordeshook (1976, 1986), Kramer (1977a), Frey (1978), Frohlich and Oppenheimer (1978), van den Doel (1978), Abrams (1980), Aranson (1981), Austen-Smith (1983), Borooah and van der Ploeg (1983), Fishburn (1983), Enelow and Hinich (1984a), Calvert (1986), and Arrow (1990).

1.4   Some alternative election models and equilibrium concepts

A synthesis and extension of the election models developed by Downs (1957a,b) and Davis and Hinich (1966, 1967, 1968) was put forward by Hinich and Pollard (1981). In their model, they treated the single dimension in Downs's model as a "predictive dimension" and included "predictive maps" (which may vary from voter to voter) that go from candidate labels on the predictive dimension to a multidimensional policy space. Among other things, Hinich and Pollard's model allow voters' perceptions of candidates' policy positions to differ. They showed that the particular assumptions they made were sufficient to imply a median-voter result on the predictive dimension. In addition, they showed that in their model both incumbents and incremental policy changes are favored when there is a great deal of heterogeneity in the voters' perceptions of the candidates. Coughlin and Hinich (1984) subsequently derived conditions (on the voters' predictive maps) that are necessary and sufficient for the voters' preferences on the predictive dimension to be single-peaked.

Enelow and Hinich (1981) studied the implications of the voters' viewing the candidates' positions as random variables on the underlying evaluative dimension. They showed that when voters perceive the candidates' positions this way, each voter's ideal point is effectively shifted on the underlying dimension and that, as a consequence, the candidates' optimal strategies can also be shifted either toward or away from the center of the underlying dimension. In a further study of election models with varying voter perceptions, Enelow and Hinich (1982a) obtained additional results on the conditions that favor incumbents and the conditions that do not. Their results shed light on the importance of the expected policy difference between the candidates in determining who will win the election. They also extended their analysis to include multiple predictive dimensions. The models and results that have been mentioned in this and the preceding paragraph are summarized and illustrated in Enelow and Hinich (1984a). They are also careful to point out there (viz., on p. 59) that the general equilibrium existence results that have been developed for models with varying voter predictions are specifically for models with a single predictive dimension, and that when there are two or more predictive dimensions, the conditions required for an equilibrium to exist are analogous to those required by the pioneering multidimensional election models discussed in Section 1.3. For further discussion see Austen-Smith (1983), Calvert (1986), and Enelow and Hinich (1990).

In addition to the work by Enelow and Hinich (1981), a number of other analyses of election models with voter uncertainty should be mentioned: in particular, Shepsle (1972a,b); McKelvey and Richelson (1974); Coughlin (1976, 1977, 1980); McKelvey (1980); McKelvey and Ordeshook (1984, 1985a,b, 1986, 1987); Bernhardt and Ingberman (1985); Austen-Smith (1986); Bowden (1987, 1989); Ordeshook (1987); Collier, Ordeshook, and Williams (1989); and Ingberman (1989). Significantly, in these models also, electoral equilibria rarely exist when the policy space has two or more dimensions. It has even been shown that the introduction of voter uncertainty into a unidimensional model can cause equilibria to disappear (see McKelvey, 1980, pp. 391–2, and the earlier papers by Zeckhauser, 1969, Shepsle, 1970, 1972c, and Fishburn, 1972, on the properties of majority rule when the alternatives are lotteries).[12] It should also be mentioned that in addition to analyzing models in which voters make their choices by looking forward with predictions of what candidates will do in office, public-choice scholars have analyzed models in which voters make their choices by looking back to the parties' past performance in office (e.g., see Fair, 1978; Fiorina, 1981; Ferejohn, 1986; Ledyard, 1986; Slutsky, 1986; Collier et al., 1987; and Reed, 1990).

Other studies have analyzed election models that are similar to those discussed in Section 1.3, except that they do not assume that there are two (predetermined) candidates. In analyses of these models, a number of scholars have considered the implications of having a fixed number of candidates (exceeding two) in plurality and related voting systems (e.g., Downs, 1957a,b; Tullock, 1976b; Hinich and Ordeshook, 1970; Selten, 1971; Aranson, Hinich, and Ordeshook, 1973, 1974; Eaton and Lipsey, 1975; Mueller, 1976, 1979, 1989a; Austen-Smith, 1981, 1984a, 1986, 1987; Cox 1984c,d, 1985, 1987; Wittman 1984, 1987; Denzau, Kats, and Slutsky, 1985; Ordeshook 1986; Snyder 1989, 1990; de Palma, Hong, and Thisse, 1990; and Myerson and Weber, 1990). Alternatively, other scholars have considered the implications of having potential candidates who decide where to locate and/or whether or not to run on the basis of the strategic choices of the current candidates in plurality and related voting systems (e.g., Brams, 1978, 1985; Brams and Straffin 1982; Palfrey, 1984; Greenberg and Weber, 1985b; and Greenberg and Shepsle, 1987).

These articles have provided a number of insights into the following related topics: how strategies are affected by the presence of other candidates, the decisions that political parties have to make when they simultaneously field different candidates in different districts, how

---

[12] For further information about models with voter uncertainty, see Fishburn (1973), Riker and Ordeshook (1973), Shepsle (1974), Kramer and Hertzberg (1975), Ordeshook (1976, 1986), Kramer (1977a), Aranson (1981), Austen-Smith (1983), Enelow and Hinich (1984a), Calvert (1986), and McKelvey and Ordeshook (1990).

candidates are affected by the threat of entry by another (potential) candidate, when it is rational for an additional candidate to enter a race (and when it is not), the best locations when it is rational to enter, and the circumstances in which candidates will not select the median. Most of the analyses, however, have been limited to models with single-peakedness (as with the median-voter theorem) because neither the actual presence of additional candidates nor the threat of other candidates entering the race ameliorates the problem of equilibria rarely existing in multidimensional models with plurality rule (e.g., see Cox 1987, pp. 99–100). Indeed, even for models in which single-peakedness is assumed, Greenberg and Shepsle have shown that with some voting rules "the mere prospect of entry . . . may destroy equilibrium altogether" (1987, p. 526); and Denzau, Kats, and Slutsky (1985) have shown that there may be no equilibrium in models with a fixed number of candidates (exceeding two).[13]

The fact that the equilibrium existence problem is at least as problematic in multidimensional *multicandidate* models as it is in multidimensional *two-candidate* models has led Cox (1984c, 1987) and other scholars to explore alternative institutional arrangements in which equilibria do exist. But this type of approach (which focuses on "institutional perturbations"), it is important to emphasize, is (like the study of variations on majority rule) one that tells us a lot about what will happen if existing institutional arrangements based on majority rule are altered, but tells us little about majority-rule–based institutions themselves.

Enelow and Hinich (1984a) have observed that, in the *absence* of an electoral equilibrium for political parties, "the process of trying to second-guess the other party is hopeless. For each possible opponent, the other party should nominate a different candidate, but, given this candidate, the first party should nominate a different opponent" (p. 99). Thus, when there is no electoral equilibrium, there is no definite prediction about what will happen. This fact has led Ordeshook (1986) to argue that "it is unsatisfactory to conclude that pure-strategy equilibria need not exist in two-candidate elections, since this conclusion leaves us without any hypotheses about eventual strategies and outcomes for a wide class of situations" (p. 180).

Because of the dearth of pure-strategy equilibria in the multidimen-

---

[13] In particular, see the last column in table 1 on p. 105 in their article, which identifies when a multicandidate equilibrium will exist and when it will not. For further discussions of models that do not have two (predetermined) candidates, see Ordeshook (1986, sect. 4.11), Cox (1990), and Shepsle and Cohen (1990).

sional election models that were discussed in Section 1.3 and in the multidimensional versions of the models discussed in this section, some scholars have concluded that "analysis of electoral competition in the general and substantively important multidimensional case must be based either on explicit hypotheses about disequilibrium behavior . . . or else on a more general equilibrium concept, such as that involving the use of mixed strategies" (Kramer, 1978a, pp. 375–6). That is, they have concluded that only a fundamental reformulation of how the competitive process works, including giving up studying pure-strategy equilibria, will allow for meaningful predictive deductions about candidate decisions in multidimensional election models.

Research that has this view as its starting point includes (i) work that has replaced the concept of a pure-strategy equilibrium for the candidates with the concept of a mixed-strategy equilibrium (e.g., Shubik, 1968, 1971, 1984; Ordeshook, 1971; McKelvey and Ordeshook, 1976; Kramer, 1978a; and Lindbeck and Weibull, 1990); (ii) work studying dynamical trajectories of changing policies (e.g., Kramer, 1977b, pts. 1–5; and Wittman, 1977); (iii) work studying the so-called uncovered set (which contains a given alternative if and only if, for each other alternative, a majority prefers the given alternative to either the other alternative or a third alternative that the majority prefers to the other alternative) in the context of election models (e.g., McKelvey, 1986, sect. 6; Ordeshook, 1986, pp. 184 –7; Feld et al., 1988; and Mueller, 1989a, chap. 10); and (iv) work on undominated candidate strategies (e.g., Cox, 1989). These studies have revealed that under some circumstances, when analysis of the majority-rule relation has led to the conclusion that policies can wander anywhere, these alternative equilibrium concepts lead to the prediction that policies tend to be in an identifiable subset of the policy space.

As was pointed out in Section 1.3, the conclusions about the pioneering election models discussed in that section revealed that the features of elections that were included in those models are not sufficient in and of themselves to assure that an electoral equilibrium in pure strategies exists when the candidates have multidimensional strategy sets. The conclusions described in the preceding paragraphs have shown that including further considerations in analyses of elections can significantly alter the deductions that are made. Nevertheless, the additional modeling features and alternative equilibrium concepts discussed in this section still do not lead to deductions that match the empirical observation that candidate positions tend to be stable. The reason: Any candidate who confidently selects a policy position using one of these approaches will (usually) subsequently want to change his position because his opponent will (usually) be able to respond with a position that is preferred by a majority of voters.[14]

1.5   Abstentions and candidate uncertainty about voters' choices

Of course, many empirically relevant aspects of elections have been left out of the models just described. Therefore, those models do not exhaust the list of models of potential interest and, hence, do not exhaust the list of models that could potentially lead to the stability of public choices observed in the world. Two prominent aspects that have been left out of the models discussed and which have been incorporated into election models in similar ways are (i) the fact that some individuals are not indifferent between the policy proposals of the candidates but nonetheless abstain from voting, and (ii) the fact that candidates are usually uncertain about the choices that some (or even all) of the voters are going to make on election day. With reference to (ii) in particular, it should be noted that even though candidates pay large sums for polls, the best estimates are unreliable, and even though economists and political scientists have carried out statistical analyses of past voting decisions, there has consistently been a substantial amount of unexplained variation (e.g., see Kramer, 1971; Stigler, 1973; Fair, 1978; Fiorina, 1981; Enelow and Hinich 1984a, 1989a; Peltzman, 1987; and Alesina and Rosenthal, 1989).

Abstentions have been incorporated into election models in four ways. The first significant analyses with abstentions by nonindifferent voters (viz., Smithies, 1941; Downs, 1957a,b; Hinich and Ordeshook, 1969, 1970, 1971; and Ordeshook, 1970) assumed that the candidates are uncertain about whether any given voter will vote but are certain that *if* he votes, *then* he will vote for the candidate whose position gives him more utility. These models also included some of the symmetry conditions discussed in Section 1.1. The presence of these symmetry conditions made it possible for Hinich and Ordeshook to consider candidate uncertainty about who will vote and assess its impact on situations in which equilibria exist when there are no abstentions. At the same time, however, these conditions also severely limited the scope of their models.

The second way in which nonindifferent abstentions have been included in election models is by assuming that the candidates are certain about who will abstain from voting and who will receive the votes of

---

[14] For particularly telling critiques of the idea of using a mixed strategy equilibrium as the equilibrium concept for election models, see Riker and Ordeshook (1973, p. 340), Ordeshook (1976, pp. 292–3; 1986, pp. 180–2), and Aranson (1981, p. 285).

those who do vote (e.g., McKelvey, 1975, esp. defn. 2.2, p. 818). McKelvey specifically formulated this assumption by assigning to each voter one of three choices: abstain from voting, vote for candidate 1, or vote for candidate 2. As with the first category of abstention models, his approach led to new electoral equilibrium existence results only under assumptions that are even stronger than the (severe) symmetry assumptions that were made in the pioneering studies of multidimensional election models.[15] McKelvey's theorems include (as special cases) deterministic versions of some of the results in Hinich and Ordeshook (1969, 1971) and Ordeshook (1970).

The third approach to including abstentions by nonindifferent voters have been (as in the first approach) to assume that, for each voter, the candidates are uncertain about whether the person will vote and are certain about who will receive the vote if the person does vote; but the approach does not make symmetry assumptions about the distribution of voters' preferences (e.g., Hinich, Ledyard, and Ordeshook, 1972). The fourth approach (again) does not make any symmetry assumptions and (alternatively) assumes that, for each voter, the candidates are uncertain about whether he will vote and whom he will vote for if he does vote (e.g., Hinich, Ledyard, and Ordeshook (1973); Comaner, 1976; Denzau and Kats, 1977; Austen-Smith 1982, 1984b; Ledyard, 1981, 1984, 1989; Coughlin, 1982, 1983, 1984a, 1985; Enelow and Hinich 1984b; Coughlin and Palfrey, 1985; Morton 1987; and Coughlin and Howe, 1989).

Public-choice scholars have also analyzed models in which (i) all voters vote *or* all voters abstain only when indifferent and (ii) the candidates are uncertain about who will receive the vote of any given individual (e.g., Brams and Davis, 1973, 1974, 1982); Hinich, 1977, 1978; Kramer, 1978b; Lake, 1979; Coughlin and Nitzan, 1981a,b; Enelow and Hinich, 1982b, 1989b; Samuelson, 1984; Wittman 1983, 1984; Coughlin, 1979, 1984b,c, 1986b,c,d, 1990c, 1991; Ledyard 1986; Slutsky, 1986; Lindbeck and Weibull, 1987, 1990; Feldman and Lee, 1988; Glazer, Grofman, and Owen, 1989; and Coughlin, Mueller, and Murrell, 1990a,b). These election models also do not contain symmetry assumptions. As a consequence, they have the feature that the only factor that can affect whether an equilibrium exists is the candidates' uncertainty about for whom a given voter will vote.

---

[15] See, in particular, McKelvey's theorems, all of which start with the assumption of radial symmetry for the distribution of voter ideal points, as in Davis and Hinich (1966, 1967, 1968), and then have further assumptions added on before the existence of an equilibrium is established.

Significantly, the last two approaches to modeling abstentions and the work that has been solely concerned with uncertainty about whom voters will vote for have led to some important new results: (i) Equilibrium existence results have been derived for distributions of voter preferences that have no equilibria when voting is fully determined by the candidates' strategies; (ii) when there is an equilibrium with candidate certainty, candidate uncertainty can lead to the equilibrium being in a different location; and (iii) equilibria that occur when there is candidate uncertainty have been shown to have desirable normative characteristics. The fact that such results have been derived with each of these approaches has made it clear that candidate uncertainty about voter behavior (i.e., about whether a voter will vote and/or whom she will vote for, if she does vote) is of central importance for election models. In addition, the analogous results that have been obtained with these separate (albeit related) approaches have also made it clear that, even though nonindifferent abstentions were important for the first results along these lines (and for the specific conclusions that were derived from the models that included abstentions), uncertainty about voter behavior is, in and of itself, a potent feature for an election model. The main reason why this is important for elections, as distinguished from committees, is because the "layer" of representative government where the uncertainty comes in is an important feature of elections that is not present in committees. Indeed, it is the presence of this layer that opened up the possibility of obtaining results about election models that do not correspond to the main results about the majority-rule relation, described in Section 1.1.[16]

1.6   Deterministic versus probabilistic voting models

As the preceding sections have made clear, in a given election model the candidates may or may not have "best" decisions. What is more, as has been emphasized, the existence of such decisions hinges crucially on the candidates' beliefs about the relation between the decisions they make and the choices the voters will make on election day. These beliefs play such an important role because they (in turn) determine what

---

[16] For further discussion about election models with abstentions and/or candidate uncertainty about voter choices, the reader is referred to Davis et al. (1970), Riker and Ordeshook (1973), Mayston (1974), Shepsle (1974), Brams (1975, 1978), Mueller (1976, 1979, 1986, 1989a), Ordeshook (1976, 1986), Kramer (1977a), Frohlich and Oppenheimer (1978), van den Doel (1978), Abrams (1980), Aranson (1981), Austen-Smith (1983), Borooah and van der Ploeg (1983), Enelow and Hinich (1984a), Blumel, Pethig, and von dem Hagen (1986), Calvert (1986), and Coughlin (1986e, 1990a).

the candidates believe about the relation between their decisions and the outcome of the election.

Because of their importance to candidates' decisions, the candidates' beliefs about how their choices relate to the voters' choices provide a natural dividing line for the economic models of elections that have been developed. The first category consists of the election models in which each candidate believes that, once the decisions of both candidates in the race have been made and are known to them, they will be able to predict exactly what all of the (or all of the nonindifferent) voters' decisions will be; and they can do this no matter what strategies the two rivals may happen to choose. These models are called *deterministic voting models* because the candidates' decisions fully determine the choices they expect all (or all of the nonindifferent) voters to make. The second category consists of models in which, even after learning the decisions of both of the candidates in the race, both candidates are still uncertain about the voters' decisions. These election models are called *probabilistic voting models* (reflecting the fact that the candidates' uncertainty requires a probabilistic description of the voters' choice behavior).

Deterministic voting models are most appropriate for elections with candidates who are well informed about the voters and their preferences. These circumstances, of course, arise most frequently in elections in small organizations (such as small clubs or small communities). The probabilistic voting models, on the other hand, are most appropriate for elections in which candidates have incomplete information about voters' preferences and/or there are random factors that can potentially affect voters' decisions (such as the possibility of some of a nation's citizens being taken hostage abroad or the possibility of unemployment and/or inflation suddenly reaching an unacceptable level). These circumstances arise most frequently in elections in which a sizable number of voters and candidates rely on polls to learn about the voter decisions they can expect. Because most elections clearly fall in the second category, it seems appropriate to agree with Calvert (1986) that assuming "that candidates cannot perfectly predict the response of the electorate to their platforms is appealing for its realism" (p. 14), a conclusion that, as he points out, is in harmony with the "importance attached by traditional political scientists to the role of imperfect information in politics" (p. 54).[17]

---

[17] Ordeshook (1986) has also expressed a similar view, stating that "probabilistic assumptions are reasonable if we consider that candidates are rarely certain about voter preferences" (p. 179). Elaborating, he pointed out that "Information from public opinion surveys is not error-free and is best represented as statistical. Hence, if we want to design models that take cognizance of the kind of data that the candidates are likely to possess, probabilistic models seem more reasonable" (p. 179).

1.7   This book

The purpose of this section is to preview the remainder of this book. Chapters 2–7 provide an analysis of voting models that satisfy the binary version of the most famous axiom for probabilistic choice models, the *Luce axiom* (introduced by Luce, 1959). The binary version of this axiom is studied because of my assumption that there are two candidates (implying that each voter has a binary choice between them). The analysis is primarily concerned with the question "What is rational for candidates to do, given that they have probabilistic beliefs (about how voters will behave) that satisfy the binary Luce axiom?" Thus, I specifically derive results about candidate choices (rather than, say, deriving results about the choices that voters make or results about why individuals vote the way they do).

One of the most important premises of this book is my assumption that there is an inherent unpredictability about voters' choices in the minds of candidates. Given this uncertainty about voter behavior, the central questions that the book addresses are the following: Are there optimal strategies for the candidates, and if so, what is the nature of the strategies that candidates will choose in their headlong pursuit of votes? Specifically I unify and extend a series of earlier analyses of and discussions about electoral equilibria in probabilistic voting models that I wrote with Nitzan (Coughlin and Nitzan 1981a,b) and alone (Coughlin, 1986b,c,d,e). Because those earlier publications are unified and extended here, the ensuing chapters contain a mix of "some things old and some things new."

Chapter 2, which develops and analyzes an election model in which the candidates' strategies are redistributional reputations, is based on Coughlin (1986b, sects. 1–5) and the two examples in Coughlin (1986c) (variations on those examples appear here as Examples 2.1 and 2.2 in Section 2.6). Chapter 3, which analyzes the nature of the redistributional equilibria whose existence is assured by Theorem 2.2 in Chapter 2, is based on Coughlin (1986b, sects. 6–10). Chapters 2 and 3 also include some arguments and observations from Coughlin (1986d,e).

The ideas behind the material in Chapter 4 were originally developed in Coughlin and Nitzan (1981a), but in their present form they go well beyond that article. More specifically, the logical argument used to establish the welfare maximization result in Chapter 4 (viz., Theorem 4.2) is essentially the same as that used to establish the corresponding theorem in Coughlin and Nitzan (1981a). Here, however, the argument is used to establish a new theorem that extends the earlier welfare maximization result to many more cases. Among other extensions, the new theorem covers cases that do not have the particular link between voters' utilities and their selection probabilities that was assumed in Coughlin and Nitzan (1981a), and it applies to models with "groups." These groups, it should be noted, could be entities such as the states in the electoral college system or could be [as in Borooah and van der Ploeg (1983, chap. 6), Enelow and Hinich (1984a, sect. 5.2), Mueller and Murrell (1985), and Morton (1987)] latent interest groups – that is, groups that do not take explicit collective actions of the sort studied in Olson (1965, 1982) but still have a common interest. The new results in Chapter 4 also lead to Nash social welfare maximization as an important special case rather than (as in Coughlin and Nitzan, 1981a) the only case.

The equilibrium existence proofs in Chapters 2 and 4 boil down to showing that a "fundamental theorem" (Ordeshook 1986, p. 129) from game theory applies to the election models that have been specified in those chapters. An important part of accomplishing this is establishing that each candidate's payoff function is a concave function of his strategy (holding the other candidate's strategy fixed). The reason is that, once the other conditions in the game-theoretic result being used are established, this concavity property is "a sufficient condition for the existence of equilibria" (Ordeshook, 1986, p. 133), though, of course, it is "not a necessary condition" (Ordeshook, 1986, p. 133). The proofs of the location theorems in Chapters 2 and 4 similarly involve showing that the implicit social objective functions (which are implicitly maximized by the candidates' equilibrium strategies) are concave. This focus on concave candidate and social objectives is, of course, compatible with the approaches used in other areas because "in economic analysis . . . the basic objective functions economists use are concave" (Weintraub, 1982, p. 148).

Chapter 5 focuses on the possibility of identifying alternative assumptions about the groups' scaling functions (i.e., assumptions other than the assumption in Chapter 4 that each group's scaling function is concave), which imply concavity properties for the implicit social objective functions and for the candidates' payoff functions. At the end of the chapter, we use the results that have been derived to identify how far theorems about symmetric, concave-convex, two-person, zero-sum games can be pushed in establishing equilibrium results such as the ones in Chapters 2 and 4; we show that all such equilibria are maxima for an implicit social objective function; and an example illustrates the fact that when the concavity and convexity assumptions that have been used up to that point are dropped, there may be no electoral equilibrium (as defined in Chapter 2).

The analysis in Chapter 5 leads directly into Chapter 6, where the concept of electoral equilibrium used in Chapters 2–5 is weakened (viz., to also include directional and stationary pure strategy equilibria). The model of Chapter 6 is also more general than the models studied earlier in that it is no longer assumed that there is a finite set of groups, and it is no longer assumed that the set of possible locations for the candidates is convex. The theorems about directional and stationary electoral equilibria derived in Chapter 6 are generalizations of the results about such equilibria that were derived in Coughlin and Nitzan (1981b, sect. 3). The logic used to obtain these new theorems is similar to the logic previously used in that paper. The results obtained here are, however, more general, because the model that is analyzed has a probability measure on the set of groups, rather than just a probability distribution for which a density function exists. The theorems about stationary electoral equilibria in Chapter 6 are also used to obtain some further results about global electoral equilibria.

Chapter 7 closes the book with a general discussion of what has been learned about candidates' choices, concentrating on the broad significance of what has been established in the detailed analyses in Chapters 2–6.

CHAPTER 2

Income redistribution and electoral equilibria

Aranson and Ordeshook (1981) have pointed out that "the fragility of spatial models is apparent in the context of redistribution." Phrasing their observation more precisely, they go on to state that (by their nature) "elections entailing issues of pure redistribution are overwhelmingly characterized by disequilibrium." Mueller (1982) has also made the same basic observation, stating: "Political instability seems likely ... when issues or platforms are constrained to distributional issues." To make sure that no one mistakenly thinks that these observations have little relevance, Aranson and Ordeshook (1981) also stated that "most imaginable elections allocating private goods are precisely elections entailing redistributive issues," and Mueller (1982) added: "redistribution emerged as a major political issue in Europe during the 1970s just as it did in the United States in the 1960s." This view was stated even more emphatically in Mueller (1983), where he wrote: "Since the mid-1960s, redistribution has emerged in virtually every developed country as *the* political issue."

In Section 2.1, a model of elections is specified in which, when deciding for which candidate to vote, voters are primarily concerned with the redistributional consequences of the outcome of the election. In the formulation of this model it is explicitly acknowledged that, though voters may be primarily concerned with what their income (or the income of similar individuals) will be after the election, candidates usually do not directly communicate in detail just what income distribution can be expected if they are elected. Rather, candidates usually concentrate on communicating their positions on the issues of the day and let the voters infer what income distribution they can expect after the election. For instance, neither candidate in the 1984 U.S. presidential election spent the campaign declaring in his speeches what his election would mean for the income distribution in the United States during his time in office. Nonetheless, on election day, each candidate had a reputation for the type of income redistribution that could be expected subsequent to his election, and these reputations were sufficiently clear for voters to use them in deciding how to vote.

Reagan had the reputation of being the candidate of the upper-income voters in the United States; that is, it was widely believed that his re-election would lead to tax reforms and to reductions in social programs that would result in income being transferred from the people who were in the lower third of the income distribution to the people who were in the upper third of the distribution. Mondale's reputation, on the other hand, was that he was the candidate of the lower-income voters; that is, it was widely believed that his election would lead to tax increases and to increases in social programs that would result in income being transferred from the individuals who were in the upper third of the income distribution to the individuals who were in the lower third of the distribution.

Because there is an important distinction between a candidate's platform and redistributional reputation in actual elections, there is also a distinction between the policy space in which a candidate can take positions and the space that contains the redistributional reputations that the candidates can potentially acquire in the model developed. In specifying this model, we make it clear at the start, in Eq. (2.1), that if a candidate's choice of positions on policy issues is viewed as implicitly being the choice of the distribution of income in the economy that can be expected if that candidate is elected, then the set of possible strategies for the candidates is inherently spatial (and multidimensional).

After a discussion of the nature of the reputations being studied (Section 2.2), the implicit two-candidate game and the corresponding definition of an electoral equilibrium are made explicit (Section 2.3). We then focus on an assumption about candidates' beliefs about voters' choices that leads exactly to the conclusions that Aranson and Ordeshook (1981) and Mueller (1982) described in the quotations. The assumption is that a candidate (i) expects to get an individual's vote if the voter's utility function on the set of possible redistributional reputations assigns a higher utility to his reputation than to his rival's reputation; (ii) expects his rival to get the individual's vote if the voter's utility function on the set of possible redistributional reputations assigns a lower utility to his reputation than to his rival's reputation; and (iii) otherwise, views the voter's choice between the candidates as being equivalent to the toss of a fair coin. Phrased differently, the assumption is that (except for those voters who are indifferent between the candidates' reputations) the voters' choices between the candidates are determined fully and completely by the voters' preferences on the candidates' redistributional reputations. The conclusion that Aranson and Ordeshook (1981) and Mueller (1982) described shows up in Theorem 2.1 (Section 2.4), which states that when there are three or more groups of voters and no single group has half or more of the voters, there is no electoral equilibrium, no matter what special case of the model may arise.

Section 2.5 follows up on a suggestion made in McFadden (1976) by incorporating a qualitative response model of voters' choices into the election model. This consists of two parts. The first part is the assumption that unobservable factors enter into the determination of voters' choices. This is formulated by adding a random-error term to the voters' utility functions on the candidates' redistributional reputations. In the second part, it is assumed that the specific qualitative response model that the candidates use is the logit model. This section closes with an equilibrium existence theorem for the resulting model (Theorem 2.2). Section 2.6 gives some simple examples to illustrate Theorems 2.1 and 2.2. Section 2.7 provides some concluding remarks.

2.1   An election with redistributional reputations

This section provides a precise statement of what will be meant by the phrase "an election with redistributional reputations" in this and the next chapter. The convention of using this single phrase to refer simultaneously to all of the assumptions used has the advantage of making it possible to invoke all of them repeatedly without constantly relisting them. It also makes it easier to concentrate later on the implications of alternative assumptions about the candidates' expectations about the voters' choice behavior (which, as will be seen, are of crucial importance in determining whether there is an equilibrium for the candidates' strategies).

There are two candidates $c = 1, 2$ in the election. Both candidates believe that there is a set N of individuals who will vote in the election and that the individuals in N will cast all of the votes that will be cast in the election. This set N is the same for both candidates. The candidates partition the set N into a finite number of groups. Both candidates use the same partition $\theta = \{1, \ldots, m\}$ (where each group θ in the set Θ is nonempty). One example is the partition obtained when N is a finite set and each voter is a group. In this case, $m = |N|$. As an alternative example, the voters could be classified according to age and/or race and/or sex and/or geographic location and/or current income, as long as the number of categories remains finite and each individual i in the set N falls into exactly one category. In this case, of course, we usually have $m < |N|$. The candidates have a (common) subjective discrete probability distribution $g(\theta)$ on the sets in the partition Θ, where, for each $\theta \in \Theta$, the corresponding $g(\theta)$ is (what both candidates believe is) the proportion of N contained in θ. It is assumed that $g(\theta) > 0$, $\forall \theta \in \Theta$. The same basic approach to modeling an electorate has also recently been used in Borooah and Van der Ploeg (1983, chap. 6), Enelow and Hinich (1984a, chap. 5), Mueller and Murrell (1985), and Morton (1987).

A (fixed) total amount of income is available (denoted by Y); that is, the total income in the economy is independent of the choices made by the candidates. This implies that any income redistribution that takes place is a *zero-sum situation* (e.g., as defined in Riker, 1962). This assumption, of course, abstracts from reality because, for instance, alternative tax laws can provide alternative incentives for engaging in various types of productive activity and hence can lead to different levels of total income for the economy. Nevertheless, assuming that the total income is constant has the advantage that the focus is entirely on redistribution (the intended subject of study) instead of, say, on combinations of redistribution and growth or on tradeoffs between equality and total output (e.g., as discussed in Arrow, 1979).

The candidates believe that, on election day, each of them will have a redistributional reputation; that is, for each candidate there will be a particular income distribution that every voter believes will occur if that candidate is elected. Each candidate's redistributional reputation is, specifically, an element of the following set of (legally) possible income distributions:

$$S = \{(s_1, \ldots, s_m) \in E^m : \sum_{\theta \in \Theta} s_\theta = Y \quad \text{and} \quad s_\theta \geq k_\theta, \forall \ \theta \in \Theta\}$$

(2.1)

where s_θ denotes the total amount of income received by the individuals in group θ and k_θ is a parameter that specifies the smallest amount of (total) income that the individuals in θ can get. It is assumed that each k_θ has been determined by existing laws and that these laws are not at issue in the election, hence the treatment of the k_θ as parameters (rather than as choice variables). It is also assumed that $k_\theta > 0, \forall \ \theta \in \Theta$, and $\sum_{\theta \in \Theta} k_\theta > Y$. When each individual is a group the specification of S given in (2.1) corresponds to Kramer's (1973, p. 287) suggestion for modeling "distributional choices": "The ith component of the vector might represent the post-transfer income of the ith citizen." The same basic formulation of the distribution of income also appears in Arrow (1969, 1981), Sen (1969b, 1973, 1974), and elsewhere. For related approaches that emphasize the redistribution per se rather than the final distribution that results, see Intriligator (1979) and Lindbeck and Weibull (1987).

In models of electoral competition, it is (of course) common to include a set of possible positions on policy issues (e.g., see Davis and

Hinich, 1966, 1967, 1968; Riker and Ordeshook, 1973; McKelvey, 1975; or Coughlin and Nitzan, 1981a,b). In the model being specified here, the set of possible positions on policy issues (or the *policy space*) is separate from S. The link between the two is as follows: During the election campaign, the candidates take positions in the policy space and communicate them to the voters; because of the positions that they take, they acquire redistributional reputations in S. Both candidates believe that each of them can get any particular reputation in S that he wants by an appropriate choice of issue position. More specifically, each candidate believes that, for each of them, there is a mapping from his choice of issue positions into S that is "onto" (i.e., for each $s \in S$, there exists a choice of issue positions such that the candidate ends up with the redistributional reputation s). In what follows, there is no need to have notation for the policy space or these mappings or to make any further assumptions about them because, with the assumptions that have been made, the candidates' choices of issue positions can be viewed as implicit choices of redistributional reputations. As a consequence, we can look at S as the candidates' (common) strategy set, knowing that the choices they will want to make during the election campaign will then be any choices of issue positions that lead to optimal strategies in S.

A particular redistributional reputation for a given candidate c (i.e., a particular strategy for this candidate in S) is denoted by $\psi_c \in S$. Note that the definition of S implies that it is a compact, convex subset of E^m, whereas (on the other hand) the policy space need not have any of these regularity properties. In this regard, the approach is akin to the one used in proofs that apply the Brouwer fixed-point theorem (which, of course, is for compact, convex sets) to establish the *fixed-point property* for sets that are merely homeomorphic images of compact, convex sets (e.g., see Sydsaeter, 1981, p. 158).

It is well known that Bernoulli (1738, 1954) suggested that an individual's utility for an amount of money is the natural logarithm of the amount. Indeed, Arrow (1951, 1963) has called this the Bernoulli assumption (p. 39). Bernoulli's suggestion serves as the basis for the assumption that is made here concerning the candidates' beliefs about the voters' preferences on the set S of possible redistributional reputations. In particular, both candidates believe that, for each group $\theta \in \Theta$, each voter i in the group has the following utility function on S:

$$U_i(s) = U_\theta(s) \equiv \alpha_\theta + \beta_\theta \cdot \log(s_\theta) \qquad (2.2)$$

where α_θ and β_θ are scaling factors that satisfy $\alpha_\theta \in E^1$ and $0 < \beta_\theta \leq 1$, and $\log(s_\theta)$ denotes the natural logarithm of s_θ.

Mueller and Von Furstenberg (1971) used the same basic functional form (without the constant term) for the individuals in their model who are solely interested in maximizing their own group's income and are unconcerned about the distribution (of the income they do not get) among the other groups in the economy. Because (2.2) is being used for every group here, we are implicitly assuming that this "selfish" description applies to every group in Θ. With regard to this selfish (sole concern with own-group income) assumption, note that some public-choice scholars, including Tullock (1971, 1981b, 1983) and Lindbeck (1985), have argued that "the largest single source of income redistribution is simply the desire of the recipients to receive the money" (Tullock, 1981b, p. 906).

Also note that (2.2) is a very special functional form when we think of all the ways in which a utility function on S could be specified. In light of what has already been stated, however, it seems to be a particularly appropriate assumption for a model of an election in which each voter is solely concerned about the impact of a candidate's election on the income level of voters like himself. Therefore, because this is precisely the type of election that this model is being used to study, (2.2) is being assumed.

Each candidate wants to maximize expected plurality (i.e., when the other candidate's redistributional reputation is taken as given, a candidate wants either to maximize the expected margin of victory or to minimize the expected margin of loss). For a candidate to be able to decide which redistributional reputation (if any) will be the best one for maximizing expected plurality, it is important to have a clear idea of the connection between the redistributional reputations of the two candidates and the likelihood of getting any given individual's vote. This connection has the following property: For any given pair of redistributional reputations, $(\psi_1, \psi_2) \in S \times S$, the candidates both believe that the likelihood of getting an individual's vote is solely a function of the group θ that the individual is in. More specifically, for each $(\psi_1, \psi_2) \in S \times S$ and $i \in N$, both candidates have a common (subjective) conditional probability $P_i^1(\psi_1, \psi_2) = P_\theta^1(\psi_1, \psi_2)$ for the event "i will vote for candidate 1, if $c = 1$ chooses ψ_1 and $c = 2$ chooses ψ_2" (where θ is the group that includes individual i). From the assumptions stated in the second paragraph of this section, it follows that, for each $(\psi_1, \psi_2) \in S \times S$ and $i \in N$, both candidates also have a common (subjective) conditional probability $P_i^2(\psi_1, \psi_2) = P_\theta^2(\psi_1, \psi_2) = 1 - P_\theta^1(\psi_1, \psi_2)$ for the event "i will vote for candidate 2, if $c = 1$ chooses ψ_1 and $c = 2$ chooses ψ_2" (where θ is the group that includes individual i). To keep the interpretation clear it should be emphasized that, even though for any given $(\psi_1, \psi_2) \in S \times S$ these probabilities are the same for every individual in any group, they can vary from group to group. They can also vary as ψ_1 and ψ_2 are varied. Normalizing so that the total expected vote (EV) from all of the voters in N is 1, the expected vote for a given candidate c at a particular pair of redistributional reputations $(\psi_1, \psi_2) \in S \times S$ can be written as

$$EV^c(\psi_1, \psi_2) = \sum_{\theta \in \Theta} P_\theta^c(\psi_1, \psi_2) \cdot g(\theta) \qquad (2.3)$$

$EV^c : S \times S \to R$ will be called the "expected vote function" for candidate c. Using the same normalization again, we can write the expected plurality for a candidate c at a particular $(\psi_1, \psi_2) \in S \times S$ as

$$P\ell^c(\psi_1, \psi_2) = EV^c(\psi_1, \psi_2) - EV^k(\psi_1, \psi_2) \qquad (2.4)$$

where k is the index for the "other" candidate, that is, the unique element in the set $\{1, 2\} - \{c\}$. $P\ell^c : S \times S \to R$ will be called the "expected plurality function" for candidate c.

Finally, to avoid misinterpretations that could arise in the remaining sections, it is worth repeating the fact that the phrase "there is an election with redistributional reputations" is consistently used to mean that all of the assumptions listed earlier are satisfied.

2.2 The reputations being studied

In recent years, much work has been done on so-called reputational effects in industrial organization (IO) contexts (e.g., see Kreps and Wilson, 1982; Milgrom and Roberts, 1982; and the references they cite). Therefore, to avoid misinterpretation, this section describes in some detail the relation between and (perhaps more important) the differences between the "models ... that demonstrate the reputation effect" (as they were described in Kreps and Wilson, 1982, p. 276) and the model of elections with redistributional reputations that is studied in this chapter. To begin with, the word *reputation* is used here in the same way it is used in the IO literature, that is, with the following meaning, which is given in *Webster's New World Dictionary of the American Language*, College Ed., 1966:

> reputation ... 3. The estimation of doing something specified, having specified qualities, etc.: as, he has the *reputation* of being a thief.

In the IO literature, two aspects of a firm's reputation are explicitly recognized and considered. They are first, the "role of a firm's reputation" (Kreps and Wilson, 1982, p. 253) in achieving specific goals, and second, the way in which a firm will "maintain or acquire a reputation" (Kreps and Wilson, 1982, p. 275). The distinction between the process of acquiring a particular reputation and the consequences of having a particular reputation is illustrated in the following description: "by practicing predation the firm establishes a reputation as a predator. This reputation then leads potential entrants to anticipate that the incumbent firm will behave similarly if they should enter" (Milgrom and Roberts, 1982, p. 280). To keep the interpretation of the election model in this chapter clear, it is important to emphasize that the focus here is entirely on the consequences of the candidates' having particular redistributional reputations and the implications of these alternative consequences for the redistributional reputations that the candidates want to have. To keep things completely clear, it should also be pointed out that the specific consequences of the candidates' having particular redistributional reputations that the candidates care about are the consequences for their expected pluralities, and the specific implications of these consequences (of special concern in this chapter and Chapter 3) are whether or not the candidates will have equilibrium reputations and if so what the characteristics of these reputations will be.

The question of how the candidates would actually acquire their redistributional reputations is left in the background, by assuming that they can acquire whatever legally possible redistributional reputations they want by taking suitable positions on policy issues during the election campaign. Thus, the model has an explicit assumption about which reputations the candidates can acquire but does not include the process by which they would obtain these reputations. This formulation serves to focus subsequent analyses on the question: "Given that candidates can select any reputation in S, which reputations can we expect them to select?" Note that this is analogous to what we do in consumer theory when we answer the question "Given that a consumer can select any point in his budget set, which one can we expect him to select?" without worrying about the process by which the consumer will actually acquire the goods and services. The question of how political candidates acquire particular redistributional reputations is, of course, important. But, as the following pages will reveal, many interesting results can be derived when only the implications of candidates having particular reputations in the single-period or "static" model developed here are explicitly considered. The investigation of the dynamic processes of *reputation building* (Milgrom and Roberts, 1982, p. 287), *reputation revision* (p. 293), and the *evolution of reputations* (p. 295) in electoral politics is, therefore, left for future research that is carried out with sequential models. Models that should prove to be especially useful in this regard include those developed in Aranson and Ordeshook (1972), Coleman (1972), Bernhardt and Ingberman (1985), Ferejohn (1986), and Calvert (1987).

For further discussion about redistributional reputations and related matters, see the comments by Ledyard (1986) and Slutsky (1986) and the replies given in Coughlin (1986c,d) that (simultaneously) appeared when the model in Section 2.2 first appeared in print, in Coughlin (1986b).

2.3   The two-candidate game and electoral equilibria

It follows from the assumptions made in Section 2.1 that when there is an election with redistributional reputations, the decisions that the candidates have to make constitute a two-person game

$$(S, S; P\ell^1, P\ell^2) \tag{2.5}$$

By the definition of expected plurality given in (2.4), this game is zero-sum, thereby corresponding, it should be noted, to Riker's (1962) view that "in discussing elections ... the zero-sum model is probably best." As a consequence, a pair of redistributional reputations is an equilibrium pair of choices for the candidates if and only if the pair is a saddle point for the two-person zero-sum game $(S, S; P\ell^1, -P\ell^1)$. Any such pair is called an *electoral equilibrium*; that is, more explicitly, a pair of redistributional reputations, $(\psi_1^*, \psi_2^*) \in S \times S$, is an electoral equilibrium if and only if

$$P\ell^1(\psi_1, \psi_2^*) \le P\ell^1(\psi_1^*, \psi_2^*) \le P\ell^1(\psi_1^*, \psi_2), \ \forall \ \psi_1, \psi_2 \in S \tag{2.6}$$

From (2.3), (2.4), and (2.6), it is clear that the decisions that candidates make depend crucially on the relation between their redistributional reputations, $(\psi_1, \psi_2) \in S \times S$, and the corresponding probabilities $P_\theta^1(\psi_1, \psi_2)$ and $P_\theta^2(\psi_1, \psi_2)$ (for the various groups in Θ). Section 2.4 identifies one possible way of specifying this relation and gives the implications of using this alternative.

2.4   Voting determined by redistributional reputations

One possible assumption about the relation between the candidates' reputations, $(\psi_1, \psi_2) \in S \times S$, and the corresponding probabilities $P_\theta^1(\psi_1, \psi_2)$ and $P_\theta^2(\psi_1, \psi_2)$ (for the various groups in Θ) is that both candidates believe that, for each candidate c and each voter $i \in N$,

$$P_i^c(\psi_1, \psi_2) = P_\theta^c(\psi_1, \psi_2) = \begin{cases} 1 & \text{if} & U_\theta(\psi_c) > U_\theta(\psi_k) \\ \frac{1}{2} & \text{if} & U_\theta(\psi_c) = U_\theta(\psi_k) \\ 0 & \text{if} & U_\theta(\psi_c) < U_\theta(\psi_k) \end{cases} \tag{2.7}$$

where, as before, θ is the group that voter i is in and k is the index for the other candidate. That is, the candidates believe that if a voter prefers the redistributional reputation of one candidate to the redistributional reputation of the other, then the voter's choice is fully determined by that preference, and that otherwise the voter's choice is equivalent to the toss of a fair coin [leading to an expected plurality (from that voter) of zero, for each candidate]. The same basic formulation of expectations about voters' choices has been used in a large number of voting models including most of those surveyed in Davis, Hinich, and Ordeshook (1970), Plott (1971), Mueller (1976, 1979), Kramer (1977a), and Enelow and Hinich (1984a). When the assumption about the candidates' expectations about voters' choices that is specified by (2.7) is satisfied, it is said that "the candidates believe that the voters' choices are determined by the candidates' redistributional reputations."

In some elections with redistributional reputations in which the candidates believe that the voters' choices are determined by the candidates' redistributional reputations, there is an electoral equilibrium. The simplest case for which an electoral equilibrium exists is any election in which there is exactly one group, because then each candidate has exactly one strategy and the definition of an electoral equilibrium, given in (2.6), is trivially satisfied at the one possible pair of strategies. The next simplest case for which an electoral equilibrium exists is any election in which there are two groups of equal size (i.e., $\Theta = \{1, 2\}$ and $g(1) = g(2) = \frac{1}{2}$). Consider any pair of strategies $(x, y) \in S \times S$. By (2.1), one of the following three statements must hold: (i) $x_1 > y_1$ and $x_2 = Y - x_1 < Y - y_1 = y_2$, (ii) $x_1 = y_1$ and $x_2 = Y - x_1 = Y - y_1 = y_2$, or (iii) $x_1 < y_1$ and $x_2 = Y - x_1 > Y - y_1 = y_2$. By (2.7), this implies that one of the following three statements must hold: (i) $P_1^1(x, y) = 1$, $P_1^2(x, y) = 0$, $P_2^1(x, y) = 0$, and $P_2^2(x, y) = 1$; (ii) $P_1^1(x, y) = P_2^1(x, y) = P_1^2(x, y) = P_2^2(x, y) = \frac{1}{2}$; or (iii) $P_1^1(x, y) = 0$, $P_1^2(x, y) = 1$, $P_2^1(x, y) = 1$, and $P_2^2(x, y) = 0$. Therefore, by (2.3) and (2.4) and since $g(1) = g(2)$, $P\ell^1(x, y) = 0$. Because this is true for each pair $(x, y) \in S \times S$, the definition of an electoral equilibrium given in (2.6) is trivially satisfied for each $(\psi_1^*, \psi_2^*) \in S \times S$. Hence, each $(\psi_1^*, \psi_2^*) \in S \times S$ is an electoral equilibrium.

The one remaining case for which it is easy to verify that an electoral equilibrium exists is any other election where there are two or more groups and group j has half or more of the voters (i.e., $g(j) \geq \frac{1}{2}$). In particular, consider the strategy pair for which each candidate has the following reputation: If $\theta \neq j$, then $\psi_{c\theta}^* = k_\theta$; if $\theta = j$, then $\psi_{cj}^* = 1 - \sum_{\theta \in \Theta - \{j\}} k_\theta$. Since the candidates have the same redistributional reputations, (2.7) implies $P_\theta^1(\psi_1^*, \psi_2^*) = P_\theta^2(\psi_1^*, \psi_2^*) = \frac{1}{2}$, $\forall \theta \in \Theta$. Therefore, by (2.3) and (2.4), $P\ell^1(\psi_1^*, \psi_2^*) = 0$. Suppose candidate 1 uses any strategy

$\psi_1 \neq \psi_1^*$. By (2.1), he must then have $\psi_{cj} < 1 - \Sigma_{\theta \in \Theta - \{j\}} k_\theta$. By (2.7), this implies $P_j^1(\psi_1, \psi_2^*) = 0$ and $P_j^2(\psi_1, \psi_2^*) = 1$, Therefore, from (2.3) and (2.4) and because group j contains half or more of the voters, $P\ell^1(\psi_1, \psi_2^*) \leq 0$. Similarly, for any $\psi_2 \neq \psi_2^*$, it follows that $P\ell^1(\psi_1^*, \psi_2) \geq 0$. Therefore, (2.6) is satisfied. Hence, (ψ_1^*, ψ_2^*) is an electoral equilibrium. It is also easy to verify that (ψ_1^*, ψ_2^*) is the only electoral equilibrium. In all remaining cases, however, the following result applies:

Theorem 2.1

Suppose there is an election with redistributional reputations in which $m \geq 3$ and $g(\theta) < \frac{1}{2}$, $\forall\ \theta \in \Theta$. If the candidates believe that the voters' choices are determined by the candidates' redistributional reputations, then there is no electoral equilibrium.

To keep the interpretation of this result clear, we emphasize that its negative conclusion applies to each and every special case of the model specified in Section 2.2 where there are three or more groups, and no single group has half or more of the voters. It should also be noted that Theorem 2.1 contains exactly the conclusion that Aranson and Ordeshook (1981) and Mueller (1982, 1983) have indicated we should expect from a model like the one in Section 2.1. Thus, this theorem captures (in a fully specified model) an important part of the conventional wisdom about elections with income redistribution.

Theorem 2.1 is proven in Appendix 2.1. The basic approach used in the proof of this result for the noncooperative game $(S, S; P\ell^1, P\ell^2)$ for the candidates is similar to the approach used in logical arguments that have appeared in analyses of the cooperative simple game that arises when a committee uses majority rule to divide a fixed amount of money. These cooperative game analyses go back at least as far as Von Neumann and Morgenstern (1944, sect. 21) and Luce and Raiffa (1957, sect. 9.1) for three-person committees and Ward (1961) for n-person committees. A more recent discussion of these cooperative games and their relation to various issues in the public-choice literature appears in Mueller (1979).

2.5 Logit models and the existence of equilibria

Taking a broad perspective on decision making, McFadden (1976, p. 363) noted that "decision problems ... often lead to acts or outcomes indexed by finite or countable sets; we term these qualitative or quantal response problems. Examples [include] ... voting behavior." Then, in closing his survey of the research that had been done on qualitative (or quantal) response models up to that time, McFadden pointed out: "Areas in which quantal choice models have been used on only a limited basis and in which substantial potential exists for useful exploitation of these methods (include) . . . voting behavior" (p. 382).

Since his 1976 survey of qualitative response models was published, McFadden and others have derived implications of using qualitative choice models and have empirically estimated and tested these models in a variety of contexts including commuters' choices of their modes of transportation to work, consumers' choices of residential location, and bureaucrats' choices. Little work on qualitative voter response models has appeared, however; as a consequence, there is virtually no empirical research that either justifies or rejects the approach of formulating voting decisions in this way. Nonetheless, these models do have the following relevant feature: They include the assumption that the observer (who, here, is a candidate) cannot fully determine the choices that individuals will make (here, the way in which voters will cast their ballots) from available data. In actual elections, candidates usually base their beliefs about voters' choices on polls – which are known to be unable to predict voters' choices precisely, thus leaving an element of uncertainty as to just what their actual choices will be. Therefore, the uncertainty about voters' choices that is built into a qualitative response model of voting behavior captures an important element of actual elections. The specific qualitative response model on which McFadden has concentrated in his own research is, of course, the logit model (e.g., see McFadden, 1974, 1976, 1978, 1981, 1982). In following McFadden's suggestion, this model is used here as well.

From the formulation of qualitative response models in McFadden (1974, 1982), it is assumed that the utility of a voter i for the redistributional reputation ψ_c of a given candidate c is an unobserved (or latent) variable that can be written as

$$u_i(\psi_c) = U_\theta(\psi_c) + \varepsilon_{ic}(\psi_c) \tag{2.8}$$

where θ is the group that includes voter i and $\varepsilon_{ic}(\psi_c)$ is a random variable. It should be noted that similar formulations of voters' utility functions have been used in Hinich and Ordeshook (1969), Hinich (1978), Enelow and Hinich (1982b; 1984a, chap. 5), Lindbeck and Weibull (1987), and elsewhere. In discussing McFadden's use of this formulation of an individual's utility in studies of commuters' choices of modes of transportation to work, Amemiya (1981, p. 1490) pointed out that "McFadden interprets the error terms as those mode characteristics and individual socio-economic characteristics which are unobservable to the researcher. This is analogous to the omitted variables interpretation of the error term in a regression." McFadden (1982, pp. 4–5) repeats and adds to this interpretation: "The disturbance term ε ... may have the conventional econometric interpretation of the impact of factors known to the decision-maker but not to the observer. However, it is also possible that a disturbance exists in the decision protocol of the economic agent, yielding stochastic choice behavior." Here, of course, the decision maker (or economic agent) is an individual voter and the observer is a political candidate. Thus, the qualitative response model used here allows for both the possibility that voters vote deterministically but candidates are uncertain about what these choices will be and the possibility that voters' choices are genuinely stochastic in nature.

Assuming that the choices of each voter i correspond to the voter's "complete" utility function u_i (rather than to the utility function U_i, which measures his preferences on redistributional reputations but leaves out other relevant factors) means, of course, that (2.7) gets replaced by the following (analogous) equation:

$$P_j^c(\psi_1, \psi_2) = \begin{cases} 1 & \text{if} & u_i(\psi_c) > u_i(\psi_k) \\ \frac{1}{2} & \text{if} & u_i(\psi_c) = u_i(\psi_k) \\ 0 & \text{if} & u_i(\psi_c) < u_i(\psi_k) \end{cases} \qquad (2.9)$$

Taken together with (2.8), this implies that for each candidate c and each voter i,

$$P_j^c(\psi_1, \psi_2) = \begin{cases} 1 & \text{if} & \varepsilon_{ic}(\psi_c) - \varepsilon_{ik}(\psi_k) > U_\theta(\psi_k) - U_\theta(\psi_c) \\ \frac{1}{2} & \text{if} & \varepsilon_{ic}(\psi_c) - \varepsilon_{ik}(\psi_k) = U_\theta(\psi_k) - U_\theta(\psi_c) \\ 0 & \text{if} & \varepsilon_{ic}(\psi_c) - \varepsilon_{ik}(\psi_k) < U_\theta(\psi_k) - U_\theta(\psi_c) \end{cases} \qquad (2.10)$$

where, as before, θ is the group that includes voter i and k is the index for the other candidate. When the assumption that unobservable factors enter into voters' choices has been cast in this form, it becomes clear that, for the selection probabilities for a given voter i to be fully specified, the only thing that has to be added at this point is an appropriate assumption about the distribution of the random variable $\varepsilon_{ic}(\psi_c) - \varepsilon_{ik}(\psi_k)$.

The distributional assumption added to the assumption already made (i.e., to the assumption that unobservable factors enter into the determination of voters' choices) is that the candidates use a logit model for the voters' selection probabilities. More specifically, we assume that, for each candidate c and each voter $i \in N$, the random variable $\varepsilon_{ic}(\psi_c) - \varepsilon_{ik}(\psi_k)$ – where, as in (2.7), k is the index for the other candidate – has a logistic distribution. This implies that, as on p. 113 of McFadden (1974) and p. 4 of McFadden (1982), the candidates believe that, for each candidate c and each voter $i \in N$,

$$P_i^c(\psi_1, \psi_2) = P_\theta^c(\psi_1, \psi_2) = \frac{\exp[U_\theta(\psi_c)]}{\exp[U_\theta(\psi_c)] + \exp[U_\theta(\psi_k)]}$$

$$= \frac{\exp\{\alpha_\theta + \beta_\theta \cdot z_\theta^c\}}{\exp\{\alpha_\theta + \beta_\theta \cdot z_\theta^c\} + \exp\{\alpha_\theta + \beta_\theta \cdot z_\theta^k\}} \quad (2.11)$$

where θ is the group that includes voter i, k is the index for the other candidate, and z_θ^j is used to denote the natural log of the θth component of ψ_j $(j = c, k)$. Note that it is easy to show (using a simple example) that this assumption does not include (2.7) as a special case. For instance, suppose that a group θ has $\alpha_\theta = 0$ and $\beta_\theta = 1$ and consider any (ψ_1, ψ_2) with $\psi_{1\theta} = .1$ and $\psi_{2\theta} = .2$. For (2.7) to be satisfied, we must have $P_\theta^1(\psi_1, \psi_2) = 0$ and $P_\theta^2(\psi_1, \psi_2) = 1$, but by (2.9) the assumptions in this section lead to $P_\theta^1(\psi_1, \psi_2) = .1 / (.1 + .2) = \frac{1}{3}$ and $P_\theta^2(\psi_1, \psi_2) = .2 / (.2 + .1) = \frac{2}{3}$.

When the two assumptions just stated are satisfied, we say that "the candidates use a binomial logit model for the voters' selection probabilities." When this feature is added to the model specified in Section 2.1, the following result holds:

Theorem 2.2

Suppose there is an election with redistributional reputations. If the candidates use a binomial logit model for the voters' selection probabilities, then an electoral equilibrium exists.

Theorem 2.2 establishes that when there is an election with redistributional reputations, *if* candidates have probabilistic expectations (about voters' choices) that can be described by the binomial logit model, *then* there is an equilibrium. As with Theorem 2.1, to keep the interpretation of this result clear, it is important to emphasize that its conclusion always applies to the model specified in Section 2.1, no matter what special case may arise. It should also be noted that this conclusion is exactly the opposite of what Aranson and Ordeshook (1981) and Mueller (1982, 1983) have told us we should expect from a model like the one in Section 2.1.

The proof of Theorem 2.2 is given in Appendix 2.2. The basic approach used in the proof is similar to approaches used in proofs of equilibrium existence results in Hinich et al. (1972, 1973), Riker and Ordeshook (1973, chap. 12), Hinich (1978), Enelow and Hinich (1982b; 1984a, appendix to chap. 5; 1989b), Wittman (1983), Samuelson (1984), and Lindbeck and Weibull (1987).

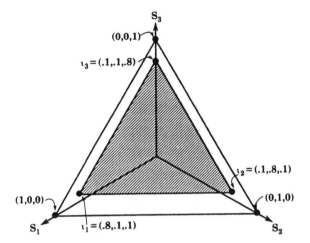

Fig. 2.1 The possible redistributional reputations.

2.6   Two examples

In this section, an election with redistributional reputations in which
there are three groups, $\theta = 1, 2, 3$, is used to illustrate Theorems 2.1
and 2.2. It is assumed throughout that the total income Y has been
normalized so that $Y = 1$. It is also assumed that (measuring in these
normalized units of income) the smallest amount of income that the
individuals in any given group can get is .1 (i.e., $k_1 = k_2 = k_3 = .1$). With
these assumptions, (2.1) implies that the strategy space (of possible
redistributional reputations) for the candidates is

$$S = \left\{ (s_1, s_2, s_3) \in E^3 : \sum_{\theta=1}^{3} s_\theta = 1 \quad \text{and} \quad s_\theta \geq .1, \forall\, \theta \in \Theta \right\} \qquad (2.12)$$

that is, the (common) set of possible strategies for the candidates is the
shaded subset of E^3 in Fig. 2.1. In this and subsequent figures, ι_θ is used
to denote the ideal point for an individual in the group θ.

By (2.12), S is contained in the same plane as, and is a proper sub-
set of, the familiar *unit simplex*, $\{(x_1, x_2, x_3) \in E^3 : x_1 \geq 0, x_2 \geq 0, x_3 \geq 0,$
and $x_1 + x_2 + x_3 = 1\}$ (e.g., see Sydsaeter, 1981, pp. 158–9). Therefore, to
make this three-dimensional figure easier to interpret, the boundary of
the unit simplex is also drawn. It should be noted that S "floats above"
the axes in the diagram (instead of resting on them) because of the legal

minima for the total incomes for the three groups (i.e., because of the positive k_θ parameters). In Fig. 2.1 it is easy to see that S can be drawn as a two-dimensional object. Because a two-dimensional diagram on a flat surface is easier to interpret than a three-dimensional diagram, S is drawn as a two-dimensional object in Fig. 2.2 and in the diagrams in Chapter 3.

We also assume throughout that $\beta_1 = \beta_2 = \beta_3 = 1$, implying by (2.2) that, for each group $\theta \in \Theta$, the utility function on S for each individual i in the group is

$$U_i(s) = U_\theta(s) \equiv \alpha_\theta + \log(s_\theta) \tag{2.13}$$

(where α_θ is any real number). Finally, it is also assumed that the three groups are of equal size (i.e., that $g(1) = g(2) = g(3) = \frac{1}{3}$).

EXAMPLE 2.1

Assume that the candidates believe the voters' choices are determined by the candidates' redistributional reputations. Theorem 2.1 implies that there is no electoral equilibrium. This conclusion can be derived in the context of this example as follows.

Choose any $(x, y) \in S \times S$. Since the game is zero-sum, there are three possibilities: (i) $P\ell^1(x, y) > 0 > P\ell^2(x, y)$, (ii) $P\ell^1(x, y) = P\ell^2(x, y) = 0$, or (iii) $P\ell^1(x, y) < 0 < P\ell^2(x, y)$. Suppose (i) or (ii) holds. Identify a group of voters i who get more income at x than the minimum they must get (i.e., for whom we have $x_i > .1$). Let w be the alternative in which this group gets $w_i = .1$ and the others get $w_j = x_j + \frac{1}{2}(x_i - .1)$ (i.e., the other groups split the decrease in i's income).

The voters' preferences on x and w can now be determined by comparing their utility levels at these two alternatives. In particular, since $x_i > .1$ and $\log(\cdot)$ is a strictly increasing function,

$$U_i(w) = \alpha_i + \log(w_i) < \alpha_i + \log(x_i) = U_i(x) \tag{2.14}$$

and

$$U_j(w) = \alpha_j + \log(w_j) > \alpha_j + \log(x_j) = U_j(x), \qquad \forall j \neq i \tag{2.15}$$

These pairwise comparisons are shown in Fig. 2.2 (where, for illustrative purposes, x has been located in the interior of S and we have taken i to be group 3). In particular, this figure contains the voters' (straight-line) indifference curves through x and w and arrows that point in the direction of increasing utility. Finally, because the candidates believe that voting is determined by redistributional reputations [i.e., the candidates' expectations are specified by (2.7)] the inequalities in (2.14)

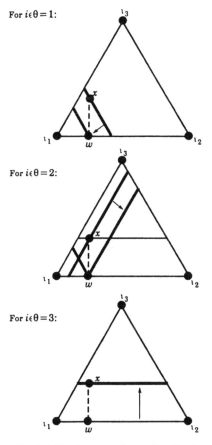

For $i \epsilon \theta = 1$:

For $i \epsilon \theta = 2$:

For $i \epsilon \theta = 3$:

Fig. 2.2 Preferences for redistributional reputations: (a) for $i \in \theta = 1$, (b) for $i \in \theta = 2$, (c) for $i \in \theta = 3$.

and (2.15) imply $P_i^2(x, w) = 0$ and $P_i^1(x, w) = 1$ and, in addition, $P_j^2(x, w) = 1$ and $P_j^1(x, w) = 0$ for each $j \neq i$. Therefore, with the definitions of expected vote and expected plurality given in (2.3) and (2.4), it follows that $P\ell^1(x, w) = g(i) - \sum_{\theta \in \Theta - \{j\}} g(j) = -\frac{1}{3}$. Hence, because we are specifically considering any case in which $P\ell^1(x, y) > 0$, it follows that $P\ell^1(x, y) > P\ell^1(x, w)$ (i.e., if candidate 2 were to choose w rather than y, then candidate 1 would have a lower expected plurality; hence, since the game is zero-sum, candidate 2 would have a larger expected plurality). Therefore, by the definition of an electoral equilibrium given in (2.6), (x, y) is not an electoral equilibrium. Therefore, if (i) or (ii) holds, then no pair of strategies is an electoral equilibrium. By similar reasoning, the same conclusion also follows when (iii) holds. Therefore, there is no electoral equilibrium.

The preceding example can be thought of as being a game-theoretic version of the "paradox of voting" which was discussed in Chapter 1; that is, the fact that when majority rule is used to make collective decisions, a society can find itself in a situation in which, for each social choice that could be made, there is a feasible alternative that a majority of the voters prefer (and, hence, any choice can be overturned by a majority vote). More specifically, this example illustrates how easy it is for this form of the paradox of voting (and the corresponding absence of equilibrium policies) to occur when the issues to be resolved involve the distribution of income in the society.

EXAMPLE 2.2

Assume that the candidates use a binomial logit model for the voters' selection probabilities. Theorem 2.2 implies that there is an electoral equilibrium. This conclusion can also be derived in the context of this example as follows.

Recall that the key implication of the binomial logit model for our purposes, stated in (2.11), is the fact that for each $i \in N$,

$$P_i^1(x, y) = P_\theta^1(x, y) = \frac{\exp\{U_\theta(x)\}}{\exp\{U_\theta(x)\} + \exp\{U_\theta(y)\}}, \qquad \forall \ x, y \in S \qquad (2.16)$$

and

$$P_i^2(x, y) = P_\theta^2(x, y) = \frac{\exp\{U_\theta(y)\}}{\exp\{U_\theta(y)\} + \exp\{U_\theta(x)\}}, \qquad \forall \ x, y \in S \qquad (2.17)$$

where θ is the group that i is in. If we plug in the utility functions on S for the voters in this example, given in (2.13), and then use the properties of the exponential function, it follows that

$$P_\theta^1(x, y) = \frac{\exp\{\alpha_\theta + \log(x_\theta)\}}{\exp\{\alpha_\theta + \log(x_\theta)\} + \exp\{\alpha_\theta + \log(y_\theta)\}} = \frac{x_\theta}{x_\theta + y_\theta} \qquad (2.18)$$

and

$$P_\theta^2(x, y) = \frac{\exp\{\alpha_\theta + \log(y_\theta)\}}{\exp\{\alpha_\theta + \log(y_\theta)\} + \exp\{\alpha_\theta + \log(x_\theta)\}} = \frac{y_\theta}{y_\theta + x_\theta} \qquad (2.19)$$

hold for each $\theta \in \Theta$. This implies that each $P_\theta^1(x, y)$ is a concave function of x, and that each $-P_\theta^2(x, y)$ is also a concave function of x. By the definition of expected vote EV, given in (2.3),

$$EV^1(x, y) = P_1^1(x, y) + P_2^1(x, y) + P_3^1(x, y) \tag{2.20}$$

and

$$-EV^2(x, y) = -P_1^2(x, y) - P_2^2(x, y) - P_3^2(x, y) \tag{2.21}$$

Therefore, since the sum of concave functions is concave, $EV^1(x, y)$ and $-EV^2(x, y)$ are concave functions for x. By the definition of expected plurality, given in (2.4), $P\ell^1(x, y) = EV^1(x, y) - EV^2(x, y) = \{EV^1(x, y)\} + \{-EV^2(x, y)\}$. Therefore, it follows that $P\ell^1(x, y)$ is also the sum of concave functions of x. Hence $P\ell^1(x, y)$ is concave in x. Similarly, $P\ell^1(x, y)$ is also convex in y. From similar arguments, it follows that $P\ell^1(x, y)$ and $P\ell^2(x, y)$ are continuous functions of (x, y). Finally, as pointed out in Section 2.1, the definition of the candidates' strategy set, given in (2.2), implies that it is a compact, convex set. Therefore, by the well-known saddle-point existence theorem that immediately precedes the proof of Theorem 2.2 in Appendix 2.2, a saddle point exists for this example. Therefore, an electoral equilibrium exists.

2.7 Conclusion

This chapter has developed a model of elections in which each candidate selects a reputation for the distribution of income that can be expected if the candidate is elected; it also has analyzed the implications for the existence of equilibria of two alternative ways of formulating candidates' expectations about voters' choices. The first major result, Theorem 2.1, establishes that whenever there are three or more groups of voters and no single group has half or more of the voters, *if* the candidates believe that the voters' choices are determined solely by the candidates' redistributional reputations, *then* there is no electoral equilibrium. The second major result, Theorem 2.2, addresses the equilibrium existence question for the model that results when the candidates' expectations about the voters' choices are reformulated using the logit model. The conclusion of Theorem 2.2 is the exact opposite of the conclusion of Theorem 2.1; that is, in an election with redistributional reputations, if the candidates use a binomial logit model for the voters' selection probabilities, then an electoral equilibrium exists. In the next chapter, we study the nature of these equilibria by deriving some of their properties.

Appendix 2.1: Proof of Theorem 2.1

In the proof of Theorem 2.1 and in subsequent proofs, we use Σ_θ to denote $\Sigma_{\theta \in \Theta}$ and $\Sigma_{\theta \neq j}$ denote $\Sigma_{\theta \in \Theta - \{j\}}$ whenever this simplifies the equations that arise.

Proof of Theorem 2.1

Consider any $(x, y) \in S \times S$. We show that (x, y) is not an electoral equilibrium. By (2.6), (x, y) is not an electoral equilibrium if and only if we do not have

$$P\ell^1(v, y) \leq P\ell^1(x, y) \leq P\ell^1(x, w), \qquad \forall\, v, w, \in S \qquad \text{(A2.1)}$$

that is, if and only if either

$$\exists\, w \in S : P\ell^1(x, y) > P\ell^1(x, w) \qquad \text{(A2.2)}$$

or

$$\exists\, v \in S : P\ell^1(v, y) > P\ell^1(x, y) \qquad \text{(A2.3)}$$

Because $P\ell^1$ is a real-valued function, one of the following three statements must be true: (i) $P\ell^1(x, y) > 0$, (ii) $P\ell^1(x, y) = 0$, or (iii) $P\ell^1(x, y) < 0$.

Suppose (i) or (ii) holds. The following argument shows that (A2.2) also holds. Choose a group $\delta \in \Theta$ such that $x_\delta > k_\delta$. Because $\Sigma_\theta\, k_\theta < Y$ (see Section 2.1), there must be at least one such group. Let w be the m-vector $(w_1, \ldots, w_m)$ in which

$$w_\delta = k_\delta \qquad \text{(A2.4)}$$

and

$$w_\theta = x_\theta + \frac{x_\delta - k_\delta}{m - 1}, \qquad \forall\, \theta \neq \delta \qquad \text{(A2.5)}$$

Since $m \geq 3$, (A2.5) is defined. Adding the components in w, substituting from (A2.4) and (A2.5), rearranging terms, and then using (2.1) and the fact that $x \in S$, we get

$$w_\delta + \sum_{\theta \neq \delta} w_\theta = k_\delta + \sum_{\theta \neq \delta} \left[x_\theta + \frac{x_\delta - k_\delta}{m - 1} \right]$$

$$= k_\delta + \left[\sum_{\theta \neq \delta} x_\theta \right] + (m - 1) \cdot \frac{x_\delta - k_\delta}{m - 1}$$

$$= k_\delta + \left[\sum_{\theta \neq \delta} x_\theta \right] + x_\delta - k_\delta = \sum_\theta x_\theta = Y \qquad \text{(A2.6)}$$

In addition, we have $w_\delta = k_\delta$, by (A2.4) and also have $w_\theta > x_\theta \geq k_\theta$, $\forall\, \theta \neq \delta$, by (A2.5), plus the fact that $x_\delta > k_\delta$ and $m \geq 3$. Therefore, $w_\theta \geq k_\theta$, $\forall\, \theta \in \Theta$. Therefore, by (2.1), $w \in S$.

By (2.2) and (A2.4), $U_\delta(w) = \alpha_\delta + \beta_\delta \cdot \log(k_\delta) < \alpha_\delta + \beta_\delta \cdot \log(x_\delta) = U_\delta(x)$ (since $x_\delta > k_\delta$, $\log(\cdot)$ is a strictly increasing function, and $\beta_\delta > 0$). Therefore, by (2.7),

$$P_\delta^1(x, w) = 1 \qquad \text{and} \qquad P_\delta^2(x, w) = 0 \tag{A2.7}$$

By (2.2) and (A2.5), for each $\theta \neq \delta$,

$$U_\theta(w) = \alpha_\theta + \beta_\theta \cdot \log(x_\theta) + \frac{x_\delta - k_\delta}{m - 1} > \alpha_\theta + \beta_\theta \cdot \log(x_\theta) = U_\theta(x)$$

since $[(x_\delta - k_\delta) / (m - 1)] > 0$ (because $x_\delta > k_\delta$ and $m \geq 3$), $\log(\cdot)$ is a strictly increasing function and $\beta_\delta > 0$. Therefore, by (2.7),

$$P_\theta^1(x, w) = 0 \qquad \text{and} \qquad P_\theta^2(x, w) = 1 \qquad \forall\, \theta \neq \delta \tag{A2.8}$$

By (2.3)–(2.4) and (A2.7)–(A2.8),

$$P\ell^1(x, w) = g(\delta) - \sum_{\theta \neq \delta} g(\theta) \tag{A2.9}$$

Therefore, since $g(\delta) < \tfrac{1}{2}$ and $\sum_\theta g(\theta) = 1$, we have $P\ell^1(x, w) < 0$. Therefore, because (i) or (ii) holds,

$$P\ell^1(x, y) \geq 0 > P\ell^1(x, w) \tag{A2.10}$$

Therefore, $P\ell^1(x, y) > P\ell^1(x, w)$. Therefore, (A2.2) holds.

If, on the other hand, (iii) holds, then (by a similar argument) (A2.3) holds. Therefore, either (A2.2) or (A2.3) must hold. Therefore, (x, y) is not an electoral equilibrium.

QED

Note

As in the corresponding proofs for cooperative majority games, the logical argument given here can still be used if (2.2) is replaced with any other utility function for which $[s'_\theta > s''_\theta]$ $\Rightarrow [U_\theta(s') > U_\theta(s'')]$, $\forall s', s'' \in S$. But the focus in this chapter is on elections with redistributional reputations, where (by definition) (2.2) is satisfied. Therefore, the result that has been proven here and stated in the text is specifically for elections with redistributional reputations.

Appendix 2.2: Proof of Theorem 2.2

The following two lemmata are used in the proof of Theorem 2.2 that is given here. In stating them, we assume (as an unstated premise) that there is an election with redistributional reputations and that the candidates use a binomial logit model for the voters' selection probabilities.

Lemma 2.1

For each $(x, y) \in S \times S$,

$$P\ell^1(x, y) = 2 \cdot \sum_\theta \left[\frac{(x_\theta)^{\beta_\theta}}{(x_\theta)^{\beta_\theta} + (y_\theta)^{\beta_\theta}} \cdot g(\theta) \right] - 1 \qquad (A2.11)$$

Proof of Lemma 2.1

Consider any $(x, y) \in S \times S$. By (2.11), for each $\theta \in \Theta$,

$$\begin{aligned} P_\theta^1(x, y) &= \frac{\exp\{\alpha_\theta\} \cdot \exp\{\beta_\theta \cdot z_\theta^1\}}{\exp\{\beta_\theta \cdot z_\theta^1\} + \exp\{\alpha_\theta\} \cdot \exp\{\beta_\theta \cdot z_\theta^2\}} \\ &= \frac{\exp\{\beta_\theta \cdot z_\theta^1\}}{\exp\{\beta_\theta \cdot z_\theta^1\} + \exp\{\beta_\theta \cdot z_\theta^2\}} \end{aligned} \qquad (A2.12)$$

where $z_\theta^1 = \log(x_\theta)$ and $z_\theta^2 = \log(y_\theta)$. Therefore, since $\beta_\theta \cdot z_\theta^1 = \beta_\theta \cdot \log(x_\theta) = \log[(x_\theta)^{\beta_\theta}]$ and $\beta_\theta \cdot z_\theta^2 = \beta_\theta \cdot \log(y_\theta) = \log[(y_\theta)^{\beta_\theta}]$, (A2.12) implies

$$P_\theta^1(x, y) = \frac{(x_\theta)^{\beta_\theta}}{(x_\theta)^{\beta_\theta} + (y_\theta)^{\beta_\theta}} \qquad (A2.13)$$

Because each voter in N will vote in the election, $P_\theta^2(x, y) = 1 - P_\theta^1(x, y)$. Therefore, $P_\theta^1(x, y) - P_\theta^2(x, y) = 2 \cdot P_\theta^1(x, y) - 1$. Therefore, by (A2.13),

$$P_\theta^1(x, y) - P_\theta^2(x, y) = \frac{2 \cdot (x_\theta)^{\beta_\theta}}{(x_\theta)^{\beta_\theta} + (y_\theta)^{\beta_\theta}} - 1 \qquad (A2.14)$$

Therefore, by (2.3) and (2.4), we have (A2.11).

QED

The proof of Lemma 2.2 uses the following well-known result (e.g., see Sydsaeter, 1981, p. 252).

Theorem

Let $f(x)$ be a C^2-function of x defined on an open, convex set $A \subseteq E^n$. Let $D_r(x)$ be the determinant of the $(r \times r)$ matrix

$$\left[\frac{\partial^2 f(x)}{\partial x_h\, \partial x_j} \right] \quad (h = 1, \ldots, r; \quad j = 1, \ldots, r)$$

If $(-1)^r \cdot D_r(x) > 0$ for each $r \in \{1, \ldots, n\}$ and $x \in A$, then $f(x)$ is a strictly concave function of x on A.

Recall that the payoff function $\pi(x, y)$ in a two-person zero-sum game $(X_1, X_2; \pi, -\pi)$ is said to be

(i)   concave (strictly concave) in x if and only if, for each given $y \in X_2$, $\pi(x, y)$ is a concave (strictly concave) function of x on X_1;

(ii)   convex (strictly convex) in y if and only if, for each given $x \in X_1$, $\pi(x, y)$ is a convex (strictly convex) function of y on X_2.

Lemma 2.2

$P\ell^1(x, y)$ is strictly concave in x and strictly convex in y.

Proof of Lemma 2.2

Consider any given $y \in S$. The following argument shows that $P\ell^1(x, y)$ is a strictly concave function of x on S. To begin with, let

$$S_e = \{(s_1, \ldots, s_m) \in E^m : s_\theta > 0, \forall\, \theta \in \Theta\} \tag{A2.15}$$

This definition directly implies that $S \subset S_e$ and that S_e is an open, convex set in E^m. Also let

$$P\ell_e^1(x, y) = 2 \cdot \sum_\theta \left[\frac{(x_\theta)^{\beta_\theta}}{(x_\theta)^{\beta_\theta} + (y_\theta)^{\beta_\theta}} \cdot g(\theta) \right] - 1 \tag{A2.16}$$

for each $x \in S_e$. At each $x \in S_e$, we have

$$x_\theta > 0, \quad y_\theta > 0, \quad \text{and} \quad 0 < \beta_\theta \le 1, \quad \forall\, \theta \in \Theta \tag{A2.17}$$

by (A2.15), (2.2), and the assumption about the β_θ that appears right after (2.2). Therefore, for each $\theta \in \Theta$, the denominator $[(x_\theta)^{\beta_\theta} + (y_\theta)^{\beta_\theta}]$ in the corresponding term in the sum over θ in (A2.16) is positive.

Therefore, $P\ell_e^1(x, y)$ is defined at each $x \in S_e$. In addition, by (A2.16), Lemma 2.1, and the definition of an extension (as stated, for instance, in Debreu, 1959, p. 5), $P\ell_e^1(x, y)$ is an extension of $P\ell^1(x, y)$ onto the larger domain S_e.

The first partial derivatives of $P\ell_e^1(x, y)$ (at any given $x \in S_e$) are

$$\frac{\partial P\ell_e^1(x, y)}{\partial x_j} = 2 \cdot \frac{((x_j)^{\beta_j} + (y_j)^{\beta_j}) \cdot (\beta_j) \cdot (x_j)^{\beta_{j-1}} - (x_j)^{\beta_j} \cdot (\beta_j) \cdot (x_j)^{\beta_{j-1}}}{[(x_j)^{\beta_j} + (y_j)^{\beta_j}]^2} \cdot g(j)$$

$$= 2 \cdot \frac{(y_j)^{\beta_j} \cdot (\beta_j) \cdot (x_j)^{\beta_{j-1}}}{[(x_j)^{\beta_j} + (y_j)^{\beta_j}]^2} \cdot g(j), \qquad \forall j \in \{1, \ldots, m\}$$

$$(A2.18)$$

The second partial derivatives of $P\ell_e^1(x, y)$ (at any given x) are, therefore,

$$\frac{\partial^2 P\ell_e^1(x, y)}{\partial x_h \partial x_j} = 0, \qquad \forall j \in \{1, \ldots, m\} \qquad \text{with} \qquad j \neq h \qquad (A2.19)$$

and, for each $j \in \{1, \ldots, m\}$,

$$\frac{\partial^2 P\ell_e^1(x, y)}{\partial x_j^2} = \{2 \cdot [(x_j)^{\beta_j} + (y_j)^{\beta_j}]^2 \cdot (y_j)^{\beta_j} \cdot (\beta_j) \cdot (\beta_j - 1) \cdot (x_j)^{(\beta_j - 2)} \cdot g(j)$$

$$- 2 \cdot (y_j)^{\beta_j} \cdot (\beta_j) \cdot (x_j)^{(\beta_j - 1)} \cdot 2 \cdot [(x_j)^{\beta_j} + (y_j)^{\beta_j}] \cdot \beta_j \cdot (x_j)^{(\beta_j - 2)} \cdot g(j)\}$$

$$+ \{[(x_j)^{\beta_j} + (y_j)^{\beta_j}]^4\} \qquad (A2.20)$$

By (A2.19) and (A2.20), for each pair $j, h \in \{1, \ldots, m\}$, the corresponding second partial $[\partial^2 P\ell_e^1(x, y) / \partial x_h \partial x_j]$ is a continuous function of x on S_e. Therefore, $P\ell_e^1(x, y)$ is a C^2-function of x and S_e.

Choose any $j \in \{1, \ldots, m\}$, and $x \in S_e$. Consider the two products in the difference that defines the numerator on the right-hand side of (A2.20). From (A2.17) and the fact that $g(j) > 0$, it follows that every term in the first product is positive except $(\beta_j - 1)$, which can be either negative or zero. Therefore, the first product is either negative or zero. From (A2.17) and the fact that $g(j) > 0$ again, it follows that every term in the second product is positive. Therefore, the difference that defines the numerator is a nonpositive number minus a positive number. Therefore, the numerator is negative. From (A2.17) again, $[(x_j)^{\beta_j} + (x_j)^{\beta_j}] > 0$. Therefore, the denominator is positive. Hence, for any given $j \in \{1, \ldots, m\}$ and $x \in S_e$, we must have

$$\frac{\partial^2 P\ell_e^1(x, y)}{\partial x_j^2} < 0 \qquad (A2.21)$$

Consider any given $r \in \{1, \ldots, m\}$ and $x \in S_e$. By (A2.19) and (A2.20), the determinant of the $(r \times r)$ matrix

$$\left[\frac{\partial^2 P\ell_e^1(x, y)}{\partial x_h\, \partial x_j}\right] \qquad (h = 1, \ldots, r; j = 1, \ldots, r)$$

is given by the product $\Pi_{j=1}^r (\partial^2 P\ell_e^1(x, y)/\partial x_j^2)$. By (A2.21), this product is negative if r is odd and positive if r is even. Therefore (using the notation in the theorem that immediately precedes this proof), $(-1)^r \cdot D_r(x) > 0$.

Gathering together what has already been proven, we know that $P\ell_e^1(x, y)$ is a C^2-function of x defined on the open, convex set $S_e \subseteq E^m$ and that $(-1)^r \cdot D_r(x) > 0$ for each $r \in \{1, \ldots, m\}$ and $x \in S_e$. Therefore, by the theorem that precedes this proof, $P\ell_e^1(x, y)$ is a strictly concave function of x on S_e. Hence, since $P\ell_e^1(x, y)$ is an extension of $P\ell^1(x, y)$ onto the larger domain S_e, $P\ell^1(x, y)$ is a strictly concave function of x on S. Hence, $P\ell^1(x, y)$ is strictly concave in x.

Consider any given $x \in S$. The following argument shows that $-P\ell^1(x, y)$ is a strictly concave function of y on S. By (A2.14),

$$P_\theta^1(x, y) - P_\theta^2(x, y) = \frac{2 \cdot (x_\theta)^{\beta_\theta} - (x_\theta)^{\beta_\theta} - (y_\theta)^{\beta_\theta}}{(x_\theta)^{\beta_\theta} + (y_\theta)^{\beta_\theta}}$$

$$= \frac{(x_\theta)^{\beta_\theta} + (y_\theta)^{\beta_\theta} - 2 \cdot (y_\theta)^{\beta_\theta}}{(x_\theta)^{\beta_\theta} + (y_\theta)^{\beta_\theta}} = \frac{-2 \cdot (y_\theta)^{\beta_\theta}}{(x_\theta)^{\beta_\theta} + (y_\theta)^{\beta_\theta}} + 1$$

$$\text{(A2.22)}$$

Therefore, by (2.3) and (2.4),

$$P\ell^1(x, y) = 2 \cdot \sum_\theta \left[\frac{(y_\theta)^{\beta_\theta}}{(y_\theta)^{\beta_\theta} + (x_\theta)^{\beta_\theta}} \cdot g(\theta)\right] - 1 \qquad \text{(A2.23)}$$

analogous to (A2.11). Therefore, by an argument similar to the one used previously, $-P\ell^1(x, y)$ is a strictly concave function of y on S. Hence, from the definition of a strictly convex function (e.g., as stated on p. 247 of Sydsaeter, 1981), it follows that $P\ell^1(x, y)$ is a strictly convex function of y on S. Hence, $P\ell^1(x, y)$ is strictly convex in y.

QED

The proof of Theorem 2.2 uses the following well-known result (e.g., see Riker and Ordeshook, 1973, pp. 216–18; Roberts and Varberg, 1973, p. 131; Moulin, 1982, p. 107; Owen, 1982, p. 78; and/or Ordeshook, 1986, p. 154).

Theorem

Let a two-person zero-sum game $(X_1, X_2; \pi, -\pi)$ be given. *If*, for each $i \in \{1, 2\}$, (i) X_i is a compact, convex subset of a Euclidean space E^n, (ii) $\pi(x, y)$ is a continuous function of (x, y) on $X_1 \times X_2$, and (iii) $\pi(x, y)$ is concave in x and convex in y, *then* there exists a saddle-point for the game.

This result follows, for instance, from the minimax theorem in Kakutani (1941) (i.e., theorem 3 in that paper) plus theorem 13.B* in Von Neumann and Morgenstern (1953, p. 95).

We are now in a position to prove Theorem 2.2.

Proof of Theorem 2.2

As noted in Section 2.1, $X_1 = X_2 = S$ is a compact, convex subset of E^m. By Lemma 2.1, $P\ell^1(x, y)$ is given by (A2.11). This, together with (2.1), directly implies that $P\ell^1(x, y)$ is a continuous function of (x, y). Finally, by Lemma 2.2, $P\ell^1(x, y)$ is concave in x and convex in y. Therefore, by the theorem stated immediately before this proof, there exists a saddle-point for the game $(S, S; P\ell^1, P\ell^2) = (S, S; P\ell^1, -P\ell^1)$. Because an electoral equilibrium is by definition a saddle-point for $(S, S; P\ell^1, -P\ell^1)$, an electoral equilibrium exists.

QED

CHAPTER 3

Properties of the redistributional equilibria

Theorem 2.2, the equilibrium existence theorem, has laid the ground-work for the analysis in this chapter. Specifically, with Theorem 2.2 established, we can now analyze electoral equilibria. In particular, we derive the most important properties of the redistributional equilibria whose existence is assured by Theorem 2.2.

Section 3.1 starts the analysis by deriving the following five properties: (i) In an equilibrium, each candidate's strategy is the unique best response to the strategy being used by the other candidate (Theorem 3.1); (ii) for any given electorate, there is a unique electoral equilibrium (Theorem 3.2); (iii) in the unique equilibrium, both candidates have the same redistributional reputations (Theorem 3.3); (iv) in the unique equilibrium, the expected plurality for each candidate is zero (corollary to Theorem 3.3); (v) the common redistributional reputation of the candidates in the unique equilibrium can be viewed as the solution of a particular optimization problem that involves candidate 1's expected plurality function (Theorem 3.4).

Two theorems in Section 3.2 identify the locations of the electoral equilibria in all of the special cases that can arise. In particular, Theorem 3.5 covers special cases in which the location can be identified by using a Lagrangian, and Theorem 3.6 covers all remaining cases. These location theorems identify the exact redistributional reputation that each candidate wants to have, for each possible electorate. Section 3.3 provides a different perspective on the redistributional equilibria being studied, by establishing that, for each possible electorate, the location of the electoral equilibrium is also the maximum of the sum of the voters' utility functions (analogous to the conclusion in theorem 1 in Ledyard 1984).

Section 3.4 contains some simple example that illustrate the main results in the chapter and, simultaneously, also illustrate how the equilibria that occur (when candidates use a binomial logit model) depend on the underlying parameters. Section 3.5 then discusses both the broad implications and the interpretation of the properties (of the redistributional equilibria) that have been turned up in the preceding sections.

In this discussion, special attention is paid to how the mathematical results that have been derived are related to the politics of redistribution. Section 3.6 provides an overview of the chapter and a description of how the analysis that is carried out here is related to the next chapter.

3.1   Some properties of the electoral equilibria

Theorem 2.2, as an existence theorem, tells us that when there is an election with redistributional reputations in which the candidates use a binomial logit model for the voters' selection probabilities, an equilibrium exists; but it does not tell us what its other properties are. This section draws out some of these, as yet unidentified, properties – including uniqueness, "convergence," and the relation between an equilibrium and a specific optimization problem (which is used to turn up more properties in Section 3.2). The proofs of the theorems in this section are given in Appendix 3.1.

The first two properties are implications of the fact that candidate 1's expected plurality function $P\ell^1(x, y)$ (which is also the payoff function for the two-candidate zero-sum game being analyzed) is strictly concave in x and strictly convex in y, as established in Lemma 2.2 in Appendix 2.2. The first of these properties is the fact that the weak inequalities in (2.6) can be replaced by strict inequalities. More precisely, the first property is given in Theorem 3.1.

> *Theorem 3.1*
>
> Suppose that there is an election with redistributional reputations and the candidates use a binomial logit model of the voters' selection probabilities. A pair of redistributional reputations $(\psi_1^*, \psi_2^*) \in S \times S$ is an electoral equilibrium if and only if
>
> $$P\ell^1(\psi_1^*, \psi_2^*) > P\ell^1(\psi_1, \psi_2^*), \qquad \forall\, \psi_1 \in S - \{\psi_1^*\} \tag{3.1}$$
>
> and
>
> $$P\ell^2(\psi_1^*, \psi_2^*) > P\ell^2(\psi_1^*, \psi_2), \qquad \forall\, \psi_2 \in S - \{\psi_2^*\} \tag{3.2}$$

The second property is given in the following uniqueness result, Theorem 3.2.

> *Theorem 3.2*
>
> Suppose that there is an election with redistributional reputations and the candidates use a binomial logit model for the

voters' selection probabilities. There is exactly one electoral equilibrium.

Theorem 3.2 establishes that (for each special case of the model specified in Section 2.1), if the candidates use a binomial logit model for the voters' selection probabilities, there is a unique electoral equilibrium. Therefore, under these circumstances it is appropriate to talk about *the* electoral equilibrium. Stated more precisely, for any given election with redistributional reputations in which the candidates use a binomial logit model for the voters' selection probabilities, a particular pair of candidate strategies, (ψ_1^*, ψ_2^*), are said to be the electoral equilibrium if and only if (ψ_1^*, ψ_2^*) is an electoral equilibrium. This terminology is used in the next theorem, which establishes that the candidates' strategies "converge" in the sense in which this term was used in McKelvey (1975).

Theorem 3.3

Suppose that there is an election with redistributional reputations and the candidates use a binomial logit model for the voters' selection probabilities. The electoral equilibrium $(\psi_1^*, \psi_2^*) \in S \times S$ has $\psi_1^* = \psi_2^*$.

We also note the following corollary of Theorem 3.3:

Corollary

Suppose that there is an election with redistributional reputations and the candidates use a binomial logit model for the voters' selection probabilities. At the electoral equilibrium, $(\psi_1^*, \psi_2^*) \in S \times S$,

$$P\ell^1(\psi_1^*, \psi_2^*) = P\ell^2(\psi_1^*, \psi_2^*) = 0 \tag{3.3}$$

Because Theorem 3.3 establishes that the electoral equilibrium $(\psi_1^*, \psi_2^*) \in S \times S$ (in an election with redistributional reputations in which the candidates use a binomial logit model for the voters' selection probabilities) necessarily has $\psi_1^* = \psi_2^*$, it is appropriate to talk about the common strategy, $z = \psi_1^* = \psi_2^*$, as "the location" of the electoral equilibrium. Stated more precisely, for any given election with redistributional reputations in which the candidates use a binomial logit model for the voters' selection probabilities, z is said to be the location of the electoral equilibrium if and only if (z, z) is the electoral equilibrium in the election. The next theorem identifies a particular optimization problem (involving candidate 1's expected plurality function) that is solved by the location of the electoral equilibrium in a particular election. The proof of this theorem (in Appendix 3.1) reveals that this result follows from Theorem 3.3 plus the fact that the game $(S, S; P\ell^1, -P\ell^1)$ is "symmetric" in the sense in which this term is used in Von Neumann and Morgenstern (1953, pp. 165–6) and Owen (1982, sect. II.6), for instance.

Theorem 3.4

Suppose that there is an election with redistributional reputations and the candidates use a binomial logit model for the voters' selection probabilities. Then z is the location of the electoral equilibrium if and only if z solves

$$\max_{x} P\ell^1(x, z) \tag{3.4}$$

subject to $\sum_{\theta \in \Theta} x_\theta = Y$

and $x_\theta \geq k_\theta, \qquad \forall\, \theta \in \Theta$

3.2   The equilibrium location

Of course, it would also be nice to be able to say, for any given electorate, just where the redistributional equilibrium is located. This section contains two important theorems that enable us to do just that; that is, the two theorems precisely identify the location of the electoral equilibrium that occurs in an election with redistributional reputations in which the candidates use a binomial logit model for the voters' selection probabilities. The first, Theorem 3.5, deals with cases in which a Lagrangian can be used to identify the location of the electoral equilibrium (indeed, it is proven in Appendix 3.2 using the familiar method of Lagrange). The second, Theorem 3.6, extends Theorem 3.5 to all remaining cases. Theorem 3.6 shows that, to find the location of the electoral equilibrium in any of these cases, all you have to do is remove certain groups from consideration (by assuming that they will get only the minimum income required by law) and then analyze the resulting "reduced" election just as in Theorem 3.5. Theorem 3.6 states that the resulting location is precisely the location of the electoral equilibrium. This result is derived in Appendix 3.3 using a Kuhn–Tucker theorem.

The specific elections studied in Theorem 3.5 are those in which the vector $(d_1, \ldots, d_m) \in E^m$ that satisfies

$$d_j = \frac{\beta_j \cdot g(j)}{\sum_{\theta \in \Theta} \beta_\theta \cdot g(\theta)} \cdot Y, \quad \forall j \in \Theta \tag{3.5}$$

is contained in S. That is, we first study the elections in which this d-vector of potential income levels (for the groups $j \in \theta$) specified by (3.5) is a feasible redistributional reputation for the candidates. In particular, Theorem 3.5 tells us that the d-vector is the location of the electoral equilibrium. Thus, when all of the portions given in (3.5) are simultaneously feasible, they identify the portions (or shares) of the total income that everyone believes will go to the various groups in Θ after the election.

Theorem 3.5

Suppose that there is an election with redistributional reputations and the candidates use a binomial logit model for the voters' selection probabilities. If the vector $d \in E^m$ that satisfies (3.5) is contained in S, then d is the location of the electoral equilibrium.

Theorem 3.5 establishes that (in an election with redistributional reputations in which the candidates use a binomial logit model for the voters' selection probabilities) if the vector d defined by (3.5) is a feasible redistributional reputation, then each candidate will choose d as his strategy. That is, in any such election, d is the location of the electoral equilibrium. This result, however, leaves open the question: Where is the electoral equilibrium located if d is not a feasible redistributional reputation for the candidates? Theorem 3.6 tells us that in any such election (i) the groups in Θ will be divided into the two sets

$$A = \left\{ j \in \Theta : \frac{\beta_j \cdot g(j)}{\sum_{\theta \in \Theta} \beta_\theta \cdot g(\theta)} \cdot Y > k_j \right\} \tag{3.6}$$

and

$$B = \Theta - A$$

and (ii) the candidates will ignore the groups in B by giving them only what is required by law (i.e., $z_\theta = k_\theta$) and will concentrate entirely on the groups in A. In particular, Theorem 3.6 says that the candidates will view the election as one in which (for all intents and purposes) the only groups in the electorate are the groups in A; and, accordingly, they will acquire the same basic redistributional reputations as those Theorem 3.5 tells us they would acquire if it actually were the case that the only groups in the electorate were the groups in A and the total income available for distribution was $Y - \sum_{\theta \in B} k_\theta$.

Theorem 3.6

Suppose that there is an election with redistributional reputations and the candidates use a binomial logit model for the voters' selection probabilities. The location of the electoral equilibrium is the vector $z \in E^m$ that satisfies

$$z_j = k_j, \qquad \forall j \in B \tag{3.7}$$

and

$$z_j = \frac{\beta_j \cdot g(j)}{\sum_{\theta \in A} \beta_\theta \cdot g(\theta)} \cdot \left(Y - \sum_{\theta \in B} k_\theta \right), \qquad \forall j \in A \tag{3.8}$$

For any specification of the parameters (for an election with redistributional reputations where the candidates use a binomial logit model for the voters' selection probabilities), the theorems in this section pick out a specific point in the set of possible redistributional reputations as *the* location of the electoral equilibrium. To keep the interpretation of these results clear, note that the locations picked out are specific by-products of the assumptions that have been used in proving the theorems, most importantly, the Bernoulli assumption and the use of the logit model. Indeed, the proofs of Theorems 3.5 and 3.6 make it clear that if the assumptions that have been used are changed, then the conclusions about the location of the equilibrium that can be derived can also change.

3.3   The implicit social objective function

In the election model that was developed by Ledyard (1981, 1984), a necessary condition for an equilibrium is that each candidate chooses a strategy that implicitly maximizes a weighted sum or integral of the voters' possible utility functions on the society's policy space (see Ledyard, 1984, theorem 1, p. 25); that is, the candidates implicitly maximize a social utility function that has the same functional form as a *Benthamite* utilitarian social welfare function (e.g., see Arrow, 1951, 1963, p. 4; 1973b, p. 278). It is, therefore, natural to wonder whether the candidate strategies identified in Theorems 3.5 and 3.6 implicitly maximize a social utility function with a similar functional form. The answer (in the affirmative) is provided by the following theorem.

Theorem 3.7

Suppose that there is an election with redistributional reputations and the candidates use a binomial logit model for the voters' selection probabilities. Then z is the location of the electoral equilibrium if and only if z maximizes

$$\omega(x) = \sum_{\theta \in \Theta} U_\theta(x) \cdot g(\theta) = \sum_{\theta \in \Theta} [\alpha_\theta + \beta_\theta \cdot \log(x_\theta)] \cdot g(\theta) \qquad (3.9)$$

on the set S.

A proof of this theorem is given in Appendix 3.4.

Theorem 3.7 establishes that (in the model that is being analyzed in this chapter) the competition for votes between the candidates leads not only to an equilibrium, but to one that implicitly maximizes a familiar social welfare function. Importantly, the Benthamite utilitarian social welfare function identified by Theorem 3.7 has known and potentially appealing normative properties. Thus, the redistributional equilibria being analyzed can be considered desirable when evaluated from a normative point of view.

3.4 Some examples

Three examples illustrate the main results that have been stated in this chapter (and derived in the accompanying appendices). Since the premises for these results have all included both the assumption that there is an election with redistributional reputations and the assumption that the candidates use a binomial logit model for the voters' selection probabilities, these assumptions will also be made in each of the examples analyzed.

The first example also includes all of the common assumptions for the examples in Chapter 2 (i.e., the assumptions in the first paragraph of Section 2.6). As a consequence, the assumptions for Example 3.1 are exactly the same as those for Example 2.2. However, the analysis in this example will (as in the preceding sections) move beyond the equilibrium existence question (resolved in Chapter 2) and will focus on the nature of the equilibrium. Starting with the assumptions that were used in Example 2.2 has the advantage that it leads to our carrying out the analysis on familiar ground. It also makes this analysis and the earlier analyses in Section 2.6 more comparable than would otherwise be the case.

The last two examples differ from Example 3.1 only in the values that are assumed for the β and g parameters. More specifically, in Example 3.2 the β coefficient for one of the utility functions has been changed, whereas in Example 3.3 the relative sizes of the groups (i.e., the g's) have been changed. Among other things, examples of this sort illustrate how changes in the parameters in the model can affect the location of the electoral equilibrium.

So that the reader does not have to turn back to Chapter 2 repeatedly while going through this chapter's examples, we relist the assumptions in Section 2.6 that are going to be made in the examples that follow. To start with, in each example, there are three groups ($\theta = 1, 2, 3$) in the electorate. The total income available Y has been normalized so that $Y = 1$. Finally, the legal minima for the three groups (measured in the same normalized units) are $k_1 = k_2 = k_3 = .1$. Recall also that because these three assumptions are being made, the strategy set for each candidate is

$$S = \{(s_1, s_2, s_3) \in E^3 : s_1 \geq .1, s_2 \geq .1, s_3 \geq .1, \quad \text{and} \quad s_1 + s_2 + s_3 = 1\}$$

EXAMPLE 3.1

As in the examples in Section 2.6, it is assumed in this example that $g(1) = g(2) = g(3) = \frac{1}{3}$ (i.e., the groups are of equal size) and that $\beta_1 = \beta_2 = \beta_3 = 1$. Recall that the latter assumption (in turn) implies that for any group θ the utility function on S for each individual i in the group is $U_i(s) = U_\theta(s) = \alpha_\theta + \log(s_\theta)$.

In what follows, we carry out three closely related analyses of this example. The first two are indirect analyses (of its two-candidate game) that take advantage of results that have been established in this chapter. The first time around we specifically make use of the location theorems in Section 3.2. The second indirect analysis uses the implicit social objective function that was identified in Section 3.3. The last time around, we use the alternative approach of directly analyzing the two-candidate game to which this example leads.

The three approaches provide three separate confirmations that the location of the electoral equilibrium in this example is the egalitarian outcome, $(\frac{1}{3}, \frac{1}{3}, \frac{1}{3})$, which is suggested by intuition (in particular, since, from the candidate's point of view, the three groups are identical and interchangeable). The ensuing formal analyses should help to bolster the reader's confidence in the correctness of the theorems in the preceding sections. More importantly, they provide three perspectives on this example and, in the process, illustrate how these three perspectives can be used in studying any special case that arises. Finally, the three analyses show that these alternative perspectives are not created equal since they require increasing amounts of work.

We now turn to our first analysis of this example (using Theorems 3.5 and 3.6). As stated in Section 3.2, the first step in using Theorems 3.5 and 3.6 to determine the location of the electoral equilibrium is to calculate the vector $d^1 \in E^3$ that satisfies (3.5). In this example, for each $j \in \Theta = \{1, 2, 3\}$,

$$d_j^1 = \frac{\beta_j \cdot g(j)}{\sum_{\theta \in \Theta} \beta_\theta \cdot g(\theta)} \cdot Y = \frac{1 \cdot (\frac{1}{3})}{1 \cdot (\frac{1}{3}) + 1 \cdot (\frac{1}{3}) + 1 \cdot (\frac{1}{3})} \cdot 1 = \frac{1}{3} \quad (3.10)$$

Therefore, $d^1 = (\frac{1}{3}, \frac{1}{3}, \frac{1}{3})$. Since this vector is in S, Theorem 3.5 implies that the egalitarian distribution $s^1 = (\frac{1}{3}, \frac{1}{3}, \frac{1}{3})$ is the location of the electoral equilibrium.

We now analyze this example using Theorem 3.7. By the implication of the common assumptions for S stated just before this example, we have $x_3 = 1 - x_1 - x_2$. Therefore, we can rewrite the implicit social objective function, $\omega(x) = \sum_{\theta \in \Theta} U_\theta \cdot g(\theta) = \sum_{\theta \in \Theta} [\alpha_\theta + \beta_\theta \cdot \log(x_\theta)] \cdot g(\theta)$, which was identified in Theorem 3.7 as the following two-variable objective function:

$$W(x_1, x_2) = [\alpha_1 + \log(x_1)] \cdot \left(\frac{1}{3}\right) + [\alpha_2 + \log(x_2)] \cdot \left(\frac{1}{3}\right)$$

$$+ [\alpha_3 + \log(1 - x_1 - x_2)] \cdot \left(\frac{1}{3}\right) \quad (3.11)$$

For this function, the first-order necessary conditions for a maximum are

$$\frac{\partial W}{\partial x_1} = \frac{1}{3 \cdot x_1} + \frac{-1}{3 \cdot (1 - x_1 - x_2)} = 0 \quad (3.12)$$

and

$$\frac{\partial W}{\partial x_2} = \frac{1}{3 \cdot x_2} + \frac{-1}{3 \cdot (1 - x_1 - x_2)} = 0 \quad (3.13)$$

Equations (3.12) and (3.13) imply $(1 - x_1 - x_2) - x_1 = 0$ and $(1 - x_1 - x_2) - x_2 = 0$, which in turn imply $x_1 = \frac{1}{3}$ and $x_2 = \frac{1}{3}$. With this established, we turn to the second-order conditions for this problem.

The Hessian of $W(x_1, x_2)$ is

$$H = \left[\frac{\partial^2 W_{ij}}{\partial x_i \, \partial x_j}\right] (i, j \in \{1, 2\})$$

$$= \left(\frac{1}{3}\right) \cdot \left[\begin{array}{c:c} \dfrac{-1}{(x_1)^2} + \dfrac{-1}{(1 - x_1 - x_2)^2} & \dfrac{-1}{(1 - x_1 - x_2)^2} \\ \hdashline \dfrac{-1}{(1 - x_1 - x_2)^2} & \dfrac{-1}{(x_1)^2} + \dfrac{-1}{(1 - x_1 - x_2)^2} \end{array}\right] \quad (3.14)$$

Therefore, simplifying (3.14),

$$H = \frac{-1}{3 \cdot (1 - x_1 - x_2)^2} \cdot \begin{bmatrix} 1 & 1 \\ 1 & 1 \end{bmatrix} + \left(\frac{1}{3}\right) \cdot \begin{bmatrix} \dfrac{-1}{(x_1)^2} & 0 \\ 0 & \dfrac{-1}{(x_2)^2} \end{bmatrix} \tag{3.15}$$

The first term on the right-hand side of (3.15) is defined and negative *semidefinite* at every feasible (x_1, x_2). The second term is defined and negative *definite* at every feasible (x_1, x_2). Therefore, H is negative definite at every feasible (x_1, x_2). This implies that $(\frac{1}{3}, \frac{1}{3})$ is a local maximum for $W(x_1, x_2)$ and that $W(x_1, x_2)$ is a strictly concave function of (x_1, x_2). Since the domain of $W(x_1, x_2)$ – namely, $\{(x_1, x_2) \in E^2 : x_1 \geq .1, x_2 \geq .1, x_1 + x_2 \leq .9\}$ – is convex, this (in turn) implies that $(\frac{1}{3}, \frac{1}{3})$ is the unique global maximum for $W(x_1, x_2)$. Therefore, $(x_1, x_2, x_3) = (\frac{1}{3}, \frac{1}{3}, \frac{1}{3})$ is the unique maximum for the implicit social objective function given in (3.9), which was identified in Theorem 3.7. This conclusion confirms, by Theorem 3.7, that $(\frac{1}{3}, \frac{1}{3}, \frac{1}{3})$ is the location of the electoral equilibrium.

The third way in which we analyze this example is by directly examining the two-candidate zero-sum game that it leads to. So that we can do this, we derive the payoff function for candidate 1. By the definition of expected plurality given by (2.3) and (2.4), we know that this payoff function is

$$P\ell^1(\psi_1, \psi_2) = \text{EV}^1(\psi_1, \psi_2) - \text{EV}^2(\psi_1, \psi_2)$$

$$= [P_1^1(\psi_1, \psi_2) + P_2^1(\psi_1, \psi_2) + P_3^1(\psi_1, \psi_2)] \cdot \left(\frac{1}{3}\right)$$

$$- [P_1^2(\psi_1, \psi_2) + P_2^2(\psi_1, \psi_2) + P_3^2(\psi_1, \psi_2)] \cdot \left(\frac{1}{3}\right) \tag{3.16}$$

Therefore, we first want to derive the probabilities $P_\theta^1(\psi_1, \psi_2)$ and $P_\theta^1(\psi_1, \psi_2)$ for each $\theta \in \Theta$ (i.e., what the candidates believe are the probabilities for the events "a given voter i in the group θ will vote for candidate 1" and "a given voter i in the group θ will vote for candidate 2," respectively, as a function of ψ_1 and ψ_2).

Because the candidates use a binomial logit model for the voters' selection probabilities, the probabilities of interest must satisfy (2.11). Since $\beta_1 = \beta_2 = \beta_3 = 1$, (2.11) can be written as

$$P_1^c(\psi_1, \psi_2) = P_\theta^c(\psi_1, \psi_2) = \frac{\exp\{\alpha_\theta + \log(\psi_{c\theta})\}}{\exp\{\alpha_\theta + \log(\psi_{c\theta})\} + \exp\{\alpha_\theta + \log(\psi_{k\theta})\}}$$

$$= \frac{\exp\{\alpha_\theta\} \cdot \exp\{\log(\psi_{c\theta})\}}{\exp\{\alpha_\theta\} \cdot \exp\{\log(\psi_{c\theta})\} + \exp\{\alpha_\theta\} \cdot \exp\{\log(\psi_{k\theta})\}} \tag{3.17}$$

Therefore, it follows that the likelihoods of interest are, analogous to (2.18) and (2.19),

$$P_1^1(\psi_1, \psi_2) = \frac{\psi_{11}}{\psi_{11} + \psi_{12}}; \qquad P_2^1(\psi_1, \psi_2) = \frac{\psi_{12}}{\psi_{12} + \psi_{22}};$$

$$P_3^1(\psi_1, \psi_2) = \frac{\psi_{13}}{\psi_{13} + \psi_{23}} \qquad (3.18)$$

and

$$P_1^2(\psi_1, \psi_2) = \frac{\psi_{21}}{\psi_{21} + \psi_{11}}; \qquad P_2^2(\psi_1, \psi_2) = \frac{\psi_{22}}{\psi_{22} + \psi_{12}};$$

$$P_3^1(\psi_1, \psi_2) = \frac{\psi_{23}}{\psi_{23} + \psi_{13}} \qquad (3.19)$$

If we plug (3.18) and (3.19) into (3.16) and rearrange terms, it follows that candidate 1's payoff function is

$$P\ell^1(\psi_1, \psi_2) = \frac{\psi_{11} - \psi_{21}}{\psi_{11} + \psi_{21}} \cdot \left(\frac{1}{3}\right) + \frac{\psi_{12} - \psi_{22}}{\psi_{12} + \psi_{22}} \cdot \left(\frac{1}{3}\right) + \frac{\psi_{13} - \psi_{23}}{\psi_{13} + \psi_{23}} \cdot \left(\frac{1}{3}\right)$$

$$(3.20)$$

By the implication of the common assumptions for S that is stated just before this example, $\psi_{13} = 1 - \psi_{11} - \psi_{12}$ and $\psi_{23} = 1 - \psi_{21} - \psi_{22}$. As a consequence, we can rewrite candidate 1's payoff function as

$$P(\psi_{11}, \psi_{12}; \psi_{21}, \psi_{22}) = \frac{\psi_{11} - \psi_{21}}{\psi_{11} + \psi_{21}} \cdot \left(\frac{1}{3}\right) + \frac{\psi_{12} - \psi_{22}}{\psi_{12} + \psi_{22}} \cdot \left(\frac{1}{3}\right)$$

$$+ \frac{\psi_{21} + \psi_{22} - \psi_{11} - \psi_{12}}{2 - \psi_{11} - \psi_{12} - \psi_{21} - \psi_{22}} \cdot \left(\frac{1}{3}\right) \qquad (3.21)$$

The first-order necessary conditions for ψ_1 to be a local maximum for candidate 1 can, therefore, be written as

$$\frac{\partial P}{\partial \psi_{11}} = \frac{(\psi_{11} + \psi_{21}) - (\psi_{11} - \psi_{21})}{(\psi_{11} + \psi_{22})^2} \cdot \left(\frac{1}{3}\right)$$

$$+ \frac{(2 - \psi_{11} - \psi_{12} - \psi_{21} - \psi_{22}) \cdot (-1) - (\psi_{21} + \psi_{22} - \psi_{11} - \psi_{12}) \cdot (-1)}{(2 - \psi_{11} - \psi_{12} - \psi_{21} - \psi_{22})^2}$$

$$\cdot \left(\frac{1}{3}\right) = 0 \qquad (3.22)$$

$$\frac{\partial P}{\partial \psi_{12}} = \frac{(\psi_{12} + \psi_{22}) - (\psi_{12} - \psi_{22})}{(\psi_{12} + \psi_{22})^2} \cdot \left(\frac{1}{3}\right)$$

$$+ \frac{(2 - \psi_{11} - \psi_{12} - \psi_{21} - \psi_{22}) \cdot (-1) - (\psi_{21} + \psi_{22} - \psi_{11} - \psi_{12}) \cdot (-1)}{(2 - \psi_{11} - \psi_{12} - \psi_{21} - \psi_{22})^2}$$

$$\cdot \left(\frac{1}{3}\right) = 0 \tag{3.23}$$

With $\psi_1 = \psi_2 = x$, (3.22) and (3.23) become

$$\frac{x_1}{6 \cdot (x_1)^2} + \frac{-2 + 2 \cdot x_1 + 2 \cdot x_2}{3 \cdot (2 - 2 \cdot x_1 - 2 \cdot x_2)^2} = \frac{1}{6 \cdot x_1} - \frac{1}{6 \cdot (1 - x_1 - x_2)} = 0 \tag{3.24}$$

and

$$\frac{1}{6 \cdot x_2} - \frac{1}{6 \cdot (1 - x_1 - x_2)} = 0 \tag{3.25}$$

Equations (3.24) and (3.25), in turn, imply $(1 - x_1 - x_2) - x_1 = 0$ and $(1 - x_1 - x_2) - x_2 = 0$. Therefore, $x_1 = \frac{1}{3}$ and $x_2 = \frac{1}{3}$.

At $(\psi_{21}, \psi_{22}) = (\frac{1}{3}, \frac{1}{3})$, (3.22) and (3.23) become

$$\frac{\partial P}{\partial \psi_{11}} = \frac{(\frac{2}{3})}{3 \cdot [\psi_{11} + (\frac{2}{3})]^2} + \frac{-2 + \psi_{11} + \psi_{12} + (\frac{2}{3}) + (\frac{2}{3}) - \psi_{11} - \psi_{12}}{3 \cdot [2 - \psi_{11} - \psi_{12} - (\frac{2}{3})]^2}$$

$$= \frac{(\frac{2}{3})}{3 \cdot [\psi_{11} + (\frac{1}{3})]^2} - \frac{(\frac{2}{3})}{3 \cdot [(\frac{4}{3}) - \psi_{11} - \psi_{12}]^2} \tag{3.26}$$

and

$$\frac{\partial P}{\partial \psi_{12}} = \frac{(\frac{2}{3})}{3 \cdot [\psi_{12} + (\frac{1}{3})]^2} - \frac{(\frac{2}{3})}{3 \cdot [(\frac{4}{3}) - \psi_{11} - \psi_{12}]^2} \tag{3.27}$$

Therefore, the Hessian for $P[\psi_{11}, \psi_{12}; \frac{1}{3}, \frac{1}{3}]$ is

$$H = \left(\frac{2}{9}\right)$$

$$\cdot \begin{bmatrix} \dfrac{-2 \cdot [\psi_{11} + (\frac{1}{3})]}{[\psi_{11} + (\frac{1}{3})]^4} - \dfrac{2 \cdot [(\frac{4}{3}) - \psi_{11} - \psi_{12}]}{[(\frac{4}{3}) - \psi_{11} - \psi_{12}]^4} & \dfrac{-2 \cdot [(\frac{4}{3}) - \psi_{11} - \psi_{12}]}{[(\frac{4}{3}) - \psi_{11} - \psi_{12}]^4} \\[2em] \dfrac{-2 \cdot [(\frac{4}{3}) - \psi_{11} - \psi_{12}]}{[(\frac{4}{3}) - \psi_{11} - \psi_{12}]^4} & \dfrac{-2 \cdot [\psi_{12} + (\frac{1}{3})]}{[\psi_{12} + (\frac{1}{3})]^4} - \dfrac{2 \cdot [(\frac{4}{3}) - \psi_{11} - \psi_{12}]}{[(\frac{4}{3}) - \psi_{11} - \psi_{12}]^4} \end{bmatrix} \tag{3.28}$$

At $(\psi_{11}, \psi_{12}) = (\frac{1}{3}, \frac{1}{3})$, this is

$$\begin{bmatrix} -3 & -(\frac{3}{2}) \\ -(\frac{3}{2}) & -3 \end{bmatrix}$$

We have $\det[-3] = -3 < 0$ and $\det H = 9 - (\frac{9}{4}) > 0$. Therefore, $(\psi_{11}, \psi_{12}) = (\frac{1}{3}, \frac{1}{3})$ is a local maximum for $P(\psi_{11}, \psi_{12}; \frac{1}{3}, \frac{1}{3})$. By a symmetric argument, $(\frac{1}{3}, \frac{1}{3})$ is also a local minimum for $P(\frac{1}{3}, \frac{1}{3}; \psi_{21}, \psi_{22})$. Therefore, we also know that $\psi_1 = (\frac{1}{3}, \frac{1}{3}, \frac{1}{3})$ is a local maximum for $P\ell^1[\psi_1, (\frac{1}{3}, \frac{1}{3}, \frac{1}{3})]$ and that $\psi_2 = (\frac{1}{3}, \frac{1}{3}, \frac{1}{3})$ is a local minimum for $P\ell^1[(\frac{1}{3}, \frac{1}{3}, \frac{1}{3}), \psi_2]$. By Lemma 2.2 in Appendix 2.2, $P\ell^1(x, y)$ is strictly concave in x and strictly convex in y. Therefore, since S is convex, it follows that $\psi_1 = (\frac{1}{3}, \frac{1}{3}, \frac{1}{3})$ is a global maximum for $P\ell^1[\psi_1, (\frac{1}{3}, \frac{1}{3}, \frac{1}{3})]$ and that $\psi_2 = (\frac{1}{3}, \frac{1}{3}, \frac{1}{3})$ is a global minimum for $P\ell^1[(\frac{1}{3}, \frac{1}{3}, \frac{1}{3}), \psi_2]$. Hence,

$$P\ell^1[\psi_1, (\tfrac{1}{3}, \tfrac{1}{3}, \tfrac{1}{3})] \le P\ell^1[(\tfrac{1}{3}, \tfrac{1}{3}, \tfrac{1}{3}), (\tfrac{1}{3}, \tfrac{1}{3}, \tfrac{1}{3})]$$

$$\le P\ell^1[(\tfrac{1}{3}, \tfrac{1}{3}, \tfrac{1}{3}), \psi_2], \quad \forall \; \psi_1, \psi_2 \in S \quad (3.29)$$

Therefore, by the definition of an electoral equilibrium, stated in (2.6), $(\psi_1^*, \psi_2^*) = [(\frac{1}{3}, \frac{1}{3}, \frac{1}{3}), (\frac{1}{3}, \frac{1}{3}, \frac{1}{3})]$ is the electoral equilibrium (which we know is unique by Theorem 3.2). Therefore, our direct examination of the two-candidate zero-sum game that this example leads to also confirms that $(\frac{1}{3}, \frac{1}{3}, \frac{1}{3})$ is the location of the electoral equilibrium.

Theorems 3.5–3.7 imply that with alternative values of $g(1), g(2), g(3)$, β_1, β_2, and/or β_3, the location of the electoral equilibrium may be different from the one in our analyses of Example 3.1. This possibility is illustrated in the next example.

EXAMPLE 3.2

Make the same assumptions as in Example 3.1 except that this time $\beta_3 = \frac{1}{2}$. Thus, the assumptions being added to the election model specified in Section 2.1 are (i) the candidates use a binomial logit model for the voters' selection probabilities; (ii) there are three groups $\theta = 1, 2, 3$; (iii) the total income available is $Y = 1$; (iv) the minimum possible values for the total income received by the groups are $k_1 = k_2 = k_3 = .1$; (v) the groups are of equal size (i.e., $g(1) = g(2) = g(3) = \frac{1}{3}$); (vi) $\beta_1 = \beta_2 = 1$ and $\beta_3 = (\frac{1}{2})$.

In this example, the vector $d^2 \in E^3$ that satisfies (3.5) has (by definition) the following three components:

$$d_1^2 = \frac{\beta_1 \cdot g(1)}{\beta_1 \cdot g(1) + \beta_2 \cdot g(2) + \beta_3 \cdot g(3)} \cdot Y = \frac{(1) \cdot (\frac{1}{3})}{(1) \cdot (\frac{1}{3}) + (1) \cdot (\frac{1}{3}) + (\frac{1}{2}) \cdot (\frac{1}{3})} \cdot 1$$

$$(3.30)$$

$$d_2^2 = \frac{\beta_2 \cdot g(2)}{\beta_1 \cdot g(1) + \beta_2 \cdot g(2) + \beta_3 \cdot g(3)} \cdot Y = \frac{(1) \cdot (\frac{1}{3})}{(1) \cdot (\frac{1}{3}) + (1) \cdot (\frac{1}{3}) + (\frac{1}{2}) \cdot (\frac{1}{3})} \cdot 1$$

(3.31)

$$d_3^2 = \frac{\beta_3 \cdot g(3)}{\beta_1 \cdot g(1) + \beta_2 \cdot g(2) + \beta_3 \cdot g(3)} \cdot Y = \frac{(\frac{1}{2}) \cdot (\frac{1}{3})}{(1) \cdot (\frac{1}{3}) + (1) \cdot (\frac{1}{3}) + (\frac{1}{2}) \cdot (\frac{1}{3})} \cdot 1$$

(3.32)

Hence, $(d_1^2, d_2^2, d_3^2) = (\frac{2}{5}, \frac{2}{5}, \frac{1}{5})$. This d-vector is also in S. Therefore (using Theorem 3.5 again), in this example the location of the electoral equilibrium is $s^2 = (\frac{2}{5}, \frac{2}{5}, \frac{1}{5})$. This location and the location of the electoral equilibrium in Example 3.1 are illustrated in Fig. 3.1. In this figure (as in Fig. 2.2), S is drawn as a two-dimensional (rather than three-dimensional) object so that (as before) the diagram is easier to interpret. With the diagram drawn this way, it is easy to see that the decrease in the parameter β for group 3 has led to the equilibrium shifting away from the ideal point for group 3 and toward the ideal points for groups 1 and 2.

In Section 3.3, it was pointed out that the d-vector given by (3.5) can sometimes fall outside of S. This possibility and the impact that it has on the location of the redistributional equilibrium are illustrated in the final example.

EXAMPLE 3.3

As in Example 3.1, assume that $\beta_1 = \beta_2 = \beta_3 = 1$. This time, however, assume that $g(1) = .01$ and $g(2) = g(3) = .495$. The vector d^3 that satisfies (3.5) in this example has the following three components:

$$d_1^3 = \frac{\beta_1 \cdot g(1)}{\beta_1 \cdot g(1) + \beta_2 \cdot g(2) + \beta_3 \cdot g(3)} \cdot Y$$

$$= \frac{(1) \cdot (.01)}{(1) \cdot (.01) + (1) \cdot (.495) + (1) \cdot (.495)} \cdot 1$$

(3.33)

$$d_2^3 = \frac{\beta_2 \cdot g(2)}{\beta_1 \cdot g(1) + \beta_2 \cdot g(2) + \beta_3 \cdot g(3)} \cdot Y$$

$$= \frac{(1) \cdot (.495)}{(1) \cdot (.01) + (1) \cdot (.495) + (1) \cdot (.495)} \cdot 1$$

(3.34)

$$d_3^3 = \frac{\beta_3 \cdot g(3)}{\beta_1 \cdot g(1) + \beta_2 \cdot g(2) + \beta_3 \cdot g(3)} \cdot Y$$

$$= \frac{(1) \cdot (.495)}{(1) \cdot (.01) + (1) \cdot (.495) + (1) \cdot (.495)} \cdot 1$$

(3.35)

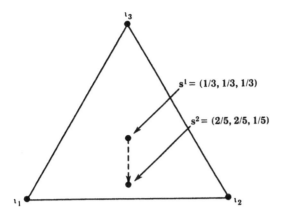

Fig. 3.1 The equilibria in Examples 3.1 and 3.2.

Therefore, $(d_1^3, d_2^3, d_3^3) = (.01, .495, .495)$. Since $d_1^3 = .01 < .1 = k_1$, Theorem 3.5 cannot be applied directly. The location of the electoral equilibrium is, therefore, determined by using Theorem 3.6. By that theorem, since $d_1^3 < k_1$, the first step is to set $s_1^3 = k_1 = .1$. The second step is to solve the reduced election, which has the two groups $\theta = 2$ and $\theta = 3$ and a total income of $Y - k_1 = .9$. Computing the vector d^4 that solves (3.5) in this reduced election [or, equivalently, by solving (3.8)], we get $(d_2^4, d_3^4) = (.45, .45)$. Therefore, by Theorem 3.6, the location of the electoral equilibrium is $(s_1^3, s_2^3, s_3^3) = (.1, .45, .45)$. The resulting equilibrium is illustrated in Fig. 3.2 (where the border of the unit simplex has also been drawn in for reference). In particular, this figure makes it easy to see that the equilibrium is the point in S that is closest to d^3 (or, equivalently, the point that is obtained by dropping a perpendicular bisector from d^3 to the closest edge of S).

3.5 The politics of redistribution

One of the best-known hypotheses about the way in which income is redistributed in an economy with elections is Director's law, which asserts that income tends to be transferred from both high-income and low-income voters to voters who are in the center of the income distribution (e.g., see Stigler, 1970; Tullock, 1971, p. 381; and Mueller, 1976, p. 410; 1979, p. 106). A related hypothesis is the Downsian view, which states that "in a democracy the poor are able to use their votes to obtain transfers from the rest of society" (Tullock, 1971, p. 379; also see Downs, 1957b, pp. 198–201). Because of the attention that these hypotheses have received, it seems worth pointing out that neither of

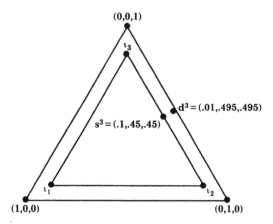

Fig. 3.2 The *d*-vector and the equilibrium in Example 3.3.

them follows as a general implication of the results derived in this and the preceding chapter.

The premise in Theorem 2.1 includes the same basic assumption about voters' choices as the median-voter theorem and the Downsian model (e.g., see Mueller, 1979, pp. 40–1 and 98–9). However, the conclusion in Theorem 2.1 is that there is no equilibrium for the candidates, rather than a tendency for income to be transferred to median-income voters, low-income voters, or any other identifiable income group. What is more, the proof of Theorem 2.1 (in Appendix 2.1) has made it clear that when voting is determined by redistributional reputations, any candidate who adopts either the redistributional strategy identified by Director's law or the redistributional strategy identified by the Downsian view can be beaten by one who does not. Indeed, the familiar logic used in that proof implies that, in considering almost any pair of possible strategies, a candidate will find that he can do better for himself by (alternatively) selecting a reputation for planning to redistribute income in a way other than the ones suggested by Director's law and the Downsian view.

The premises of Theorem 2.2 and the theorems in this chapter included the alternative assumption that the candidates use a binary logit model for the voters' selection probabilities. This assumption turns out to be sufficient for the existence of equilibria for the candidates. These equilibria, however, only rarely exhibit the redistribution pattern in Director's law and the Downsian view. Indeed, there are far more cases in which income is redistributed to groups of voters that do not make up any particular stratum of the income distribution than cases in which income is redistributed from the ends of the income distribution to the center or from the upper to the lower end of the distribution. In this respect, the model and the redistributional equilibria studied in this chapter are closer to Tullock's (1971) view that "the bulk of the transfers are made to groups not defined by income" (p. 383). Additionally, it is worth noting that if we also accept his view that "groups receive their transfers largely in terms of their political power" (p. 383), then the political power of the groups in the model is captured by the coefficients that specify the income shares in equilibrium (i.e., by the $[\beta_j \cdot g(j)] / [\Sigma \ \beta_\theta \cdot g(\theta)]$ terms).

To keep the interpretation of the location results in this chapter clear, it should be emphasized that Theorems 3.5 and 3.6 show that in the model analyzed in this chapter three and only three factors enter into the determination of how the income pie is sliced: (i) the minimum levels of income for the various groups required by law; (ii) the candidates' beliefs about the proportions of the total number of voters in the various groups in the electorate; and (iii) the candidates' beliefs about the parameters $\beta_1, \ldots, \beta_m$ that appear in the voters' utility functions specified in (2.2) in Section 2.1. The minimum requirements for the groups' income levels serve to establish threshold levels for the groups' incomes. In particular, if the value of d_j given by (3.5) turns out to be below the minimum income required for the group j, then the group gets only this minimum amount. On the other hand, if the value of d_j given by (3.5) turns out to be above the groups' minimum, then the income for the group is positively related to the size of its parameter β_θ and the proportion of the voters contained in the group.

The conclusion that (above the threshold level) a group's income is a strictly increasing function of the proportion of the electorate in the group reflects the fact that each candidate wants to win over as many voters as possible. The parameter β_θ that appears in any voter's utility function, in a sense, measures the strength of his preference for income relative to the other factors that can affect his vote. In particular, the larger β_θ is, the more difficult it is for other factors to outweigh the voter's utility from his income. As a consequence, the larger β_θ is, the more likely it is that the voter's choice will be determined solely on the basis of the candidates' redistributional reputations. This conclusion, in turn, implies that the larger β_θ is, the greater the incentive for a candidate to obtain a redistributional reputation that would make the voter expect a large income. These observations summarize why a group's income is a strictly increasing function of its parameter β_θ (again, above the threshold level where the candidates start to concern themselves with the group).

To keep the interpretation of Theorems 3.5 and 3.6 as clear as possible, it is important to emphasize that the analysis in this chapter has determined the optimal strategies for the candidates as a function of the g's and β's in the model; that is, the location for the candidates identified by Theorems 3.5 and 3.6 is contingent on the particular g's and β's that the candidates believe are correct. It is also important to emphasize that the entire analysis up to this point has been based on the assumption that the candidates have definite, established beliefs about what the values of $g(1), \ldots, g(m)$ and $\beta_1, \ldots, \beta_m$ are, leaving in the background the question of just where these beliefs came from. Thus, there is no theory about how the g's and β's are formed. It seems natural to suggest that the candidates' beliefs about what these parameters are will come, at least in part, from efforts by the groups in the electorate to influence these beliefs. Indeed, the remarks in the previous paragraph make it clear that, if a group has the opportunity to convince the candidates that its $g(j)$ or its β_j is higher than they currently believe it is, bringing about such a change in their beliefs would usually lead to a higher income for the group (in particular, when the resulting value of d_j given by (3.5) exceeds the minimum income that the group has to get). What is more, we commonly see both of these phenomena in practice. When the farmers march on Washington, they are saying, "I'm hurting more than you think; please give me a bigger share of the pot." Census fraud and fraudulent lists of registered voters are legendary in Chicago, Philadelphia, and other communities. It therefore seems worthwhile to point out that if the voters have an opportunity to manipulate the candidates' beliefs about $g(1), \ldots, g(m)$ and $\beta_1, \ldots, \beta_m$, the effect is (in general) to make the candidates' equilibrium dependent on the voters' efforts. In particular, the equilibrium will be the one that corresponds to the parameters that result once the voters have done all that they can to influence the candidates' beliefs about them; that is, the candidates' strategies will be at the point that Theorems 3.5 and 3.6 identify as the equilibrium location for the resultant parameters.

The observations in the preceding paragraph should make it clear that there still needs to be some n-person noncooperative modeling of the game over g and β formation before it will be possible to say precisely which of the possible values for these parameters can be expected to be the relevant ones in a particular empirical context. It should also be pointed out that the g's and β's would also have to be estimated (presumably using standard statistical methods and appropriate data sets) before actual candidates would be able to know what their optimal strategies are.

It should also be noted that if (in a particular context) there is no a priori reason to rule out any possible values for the g's and the β's in the model, then the theorems that have been derived do not rule out a priori any particular income distribution (since, for each possible income distribution there is a corresponding choice of g's and β's that leads to this distribution being the optimal strategy for each candidate). This conclusion, of course, is not surprising since it says that if we do not know anything about the distribution of voters and also do not know what their utilities for redistributional reputations are, then we do not know what redistributional reputations will be adopted by the candidates. However, when there is reason to restrict the g and β parameters to certain specific subsets of their possible values, Theorems 3.5 and 3.6 will (generally) also reduce the set of outcomes predicted by the model. What is more, as these beliefs become better known (in the sense of the subsets of possible values shrinking), the set of predicted outcomes will also (generally) become smaller. Finally, in the limit where these beliefs become known to a person testing the model or are assumed to have specific values by a person using the model for a theoretical analysis, Theorems 3.5 and 3.6 have the virtue that they give a very precise prediction by ruling out a priori every possible equilibrium except the unique distribution of income identified by (3.7) and (3.8).

Finally, it is also worthwhile to point out that though Theorem 3.3 states that (in the model it applies to) the candidates will choose the same redistributional reputations, the redistributional reputations of Mondale and Reagan described in the opening discussion in Chapter 2 are, in fact, different from each other. This naturally leads to the question of whether their campaign strategies were simply not in equilibrium or (as seems to be more likely) there were constraints or asymmetries present in the 1984 presidential election that are not reflected in the election model studied in this chapter. If the latter is true, then there is clearly some potential for future research that explicitly incorporates these factors into the model.

3.6   Conclusion

This chapter has provided an in-depth analysis of the model of an election with redistributional reputations that results when the assumptions in Section 2.1 are combined with a logit model for the candidates' expectations (in place of the assumption that they expect the voters' choices to be fully determined by the candidates' redistributional reputations, which was studied in Section 2.4). Among other things, the results established that there is always a unique equilibrium, provided a simple procedure for finding the precise location of this equilibrium, and showed that this location implicitly maximizes the sum of the voters' utility functions on the set of possible income distributions. The penultimate sections provided some simple examples that illustrate the main results in the chapter plus a discussion of these results and the results in Chapter 2 in terms of the politics of redistribution.

The next chapter develops and analyzes a model in which the assumptions used thus far, which are special to income redistribution and the logit model, are replaced by more general assumptions. Among other things, the more general results that are then derived make it clear that neither the assumption that the candidates' strategies are redistributional reputations nor the logit model is crucially needed for an electoral equilibrium to exist or for the equilibrium strategies to be social alternatives that maximize an implicit social objective function.

Appendix 3.1: Proofs of Theorems 3.1–3.4

Proof of Theorem 3.1

("If")   This part follows directly from the definition of an electoral equilibrium in Section 2.3 plus the fact that $P\ell^2(x, y) = -P\ell^1(x, y)$, $\forall (x, y) \in S \times S$.

("Only if")   Assume $(\psi_1^*, \psi_2^*) \in S \times S$ is an electoral equilibrium. Then, by (2.6), we have $P\ell^1(\psi_1^*, \psi_2^*) \geq P\ell^1(\psi_1, \psi_2^*)$, $\forall \psi_1 \in S - \{\psi_1^*\}$. Suppose $\exists \psi_1 \in S - \{\psi_1^*\}$ such that $P\ell^1(\psi_1^*, \psi_2^*) = P\ell^1(\psi_1, \psi_2^*)$. Consider $w = \frac{1}{2} \cdot \psi_1^* + \frac{1}{2} \cdot \psi_1$. Since S is convex, $w \in S - \{\psi_1^*\}$. Since, by Lemma 2.2, $P\ell^1(x, \psi_2^*)$ is a strictly concave function of x on S, we have $P\ell^1(w, \psi_2^*) > \frac{1}{2} \cdot P\ell^1(\psi_1^*, \psi_2) + \frac{1}{2} \cdot P\ell^1(\psi_1, \psi_2)$. Therefore, since $P\ell^1(\psi_1^*, \psi_2^*) = P\ell^1(\psi_1, \psi_2^*)$, we have $P\ell^1(w, \psi_2^*) > P\ell^1(\psi_1^*, \psi_2^*)$, contradicting (2.6). Hence, (3.1) holds. Since $P\ell^2(x, y) = -P\ell^1(x, y)$, $\forall (x, y) \in S \times S$, (i) (2.6) implies $P\ell^2(\psi_1^*, \psi_2^*) \geq P\ell^2(\psi_1^*, \psi_2)$, $\forall \psi_2 \in S - \{\psi_2^*\}$ and (ii) Lemma 2.2 implies that $P\ell^2(\psi_1^*, y)$ is a strictly concave function of y on S. Therefore, by an argument similar to that used to obtain (3.1) (with the roles of ψ_1 and ψ_2 reversed), (3.2) holds.

QED

Proof of Theorem 3.2

By Theorem 2.2 there exists at least one electoral equilibrium. Suppose that two distinct pairs $(x, y) \in S \times S$ and $(w, z) \in S \times S$ are both electoral equilibria. By Theorem 3.1 and the fact that $P\ell^1(s, t) = -P\ell^2(s, t)$, $\forall (s, t) \in S \times S$,

$$P\ell^1(x, y) > P\ell^1(\psi_1, y), \qquad \forall \psi_1 \in S - \{x\} \tag{A3.1}$$

$$P\ell^1(x, y) < P\ell^1(x, \psi_2), \qquad \forall\, \psi_2 \in S - \{y\} \tag{A3.2}$$

$$P\ell^1(w, z) > P\ell^1(\psi_1, z), \qquad \forall\, \psi_1 \in S - \{w\} \tag{A3.3}$$

$$P\ell^1(w, z) < P\ell^1(w, \psi_2), \qquad \forall\, \psi_2 \in S - \{z\} \tag{A3.4}$$

If $x = w$, then, since (x, y) and (w, z) are distinct pairs, $y \neq z$. Therefore, by (A3.2) and the fact that $y \neq z$, $P\ell^1(x, y) < P\ell^1(x, z)$; and by (A3.4) and the fact that $x = w$ and $y \neq z$, $P\ell^1(x, z) < P\ell^1(x, y)$, implying $P\ell^1(x, y) < P\ell^1(x, y)$, a contradiction. Therefore, we must have $x \neq w$. If $y = z$, then, since $x \neq w$, we have by (A3.1) $P\ell^1(x, y) > P\ell^1(w, y)$ and by (A3.3) $P\ell^1(w, y) > P\ell^1(x, y)$, again implying $P\ell^1(x, y) > P\ell^1(x, y)$, a contradiction. Therefore, we must have $y \neq z$. Finally, since $x \neq w$ and $y \neq z$, we have by (A3.1), $P\ell^1(x, y) > P\ell^1(w, y)$; by (A3.4), $P\ell^1(w, y) > P\ell^1(w, z)$; by (A3.3), $P\ell^1(w, z) > P\ell^1(x, z)$; and by (A3.2), $P\ell^1(x, z) > P\ell^1(x, y)$, once again implying $P\ell^1(x, y) > P\ell^1(x, y)$, a contradiction. Hence, there cannot be more than one electoral equilibrium. Therefore, there is exactly one electoral equilibrium.

QED

Proof of Theorem 3.3

Let $(w, z) \in S \times S$ be the electoral equilibrium. Suppose $w \neq z$. By Lemma 2.1, $P\ell^1(z, z) = 0$. Therefore by Theorem 3.1, since $w \neq z$,

$$P\ell^1(w, z) > P\ell^1(z, z) = 0 \tag{A3.5}$$

Using Lemma 2.1 again gives $P\ell^2(w, w) = -P\ell^1(w, w) = 0$. Therefore, using Theorem 3.1 again gives $P\ell^2(w, z) > P\ell^2(w, w) = 0$. Since $P\ell^2(w, z) = -P\ell^1(w, z)$, this implies $P\ell^1(w, z) < 0$. By (A3.5), this implies $P\ell^1(w, z) > P\ell^1(w, z)$, a contradiction. Therefore, $w = z$.

QED

Proof of the Corollary to Theorem 3.3

Theorem 3.3 plus Lemma 2.1 directly imply $P\ell^1(\psi_1^*, \psi_2^*) = 0$. Since $P\ell^2(\psi_1^*, \psi_2^*) = -P\ell^1(\psi_1^*, \psi_2^*)$ this, in turn, implies $P\ell^2(\psi_1^*, \psi_2^*) = 0$.

QED

Proof of Theorem 3.4

("Only if") Assume z is the location of the electoral equilibrium. Then, by definition (z, z) is the electoral equilibrium. Therefore, by (2.6) and (2.1), z solves (3.4).

("If") Assume z solves (3.4). Let $\psi_1^* = z$ and $\psi_2^* = z$. By (2.1), the fact that z solves (3.4) immediately implies that the inequalities on the left-hand side of (2.6) are satisfied. By (2.1) and Lemma 2.1, the fact that z solves (3.4) implies that z solves

$$\max_{x} 2 \cdot \sum_{\theta \in \Theta} \left[\frac{(x_\theta)^{\beta_\theta}}{(x_\theta)^{\beta_\theta} + (z_\theta)^{\beta_\theta}} \cdot g(\theta) \right] - 1 \qquad (A3.6)$$

subject to $\qquad \sum_{\theta \in \Theta} x_\theta = Y$

and $\qquad x_\theta \geq k_\theta, \qquad \forall\, \theta \in \Theta$

Therefore (changing symbols), z solves

$$\max_{y} 2 \cdot \sum_{\theta \in \Theta} \left[\frac{(y_\theta)^{\beta_\theta}}{(y_\theta)^{\beta_\theta} + (z_\theta)^{\beta_\theta}} \cdot g(\theta) \right] - 1 \qquad (A3.7)$$

subject to $\qquad \sum_{\theta \in \Theta} y_\theta = Y$

and $\qquad y_\theta \geq k_\theta, \qquad \forall\, \theta \in \Theta$

Therefore by (A2.23) (in the proof of Lemma 2.2 in Appendix 2.2), z solves

$$\max_{y} -P\ell^1(z, y) \qquad (A3.8)$$

subject to $\qquad \sum_{\theta \in \Theta} y_\theta = Y$

and $\qquad y_\theta \geq k_\theta, \qquad \forall\, \theta \in \Theta$

Hence, by (2.1), z solves

$$\min_{y \in S} P\ell^1(z, y) \qquad (A3.9)$$

Therefore, the inequalities on the right-hand side of (2.6) are satisfied. Therefore, $(\psi_1^*, \psi_2^*) = (z, z)$ is an electoral equilibrium. Therefore, by Theorem 3.2, (z, z) is the only electoral equilibrium. Therefore, by definition, z is the location of the electoral equilibrium.

QED

Appendix 3.2: Proof of Theorem 3.5

The following lemma will be used in the proof of Theorem 3.5. [Note: The two equations (A2.15) and (A2.16) that appear in the statement of the lemma are in the proof of Lemma 2.2 in Appendix 2.2.] The unstated premise used in Lemmata 2.1 and 2.2 in Appendix 2.2 will once again be taken as given.

Lemma 3.1

Let S_e be defined by (A2.15); let $P\ell_e^1(x, z)$ be defined by (A2.16); $z \in S_e$ solves

$$\max_{x \in S_e} P\ell_e^1(x, z) \tag{A3.10}$$

subject to $\quad \sum_{\theta \in \Theta} x_\theta = Y$

if and only if

$$z_j = \frac{\beta_j \cdot g(j)}{\sum_{\theta \in \Theta} \beta_\theta \cdot g(\theta)} \cdot Y, \qquad \forall\, j \in \Theta$$

For the proof of Lemma 3.1, recall that the "general Lagrangian problem" (see Sydsaeter, 1981, p. 272) is

$$\max_x f(x) \tag{A3.11}$$

subject to $\quad \gamma_1(x) = b_1$

$$\vdots \qquad (t < n)$$

$$\gamma_t(x) = b_t$$

where (i) f and $\gamma_1, \ldots, \gamma_t$ are real-valued functions on a set $A \subseteq E^n$; (ii) $b_1, \ldots, b_t \in E^1$; and (iii) $x = (x_1, \ldots, x_n) \in A$. In proving Lemma 3.1, we use the following well-known result about the general Lagrangian problem (which can be obtained, for instance, from theorems 5.20 and 5.21 plus remark 5.62 in Sydsaeter, 1981, sect. 5.10).

Theorem

Suppose f is a concave, C^1, real-valued function and $\gamma_1, \ldots, \gamma_t$ are linear, real-valued functions on a convex set A in E^n. Let x^o be an interior point of A at which the Jacobian matrix

$$\left[\frac{\partial \gamma_h(x^o)}{\partial x_j} \right] \qquad (h = 1, \ldots, t; \quad j = 1, \ldots, n)$$

has rank t; x^o is a global maximum for the general Lagrangian problem (A3.11) if and only if

$$\exists \text{ a unique } (\lambda_1, \ldots, \lambda_t) \in E^t : \frac{\partial f(x^o)}{\partial x_j} - \sum_{h=1}^{t} \lambda_h \cdot \frac{\partial \gamma_h(x^o)}{\partial x_j} = 0,$$

$$j = 1, \ldots, n \qquad\qquad\qquad\qquad\qquad\qquad\qquad\qquad (A3.12)$$

and

$$\gamma_h(x^o) = b_h, \qquad h = 1, \ldots, t \qquad\qquad\qquad\qquad\qquad (A3.13)$$

Proof of Lemma 3.1

By (A2.16) and the proof of Lemma 2.2, $P\ell_e^1(x, z)$ is a concave, C^1, real-valued function on S_e. The function $\gamma_1(x) = \sum_\theta x_\theta$ is clearly a linear, real-valued function on S_e (e.g., see the definition of a linear transformation on pp. 99–100 in Sydsaeter, 1981). It was noted in the proof of Lemma 2.2 that S_e is an open, convex subset of E^m. Since S_e is open, each $z \in S_e$ is an interior point of S_e. The Jacobian matrix for the one function $\gamma_1(x) = \sum_\theta x_\theta$ is

$$\left[\frac{\partial \gamma_1(x)}{\partial x_j} \right] = [1, \ldots, 1]$$

That is, it is the $(1 \times m)$ matrix of all ones. This matrix has rank 1. Therefore, by the theorem that immediately precedes this proof, $z \in S_e$ solves (A3.10) if and only if

$$\exists \text{ a unique } \lambda \in E^1 : \frac{\partial P\ell_e^1(x, z)}{\partial x_j}\bigg|_{x=z} - \lambda = 0, \qquad j = 1, \ldots, m \qquad (A3.14)$$

and

$$\sum_\theta z_\theta = Y \qquad\qquad\qquad\qquad\qquad\qquad\qquad\qquad (A3.15)$$

We are now ready to directly derive the "only if" (and then the "if") statement in Lemma 3.1.

("Only if")   Assume $z \in S_e$ solves (A3.10). Then, by what was proven in the opening paragraph in this proof, (A3.14) and (A3.15) must hold. By (A3.14) and (A2.18), $\exists$ a unique number λ such that

$$2 \cdot \frac{(z_j)^{\beta_j} \cdot \beta_j \cdot (x_j)^{\beta_j-1}}{[(x_j)^{\beta_j} + (z_j)^{\beta_j}]^2} \cdot g(j) \bigg|_{x=z} - \lambda = 0, \qquad j = 1, \ldots, m \qquad (A3.16)$$

Evaluating the leftmost term at $x = z$, (A3.16) can be rewritten as

$$2 \cdot \frac{\beta_j \cdot (z_j)^{2\beta_j-1}}{[2 \cdot (z_j)^{\beta_j}]^2} \cdot g(j) - \lambda = 0, \qquad \forall j \in \Theta \qquad\qquad (A3.17)$$

which is equivalent to

$$\lambda = \frac{\beta_j \cdot g(j)}{2 \cdot z_j}, \qquad \forall j \in \Theta \tag{A3.18}$$

Therefore,

$$\frac{\beta_j \cdot g(j)}{2 \cdot z_j} = \frac{\beta_h \cdot g(h)}{2 \cdot z_h}, \qquad \forall h, j \in \Theta$$

Therefore, for any given $j \in \Theta$, we have

$$z_\theta = \frac{\beta_\theta \cdot g(\theta)}{\beta_j \cdot g(j)} \cdot z_j \theta \qquad \forall \theta \in \Theta$$

Therefore by (A3.15)

$$Y = \sum_\theta z_\theta = \sum_\theta \frac{\beta_\theta \cdot g(\theta)}{\beta_j \cdot g(j)} \cdot z_j$$

Therefore,

$$z_j = \frac{\beta_j \cdot g(j)}{\sum_\theta \beta_\theta \cdot g(\theta)} \cdot Y$$

("If")   Assume

$$z_j = \frac{\beta_j \cdot g(j)}{\sum_\theta \beta_\theta \cdot g(\theta)} \cdot Y, \qquad \forall j \in \Theta$$

We immediately have $\sum z_\theta = Y$. Therefore, (A3.15) is satisfied. By (A2.18) and (A3.16)–(A3.18),

$$\left. \frac{\partial P\ell_e^1(x, z)}{\partial x_j} \right|_{x=z} - \lambda = 0, \qquad j = 1, \ldots, m \tag{A3.19}$$

if and only if

$$\lambda = \frac{\beta_j \cdot g(j)}{2 \cdot z_j} \qquad \forall j \in \Theta$$

Therefore, by our starting assumption about z_j, (A3.19) holds for

$$\lambda = \frac{\sum_\theta \beta_\theta \cdot g(\theta)}{2 \cdot Y}$$

Therefore, (A3.14) is satisfied. Therefore, by what was proven in the opening paragraph in this proof, z solves (A3.10).

QED

Proof of Theorem 3.5

Assume that the vector $d \in E^m$ that satisfies (3.5) is contained in S. By Lemma 3.1, d solves (A3.10). Therefore, since $S \subset S_e$, the vector d also solves (3.4). Therefore, by Theorem 3.4, d is the location of the electoral equilibrium.

QED

Appendix 3.3: Proof of Theorem 3.6

The following lemma will be used in the proof of Theorem 3.6. As with the earlier lemmata, it will be assumed as an unstated premise that there is an election with redistributional reputations in which the candidates use a binomial logit model for the voters' selection probabilities.

Lemma 3.2

Let $P\ell_e^1(x, z)$ be defined by (A2.16); z solves

$$\max_{x} P\ell_e^1(x, z) \tag{A3.20}$$

$$\text{subject to} \quad \sum_{\theta \in \theta} x_\theta \leq Y$$

$$\text{and} \quad x_\theta \geq k_\theta, \quad \forall \, \theta \in \Theta$$

if and only if z satisfies (3.7) and (3.8).

For the proof of Lemma 3.2, recall the following:

1.   The nonlinear programming problem (see Sydsaeter, 1981, p. 297) is

$$\max_{(x_1, \ldots, x_n)} f(x_1, \ldots, x_n) \tag{A3.21}$$

$$\text{subject to} \quad \gamma_1(x_1, \ldots, x_n) \leq b_1$$

$$\vdots$$

$$\gamma_t(x_1, \ldots, x_n) \leq b_t$$

$$x_1 \geq 0, \ldots, x_n \geq 0$$

where (i) f and $\gamma_1, \ldots, \gamma_t$ are real-valued functions on a set $A \subseteq E^n$, which contains every $(x_1, \ldots, x_n) \in E^n$ that satisfies the $t + n$ inequalities in (A3.21), and (ii) $b_1, \ldots, b_t \in E^1$.

2. $E_+^n = \{(x_1, \ldots, x_n) \in E^n : x_j \leq 0, j = 1, \ldots, n\}$
3.   The Slater condition (see Sydsaeter, 1981, p. 307) is

$$\exists \, x' \in E^n_+ : \gamma_h(x') < b_h, \qquad h = 1, \ldots, t \qquad\qquad\text{(A3.22)}$$

In proving Lemma 3.2, we use the following well-known result about the nonlinear programming problem (which follows, for instance, from Theorem 5.30 in Sydsaeter, 1981, sect. 5.15).

Theorem

Suppose that f is a concave, C^1, real-valued function and $\gamma_1, \ldots,$ γ_t are linear, real-valued functions on E^n_+. Assume the Slater condition is satisfied. $x^o \in E^n_+$ is a global maximum for the nonlinear programming problem, (A3.21), if and only if $\exists (\lambda_1, \ldots, \lambda_t)$ $\in E^t_+$ such that

$$\frac{\partial f(x^o)}{\partial x_j} - \sum_{h=1}^{t} \lambda_h \cdot \frac{\partial \gamma_h(x^o)}{\partial x_j} \leq 0, \qquad j = 1, \ldots, n \qquad\qquad\text{(A3.23)}$$

$$x^o_j = 0 \quad \text{or} \quad \frac{\partial f(x^o)}{\partial x_j} - \sum_{h=1}^{t} \lambda_h \cdot \frac{\partial \gamma_h(x^o)}{\partial x_j} = 0, \qquad j = 1, \ldots, n$$

$$\text{(A3.24)}$$

$$\gamma_h(x^o) \leq b_h, \qquad h = 1, \ldots, t \qquad\qquad\text{(A3.25)}$$

$$\lambda_h = 0 \quad \text{if} \quad \gamma_h(x^o) < b_h, \qquad h = 1, \ldots, t \qquad\qquad\text{(A3.26)}$$

Proof of Lemma 3.2

("If")   Assume z satisfies (3.7) and (3.8). In this proof, w_θ is used to denote the variable obtained when x_θ is rescaled by subtracting k_θ from it, that is, $w_\theta = x_\theta - k_\theta$, $\forall \, \theta \in \Theta$. In this notation, $x_\theta \geq k_\theta$, $\forall \, \theta \in \Theta$, becomes $w_\theta \geq 0$, $\forall \, \theta \in \Theta$, and $\sum_\theta x_\theta \leq Y$ becomes $\sum_\theta (w_\theta + k_\theta) \leq Y$ or, equivalently, $\sum_\theta w_\theta \leq Y - \sum_\theta k_\theta$. In what follows, we denote $\sum_\theta w_\theta$ by $\gamma_1(w)$ and $Y - \sum_\theta k_\theta$ by b_1, making the corresponding constraint $\gamma_1(w) \leq b_1$. In addition, we let

$$P\ell^1_k(w, v) = P\ell^1_e(w + k, v + k) \qquad\qquad\text{(A3.27)}$$

where $k = (k_1, \ldots, k_m)$ and $r + k = (r_1 + k_1, \ldots, r_m + k_m)$. Using this new notation, we can restate (A3.20) as

$$\max_w \; P\ell^1_k(w, z - k) \qquad\qquad\text{(A3.28)}$$

$$\text{subject to} \qquad \gamma_1(w) \leq b_1$$

$$\text{and} \qquad w_1 \geq 0, \ldots, w_m \geq 0$$

By (A3.27), (A2.16), and (A2.15), $P\ell_k^1(x, y)$ is a C^1, real-valued function of x on S_e for any given $y \in S_e$. By the proof of Lemma 2.2, $P\ell_e^1(x, y)$ is a strictly concave function of x on S_e for any given $y \in S_e$. Therefore, for and given $v \in E_+^m$, we have

$$P\ell_k^1(\lambda \cdot w' + (1 - \lambda) \cdot w'', v)$$
$$= P\ell_e^1(\lambda \cdot w' + (1 - \lambda) \cdot w'' + k, v + k)$$
$$= P\ell_e^1(\lambda \cdot (w' + k) + (1 - \lambda) \cdot (w'' + k), v + k)$$
$$> \lambda \cdot P\ell_e^1(w' + k, v + k) + (1 - \lambda) \cdot P\ell_e^1(w'' + k, v + k)$$
$$= \lambda \cdot P\ell_k^1(w', v) + (1 - \lambda) \cdot P\ell_k^1(w'', v)$$

for each distinct pair w', $w'' \in E_+^m$, and $\lambda \in (0, 1)$. Therefore, $P\ell_k^1(w, v)$ is a strictly concave function of w, for any given $v \in E_+^m$ (e.g., see the definition of a strictly concave function on p. 247 of Sydsaeter, 1981). The function $\gamma_1(w) = \sum_\theta w_\theta$ is clearly a linear, real-valued function on E_+^m. Furthermore, since $\sum_\theta k_\theta < Y$ (see Section 2.1), we have $\gamma_1(w') = \sum w_\theta' = 0 < Y - \sum_\theta k_\theta = b_1$ at $w' = (0, \dots, 0) \in E_+^m$ (i.e., at the zero vector in E^m). Therefore, the Slater condition is satisfied for (A3.28). Therefore, by the theorem that immediately precedes this proof, a necessary and sufficient condition for $w^o = z - k$ to solve (A3.28) or, equivalently, for $z = w^o + k$ to solve (A3.20) is $\exists \lambda \in E_+^1$ such that

$$\frac{\partial P\ell_k^1(w^o, z - k)}{\partial w_j} - \lambda \cdot \frac{\partial \gamma_1(w^o)}{\partial w_j} \le 0, \qquad j = 1, \dots, m \qquad \text{(A3.29)}$$

$$w_j^o = 0 \quad \text{or} \quad \frac{\partial P\ell_k^1(w^o, z - k)}{\partial w_j} - \lambda \cdot \frac{\partial \gamma_1(w^o)}{\partial w_j} = 0, \qquad j = 1, \dots, m$$
$$\text{(A3.30)}$$

$$\gamma_1(w^o) \le b_1 \qquad \text{(A3.31)}$$

$$\lambda = 0 \quad \text{if} \quad \gamma_1(w^o) < b_1 \qquad \text{(A3.32)}$$

By (A3.27), (A2.16), and the chain rule (e.g., see Sydsaeter, 1981, pp. 66–7),

$$\frac{\partial P\ell_k^1(w^o, z - k)}{\partial w_j} = \frac{\partial P\ell_e^1(w^o + k, z)}{\partial x_j} = 2 \cdot \frac{(z_j)^{\beta_j} \cdot \beta_j \cdot (w_j^o + k_j)^{\beta_j - 1}}{[(w_j^o + k_j)^{\beta_j} + (z_j)^{\beta_j}]^2} \cdot g(j),$$
$$\forall j \in \Theta \qquad \text{(A3.33)}$$

In addition,

$$\frac{\partial \gamma_1(w^o)}{\partial w_j} = 1, \qquad \forall j \in \Theta \qquad \text{(A3.34)}$$

Therefore (with the definitions given at the beginning of this proof), (A3.29)–(A3.32) can be rewritten as

$$2 \cdot \frac{(z_j)^{\beta_j} \cdot \beta_j \cdot (w_j^o + k_j)^{\beta_j - 1}}{[(w_j^o + k_j)^{\beta_j} + (z_j)^{\beta_j}]^2} \cdot g(j) \leq \lambda, \qquad \forall j \in \Theta \tag{A3.35}$$

$$w_j^o = 0 \quad \text{or} \quad 2 \cdot \frac{(z_j)^{\beta_j} \cdot \beta_j \cdot (w_j^o + k_j)^{\beta_j - 1}}{[(w_j^o + k_j)^{\beta_j} + (z_j)^{\beta_j}]^2} \cdot g(j) = \lambda, \qquad \forall j \in \Theta$$
$$\tag{A3.36}$$

$$\sum_\Theta w_\Theta^o \leq Y - \sum_\Theta k_\Theta \tag{A3.37}$$

$$\lambda = 0 \quad \text{if} \quad \sum_\Theta w_\Theta^o < Y - \sum_\Theta k_\Theta \tag{A3.38}$$

We establish that z solves (A3.20) by showing that $w^o = z - k$ solves (A3.28). Since, by the starting assumption for this proof, z satisfies (3.7) and (3.8), $\sum_\Theta w_\Theta^o = Y - \sum_\Theta k_\Theta$. Therefore, (A3.38) and (A3.37) are satisfied. Since $w_j^o = z_j - k_j$ holds for each $j \in \Theta$, (i) (3.7) immediately implies that (A3.36) holds for each $j \in B$, and (ii) for each $j \in A$, the equality on the right side of (A3.36) reduces to

$$\frac{\beta_j \cdot g(j)}{2 \cdot z_j} = \lambda \tag{A3.39}$$

Let λ be the number given by the following equation:

$$\lambda = \frac{\sum_{\Theta \in A} \beta_\Theta \cdot g(\Theta)}{2 \cdot (Y - \sum_{\Theta \in B} k_\Theta)} \tag{A3.40}$$

Then, by (3.8) we have (A3.39) for each $j \in A$. Therefore, the equality on the right-hand side of (A3.36) holds for each $j \in A$. Therefore, (A3.36) holds for each $j \in \Theta$. Since the equality on the right-hand side of (A3.36) holds for each $j \in A$, we also have (A3.35) for each $j \in A$. As the last step in this part of the proof, it is shown that (A3.35) holds for each $j \in B$. Once this is done, we know that (A3.35)–(A3.38) are satisfied at $w^o = z - k$. This, in turn, implies that $w^o = z - k$ solves (A3.28), which establishes that z solves (A3.20).

Since $w^o = z - k$, we have (A3.35) for each $j \in B$ if and only if

$$\frac{\beta_j \cdot g(j)}{2 \cdot z_j} \leq \lambda, \qquad \forall j \in B \tag{A3.41}$$

as in (A3.39). This inequality is established by deriving two other inequalities, (A3.43) and (A3.44), which, when taken together, imply (A3.41). First, by the definition of B,

$$\frac{\beta_j \cdot g(j)}{\sum_\Theta \beta_\Theta \cdot g(\Theta)} \cdot Y \leq k_j, \qquad \forall j \in B \tag{A3.42}$$

Therefore, from the fact that $Y > 0$ and $k_\theta > 0$, $\forall\, \theta \in \Theta$,

$$\frac{\beta_j \cdot g(j)}{2 \cdot k_j} \le \frac{\Sigma_\theta \beta_\theta \cdot g(\theta)}{2 \cdot Y}, \qquad \forall\, j \in B \tag{A3.43}$$

Second, (A3.42) $\Rightarrow$

$$\sum_{j \in B} \frac{\beta_j \cdot g(j)}{\Sigma_\theta \beta_\theta \cdot g(\theta)} \cdot Y \le \sum_{j \in B} k_j$$

$$\Rightarrow \frac{Y \cdot \Sigma_{j \in B} \beta_j \cdot g(j)}{\Sigma_\theta \beta_\theta \cdot g(\theta)} \le \sum_{j \in B} k_j$$

$$\Rightarrow Y \cdot \sum_{j \in B} \beta_j \cdot g(j) \le \left(\sum_{j \in B} k_j \right) \cdot \left[\sum_\theta \beta_\theta \cdot g(\theta) \right]$$

$$\Rightarrow Y \cdot \sum_{j \in A} \beta_j \cdot g(j) + Y \cdot \sum_{j \in B} \beta_j \cdot g(j) \le Y \cdot \sum_{j \in A} \beta_j \cdot g(j)$$

$$+ \left(\sum_{j \in B} k_j \right) \cdot \left[\sum_\theta \beta_\theta \cdot g(\theta) \right]$$

$$\Rightarrow Y \cdot \left[\sum_\theta \beta_\theta \cdot g(\theta) \right] \le Y \cdot \sum_{j \in A} \beta_j \cdot g(j) + \left[\left(\sum_{j \in B} k_j \right) \cdot \left(\sum_\theta \beta_\theta \cdot g(\theta) \right) \right]$$

$$\Rightarrow \left(Y - \sum_{j \in B} k_j \right) \cdot \left[\sum_\theta \beta_\theta \cdot g(\theta) \right] \le Y \cdot \sum_{j \in A} \beta_j \cdot g(j)$$

$$\Rightarrow \frac{\Sigma_\theta \beta_\theta \cdot g(\theta)}{Y} \le \frac{\Sigma_{j \in A} \beta_j \cdot g(j)}{Y - \Sigma_{j \in B} k_j}$$

$$\Rightarrow \frac{\Sigma_\theta \beta_\theta \cdot g(\theta)}{2 \cdot Y} \le \frac{\Sigma_{j \in A} \beta_j \cdot g(j)}{2 \cdot (Y - \Sigma_{j \in B} k_j)} \tag{A3.44}$$

By (A3.43) and (A3.44),

$$\frac{\beta_j \cdot g(j)}{2 \cdot k_j} \le \frac{\Sigma_{\theta \in A} \beta_\theta \cdot g(\theta)}{2 \cdot (Y - \Sigma_{\theta \in B} k_\theta)}, \qquad \forall\, j \in B \tag{A3.45}$$

Finally, using (A3.40) and (A3.45), we have (A3.41). Therefore, (A3.35) holds for each $j \in B$. Hence, z solves (A3.20).

("Only if")   Assume z solves (A3.20). We first show that $z \in S$. Suppose $z \notin S$. By the constraints in (A3.20), $z_\theta \ge k_\theta$, $\forall\, \theta \in \Theta$, and $\Sigma_\theta z_\theta \le Y$. Therefore, by (2.1), since $z \notin S$ we must have

$$\sum_\theta z_\theta < Y \tag{A3.46}$$

Let y be the vector in E^m that satisfies

$$y_1 = z_1 + \left(Y - \sum_\theta z_\theta\right) \tag{A3.47}$$

$$y_\theta = z_\theta, \qquad \forall\, \theta \in \Theta - \{1\} \tag{A3.48}$$

(A3.46) implies

$$\left(Y - \sum_\theta z_\theta\right) > 0 \tag{A3.49}$$

Therefore, since $z_\theta \geq k_\theta$, $\forall\, \theta \in \Theta$, we have $y_\theta \geq k_\theta$ $\forall\, \theta \in \Theta$. In addition, (A3.47) and (A3.48) imply $\sum_\theta y_\theta = z_1 + (Y - \sum_\theta z_\theta) + \sum_{\theta \neq 1} z_\theta = Y$. Therefore, y is a feasible point in (A3.20). By (A2.16), (A3.47), and (A3.48),

$$P\ell_e^1(y, z) = 2 \cdot \frac{[z_1 + (Y - \sum_\theta z_\theta)]^{\beta_1}}{[z_1 + (Y - \sum_\theta z_\theta)]^{\beta_1} + (z_1)^{\beta_1}} \cdot g(1)$$

$$+ \sum_{\theta \neq 1} \frac{(z_\theta)^{\beta_\theta}}{(z_\theta)^{\beta_\theta} + (z_\theta)^{\beta_\theta}} \cdot g(\theta) - 1 \tag{A3.50}$$

Therefore, by (A3.50) and (A2.16),

$$P\ell_e^1(y, z) - P\ell_e^1(z, z)$$

$$= 2 \cdot g(1) \cdot \left[\frac{[z_1 + (Y - \sum_\theta z_\theta)]^{\beta_1}}{[z_1 + (Y - \sum_\theta z_\theta)]^{\beta_1} + (z_1)^{\beta_1}} - \frac{(z_1)^{\beta_1}}{(z_1)^{\beta_1} + (z_1)^{\beta_1}}\right] \tag{A3.51}$$

Let

$$f(x) = \frac{[z_1 + x]^{\beta_1}}{[z_1 + x]^{\beta_1} + (z_1)^{\beta_1}}, \qquad \forall\, x \in [0, +\infty) \tag{A3.52}$$

By the constraints in (A3.20), $z_1 \geq k_1$. Therefore, since $k_1 > 0$ and $0 < \beta_1 \leq 1$ (see Section 2.2), $f(x)$ is defined. Taking the derivative, we get

$$\frac{df(x)}{dx} = \frac{([z_1+x]^{\beta_1} + (z_1)^{\beta_1}) \cdot \beta_1 \cdot [z_1 + x]^{\beta_1 - 1} - [z_1 + x]^{\beta_1} \cdot \beta_1 \cdot [z_1 + x]^{\beta_1 - 1}}{([z_1 + x]^{\beta_1} + (z_1)^{\beta_1})^2}$$

$$= \frac{(z_1)^{\beta_1} \cdot \beta_1 \cdot [z_1 + x]^{\beta_1 - 1}}{([z_1 + x]^{\beta_1} + (z_1)^{\beta_1})^2} \tag{A3.53}$$

at each x in the domain of f. Therefore, since $z_1 \geq k_1 > 0$ and $0 < \beta_1 \leq 1$, we have $df(x)\,/\,dx > 0$, $\forall\, x \in [0, +\infty)$. Therefore, using (A3.49) gives

$$\frac{[z_1 + (Y - \sum_\theta z_\theta)]^{\beta_1}}{[z_1 + (Y - \sum_\theta z_\theta)]^{\beta_1} + (z_1)^{\beta_1}} = f\left(Y - \sum_\theta z_\theta\right) > f(0) = \frac{(z_1)^{\beta_1}}{(z_1)^{\beta_1} + (z_1)^{\beta_1}}$$

$$\tag{A3.54}$$

Therefore, by (A3.51), (A3.54), and the fact that $g(1) > 0$ (see Section 2.2), $P\ell_e^1(y, z) - P\ell_e^1(z, z) > 0$. That is,

$$P\ell_e^1(y, z) > P\ell_e^1(z, z) \qquad\qquad (A3.55)$$

Therefore, z does not solve (A3.20), a contradiction. Hence, $z \in S$.

We now use the fact that z solves (A3.20), and is such that $z \in S$, to show that z must be the location of the electoral equilibrium. $P\ell_e^1(x, z)$ is an extension of $P\ell^1(x, z)$ onto S_e. Therefore, since $z \in S$ maximizes $P\ell_e^1(x, z)$ on the set $\{x \in E^m : \Sigma_\theta x_\theta \leq Y \ \& \ x_\theta \geq k_\theta, \ \forall \theta \in \Theta\}$ and S is a subset of this set, z must also solve $\mathrm{Max}_{x \in S} P\ell^1(x, z)$; that is, z solves (3.4). Therefore, by Theorem 3.4, z is the location of the electoral equilibrium. That is, (z, z) is the electoral equilibrium.

Finally, suppose that z does not satisfy (3.7) and (3.8). Let z' denote the vector that does satisfy (3.7) and (3.8). By the "if" part of this proof, z' solves (A3.20). In addition, by (3.7) and (3.8), $z' \in S$. Therefore, if we repeat the argument in the previous paragraph, z' must be the location of the electoral equilibrium. That is, (z', z') is the electoral equilibrium. This contradicts Theorem 3.2 (since, by our starting supposition and the definition of z', we have $z \neq z'$). Therefore, z satisfies (3.7) and (3.8).

QED

Proof of Theorem 3.6

By construction, for any given $z \in S$, $P\ell_e^1(x, z)$ is an extension of $P\ell^1(x, z)$ onto S_e. By Lemma 3.2, z maximizes $P\ell_e^1(x, z)$ on $\{x \in E^m : \Sigma_{\theta \in \Theta} x_\theta \leq Y \ \& \ x_\theta \geq k_\theta, \ \forall \theta \in \Theta\}$. Therefore, since $z \in S$ and $S \subset \{x \in E^m : \Sigma_{\theta \in \Theta} x_\theta \leq Y \ \& \ x_\theta \geq k_\theta, \ \forall \theta \in \Theta\}$, we know that z maximizes $P\ell^1(x, z)$ on S. Therefore, z solves (3.4). Therefore, by Theorem 3.4, z is the location for the electoral equilibrium.

QED

Appendix 3.4: Proof of Theorem 3.7

The following two lemmata will be used in the proof of Theorem 3.7. They have the same unstated premise as all previous lemmata.

Lemma 3.3

Let S_e be defined by (A2.15); $\omega(x) = \Sigma_{\theta \in \Theta}[\alpha_\theta + \beta_\theta \cdot \log(x_\theta)] \cdot g(\theta)$ is a strictly concave function of x of S_e.

Proof of Lemma 3.3

By (A2.15), $x \in S_e$ implies $x_\theta > 0$, $\forall \theta \in \Theta$. Therefore, $\omega(x)$ is a real-valued function of x on S_e.

Consider any distinct pair $(y, z) \in S_e$ and any $\lambda \in (0, 1)$. By the definition of $\omega(\cdot)$,

$$\omega[\lambda \cdot y + (1 - \lambda) \cdot z] = \sum_{\theta \in \Theta} [\alpha_\theta + \beta_\theta \cdot \log(\lambda \cdot y_\theta + (1 - \lambda) \cdot z_\theta)] \cdot g(\theta)$$
(A3.56)

Let $C = \{\theta \in \Theta : y_\theta = z_\theta\}$ and let $D = \Theta - C$. Then, by (A3.56) and the definition of C,

$$\omega[\lambda \cdot y + (1 - \lambda) \cdot z] = \sum_{\theta \in \Theta} \alpha_\theta \cdot g(\theta) + \sum_{\theta \in C} \beta_\theta \cdot \log(y_\theta) \cdot g(\theta)$$
$$+ \sum_{\theta \in D} \beta_\theta \cdot \log(\lambda \cdot y_\theta + (1 - \lambda) \cdot z_\theta) \cdot g(\theta) \qquad (A3.57)$$

By (A3.57) and the definition of C,

$$\omega[\lambda \cdot y + (1 - \lambda) \cdot z] = \sum_{\theta \in \Theta} \alpha_\theta \cdot g(\theta)$$
$$+ \sum_{\theta \in C} \beta_\theta \cdot [\lambda \cdot \log(y_\theta) + (1 - \lambda) \cdot \log(z_\theta)] \cdot g(\theta)$$
$$+ \sum_{\theta \in D} \beta_\theta \cdot \log[\lambda \cdot y_\theta + (1 - \lambda) \cdot z_\theta] \cdot g(\theta) \qquad (A3.58)$$

Since $\log(r)$ is a strictly concave function of r on $(0, +\infty)$, the definition of D implies

$$\log[\lambda \cdot y_\theta + (1 - \lambda) \cdot z_\theta] > \lambda \cdot \log(y_\theta) + (1 - \lambda) \cdot \log(z_\theta), \qquad \forall\, \theta \in D$$
(A3.59)

Therefore, by (A3.58) and (A3.59),

$$\omega[\lambda \cdot y + (1 - \lambda) \cdot z] > \sum_{\theta \in \Theta} \alpha_\theta \cdot g(\theta)$$
$$+ \sum_{\theta \in C} \beta_\theta \cdot [\lambda \cdot \log(y_\theta) + (1 - \lambda) \cdot \log(z_\theta)] \cdot g(\theta)$$
$$+ \sum_{\theta \in D} \beta_\theta \cdot [\lambda \cdot \log(y_\theta) + (1 - \lambda) \cdot \log(z_\theta)] \cdot g(\theta)$$
(A3.60)

Therefore, by (A3.60),

$$\omega[\lambda \cdot y + (1 - \lambda) \cdot z]$$
$$> \sum_{\theta \in \Theta} [\lambda \cdot \alpha_\theta + (1 - \lambda) \cdot \alpha_\theta + \lambda \cdot \beta_\theta \cdot \log(y_\theta) + (1 - \lambda) \cdot \beta_\theta \cdot \log(z_\theta)] \cdot g(\theta)$$
$$= \lambda \cdot \sum_{\theta \in \Theta} [\alpha_\theta + \beta_\theta \cdot \log(y_\theta)] \cdot g(\theta) + (1 - \lambda) \cdot \sum_{\theta \in \Theta} [\alpha_\theta + \beta_\theta \cdot \log(z_\theta)] \cdot g(\theta)$$
(A3.61)

Finally, by (A3.61) and the definition of $\omega(\cdot)$,

$$\omega[\lambda \cdot y + (1 - \lambda) \cdot z] > \lambda \cdot \omega(y) + (1 - \lambda) \cdot \omega(z) \qquad \text{(A3.62)}$$

Hence, $\omega(x)$ is strictly concave on S_e.

QED

Lemma 3.4

z solves

$$\max_{x} \sum_{\theta \in \Theta} U_\theta(x) \cdot g(\theta) \qquad \text{(A3.63)}$$

subject to $\sum_{\theta \in \Theta} x_\theta \leq Y$

and $x_\theta \geq k_\theta, \qquad \forall\, \theta \in \Theta$

if and only if z solves (A3.20).

Proof of Lemma 3.4

The notation w_θ, $\gamma_1(w)$, and b_1 will be used in the same way as in the proof of Lemma 3.1. We also let $\omega_k(w) = \omega(w + k)$, where $\omega(x)$ is defined as in Lemma 3.2. Using this notation, we can rewrite (A3.63) as

$$\max_{w} \omega_k(w) \qquad \text{(A3.64)}$$

subject to $\gamma_1(w) \leq b_1$

and $w_1 \geq 0, \ldots, w_m \geq 0$

By Lemma 3.3, and (2.2), $\omega(x) = \sum_\theta U_\theta(x) \cdot g(\theta)$ is strictly concave in x on S_e. Therefore, as in the argument following (A3.28) in the proof of Theorem 3.6,

$$\begin{aligned}
\omega_k[\lambda \cdot w' + (1 - \lambda) \cdot w''] &= \omega[\lambda \cdot w' + (1 - \lambda) \cdot w'' + k] \\
&= \omega[\lambda \cdot (w' + k) + (1 - \lambda) \cdot (w'' + k)] \\
&> \lambda \cdot \omega(w' + k) + (1 - \lambda) \cdot \omega(w'' + k) \\
&= \lambda \cdot \omega_k(w') + (1 - \lambda) \cdot \omega_k(w'')
\end{aligned}$$

for each distinct pair w', $w'' \in E_+^m$ and $\lambda \in (0, 1)$. Therefore, $\omega_k(w)$ is strictly concave in w on E_+^m. In addition, as noted in the proof of Lemma 3.2, $\gamma_1(w) = \sum_\theta w_\theta$ is a linear function on E_+^m, and since $\sum_\theta k_\theta < Y$, the constraint in (A3.64) satisfies the Slater condition. Therefore, by the theorem that immediately precedes the proof of Lemma 3.2, a necessary and sufficient condition for $w^o = z - k$ to solve (A3.64) [or equivalently, for $z = w^o + k$ to solve (A3.63)] is $\exists \, \lambda' \in E^1_+$ such that

$$\frac{\partial \omega_k(w^o)}{\partial w_j} - \lambda' \cdot \frac{\partial \gamma_1(w^o)}{\partial w_j} \leq 0, \qquad j = 1, \ldots, m \tag{A3.65}$$

$$w^o_j = 0 \quad \text{or} \quad \frac{\partial \omega_k(w^o)}{\partial w_j} - \lambda' \cdot \frac{\partial \gamma_1(w^o)}{\partial w_j} = 0, \qquad j = 1, \ldots, m \tag{A3.66}$$

$$\gamma_1(w^o) \leq b_1 \tag{A3.67}$$

$$\lambda' = 0 \quad \text{if} \quad \gamma_1(w^o) < b_1 \tag{A3.68}$$

By the definition of $\omega_k(x)$ and the definition of $\omega(x)$, in (3.9),

$$\omega_k(w) = \omega(w + k) = \sum_{\theta \in \Theta} U_\theta(w + k) \cdot g(\theta) = \sum_{\theta \in \Theta} [\alpha_\theta + \beta_\theta \cdot \log(w_\theta + k_\theta)] \cdot g(\theta) \tag{A3.69}$$

Therefore, by (A3.69) and the definition of $\gamma_1(w)$, (A3.65) and (A3.66) can be rewritten as

$$\frac{\beta_j \cdot g(j)}{w^o_j + k_j} - \lambda' \leq 0, \qquad j = 1, \ldots, m \tag{A3.70}$$

$$w^o_j = 0 \quad \text{or} \quad \frac{\beta_j \cdot g(j)}{w^o_j + k_j} - \lambda' = 0, \qquad j = 1, \ldots, m \tag{A3.71}$$

$$\sum_\theta w^o_\theta \leq Y - \sum_\theta k_\theta \tag{A3.72}$$

$$\lambda' = 0 \quad \text{if} \quad \sum_\theta w^o_\theta < Y - \sum_\theta k_\theta \tag{A3.73}$$

Therefore, $z = w^o + k$ solves (A3.63) if and only if $\exists \, \lambda' \in E^1_+$ such that

$$\frac{\beta_j \cdot g(j)}{z_j} \leq \lambda', \qquad j = 1, \ldots, m \tag{A3.74}$$

$$w_j = 0 \quad \text{or} \quad \frac{\beta_j \cdot g(j)}{z_j} = \lambda', \qquad j = 1, \ldots, m \tag{A3.75}$$

and (A3.72) and (A3.73) are satisfied. Therefore, $z = w^o + k$ solves (A3.63) if and only if $\exists \, \lambda = (\lambda' / 2) \in E^1_+$ such that

$$\frac{\beta_j \cdot g(j)}{2 \cdot z_j} \leq \lambda, \qquad j = 1, \ldots, m \tag{A3.76}$$

$$w_j^o = 0 \quad \text{or} \quad \frac{\beta_j \cdot g(j)}{2 \cdot z_j} = \lambda, \quad j = 1, \ldots, m \qquad (A3.77)$$

and (A3.72) and (A3.73) are satisfied. By the argument leading to (A3.39) in the proof of Lemma 3.2, (A3.77) is equivalent to (A3.36). Using the argument leading to (A3.41) in the proof of Lemma 3.2 again, we find that (A3.76) is equivalent to (A3.35). In addition, (A3.72) and (A3.73) are exactly the same as (A3.37) and (A3.38). Therefore, $z = w^o + k$ solves (A3.63) if and only if $\exists\, \lambda \in E_+^1$ such that (A3.35)–(A3.38) are satisfied. Finally, in the proof of Lemma 3.2, it was shown that $\exists\, \lambda \in E_1^+$ such that (A3.35)–(A3.38) are satisfied if and only if $z = w^o + k$ solves (A3.20). Therefore, $z = w^o + k$ solves (A3.63) if and only if it solves (A3.20).

QED

We are now in a position to prove Theorem 3.7.

Proof of Theorem 3.7

("Only if")   Assume that z is the location of the electoral equilibrium. This immediately implies $z \in S$. It also implies by Theorem 3.6 that z solves (3.7) and (3.8). Therefore, by Lemma 3.2, z solves (A3.20). Therefore, by Lemma 3.4, z solves (A3.63). Hence, since S is a subset of the feasible set in (A3.63), z also solves (3.9).

("If")   Assume that z solves (3.9). Suppose that z is not the location of the electoral equilibrium. Then, by Theorems 3.2 and 3.3, there exists a $z' \neq z$ that is the location of the electoral equilibrium. By the argument in the preceding paragraph, z' also solves (3.9). Since both z and z' solve (3.9), we must have

$$\sum_{\theta \in \Theta} U_\theta(z) \cdot g(\theta) = \sum_{\theta \in \Theta} U_\theta(z') \cdot g(\theta) \qquad (A3.78)$$

Consider the vector $z'' = \frac{1}{2} \cdot z + \frac{1}{2} \cdot z'$. Because $z \in S$, $z' \in S$, and S is convex, $z'' \in S$. What is more, by Lemma 3.3 and (2.2),

$$\sum_{\theta \in \Theta} U_\theta(z'') \cdot g(\theta) > \frac{1}{2} \cdot \sum_{\theta \in \Theta} U_\theta(z) \cdot g(\theta) + \frac{1}{2} \cdot \sum_{\theta \in \Theta} U_\theta(z') \cdot g(\theta) \qquad (A3.79)$$

Therefore, by (A3.78) and (A3.79),

$$\sum_{\theta \in \Theta} U_\theta(z'') \cdot g(\theta) > \sum_{\theta \in \Theta} U_\theta(z) \cdot g(\theta) \qquad (A3.80)$$

which contradicts the assumption that z solves (3.9). Hence, z is the location of the electoral equilibrium.

QED

CHAPTER 4

A more general election model

Theorem 2.2 (the equilibrium existence theorem) and Theorems 3.1–3.7 were all concerned with the implications of using a logit model to specify the candidates' beliefs about the voters' behavior in an election with redistributional reputations. In this chapter, the special assumptions that came from using a logit model and studying the problem of income redistribution with selfish voters will be generalized to make it possible to derive results that apply more broadly. In particular, the assumptions about the set of possible locations for the candidates and the candidates' expectations about the voters' choices will be replaced by less demanding assumptions. These alternative assumptions are identified in Section 4.1. The fact that these assumptions are generalizations of their counterparts in the premises for Theorems 2.2 and 3.1–3.7 is also established in that section.

Once the generalizations are made, a number of the assumptions used in Chapters 2 and 3 become obsolete for our subsequent analyses, in the sense of being possibilities that are covered without having to be explicitly assumed. To be sure that there is no confusion about exactly which assumptions from the earlier chapters are retained in full and which are subsumed, Section 4.2 provides a complete statement of all assumptions that are in the model that results from making the generalizations in Section 4.1. This explicit statement of the resulting model is also useful because it emphasizes that the resulting model can be stated more succinctly than the model it subsumes and because it makes it easier for the chapter's results to (potentially) be used in alternative applications.

Section 4.3 identifies the two-candidate game in the model in Section 4.2 and the corresponding definition of an electoral equilibrium. This is followed by a theorem that establishes that the assumptions in the model in Section 4.2 imply that an electoral equilibrium exists (Theorem 4.1). In the discussion at the end of Section 4.2 this general existence theorem is compared with results about electoral equilibria that have been derived elsewhere.

In Section 4.4 we observe that the assumptions in the model in Section 4.2 are not sufficient to ensure a unique, convergent equilibrium. Because uniqueness and convergence are not ensured, the previous chapter's notion of "the location of the electoral equilibrium" (i.e., the one and only equilibrium strategy for a candidate) is replaced in Section 4.4 by the weaker notion of the set of "electoral outcomes" (i.e., the – possibly larger than a singleton – set of equilibrium strategies for the candidates).

Section 4.5 begins with a theorem that identifies a social objective function that is implicitly maximized by the electoral equilibria in the model in Section 4.2 (Theorem 4.2). The remainder of the section is devoted to drawing a variety of implications from this result. Among other things, Theorem 4.2 is used to identify conditions under which a unique electoral equilibrium exists and to determine more fully the nature of the implicit social objective functions that arise in two particular cases that are of special interest.

Section 4.6 studies a specific example that satisfies the assumptions in Section 4.2. In doing this, emphasis is placed on illustrating how the various approaches and results in the chapter can be used to gain alternative perspectives on the example and its properties. Section 4.7 provides closing remarks.

4.1   The more general assumptions

Up to this point, it has consistently been assumed that each candidate selects a redistributional reputation in the set specified by (2.1). In this chapter, this earlier assumption about the candidates' possible locations is replaced with the following, more general assumptions: The candidates have a (common) set of possible locations S; the set S is a nonempty, compact, convex subset of a Euclidean space E^n. The second of these two assumptions is less demanding than assuming that S satisfies (2.1) because (as was pointed out in Section 2.1) assuming that S satisfies (2.1) *implies* that S is a nonempty, compact, convex subset of E^m.

To keep clear the interpretation of this chapter's more general assumptions about the possible candidate locations, it should be emphasized that here we are not assuming that the number of dimensions in the policy space is the same as the number of groups in the electorate nor that the jth component in a candidate's strategy is the income that everyone expects the jth group to receive after the election. Rather, the elements of S can now be given various additional interpretations, such as vectors that specify alternative tax structures, alternative amounts of various public goods, alternative institutional arrangements, alternative allocations of campaign resources, or combinations of these.

In reference to campaign resources in particular, it is worth pointing out that this chapter's assumption about the set of possible locations for the candidates (and each of the other assumptions in the model that will be specified in Section 4.2) is satisfied by the popular-vote model with campaign resources suggested in Luenberger (1969, p. 7) and analyzed in detail in Brams and Davis (1973, 1974) and Brams (1975, 1978) whenever (i) each voter is uncommitted before the election campaign and (ii) the candidates have equal budgets. With respect to (ii), note that Brams and Davis (1974, pp. 120–1) and Brams (1975, pp. 257–8; 1978, pp. 103–4) defended the "equal budgets" assumption by arguing for the stronger assumption that the "candidates match each other's resources in each state," on the basis of "the fact that the candidates tend to agree on which states (usually large and heterogeneous) are the most attractive campaign targets." Colantoni, Levesque, and Ordeshook (1975, pp. 158–9) have also expressed the view that the assumption that "candidates have equal budgets . . . is, admittedly, a reasonable and convenient starting point for modeling election competition."

The assumptions about the candidates' expectations about the voters' choice behavior used in Theorem 2.2 and Theorems 3.1–3.7 are replaced by the following, more general assumptions: For each group, $\theta \in \Theta$, there exist two *probabilistic voting functions*, $P_\theta^1 : S \times S \rightarrow [0, 1]$ and $P_\theta^2 : S \times S \rightarrow [0, 1]$ and a C^1, positive, real-valued function $f(x \mid \theta)$ on a set X that has $S \subset \text{int}(X)$ such that $f(x \mid \theta)$ is concave on S and

$$P_\theta^1(\psi_1, \psi_2) = \frac{f(\psi_1 \mid \theta)}{f(\psi_1 \mid \theta) + f(\psi_2 \mid \theta)} \tag{4.1}$$

and

$$P_\theta^2(\psi_1, \psi_2) = \frac{f(\psi_2 \mid \theta)}{f(\psi_1 \mid \theta) + f(\psi_2 \mid \theta)} \tag{4.2}$$

for each $(\psi_1, \psi_2) \in S \times S$. This formulation is compatible with three alternative interpretations that have been used in various election models. First, it includes models like that specified in Section 2.1 where, for each $(\psi_1, \psi_2) \in S \times S$ and $i \in N$, the candidates have (i) a common (subjective) conditional probability $P_i^1(\psi_1, \psi_2) = P_\theta^1(\psi_1, \psi_2)$ for the event "i will vote for candidate 1, if candidate 1's location is ψ_1 and candidate 2's location is ψ_2" (where θ is the group containing i), and (ii) a common (subjective) conditional probability $P_i^2(\psi_1, \psi_2) = P_\theta^2(\psi_1, \psi_2)$ for the event "i will vote for candidate 1, if candidate 1's location is ψ_1

and candidate 2's location is ψ_2 (where, again, θ is the group containing individual i). Second, it includes models in which, for each $\theta \in \Theta$, $(\psi_1, \psi_2) \in S \times S$ and $c \in C$, the candidates have a (common) subjective probability $P_\theta^c(\psi_1, \psi_2)$ for the event "an individual randomly selected from the group θ will vote for c, given that the candidates choose ψ_1 and ψ_2 (respectively)." Third, the assumptions being made also cover models in which $P_\theta^c(\psi_1, \psi_2)$ is the probability that candidate c will win a "bloc of votes" that the group θ has – as, for instance, in the electoral college model (with campaign resource allocation) in Brams and Davis (1973, p. 113; 1974, p. 120) and Brams (1975, p. 257; 1978, p. 103), which was included in Ordeshook (1986, pp. 112–13 and pp. 155–8).

It can be seen that the assumptions about the candidates' expectations about the voters' choice behavior that were used in Theorem 2.2 and Theorems 3.1–3.7 satisfy these alternative assumptions by letting $n = m$; letting X be the set S_e defined in (A2.15) in Appendix 2.2 – that is, $X = \{(s_1, \ldots, s_m) \in E^m : s_\theta > 0, \theta = 1, \ldots, m\}$; and letting

$$f(\psi_c \mid \theta) = \exp\{\alpha_\theta + \beta_\theta \cdot z_\theta^c\} \tag{4.3}$$

at each $\psi_c \in S$ (where z_θ^c denotes the natural logarithm of the θth component of ψ_c, as in Section 2.4). Equations (2.9) and (4.3) immediately imply that (4.1) and (4.2) are satisfied for each $\theta \in \Theta$ and each $(\psi_1, \psi_2) \in S \times S$. In addition, (4.3) also implies

$$f(\psi_c \mid \theta) = \exp\{\alpha_\theta + \beta_\theta \cdot \log(\psi_{c\theta})\} = \exp\{\alpha_\theta\} \cdot (\psi_{c\theta})^{\beta_\theta} \tag{4.4}$$

(first using the definition of z_θ^c and then using the properties of the function $\exp\{\cdot\}$). From (4.4), we can see (since we have $\psi_{c\theta} \geq k_\theta > 0$ at each $\psi_c \in S$ and $0 < \beta_\theta \leq 1$) that this $f(\psi_c \mid \theta)$ is a C^1, positive, real-valued function on $X = S_e$ that is concave on X (and, hence, also concave on S).

Note that the existence of a positive, real-valued function $f(z \mid i)$ on a set Z such that (4.1) and (4.2) hold (with θ set equal to i) for each possible pair ψ_1, ψ_2 from the set Z is the definition of a "strict (binary) utility model" or "binary Luce model" for individual i (see Luce, 1959, sect. 1.E; Becker, DeGroot, and Marschak, 1963, p. 44; Luce, 1977, p. 216; Roberts, 1979, p. 280; Samuelson, 1985, p. 378; and/or Strauss, 1985, p. 167). Thus, in the model analyzed here the candidates use a binary Luce model, either for each individual voter or for each group of voters. It is worth noting that, as has been pointed out elsewhere (e.g., Luce, 1959, 1977; Strauss, 1985), the binary Luce model itself is mathematically equivalent to the Bradley–Terry model, which is "a basic model for paired comparisons" in biometrics (Bradley, 1976, p. 216) (for further details about Bradley–Terry models see Bradley and Terry, 1952, or Kotz and Johnson, 1982).

To keep the interpretation of this chapter's model clear, note that (as with the model in Chapter 2) the assumptions being made about the candidates' expectations about the voters' choices include (as special cases) both (i) the possibility that the voters' choices are actually deterministic in nature though the candidates are uncertain about what they are, and (ii) the possibility that the voters' choices are stochastic in nature. These possibilities are covered simultaneously because elections are "Stackelberg" in nature, in that the voters make their decisions after the candidates select their strategies. Therefore, when the candidates make their decisions what matters is what is in their minds (i.e., their beliefs or expectations about voters' choices) rather than what the voters will actually do.

The binary Luce model involves the "separability" or "independence" assumption that the likelihood of choosing one particular element in a binary set depends solely on the values assigned to the elements by an underlying scaling function. The nature of this feature has been described by Luce as follows:

> In decision theory (see, for example, Luce and Raiffa [1957]) one axiomatic idea, which may be termed "independence from irrelevant alternatives," is recurrent. The idea was brought to the fore by Arrow [1951] in a particular choice context ... The actual gist of the idea is that alternatives which *should be* irrelevant to the choice are in fact irrelevant (Luce, 1959, p. 9).

The multinomial Luce model has been criticized (e.g., see Debreu, 1960; Luce and Suppes, 1965; and McFadden, 1981) on the basis of examples in which adding similar alternatives to an individual's feasible set results in the individual having implausible selection probabilities. It is, therefore, important to point out that the binary Luce model (which is used here) is immune from these criticisms. In particular, it is immune because only binary (viz., two-candidate) sets are ever considered. Thus, the feasible sets for the voters are never expanded or contracted. The criticisms are still relevant, however, because they argue against extending this chapter's model to include additional candidates or the additional choice of not voting by making a straightforward generalization from the binomial Luce model to the multinomial logit model, as in de Palma, Hong, and Thisse (1990). Indeed, such an approach would be inadequate for handling the voters' strategic concern with the likelihood of a candidate (in a multicandidate race) winning and would also fail to adequately reflect "abstention due to alienation" and "abstention due to indifference." Because such a generalization would, therefore, be of little value, it is not carried out here.

Finally, to keep the interpretation of this chapter's assumptions clear, we emphasize that (unlike in the model specified in Section 2.1) it is not being assumed that there is necessarily a common utility function on S, such as (2.2), for all of the individuals in a group. It is, however, shown in Section 4.5 that some interesting implications follow from adding this assumption to the present model in the ways in which utility functions are usually included in binary Luce models.

4.2   The resulting model

The assumptions in the election model that results when the changes discussed in Section 4.1 are made are briefly listed here so that there is no ambiguity about the model that is being analyzed in this chapter.

There are two candidates $c = 1, 2$. There is a set N of eligible voters. The candidates partition the set N into a finite number of groups. Both candidates use the same partition $\Theta = \{1, \ldots, m\}$. Note that the elements in this set denote the sets in the partition (rather than, say, serve as indices for these sets). Thus (with this notation), $\theta \cap \zeta = \varnothing, \forall \theta, \zeta \in \Theta$, and $\cup_{\theta=1}^{m} \theta = \Theta$. The candidates have a (common) discrete, probability distribution $g(\theta)$ on the sets in the partition Θ. One possible interpretation of g is that, for each $\theta \in \Theta$, the corresponding number $g(\theta)$ is what both candidates believe is the proportion of N contained in θ. A second possible interpretation of g is that it is the ratio of the number of votes in a bloc of votes that θ has to the total number of votes in the blocs for all of the groups. It is assumed that $g(\theta) > 0, \forall \theta \in \Theta$.

There is a nonempty set S of possible locations for the candidates. Each candidate has to choose one particular location in S. The set S is contained in the interior of a set X, which is a subset of a Euclidean space E^n (where the interior of X is specifically defined with respect to E^n). This, of course, does not require either S or X to be an open set. This is important to note because S is also assumed to be compact and convex. Let $\psi_c \in S$ be a particular location for candidate c.

For each group $\theta \in \Theta$, there are two probabilistic voting functions, $P_\theta^1 : S \times S \to [0, 1]$ and $P_\theta^2 : S \times S \to [0, 1]$, which are such that normalizing (as in Chapters 2 and 3) so that the total expected vote from all voters is 1, the expected plurality for a given candidate c from a given group θ at a particular pair of candidate locations $(\psi_1, \psi_2) \in S \times S$ is

$$P\ell_\theta^c(\psi_1, \psi_2) = [P_\theta^c(\psi_1, \psi_2) - P_\theta^k(\psi_1, \psi_2)] \cdot g(\theta) \qquad (4.5)$$

where k is the index for the other candidate. This, in turn, implies that the expected plurality for candidate c at a particular pair of candidate strategies, $(\psi_1, \psi_2) \in S \times S$, is given by

$$P\ell^c(\psi_1, \psi_2) = \sum_{\theta \in \Theta} P\ell_\theta^c(\psi_1, \psi_2) \cdot g(\theta) \tag{4.6}$$

Each candidate wants to maximize his expected plurality.

Finally, for each $\theta \in \Theta$, there exists a C^1, positive, real-valued function $f(x \mid \theta)$ on X that is concave on S and such that, for each $c \in \{1, 2\}$ and $(\psi_1, \psi_2) \in S \times S$,

$$P_\theta^c(\psi_1, \psi_2) = \frac{f(\psi_c \mid \theta)}{f(\psi_c \mid \theta) + f(\psi_k \mid \theta)} \tag{4.7}$$

where (as before) k is the index of the other candidate. Note that this assumption implies $P_\theta^1(\psi_1, \psi_2) + P_\theta^2(\psi_1, \psi_2) = 1$, $\forall (\psi_1, \psi_2) \in S \times S$, $\forall \theta \in \Theta$.

To highlight the key assumptions in the model that has just been specified, I use the statement "there is an election in which (i) there is a finite set of groups, (ii) there is a compact, convex set of possible locations for the candidates, and (iii) the candidates use a C^1 concave, binary Luce model" to state that all of the assumptions listed in this section are satisfied, when doing so is appropriate. A shorter statement could be used, but this statement has the advantage that it is descriptive (i.e., provides a short description of the specified model). This descriptive statement also explicitly refers to all of the specific characteristics of the model that will be varied in subsequent chapters.

4.3   The two-candidate game and electoral equilibria

The electoral competition for the two candidates studied in this chapter fits the description in Section 2.3: the two-candidate, zero-sum game $(S, S; P\ell^1, P\ell^2) = (S, S; P\ell^1, -P\ell^1)$. Therefore, that section's definition of an electoral equilibrium, as a saddle-point for the game $(S, S; P\ell^1, -P\ell^1)$ also applies verbatim.

The first major result in this chapter is Theorem 4.1.

Theorem 4.1

Suppose there is an election in which (i) there is a finite set of groups, (ii) there is a compact, convex set of possible locations for the candidates, and (iii) the candidates use a C^1, concave, binary Luce model. Then an electoral equilibrium exists.

A proof of this theorem (using an argument that parallels the one used to prove Theorem 2.2 in Appendix 2.2) appears in Appendix 4.1. Because (by the observations in Section 4.1) each election with redistributional reputations in which the candidates use a binomial logit model for the voters' selection probabilities is a special case of the model specified in Section 4.2, Theorem 4.1 is a generalization of Theorem 2.2 (in Section 2.5).

It is also worth noting that the equilibrium existence result established in the theorem in this section (i) does not require that the candidates' strategy space be restricted to one dimension (unlike the electoral equilibrium existence results implicit in Downs, 1957b, and Black, 1958, for instance), (ii) does not use any special symmetry assumptions (unlike the electoral equilibrium existence results derived in Davis and Hinich, 1966, 1967, 1968; Hinich and Ordeshook, 1969; McKelvey, 1975; and Matthews, 1979, for instance), and (iii) follows without introducing abstentions and special assumptions about nonvoting behavior (unlike the electoral equilibrium existence results developed in Hinich and Ordeshook, 1969; Hinich et al., 1972, 1973; McKelvey, 1975; Enelow and Hinich, 1984a, sect. 5.3, 1984b; and Ledyard, 1984, for instance). Thus, among other things, Theorem 4.1 (and Theorem 2.2) make it clear that none of these specific assumptions is necessary for electoral equilibria to exist.

4.4   Electoral outcomes

In Chapter 3 it was possible to talk about *the* location of *the* electoral equilibrium for any given specification of the parameters in the model analyzed in Theorem 2.2 and Theorems 3.1–3.7, because Theorem 3.2 established that there is a unique electoral equilibrium and Theorem 3.3 established that both candidates choose the same strategy at the equilibrium. Under the assumptions listed in Section 4.2, however, neither uniqueness nor convergence is guaranteed. The fact that this statement is true can be seen in any special case in which S has more than one element and there exists a positive constant, κ such that $f(s \mid \theta) = \kappa$, $\forall s \in S$, $\forall \theta \in \Theta$. In any such case, $P\ell^1(\psi_1, \psi_2) = P\ell^2(\psi_1, \psi_2) = 0$, $\forall(\psi_1, \psi_2) \in S \times S$. This conclusion implies that each ordered pair in $S \times S$ is an electoral equilibrium. This further conclusion, in turn, implies that (in any such special case) there is more than one electoral equilibrium and the candidates' strategies diverge (i.e., are different from each other) at most of the equilibria.

Because neither uniqueness nor convergence is guaranteed, it becomes more useful to talk about the set of equilibrium strategies E_c, for a candidate c in a given electoral competition $\Gamma = (S, S; P\ell^1, P\ell^2)$. That is, the set

$$E_1 = \{\psi_1 \in S : \exists \psi_2 \in S \text{ such that } (\psi_1, \psi_2) \text{ is an electoral equilibrium in } \Gamma\}$$

$$(4.8)$$

for $c = 1$, and the set

$$E_2 = \{\psi_2 \in S : \exists\ \psi_1 \in S \text{ such that } (\psi_1, \psi_2) \text{ is an electoral equilibrium in } \Gamma\}$$
(4.9)

for $c = 2$. The following proposition identifies an important property of these sets. A proof of the proposition is given in Appendix 4.2.

Proposition 4.1

Suppose there is an election in which (i) there is a finite set of groups, (ii) there is a compact, convex set of possible locations for the candidates, and (iii) the candidates use a C^1 concave, binary Luce model. Then $E_1 = E_2$.

Throughout the remainder of this chapter, E is used to denote the candidates' (common) set of equilibrium strategies (i.e., $E = E_1 = E_2$). This set is referred to as "the set of electoral outcomes." Accordingly, the phrase "z is an electoral outcome" is used to mean that $z \in E$. Stated more informally, saying that z is an electoral outcome means that z is a strategy used by a candidate in an electoral equilibrium. Electoral outcomes have the following important property (also proven in Appendix 4.2).

Proposition 4.2

Suppose there is an election in which (i) there is a finite set of groups, (ii) there is a compact, convex set of possible locations for the candidates, and (iii) the candidates use a C^1 concave, binary Luce model. Let $s \in S$ be given. Then s is an electoral outcome if and only if (s, s) is an electoral equilibrium.

From what has already been stated, it should be clear that saying that a given z in S is *an* electoral outcome does not mean that it will necessarily be *the* strategy used by the winning candidate, but it does mean that it is in the set of equilibrium strategies for the winning candidate. Thus, if z is not an electoral outcome, we can be sure that it will not be a strategy used by the winning candidate in an electoral equilibrium. The actual strategy used by the winning candidate will, of course, depend on which electoral equilibrium actually occurs.

If we refer back to elections with redistributional reputations in which the candidates use a binomial logit model for the voters, it is easy to see that (in that model) a redistributional reputation is an electoral outcome if and only if it is the location of the electoral equilibrium.

4.5   The implicit social objective function

The second main result in this chapter establishes that, in any electoral competition that satisfies the assumptions in Section 4.2, the candidates implicitly maximize the function $W : S \rightarrow E^1$ that satisfies

$$W(v) = \sum_{\theta \in \Theta} \log[f(v \mid \theta)] \cdot g(\theta) \qquad (4.10)$$

(at each $v \in S$). That is, although each candidate sets out to maximize his own expected plurality, he ends up acting as if he is maximizing the implicit social objective function specified in (4.10). Theorem 4.2 states this more precisely.

Theorem 4.2

Suppose there is an election in which (i) there is a finite set of groups, (ii) there is a compact, convex set of possible locations for the candidates, and (iii) the candidates use a C^1, concave, binary Luce model. Let $s \in S$ be given. Then s is an electoral outcome if and only if s maximizes $W(v)$ on the set S.

A proof of Theorem 4.2 is given in Appendix 4.3.

Note that, in addition to identifying a social objective function that is implicitly being maximized when there is an election that satisfies the assumptions in Section 4.2, Theorem 4.2 also provides an alternative and very different way of proving Theorem 4.1. In particular, Lemma 4.8 (in Appendix 4.3) establishes that the function $W_e(x)$ defined by (A4.33) (in Appendix 4.3) is C^1 on S. Therefore, $W_e(x)$ is continuous on S (e.g., see Theorems 12.11 and 12.4 in Apostol, 1974). Therefore, by Weierstrass' (or the "extreme value" theorem) there exists an $s \in S$ that maximizes $W_e(x)$ on the compact set $S \subset E^n$ (e.g., see Theorem 5.1 in Sydsaeter, 1981). Next, since $W_e(x)$ is an extension of $W(v)$, s maximizes $W(v)$. Therefore, by Theorem 4.2, s is an electoral outcome. Finally, by Proposition 4.2, (s, s) is an electoral equilibrium. Therefore, an electoral equilibrium exists.

It was pointed out in Section 4.4 that the assumptions in the model specified in Section 4.2 (unlike the assumptions in the model specified in Section 2.1) are not sufficient to assure the existence of a unique electoral equilibrium. At this point it is also easy to see that the presence of a unique equilibrium is not something that occurs only when the assumptions in the model specified in Section 2.1 are satisfied. This can be seen from the following "uniqueness" result (which follows directly from Theorem 4.2 and the definition of an electoral outcome).

Corollary 4.1

Suppose there is an election in which (i) there is a finite set of groups, (ii) there is a compact, convex set of possible locations for the candidates, and (iii) the candidates use a C^1, concave, binary Luce model. There exists a unique electoral equilibrium if and only if $W(v)$ has a unique maximum in S.

This result can be used, in turn, to identify "group-level" as opposed to "aggregate-level" (see McKelvey, 1975, p. 816) assumptions that lead to the existence of a unique equilibrium. For instance, see the following corollary.

Corollary 4.2

Suppose there is an election in which (i) there is a finite set of groups, (ii) there is a compact, convex set of possible locations for the candidates, and (iii) the candidates use a C^1, concave, binary Luce model, *and* there exists at least one $\theta \in \Theta$ such that the corresponding function $f(x \mid \theta)$ is strictly concave on S. Then there exists a unique electoral equilibrium.

Corollary 4.1 can be considered to be a generalization of the uniqueness result established in Theorem 3.2 – because, by Lemma 3.3 in Appendix 3.4, the function $W(x)$ for the model specified in Section 2.1 has a unique maximum. The same is not, however, true of Corollary 4.2 – because, by (4.4), each group's scaling function is a strictly concave function of $\psi_{c\theta}$ and is concave on S, but not strictly concave on S. Therefore, Corollary 4.2 identifies a separate set of sufficient conditions for the existence of a unique electoral equilibrium.

The next result includes both the uniqueness result established in Chapter 3 and the uniqueness result established in Corollary 4.2 as special cases. To help motivate the premise for the next corollary, two important implications of the premises of Theorem 3.2 and Corollary 4.2 (respectively) are stated. These implications are specifically stated in "suggestive" notation and terminology, which is subsequently used in the statement of Corollary 4.3.

First, in the model to which Theorem 3.2 applies, for each component $k \in \{1, \ldots, n\}$, there is a group $\rho(k)$ (viz., the group k itself) such that $\log[f(s \mid \rho(k))]$ is "strictly concave over the component x_k" in the sense that $\log[f(\lambda \cdot x + (1 - \lambda) \cdot y \mid \rho(k))] > \lambda \cdot \log f(x) + (1 - \lambda) \cdot f(y), \forall \lambda \in (0, 1)$ and $x, y \in S$ with $x_k \neq y_k$. This follows, in particular, because, by (2.2), (2.11), and (4.7) we have $\log[f(s \mid k)] = \alpha_k + \beta_k \cdot \log(x_k)$ for each k.

Second, the premise for Corollary 4.2 implies that, for the set $P = \{1, \ldots, n\}$, there is a group $\rho(1) = \theta'$ such that $\log[f(s \mid \rho(1))]$ is "strictly concave over the components $x_1, \ldots, x_n$" in the sense that $\log[f(\lambda \cdot x + (1 - \lambda) \cdot y \mid \rho(1))] > \lambda \cdot \log[f(x \mid \rho(1))] + (1 - \lambda) \cdot \log[f(y \mid \rho(1))]$, $\forall \lambda \in (0, 1)$ and $x, y \in S$ with $x \neq y$. This follows, in particular, because the log of a strictly concave function is itself strictly concave.

In the statement of Corollary 4.3, we use the following (precise) definition of the notion of strict concavity over components. Let P_j be a subset of $\{1, \ldots, n\}$. We say that a function $h : S \to E^1$ is "strictly concave on S over the components covered by P_j" if and only if $h[\lambda \cdot x + (1 - \lambda) \cdot y] > \lambda \cdot h(x) + (1 - \lambda) \cdot h(y)$, $\forall \lambda \in (0, 1)$ and $x, y \in S$ such that $x_k \neq y_k$ for at least one $k \in P_j$.

Corollary 4.3

Suppose there is an election in which (i) there is a finite set of voters, (ii) there is a compact, convex set of possible locations for the candidates, and (iii) the candidates use a C^1, concave, binary Luce model, *and* there exists a partition $P = \{P_1, \ldots, P_q\}$, of the set $\{1, \ldots, n\}$ and a function $\rho : \{1, \ldots, q\} \to \Theta$ such that, for each $P_j \in P$, the corresponding function $\log[f(v \mid \rho(j))]$ is strictly concave on S over the components covered by P_j. Then there exists a unique electoral equilibrium.

To help keep the interpretation of this uniqueness condition clear, note that, in the earlier discussion of the model to which Theorem 3.2 applies, the partition P had $P_1 = \{1\}, \ldots, P_n = \{n\}$, and the function ρ was the identity map $\rho(j) = j$. In the earlier discussion of the premise for Corollary 4.2, the partition P had only one element (viz., $P_1 = \{1, \ldots, n\}$), and the function ρ simply assigned a group whose scaling function is strictly concave on S. The uniqueness condition identified in Corollary 4.3 covers all partitions "in between" and various alternative ρ's as well. Finally, note also that even though Corollary 4.2 is a special case of Corollary 4.3, Corollary 4.2 is stated as a separate result because Corollary 4.2 is of inherent interest and because, at least initially, it is easier to interpret the premise of Corollary 4.2; so the statement of Corollary 4.2 also serves as a useful intermediate step on the way to the statement of Corollary 4.3.

A utility function for an individual is included in a binary Luce model in one of two ways. The first way showed up in Section 2.5 (and, indeed, shows up in any analysis based on McFadden's choice theoretic foundations for the logit model), where, for each individual i, there is a utility function U_i on S and

$$\exp[U_i(x)] = \exp[U_\theta(x)] = f(x \mid \theta), \qquad \forall\, x \in S \tag{4.11}$$

where θ is the group that contains i. The other way in which a utility function is commonly included in a binary Luce model is to assume that there is a utility function U_i on S for each individual i and that

$$U_i(x) = U_\theta(x) = f(x \mid \theta), \qquad \forall\, x \in S \tag{4.12}$$

where θ is the group that contains i (e.g., see Block and Marschak, 1960, p. 103; Marschak, 1960, p. 323; Luce and Suppes, 1965, p. 335; Coughlin and Nitzan, 1981a, p. 114; Coughlin, 1986a, p. 206; McGuire and Radner, 1986, p. XI; and Ordeshook, 1986, p. 117).

When either of the two approaches is followed, we are still (of course) working with a binary Luce model. Indeed, it should be emphasized that these alternatives provide us with two especially interesting special cases for the binary Luce model. These cases are, of course, separate special cases. As the next two results make clear, each of these alternative ways of including a utility function in a binary Luce model has an interesting implication for the nature of the implicit social objective function identified in Theorem 4.2.

As in Section 3.3 (again, following Arrow, 1951, 1963, 1973b, for instance), we call the social objective function $W_B : S \to E^1$ that satisfies

$$W_B(x) = \sum_{\theta \in \Theta} U_\theta(x) \cdot g(\theta) \tag{4.13}$$

(at each $x \in S$) the Benthamite social welfare function. Following Kaneko and Nakamura (1979, ex. 4.1) and Coughlin and Nitzan (1981a), we call the objective function $W_N : S \to E^1$ that satisfies

$$W_N(x) = \sum_{\theta \in \Theta} \log |U_\theta(x)| \cdot g(\theta), \qquad \forall\, x \in S \tag{4.14}$$

(at each $x \in S$) the Nash social welfare function (for further discussion of the Nash social welfare function, see Sen, 1970, and Mueller, 1989a). Using this terminology, we have the following corollaries.

Corollary 4.4

Suppose there is an election in which (i) there is a finite set of groups, (ii) there is a compact, convex set of possible locations for the candidates, and (iii) the candidates use a C^1, concave, binary Luce model, *and* each voter i has a utility function that satisfies (4.11). Let $s \in S$ be given. Then s is an electoral outcome if and only if s maximizes the Benthamite social welfare function, $W_B(x)$ on the set S.

Corollary 4.5

Suppose there is an election in which (i) there is a finite set of groups, (ii) there is a compact, convex set of possible locations for the candidates, and (iii) the candidates use a C^1 concave, binary Luce model, *and* each voter i has a utility function that satisfies (4.12). Let $s \in S$ be given. Then s is an electoral outcome if and only if s maximizes the Nash social welfare function, $W_N(x)$ on the set S.

By the observations in Section 4.1, we know that each election with redistributional reputations in which the candidates use a binomial logit model for the voters' selection probabilities satisfies all of the assumptions listed in Section 4.2. In addition, by (2.11) and (4.7), in any such model each voter i has a utility function that satisfies (4.11). Therefore, Corollary 4.3 is a generalization of Theorem 3.7 (in Section 3.3).

In closing this analysis, we note that related results about the relation between electoral equilibria and the maxima of various possible implicit social objective functions have previously been established in Davis and Hinich (1966, 1968); Hinich and Ordeshook (1971); Hinich, Ledyard, and Ordeshook (1972, p. 152; 1973, p. 184); Coughlin and Nitzan (1981a); Enelow and Hinich (1982b); Ledyard (1984); and Lindbeck and Weibull (1987).

4.6   An example

Perhaps the simplest examples to analyze are those given in the first paragraph in Section 4.4. It was pointed out in those examples that each ordered pair in $S \times S$ is an electoral equilibrium. Therefore, we already have confirmation that what Theorem 4.1 tells us must be the case (viz., there exists an electoral equilibrium). Combining what we already know about these examples with Theorem 4.2 leads to the conclusion that every $v \in S$ must maximize the implicit social objective function defined by (4.10). Plugging the assumption that $f(v \mid \theta) = \kappa$, $\forall\, v \in S$, $\forall\, \theta \in \Theta$, for some positive constant κ, into (4.10), we get $W(v) = \sum_{\theta \in \Theta} \log(\kappa) \cdot g(\theta)$. Since this function always assigns the same value no matter what v is, $W(v)$ is indeed maximized by every $v \in S$.

The following example illustrates the opposite extreme that can arise in the model specified in Section 4.2, in that there is a unique equilibrium in the example. Also, because the examples analyzed in Section 3.4 illustrate the conclusion in Corollary 4.4, this example has been designed to illustrate the conclusion in Corollary 4.5.

EXAMPLE 4.1

Assume that $\Theta = \{1, 2\}$, that $g(1) = \frac{2}{3}$ and that $g(2) = \frac{1}{3}$. Assume that $S = [0, 1]$ and $X = (-\frac{1}{4}, +\frac{5}{4})$. Finally, assume that

$$U_1(x) = f(x \mid 1) = \frac{1}{2} + x \qquad (4.15)$$

$$U_2(x) = f(x \mid 2) = \frac{3}{2} - x \qquad (4.16)$$

By (4.14), the Nash social welfare function is

$$W_N(x) = \log\left(\frac{1}{2} + x\right) \cdot \frac{2}{3} + \log\left(\frac{3}{2} - x\right) \cdot \frac{1}{3} \qquad (4.17)$$

Therefore,

$$\frac{dW_N(x)}{dx} = \frac{1}{\frac{1}{2} + x} \cdot \frac{2}{3} + \frac{-1}{\frac{3}{2} - x} \cdot \frac{1}{3} \qquad \forall \, x \in X \qquad (4.18)$$

Hence, $dW_N(x)/dx = 0$ if and only if $x = \frac{5}{6}$. In addition, analyzing the function $W_e(x)$ defined in (A4.33) (in Appendix 4.2), which is an extension of $W_N(x)$, we obtain

$$\frac{d^2W_e(x)}{dx^2} = \frac{-1}{(\frac{1}{2} + x)^2} \cdot \frac{2}{3} + \frac{-1}{(\frac{3}{2} - x)^2} \cdot \frac{1}{3} < 0, \qquad \forall \, x \in X \qquad (4.19)$$

Therefore, since $W_e(x)$ is an extension of $W_N(x)$, it follows that $W_N(x)$ is a strictly concave function on the convex set $S \subset X$. Therefore, $x = \frac{5}{6}$ is the unique maximum of the Nash social welfare function. Therefore, by Corollary 4.4 and the definition of an electoral outcome, $(\frac{5}{6}, \frac{5}{6})$ is the unique electoral equilibrium.

The conclusion just obtained will now be verified by directly analyzing the two-candidate game that arises in the example. This analysis will, by necessity, be a bit more involved than the analysis of the Nash social welfare function. To begin with, by this example's special assumptions about the group's scaling functions, stated in (4.15) and (4.16), and the model's assumption about how the scaling functions are related to the voters' selection probabilities, stated in (4.7), we have the following. For candidate 1,

$$P_1^1(\psi_1, \psi_2) = \frac{\frac{1}{2} + \psi_1}{\frac{1}{2} + \psi_1 + \frac{1}{2} + \psi_2} \qquad \text{and}$$

$$P_2^1(\psi_1, \psi_2) = \frac{\frac{3}{2} - \psi_1}{\frac{3}{2} - \psi_1 + \frac{3}{2} - \psi_2} \qquad (4.20)$$

whereas for candidate 2,

$$P_1^2(\psi_1, \psi_2) = \frac{\frac{1}{2} + \psi_2}{1 + \psi_1 + \psi_2} \quad \text{and} \quad P_2^2(\psi_1, \psi_2) = \frac{\frac{3}{2} - \psi_2}{3 - \psi_1 - \psi_2}$$

(4.21)

Therefore, by (4.20) and (4.21) and the relation between the voters' selection probabilities and candidate 1's expected plurality function, specified in (4.5) and (4.6),

$$P\ell^1(\psi_1, \psi_2) = \frac{\psi_1 - \psi_2}{1 + \psi_1 + \psi_2} \cdot \frac{2}{3} + \frac{\psi_2 - \psi_1}{3 - \psi_1 - \psi_2} \cdot \frac{1}{3}$$

(4.22)

Holding ψ_2 constant – thereby making $P\ell^1(\psi_1, \psi_2)$ a function of the single variable ψ_1 – when we take the first derivative of $P\ell^1(\psi_1, \psi_2)$ with respect to its one variable, we get

$$\frac{dP\ell^1(\psi_1, \psi_2)}{d\psi_1} = \frac{(1 + \psi_1 + \psi_2) - (\psi_1 - \psi_2)}{(1 + \psi_1 + \psi_2)^2} \cdot \frac{2}{3}$$
$$+ \frac{(3 - \psi_1 - \psi_2) \cdot (-1) - (\psi_2 - \psi_1) \cdot (-1)}{(3 - \psi_1 - \psi_2)^2} \cdot \frac{1}{3}$$

(4.23)

or, equivalently,

$$\frac{dP\ell^1(\psi_1, \psi_2)}{d\psi_1} = \frac{2 + 4 \cdot \psi_1}{3 \cdot (1 + \psi_1 + \psi_2)^2} + \frac{2 \cdot \psi_2 - 3}{3 \cdot (3 - \psi_1 - \psi_2)^2}$$

(4.24)

Setting $dP\ell^1(\psi_1, \psi_2) / d\psi_1 = 0$ and letting $\psi_1 = \psi_2 = x$, we obtain

$$\frac{2 + 4 \cdot x}{3 \cdot (1 + 2 \cdot x)^2} + \frac{2 \cdot x - 3}{3 \cdot (3 - 2 \cdot x)^2} = 0$$

That is,

$$\frac{2}{(1 + 2 \cdot x)} + \frac{-1}{(3 - 2 \cdot x)} = 0$$

This implies $6 - (4 \cdot x) - 1 - (2 \cdot x) = 0$. Therefore, $x = \frac{5}{6}$. Therefore, we know that *if* $c = 2$ uses $\psi_2 = \frac{5}{6}$, *then* ψ_1 solves $dP\ell^1(\psi_1, \psi_2) / d\psi_1 = 0$ if and only if we also have $\psi_1 = \frac{5}{6}$.

Taking the second derivative of the function $P\ell^1(\psi_1, \psi_2)$ defined in (A4.26), which is an extension of $P\ell^1(\psi_1, \psi_2)$, we obtain

$$\frac{d^2 P\ell_e^1(\psi_1, \psi_2)}{d\psi_1^2} = \frac{-(2 + 4 \cdot \psi_2) \cdot (2) \cdot (1 + \psi_1 + \psi_2)}{3 \cdot (1 + \psi_1 + \psi_2)^4}$$
$$+ \frac{-(2 \cdot \psi_2 - 3) \cdot (2) \cdot (3 - \psi_1 - \psi_2)}{3 \cdot (3 - \psi_1 - \psi_2)^4}, \quad \forall \psi_1 \in S$$

(4.25)

Therefore,

$$\frac{d^2 P\ell_e^1(\psi_1, \frac{5}{6})}{d\psi_1^2} = \frac{-\frac{32}{3}}{(\frac{11}{6} + \psi_1)^3} + \frac{-3}{(\frac{13}{6} - \psi_1)^3}, \qquad \forall \ \psi_1 \in S \quad (4.26)$$

Both terms are negative at every possible $\psi_1 \in [0, 1]$ Therefore,

$$\frac{d^2 P\ell_e^1(\psi_1, \frac{5}{6})}{d\psi_1^2} < 0, \qquad \forall \ \psi_1 \in S \qquad\qquad (4.27)$$

This implies that $P\ell^1(\psi_1, \frac{5}{6})$ is a strictly concave function on the convex set S. Therefore, $\psi_1 = \frac{5}{6}$ is the unique global maximum of $P\ell^1(\psi_1, \frac{5}{6})$. By a symmetric argument, $\psi_2 = \frac{5}{6}$ is the unique global maximum of $P\ell^1(\frac{5}{6}, \psi_2)$. Therefore, $\psi_2 = (\frac{5}{6}, \frac{5}{6})$ is an electoral equilibrium.

It is also possible to prove directly that this equilibrium is unique (thereby confirming what was revealed indirectly in our initial analysis with the Nash welfare function). First of all, by (4.22),

$$P\ell^1(x, y) = -\frac{x - y}{1 + x + y} \cdot \frac{2}{3} + \frac{y - x}{3 - x - y} \cdot \frac{1}{3}$$

$$= -\left(\frac{y - x}{1 + y + x} \cdot \frac{2}{3} + \frac{x - y}{3 - y - x} \cdot \frac{1}{3} \right) = P\ell^1(y, x) \qquad (4.28)$$

Therefore, $P\ell^1(x, x) = 0, \forall x \in S$. Now let (x^*, y^*) be any electoral equilibrium. By the definition of an electoral equilibrium, stated in (2.6), $P\ell^1(x^*, y^*) \geq P\ell^1(x, y^*), \forall x \in S$ and $-P\ell^1(x^*, y^*) \geq -P\ell^1(x^*, y), \forall y \in S$. Therefore, in particular, $P\ell^1(x^*, y^*) \geq P\ell^1(y^*, y^*) = 0$ and $-P\ell^1(x^*, y^*) \geq -P\ell^1(x^*, x^*) = 0$. That is, $P\ell^1(x^*, y^*) \geq 0$ and $P\ell^1(x^*, y^*) \leq 0$. Therefore, $P\ell^1(x^*, y^*) = 0$. Suppose $y^* = \frac{5}{6}$. Then, since $\frac{5}{6}$ is the unique maximum for $-P\ell^1(\frac{5}{6}, y)$, we have $-P\ell^1(\frac{5}{6}, y^*) < -P\ell^1(\frac{5}{6}, \frac{5}{6}) = 0$. Therefore, $P\ell^1(\frac{5}{6}, y^*) > 0 = P\ell^1(x^*, y^*)$, contradicting the fact that (x^*, y^*) is an electoral equilibrium. Hence, we must have $y^* = \frac{5}{6}$. Since $\frac{5}{6}$ is the unique maximum for $P\ell^1(x^*, \frac{5}{6})$, this also implies $x^* = \frac{5}{6}$. That is, $(x^*, y^*) = (\frac{5}{6}, \frac{5}{6})$. Therefore, $(\frac{5}{6}, \frac{5}{6})$ is the unique electoral equilibrium.

4.7 Conclusion

This chapter has analyzed a model whose assumptions are more general than those used to specify an election with redistributional reputations in which the candidates use a binomial logit model for the voters' selection probabilities – in particular, allowing for more flexibility in the specification of the set of possible locations for the candidates and in the specification of the candidates' expectations about the voters' choice behavior. The first major result (Theorem 4.1) was an equilibrium existence theorem that generalizes Theorem 2.2. A simple example was then used to show that there need not be either a unique equilibrium or convergence of the candidates' strategies in this more general model, unlike in the model to which Theorem 2.2 and Theorems 3.1–3.7 apply. The earlier concept of the location of the electoral equilibrium was, therefore, generalized to the concept of an electoral outcome.

The second major result (Theorem 4.2) identified an implicit social objective function that is maximized by the set of electoral outcomes. This theorem was used to obtain further insights into the model specified in Section 4.2. First, it was shown that Theorem 4.2 provides an alternative way of proving that an electoral equilibrium exists. Next, the theorem was used to identify conditions under which there is a unique equilibrium. In addition, Theorem 4.2 was used to show that, if utility functions are explicitly introduced into this chapter's model in either of the ways in which they are usually included in binary Luce models, then the society's implicit social objective function is either a Benthamite or a Nash social welfare function. Finally, the penultimate section illustrated the main results in the context of some simple examples.

The primary concern in the next chapter is the possibility of deriving assumptions about the scaling functions for the groups that are more general than concavity but that still imply the concavity properties [for the social objective function specified in (4.10) and for the candidates' payoff functions] that were used in proving this chapter's theorems. The alternative assumptions derived will then be used to obtain further existence theorems, which extend Theorem 4.1 to cover additional cases. Examples are provided to illustrate the new results that are obtained and the fact that there may be no electoral equilibrium (using this term as it has been used up to this point) when the concavity properties used in deriving this chapter's theorems are absent.

Appendix 4.1: Proof of Theorem 4.1

The following three lemmata will be used in the proof of Theorem 4.1. In stating them, we assume (as an unstated premise) that there is an election in which (i) there is a finite set of groups, (ii) there is a compact, convex set of possible locations for the candidates, and (iii) the candidates use a C^1, concave, binary Luce model.

Lemma 4.1

$P\ell^1(v, w)$ is concave in v.

Proof of Lemma 4.1

We first note that, by $(4.5) - (4.7)$, for each $(v, w) \in S \times S$,

$$P\ell^1(v, w) = \sum_{\theta \in \Theta} \frac{f(v \mid \theta) - f(w \mid \theta)}{f(v \mid \theta) - f(w \mid \theta)} \cdot g(\theta) \qquad (A4.1)$$

Consider the function

$$h(y) = \frac{y - \kappa}{y + \kappa}, \qquad \forall \, y \in E_{++}^1 \qquad (A4.2)$$

where κ is a positive real constant. Taking the first derivative gives

$$h'(y) = \frac{(y + \kappa) - (y - \kappa)}{(y + \kappa)^2} = \frac{2 \cdot \kappa}{(y + \kappa)^2} > 0 \qquad (A4.3)$$

Therefore, $h(y)$ is strictly increasing at each $y \in E_{++}^1$. Taking the second derivative gives

$$h''(y) = \frac{-4 \cdot \kappa \cdot (y + \kappa)}{(y + \kappa)^4} < 0 \qquad (A4.4)$$

Therefore, $h(y)$ is also a concave function on E_{++}^1 (e.g., see (5.12) on p. 226 of Sydsaeter, 1981).

Next, consider any $w \in S$. Choose any $\theta \in \Theta$. Let $\kappa = f(w \mid \theta)$. Then, by (A4.2) and the assumption that $f(v \mid \theta)$ is a positive, real-valued function,

$$\frac{f(v \mid \theta) - f(w \mid \theta)}{f(v \mid \theta) + f(w \mid \theta)} = h[f(v \mid \theta)] \qquad (A4.5)$$

is defined at each $v \in S$. By the assumptions in Section 4.2, $f(x \mid \theta)$ is concave on S. Therefore – since (i) S is a convex subset of E^n, (ii) h is a strictly increasing, concave function, and (iii) for each $v \in S$, the positive real number f is in the domain of h – it follows that $h[f(v \mid \theta)]$ is a concave function of v on S (e.g., see part iv of theorem 5.14 in Sydsaeter, 1981). Since $g(\theta) > 0$, $\forall \, \theta \in \Theta$, this (in turn) implies that the function $\phi : S \to E^1$ that satisfies

$$\phi(v) = \frac{f(v \mid \theta) - f(w \mid \theta)}{f(v \mid \theta) + f(w \mid \theta)} \cdot g(\theta) \qquad (A4.6)$$

(at each $v \in S$) is a concave function of v on S (e.g., see part i of theorem 5.14 in Sydsaeter, 1981, p. 254). Finally, because this conclusion holds for each $\theta \in \Theta$ and Θ is a finite set, it follows from (A4.1) and (A4.6) that $P\ell^1(v, w)$ is a concave function of v (e.g., by part i of theorem 5.14 in Sydsaeter, 1981, p. 254). Therefore, $P\ell^1(v, w)$ is concave in v.

QED

Lemma 4.2

$P\ell^1(v, w)$ is convex in w.

Proof of Lemma 4.2

Similar to the proof of Lemma 4.1.

QED

Lemma 4.3

$P\ell^1(v, w)$ is continuous in (v, w).

Proof of Lemma 4.3

The first step is to establish that each $f(x \mid \theta)$ is continuous at each $s \in S$. Choose any $\theta \in \Theta$. By the assumptions in Section 4.2, $f(x \mid \theta)$ is C^1 on X. Therefore, $f(x \mid \theta)$ is continuous at each point in X. Therefore, since $S \subseteq \text{int}(X)$, we know that $f(x \mid \theta)$ is continuous at each $s \in S$.

The second step is to establish that, for each $\theta \in \Theta$, the corresponding function $P\ell_\theta^1 : S \times S \to E^1$ defined by

$$P\ell_\theta^1(v, w) = \frac{f(v \mid \theta) - f(w \mid \theta)}{f(v \mid \theta) + f(w \mid \theta)} \cdot g(\theta), \qquad \forall (v, w) \in S \times S \qquad (A4.7)$$

(which goes from any given pair of strategies to candidate 1's expected plurality within the group θ at that pair) is continuous in (v, w). Consider any $\theta \in \Theta$. Choose any $(v^*, w^*) \in S \times S$ and let $\{(v', w')\}$ be any infinite sequence in $S \times S$ that converges to (v^*, w^*). The assumption that $\{(v', w')\}$ converges to (v^*, w^*) implies $\lim_{t \to \infty} v' = v^*$ and $\lim_{t \to \infty} w' = w^*$ (e.g., see entry e in Debreu, 1959, p. 12). Therefore, since $f(x \mid \theta)$ is continuous at each $S \times S$ and $(v^*, w^*) \in S \times S$,

$$\lim_{t \to \infty} f(v' \mid \theta) = f(v^* \mid \theta) \quad \text{and} \quad \lim_{t \to \infty} f(w' \mid \theta) = f(w^* \mid \theta) \qquad (A4.8)$$

(e.g., see theorem 4.16 in Apostol, 1974, p. 79). Therefore, by (A4.8)

$$\lim_{t \to \infty} [f(v^t \mid \theta) + f(w^t \mid \theta)] = \lim_{t \to \infty} f(v^t \mid \theta) + \lim_{t \to \infty} f(w^t \mid \theta)$$

$$= f(v^* \mid \theta) + f(w^* \mid \theta) \tag{A4.9}$$

and

$$\lim_{t \to \infty} [f(v^t \mid \theta) - f(w^t \mid \theta)] = \lim_{t \to \infty} f(v^t \mid \theta) - \lim_{t \to \infty} f(w^t \mid \theta)$$

$$= f(v^* \mid \theta) - f(w^* \mid \theta) \tag{A4.10}$$

(e.g., see theorem 4 on p. 40 in Buck, 1978). Since $f(x \mid \theta)$ is a positive, real-valued function, (A4.9) implies that $\lim_{t \to \infty} [f(v^t \mid \theta) + f(w^t \mid \theta)] > 0$. Therefore, by (A4.9) and (A4.10),

$$\lim_{t \to \infty} \frac{f(v^t \mid \theta) - f(w^t \mid \theta)}{f(v^t \mid \theta) + f(w^t \mid \theta)} = \frac{\lim_{t \to \infty} [f(v^t \mid \theta) - f(w^t \mid \theta)]}{\lim_{t \to \infty} [f(v^t \mid \theta) + f(w^t \mid \theta)]}$$

$$= \frac{f(v^* \mid \theta) - f(w^* \mid \theta)}{f(v^* \mid \theta) + f(w^* \mid \theta)} \tag{A4.11}$$

(e.g., see theorem 12 on p. 44 in Buck, 1978). Finally, since $g(\theta)$ is a constant, (A4.11) implies

$$\lim_{t \to \infty} \frac{f(v^t \mid \theta) - f(w^t \mid \theta)}{f(v^t \mid \theta) + f(w^t \mid \theta)} \cdot g(\theta) = \frac{f(v^* \mid \theta) - f(w^* \mid \theta)}{f(v^* \mid \theta) + f(w^* \mid \theta)} \cdot g(\theta) \tag{A4.12}$$

(e.g., see the corollary to theorem 9 on p. 43 in Buck, 1978). Therefore, by (A4.7) and (A4.12),

$$\lim_{t \to \infty} P\ell_\theta^1(v^t, w^t) = P\ell_\theta^1(v^*, w^*) \tag{A4.13}$$

Therefore, by (A4.13), $P\ell_\theta^1(v, w)$ is continuous at each $(v, w) \in S \times S$ (e.g., see theorem 4.16 in Apostol, 1974, p. 79). Therefore, $P\ell_\theta^1(v, w)$ is continuous in (v, w).

Finally, because each $P\ell_\theta^1(v, w)$ is continuous and Θ is a finite set, it follows from (A4.1) and (A4.7) that $P\ell^1(v, w)$ is continuous in (v, w) (e.g., by theorem 4 on p. 40 in Buck, 1978).

QED

The proof of Theorem 4.1 also uses the following well-known theorem (previously stated in Appendix 2.2 and repeated here for convenience).

Theorem

Let a two-person zero-sum game $(X_1, X_2; \pi, -\pi)$ be given. *If*, for each $i \in \{1, 2\}$, (i) X_i is a compact, convex subset of a Euclidean space E^n, (ii) $\pi(x, y)$ is a continuous function of (x, y) on $X_1 \times X_2$, and (iii) $\pi(x, y)$ is concave in x and convex in y, *then* there exists a saddle-point for the game.

Proof of Theorem 4.1

By Lemmata 4.1–4.3, the premise of the preceding theorem is satisfied. Therefore, by its conclusion, the game $\Gamma = (S, S; P\ell^1, -P\ell^1)$ has a saddle-point. Finally, because an electoral equilibrium is (by definition) a saddle-point in Γ, an electoral equilibrium exists.

QED

Note

In the proof of Theorem 4.1, the only aspect we used of the assumption that each $f(x \mid \theta)$ is C^1 on X was the implication that each $f(x \mid \theta)$ is continuous on S. Therefore, this proof also tells us that, if the assumption that each $f(x \mid \theta)$ is C^1 on X is replaced by the assumption that each $f(x \mid \theta)$ is continuous on S, then the conclusion of Theorem 4.1 still holds. Similarly, the conclusion of this theorem still holds if, alternatively, the C^1 assumption is replaced by any other assumption that implies that each $f(x \mid \theta)$ is continuous on S. For instance, if we make use of the fact that the (unaltered) assumption that f is concave on S implies that f is continuous at each $s \in \text{int}(S)$ (e.g., see theorem D, p. 93, Roberts and Varberg, 1973), Theorem 4.1 still holds if we use the alternative assumption: f is continuous at each boundary point in S. As a second example, the assumption that f is concave on an open set T which is such that $S \subset T \subseteq X$ also implies that f is continuous on S (again, by theorem D, p. 93, Roberts and Varberg, 1973). It should, therefore, be made clear at this point that the reason that the stronger assumption that each $f(x \mid \theta)$ is C^1 on X has been used in stating the premise for Theorem 4.1 is because this assumption was satisfied in the premise for Theorems 2.2 and 3.1–3.7 and will play a more crucial role in the proof of Theorem 4.2 and in the proofs in Chapters 5 and 6. Thus, the approach used serves to link Theorem 4.1 more closely with the other results that are derived in the book.

Appendix 4.2: Proofs of Propositions 4.1 and 4.2

The following lemma is used in the proof of Proposition 4.1. In stating the lemma, we again take as given the unstated premise for Lemmata 4.1–4.3.

Recall that a two-person, zero-sum game $(X_1, X_2; \pi_1, \pi_2)$ is said to be symmetric (or symmetrical) if and only if $X_1 = X_2$ and $\pi_1(v, w) = \pi_2(w, v)$, $\forall v, w \in X_1 = X_2$ (see, for instance, Moulin, 1982, p. 45; Owen, 1982, p. 28; or Ordeshook, 1986, p. 158).

Lemma 4.4

$\Gamma = (S, S; P\ell^1, P\ell^2)$ is symmetric.

Proof of Lemma 4.4

By the definition of Γ, we immediately have $X_1 = S = X_2$. Then, by (4.5)–(4.7), for each $(\psi_1, \psi_2) \in S \times S$,

$$P\ell^1(\psi_1, \psi_2) = \sum_{\theta \in \Theta} \frac{f(\psi_1 \mid \theta)}{f(\psi_1 \mid \theta) + f(\psi_2 \mid \theta)} \cdot g(\theta)$$

$$- \sum_{\theta \in \Theta} \frac{f(\psi_1 \mid \theta)}{f(\psi_1 \mid \theta) + f(\psi_2 \mid \theta)} \cdot g(\theta) \qquad \text{(A4.14)}$$

and

$$P\ell^2(\psi_1, \psi_2) = \sum_{\theta \in \Theta} \frac{f(\psi_2 \mid \theta)}{f(\psi_1 \mid \theta) + f(\psi_2 \mid \theta)} \cdot g(\theta)$$

$$- \sum_{\theta \in \Theta} \frac{f(\psi_2 \mid \theta)}{f(\psi_1 \mid \theta) + f(\psi_2 \mid \theta)} \cdot g(\theta) \qquad \text{(A4.15)}$$

Therefore, by (A4.14) and (A4.15), for each pair $v, w \in S$,

$$P\ell^1(v, w) = \sum_{\theta \in \Theta} \frac{f(v \mid \theta)}{f(v \mid \theta) + f(w \mid \theta)} \cdot g(\theta)$$

$$- \sum_{\theta \in \Theta} \frac{f(w \mid \theta)}{f(v \mid \theta) + f(w \mid \theta)} \cdot g(\theta) = P\ell^2(w, v) \qquad \text{(A4.16)}$$

Therefore, Γ is symmetric.

QED

Proof of Proposition 4.1

We first establish that

$$E_1 \subseteq E_2 \tag{A4.17}$$

Consider any $x \in E_1$. By the definition of E_1, there exists $y \in S$ such that (x, y) is an electoral equilibrium. Therefore, by (2.6),

$$P\ell^1(a, y) \le P\ell^1(x, y) \le P\ell^1(x, b), \qquad \forall\, a, b \in S \tag{A4.18}$$

By Lemma 4.4, $P\ell^2(w, v) = P\ell^1(v, w), \forall\, v, w \in S$. Therefore, by (A4.18),

$$P\ell^2(y, a) \le P\ell^2(y, x) \le P\ell^2(b, x), \qquad \forall\, a, b \in S \tag{A4.19}$$

Since Γ is zero-sum, (A4.19) implies

$$-P\ell^1(y, a) \le -P\ell^1(y, x) \le -P\ell^1(b, x), \qquad \forall\, a, b \in S \tag{A4.20}$$

or, equivalently,

$$P\ell^1(b, x) \le P\ell^1(y, x) \le P\ell^1(y, a), \qquad \forall\, b, a \in S \tag{A4.21}$$

Therefore, by (A4.21) and the definition of an electoral equilibrium, stated in (2.6), (y, x) is an electoral equilibrium. Therefore, by the definition of E_2, we have $x \in E_2$. Therefore, (A4.17) holds. By a similar argument,

$$E_2 \subseteq E_1 \tag{A4.22}$$

holds. Therefore, by (A4.17) and (A4.22), $E_1 = E_2$.

QED

Note

The conclusion and proof of Proposition 4.1 apply not only to the model specified in Section 4.2 but also to all other symmetric, two-person, zero-sum games (e.g., see Moulin, 1982, p. 45; Owen, 1982, pp. 28–30; or Ordeshook, 1986, p. 158).

In proving Proposition 4.2 we use the following well-known theorem (e.g., Luce and Raiffa, 1957, p. 66; Owen, 1982, pp. 10–11; or Ordeshook, 1986, pp. 147–8), which states that equilibrium strategies are "interchangeable."

Theorem

Let a two-person zero-sum game $(X_1, X_2; \pi, -\pi)$ be given. If $(v, w) \in X_1 \times X_2$ and $(x, y) \in X_1 \times X_2$ are saddle-points for the game, then $(v, y) \in X_1 \times X_2$ and $(x, w) \in X_1 \times X_2$ are also saddle-points for the game.

Proof of Proposition 4.2

("If")   Follows directly from the definition of an electoral outcome.

("Only if")   Suppose that s is an electoral outcome. Then, by definition, $s \in E_1 = E_2$. Therefore, by (4.8) and (4.9), there exist $w \in S$ and $x \in S$ such that (s, w) and (x, s) are electoral equilibria. Therefore, by the theorem that precedes this proof, (s, s) is an electoral equilibrium.

QED

Note

It should be clear that the conclusion and proof of Proposition 4.2 also apply to all other symmetric, two-person, zero-sum games.

Appendix 4.3: Proofs of Theorem 4.2 and Corollary 4.3

The proof of Theorem 4.2 uses the next six lemmata. We again assume (as an unstated premise) that the assumptions listed in Section 4.2 are satisfied.

The first lemma roughly establishes that saying a location is an electoral outcome is equivalent to the statement that *if* candidate 2 were to choose the location, then candidate 1 could not do any better than he does by choosing the same location. This reflects the fact that in equilibrium each candidate's strategy is a best response to the other candidate's strategy and the fact that (because the game is symmetric), for any deduction about candidate 1, an analogous deduction about candidate 2 also holds true. Stated precisely:

Lemma 4.5

Let $s \in S$ be given. Then s is an electoral outcome if and only if s solves

$$\max_{v \in S} P\ell^1(v, s) \tag{A4.23}$$

Proof of Lemma 4.5

("If")   Suppose s solves (A4.23). This immediately implies

$$P\ell^1(s, s) \geq P\ell^1(v, s), \qquad \forall\, v \in S \tag{A4.24}$$

By (A4.24) and Lemma 4.4,

$$P\ell^2(s, s) \geq P\ell^2(s, v), \qquad \forall\, v \in S \qquad\qquad (A4.25)$$

(A4.24) and (A4.25), plus the fact that the game $(S, S, P\ell^1 P\ell^2)$ is zero-sum, imply that (2.6) holds. Therefore, (s, s) is an electoral equilibrium. Therefore, by the definition of an electoral outcome, s is an electoral outcome.

("Only if") Suppose that s is an electoral outcome. Then, by Proposition 4.2, (s, s) is an electoral equilibrium. Therefore, by (2.6), (A4.24) holds. Hence, S solves (A4.23).

QED

For any given $s \in S$, let $P\ell_e^1 \colon X \to E^1$ be the function defined by

$$P\ell_e^1(v, s) = \sum_{\theta \in \Theta} \frac{f(v \mid \theta) - f(s \mid \theta)}{f(v \mid \theta) + f(s \mid \theta)} \cdot g(\theta) \qquad\qquad (A4.26)$$

It should be noted that $P\ell_e^1(v, s)$ is an extension of $P\ell^1(v, s)$ onto the set X.

For the next lemma, recall that a function is said to be C^1 on the compact set S, if and only if it is C^1 at each point in an open set that contains S. That is, a function is C^1 on S if and only if there exists an open set T that contains S and is such that the function is continuous on T and possesses continuous first partial derivatives at each $t \in T$ (e.g., see Hestenes, 1975, p. 427).

Lemma 4.6

Let $s \in S$ be given. $P\ell_e^1(v, s)$ is C^1 on S.

Proof of Lemma 4.6

Since $S \subset \text{int}(X)$, (by definition) for each $s \in S$ there exists an open set $0(s)$ such that $s \in 0(s) \subseteq \text{int}(X)$. For any such assignment of open sets, $T = \cup_{s \in S} 0(s)$ is an open set such that $S \subset T \subseteq \text{int}(X)$. For the remainder of the proof, let T be an open set with this property; that is, let T be any open set that is a subset of $\text{int}(X)$ and a strict superset of S.

Consider any $v \in T$. Choose any $\theta \in \Theta$. Let $h : E_{++}^1 \to E^1$ be the function defined by (A4.2), with $\kappa = f(s \mid \theta)$. Since $f(x \mid \theta)$ is a positive real-valued function, $h(y)$ is defined on all of E_{++}^1, and $v \in T \subseteq \text{int}(X)$, it follows that the composition $h[f(x \mid \theta)]$ is defined in a neighborhood of v. Since $v \in \text{int}(X)$ and $f(x \mid \theta)$ is C^1 at v, the function $f(x \mid \theta)$ is differentiable at v (e.g., see theorem 12.11 in Apostol, 1974, p. 357). In addition, $h(y)$ is differentiable at each $y \in E^1_{++}$ and hence (in particular) at v. Therefore, $h[f(x \mid \theta)]$ is differentiable at v (e.g., see theorem 12.7, Apostol, 1974, p. 352). This, in turn, implies that $h[f(x \mid \theta)]$ has all of its partial derivatives at v (e.g., see theorem 12.5, Apostol, 1974, pp. 347–8). By the definition of h and the chain rule, for each $j \in \{1, \ldots, n\}$,

$$\frac{\partial h[f(x \mid \theta)]}{\partial x_j} = \frac{\partial}{\partial x_j} \left[\frac{f(x \mid \theta) - f(s \mid \theta)}{f(x \mid \theta) + f(s \mid \theta)} \right]$$

$$= \frac{[f(x \mid \theta) + f(s \mid \theta)] \cdot [\partial f(x \mid \theta) / \partial x_j] - [f(x \mid \theta) - f(s \mid \theta)] \cdot [\partial f(x \mid \theta) / \partial x_j]}{[f(x \mid \theta) + f(s \mid \theta)]^2}$$

$$= \frac{2 \cdot f(s \mid \theta) \cdot \partial f(x \mid \theta) / \partial x_j}{[f(x \mid \theta) + f(s \mid \theta)]^2} \tag{A4.27}$$

Consider any $j \in \{1, \ldots, n\}$. Since $f(x \mid \theta)$ is C^1 on X, (by definition) $\partial f(x \mid \theta) / \partial x_j$ is continuous at $v \in \text{int}(X)$. In addition, since $f(x \mid \theta)$ is C^1 on X, $f(x \mid \theta)$ is continuous at $v \in \text{int}(X)$. Therefore, since $f(x \mid \theta)$ is a positive, real-valued function, (A4.27) implies that each partial of $h[f(x \mid \theta)]$ is continuous at v (e.g., using theorem 4, p. 40, and theorem 12, p. 44, Buck, 1978).

The fact that each partial of $h[f(x \mid \theta)]$ is continuous at $v \in \text{int}(X)$ implies that $h[f(x \mid \theta)]$ is differentiable at v (e.g., from theorem 12.11, Apostol, 1974, p. 357). The fact that $h[f(x \mid \theta)]$ is differentiable at $v \in \text{int}(X)$, in turn, implies that $h[f(x \mid \theta)]$ is continuous at $v \in \text{int}(X)$ (e.g., see theorem 12.4, Apostol, 1974, p. 347).

Combining the conclusions at the ends of the two preceding paragraphs, we know that $h[f(x \mid \theta)]$ is continuous at v and possesses a continuous first partial derivative at v. Hence, for each $\theta \in \Theta$,

$$h[f(x \mid \theta)] = \frac{f(x \mid \theta) - f(s \mid \theta)}{f(x \mid \theta) + f(s \mid \theta)} \tag{A4.28}$$

is C^1 at v. Therefore, from the fact that Θ is finite, the fact that each $g(\theta)$ is positive, and (A4.26), it follows that $P\ell^1_e(v, s)$ is C^1 at v. Hence, $P\ell^1_e(v, s)$ is C^1 at each $v \in T$. Therefore, by the definition of what it means to say that a function is C^1 on the compact set S (stated right before this lemma), it follows that $P\ell^1_e(v, s)$ is C^1 on S.

QED

In the next lemma, we use the following standard notation: $\nabla\alpha(x)\big|_{x=z}$ denotes the gradient of the function $\alpha(x)$, evaluated at $x=z$; $\langle q, r\rangle$ denotes the inner product of the two vectors q and r.

Lemma 4.7

Let $s \in S$ be given. Then s solves (A4.23) if and only if

$$\langle\nabla P\ell_e^1(v, s)\big|_{v=s}, (z-s)\rangle \le 0, \qquad \forall z \in S \tag{A4.29}$$

Proof of Lemma 4.7

To begin with, $P\ell_e^1(v, s)$ is an extension of $P\ell^1(v, s)$ from S onto X. Therefore, s solves (A4.23) if and only if s maximizes $P\ell_e^1(v, s)$ on S.

In what follows, the directional derivative of $P\ell_e^1(v, s)$ in the direction $b \in E^n$ at $v = s$ (e.g., as defined in Hestenes, 1975, p. 29) is denoted by

$$D_b P\ell_e^1(v, s)\big|_{v=s} \tag{A4.30}$$

Since $P\ell_e^1(v, s)$ is an extension of $P\ell^1(v, s)$, Lemma 4.1 implies that $P\ell_e^1(v, s)$ is a concave function of v on S. In addition, Lemma 4.6 has established that $P\ell_e^1(v, s)$ is C^1 on S. Therefore, using the notation in (A4.30), s maximizes $P\ell_e^1(v, s)$ on S if and only if

$$D_{(z-s)}P\ell_e^1(v, s)\big|_{v=s} \le 0, \qquad \forall z \in S \tag{A4.31}$$

(e.g., see theorem 5.3, Hestenes, 1975, p. 31). Hence, s solves (A4.23) if and only if (A4.31) holds.

Finally, since (by Lemma 4.6) $P\ell_e^1(v, s)$ is C^1 at s and $s \in \text{int}(X)$,

$$D_{(z-s)}P\ell_e^1(v, s)\big|_{v=s} = \langle\nabla P\ell_e^1(v, s)\big|_{v=s}, (z-s)\rangle, \qquad \forall z \in S \tag{A4.32}$$

(e.g., see theorems 12.11 and 12.5, Apostol, 1974). Therefore, (A4.31) holds if and only if (A4.29) holds. Therefore, s solves (A4.23) if and only if (A4.29) holds.

QED

Let $W_e : X \to E^1$ be the function defined by

$$W_e(x) = \sum_{\theta \in \Theta} \log(f(x\mid\theta)) \cdot g(\theta) \qquad \forall x \in X \tag{A4.33}$$

Note that W_e is an extension of W, defined in (4.10), from S onto the larger set X.

Lemma 4.8

$W_e(x)$ is C^1 on S.

Proof of Lemma 4.8

Similar to the proof of Lemma 4.6, using $\log(y)$ instead of $h(y)$.

QED

Lemma 4.9

Let $s \in S$ be given. (A4.29) holds if and only if

$$\langle \nabla W_e(x)\big|_{x=s}, (z-s)\rangle \le 0, \qquad \forall\, z \in S \qquad\qquad (\text{A4.34})$$

Proof of Lemma 4.9

By (A4.26)–(A4.28), Lemma 4.6, and the fact that each $f(x \mid \theta)$ is C^1 on X,

$$
\begin{aligned}
\frac{\partial P\ell_e^1(x, s)}{\partial x_j}\bigg|_{x=s} &= \sum_{\theta \in \Theta} \frac{2 \cdot f(s \mid \theta) \cdot \partial f(x \mid \theta)\,/\,\partial x_j}{[f(x \mid \theta) + f(s \mid \theta)]^2}\bigg|_{x=s} \cdot g(\theta) \\
&= \sum_{\theta \in \Theta} \frac{2 \cdot f(s \mid \theta) \cdot [\partial f(x \mid \theta)\,/\,\partial x_j]_{x=s}}{4 \cdot [f(s \mid \theta)]^2} \cdot g(\theta) \\
&= \sum_{\theta \in \Theta} \frac{[\partial f(x \mid \theta)\,/\,\partial x_j]_{x=s}}{2 \cdot f(s \mid \theta)} \cdot g(\theta) \qquad\qquad (\text{A4.35})
\end{aligned}
$$

for each $j \in \{1, \ldots, n\}$. By (A4.33), Lemma 4.8, and the fact that each $f(x \mid \theta)$ is C^1 on X,

$$\frac{\partial W_e(x)}{\partial x_j}\bigg|_{x=s} = \sum_{\theta \in \Theta} \frac{[\partial f(x \mid \theta)\,/\,\partial x_j]_{x=s}}{f(s \mid \theta)} \cdot g(\theta) \qquad\qquad (\text{A4.36})$$

for each $j \in \{1, \ldots, n\}$. Therefore, by (A4.35), (A4.36), and the definition of a gradient,

$$
\begin{aligned}
\nabla W_e(x)\big|_{x=s} &= \left(\frac{\partial W_e(x)}{\partial x_1}\bigg|_{x=s}, \ldots, \frac{\partial W_e(x)}{\partial x_n}\bigg|_{x=s} \right) \\
&= \frac{1}{2} \cdot \left(\frac{\partial P\ell_e^1(x, s)}{\partial x_1}\bigg|_{x=s}, \ldots, \frac{\partial P\ell_e^1(x, s)}{\partial x_n}\bigg|_{x=s} \right) \\
&= \frac{1}{2} \cdot \nabla P\ell_e^1(x, s)\big|_{x=s} \qquad\qquad (\text{A4.37})
\end{aligned}
$$

Therefore, using (A4.27) and the definition of an inner product, we obtain

$$\langle \nabla W_e(x)\big|_{x=s}, (z-s)\rangle = \frac{1}{2}\cdot\langle \nabla P\ell_e^1(x,s)\big|_{x=s}, (z-s)\rangle, \qquad \forall\, z\in S \qquad (A4.38)$$

Therefore, by (A4.38), (A4.29) holds if and only if (A4.34) holds.

QED

Lemma 4.10

Let $s \in S$ be given. (A4.34) holds if and only if s maximizes $W(v)$ on S.

Proof of Lemma 4.10

To begin with, using an argument similar to the one used to prove Lemma 4.1, with $\log(y)$ replacing $h(y)$, it follows that $W_e(x)$ is a concave function on the convex set S. In addition, by Lemma 4.8, $W_e(x)$ is C^1 on the convex set S. Therefore, using an argument similar to the one used to prove Lemma 4.7, with $W(x)$ in place of $P\ell^1(v,s)$ and $W_e(x)$ in place of $P\ell_e^1(v,s)$, it follows that (A4.34) holds if and only if s maximizes $W(x)$ on S.

QED

Proof of Theorem 4.2

By Lemma 4.5, s is an electoral equilibrium if and only if s solves (A4.23). Therefore, by Lemma 4.7, s is an electoral outcome if and only if (A4.29) holds. Therefore, by Lemma 4.9, s is an electoral outcome if and only if (A4.34) holds. Therefore, by Lemma 4.10, s is an electoral outcome if and only if s maximizes $W(v)$ on S.

QED

The following lemma will be used in the proof of Corollary 4.3. The unstated assumptions in the preceding lemmata will once again be taken as given.

Lemma 4.11

If there exists a partition $P = \{P_1, \ldots, P_q\}$ of the set $\{1, \ldots, n\}$ and a function $\rho : \{1, \ldots, q\} \to \Theta$ such that, for each $P_j \in P$, the corresponding function $\log f[v \mid \rho(j)]$ is strictly concave on S over the components covered by P_j, *then* $W(v)$ is strictly concave on S.

Proof of Lemma 4.11

Recall that, by definition, $W(v)$ is strictly concave on S if and only if

$$W(\lambda \cdot x + (1 - \lambda) \cdot y) > \lambda \cdot W(x) + (1 - \lambda) \cdot W(y) \qquad (A4.39)$$

holds for each $\lambda \in (0, 1)$ and distinct pair $x, y \in S$.

Consider any particular $\lambda \in (0, 1)$ and $x, y \in S$ with $x \neq y$. Let

$$P^1 = \{P_j \in P : \exists\, k \in P_j \text{ with } x_k \neq y_k\} \qquad (A4.40)$$

and

$$P^0 = P - P^1 \qquad (A4.41)$$

In turn, let

$$\Theta_1 = \{\theta_j \in \Theta : \exists\, P_j \in P^1 \text{ such that } \rho(j) = \theta\} \qquad (A4.42)$$

and

$$\Theta_0 = \Theta - \Theta_1 \qquad (A4.43)$$

By (4.10) and the fact that $\{\Theta_0, \Theta_1\}$ is a partition of Θ,

$$W(v) = \sum_{\theta \in \Theta_0} \log(f(v \mid \theta)) \cdot g(\theta) + \sum_{\theta \in \Theta_1} \log(f(v \mid \theta)) \cdot g(\theta) \qquad (A4.44)$$

Consider any $\theta \in \Theta_0$. Since $f(v \mid \theta)$ is concave and $g(\theta)$ is positive, $\log[f(v \mid \theta)] \cdot g(\theta)$ is concave. Therefore, $\sum_{\theta \in \Theta_0} \log[f(v \mid \theta)] \cdot g(\theta)$ is concave. Therefore,

$$\sum_{\theta \in \Theta_0} \log[f(\lambda \cdot x + (1 - \lambda) \cdot y \mid \theta)] \cdot g(\theta) \geq \lambda \cdot \sum_{\theta \in \Theta_0} \log f(x \mid \theta) \cdot g(\theta)$$

$$+ (1 - \lambda) \cdot \sum_{\theta \in \Theta_0} \log[f(y \mid \theta)] \cdot g(\theta) \qquad (A4.45)$$

Now consider any $\theta \in \Theta_1$. By (A4.42), there exists $P_j \in P^1$ such that

$$\rho(j) = \theta \qquad (A4.46)$$

By the definition of ρ (stated in the premise of this lemma) the function $\log[f(v \mid \rho(j))]$ is strictly concave on S over the components covered by P_j. Therefore, from the definition given before Corollary 4.3,

$$\log f[\lambda \cdot x + (1 - \lambda) \cdot y \mid \rho(j)] > \lambda \cdot \log f[x \mid \rho(j)] + (1 - \lambda) \cdot \log f[y \mid \rho(j)] \qquad (A4.47)$$

holds for each $\lambda \in (0, 1)$ and $x, y \in S$ such that $x_k \neq y_k$ for at least one $k \in P_j$. Since $P_j \in P^1$ by (A4.40), there exists $k \in P_j$ with $x_k \neq y_k$. Therefore, (A4.47) holds for the particular $x, y,$ and λ under consideration. Hence, from (A4.46), it follows that $\log[f(v \mid \theta)]$ is strictly concave. Therefore, by an argument analogous to the one that precedes (A4.45),

$$\sum_{\theta \in \Theta_1} \log f[\lambda \cdot x + (1 - \lambda) \cdot y \mid \theta] \cdot g(\theta) > \lambda \cdot \sum_{\theta \in \Theta_1} \log [f(x \mid \theta)] \cdot g(\theta)$$

$$+ (1 - \lambda) \cdot \sum_{\theta \in \Theta_1} \log [f(y \mid \theta)] \cdot g(\theta) \qquad (A4.48)$$

Therefore, using (A4.44), (A4.45), and (A4.48), we have (A4.39).

Finally, since we have established that (A4.39) holds for each $\lambda \in (0, 1)$ and distinct pair $x, y \in S$, the function $W(v)$ is (by definition) strictly concave on S.

QED

Proof of Corollary 4.3

By Lemma 4.11, $W(v)$ is strictly concave. This result and the assumption that S is convex (together) imply that W has a unique maximum on S. Therefore, by Corollary 4.1, there exists a unique electoral equilibrium.

QED

CHAPTER 5

Concave social and candidate
objective functions

A key step in the derivation of Chapter 4's equilibrium existence theorem was to establish that the assumptions (in the model specified in Section 4.2) were sufficient for each candidate's payoff function to be concave in her possible strategies. Then, in deriving the theorem that identified the implicit social objective function that is maximized by these equilibria, a key step was to establish that the assumptions (in the model specified in Section 4.2) were sufficient for the implicit social objective function to be concave. What is more, concavity for a (social or individual) objective function is also of inherent interest in and of itself; as Avriel et al. (1981, p. 24) put it, "In utility theory, the definition of concavity is precisely equivalent to the notion that an individual would never prefer an actuarially fair gamble."

The assumption in Section 4.2 that played the greatest role in the derivation of the (intermediate) "concavity results" was, not surprisingly, the assumption that, for each group $\theta \in \Theta$, the corresponding scaling function $f(s \mid \theta)$ is concave on S. Because of the important role that this assumption played in the derivation of those key concavity results, we now concern ourselves with the possibility of identifying alternative conditions on the groups' scaling functions, which (when all of the other assumptions in Section 4.2 are maintained) also assure either that the society's implicit social objective function is necessarily concave or that the candidates' objective functions are necessarily concave. The approach used to obtain these alternative conditions is described in Section 5.1.

This approach applied in Section 5.2 to deal with the question: "Which conditions assure concavity for the implicit social objective function which was identified in Theorem 4.2?" Proposition 5.1 provides a precise statement of the partial answer that was described in the opening paragraph in this chapter (i.e., the partial answer provided by Chapter 4's intermediate concavity result for the implicit social objective function). Theorem 5.1 then goes beyond Proposition 5.1's sufficient condition for concavity (for the society's implicit objective function) by identifying a condition that is necessary and sufficient to assure that the implicit social objective function is concave.

We then question (Section 5.3) whether the condition that has been identified as being necessary and sufficient for assuring a concave social objective function is also sufficient to assure that the candidates' objective functions are concave. After we show that the answer is no, we turn to some closely related questions that this answer raises. Section 5.4 goes beyond this analysis by identifying necessary and sufficient conditions for assuring concave candidate objective functions. This is first carried out for models in which (as in Chapter 4) it is assumed that each possible scaling function is continuously differentiable (viz., in Theorem 5.2). Very different necessary and sufficient conditions are then derived for models in which we assume that each possible scaling function is twice continuously differentiable (viz., in Theorems 5.3 and 5.4).

The results of Section 5.4 are then used to obtain some new sufficient conditions for the existence of an electoral equilibrium; the locations of those equilibria are then characterized (viz., in Theorems 5.5–5.7). Section 5.5 closes with an example to illustrate the fact that, when the convexity assumptions that have been used to that point are dropped, there may be no electoral equilibrium (as defined in Section 2.3). The last section provides an overview of the results in this chapter and discusses how they relate to the questions addressed in Chapter 6.

5.1   The basic approach

The basic approach used here is similar to that of Inada (1969), Sen and Pattanaik (1969), Sen (1970), and Pattanaik (1971) when they derived necessary and sufficient conditions for a transitive majority rule relation and a choice function generated by the majority rule relation. By way of review, the approach that Inada, Pattanaik, and Sen used in their analyses was to hold every component in their model constant except for the "profile" (or m-tuple) of preference orderings for the m individuals. As Sen (1970, p. 183) put it: "the restrictions that [are] consider[ed] are those that apply only to types of permissible preference orderings and not on numbers holding them." This approach specifically enabled them to "clear up the extent to which qualitative patterns (as opposed to numerical distributions) of individual preferences can guarantee transitivity of the majority relation and the existence of a majority winner in each subset" (Sen, 1970, p. 170).

In this chapter, all of the assumptions of Section 4.2 are retained except the assumption that each $f(x \mid \theta)$ is concave on S. In the ensuing analyses, all of the components in the resulting model are held constant except the profile (or m-tuple) of scaling functions for the m groups. The assumptions from Section 4.2 that are being retained are divided into two parts, each part being (separately) brought into the subsequent analysis at the most appropriate point. The first part consists of all of the assumptions that are listed from the beginning of Section 4.2 up through (and including) the objectives of the two candidates. We refer to this set of assumptions by saying that "there is an election in which (i) there is a finite set of groups and (ii) there is a compact, convex set of possible locations for the candidates," that is, by using the phrase that results when the references to the assumptions about the groups' scaling functions are dropped from our phrase for the entire model specified in Section 4.2.

The preceding descriptive phrase emphasizes that we are starting with a framework that is the same as the one in Section 4.2 in all respects except one: The starting framework does not include the assumptions about the groups' scaling functions that were made in specifying the entire model in Chapter 4. The remaining assumptions from Section 4.2 that are retained are brought in via the following notation (which also makes it easier for us to refer to a particular set of possible profiles): $\mathcal{F}$ denotes a set of functions such that each $f \in \mathcal{F}$ either satisfies all of the assumptions about the group-scaling functions given in Section 4.2 or satisfies all of the assumptions about the group-scaling functions given in Section 4.2 except the assumption that f is concave on S. That is (restating the condition on the elements in $\mathcal{F}$ in more explicit terms), each $f \in \mathcal{F}$ is a C^1 positive, real-valued function on a set X, which has $S \subset \text{int}(X)$, such that (4.1) and (4.2) are satisfied for each $i \in \theta$ and each $(\psi_1, \psi_2) \in S \times S$. We also let

$$\mathcal{F}^m = \underset{\theta=1}{\overset{m}{\times}} \mathcal{F} \tag{5.1}$$

(i.e., $\mathcal{F}^m$ denotes the m-fold Cartesian product of $\mathcal{F}$ with itself).

The results established (viz., in Theorems 5.1–5.4) identify necessary and sufficient conditions for a particular function or functions to be concave: the implicit social objective function (Section 5.2) and each candidate's payoff function in his possible strategies (Section 5.4). In obtaining these conditions, the possible restrictions that are considered are those that apply to types of permissible scaling functions for the groups. Therefore, they will clear up, in a way that is analogous to what was accomplished by Inada et al., the extent to which qualitative patterns (as opposed to numerical distributions of group scaling functions) can guarantee concavity for the function (or functions) under consideration. What is more, the approach specified in this section provides some results about electoral competitions and the societies in which they occur that are not directly analogous to any of the results that Inada et al. derived.

5.2   Concave social objective functions

If a society explicitly used a concave social objective function, then it would always be able to do at least as well by restricting itself to a given set of alternatives S as it could if it expanded its set of alternatives to include lotteries over S (e.g., as in Zeckhauser, 1969; Shepsle, 1970, 1972c; and Fishburn, 1972, 1973). That is, the society would always be able to do at least as well as it could have done if it had considered options in which its final choice is determined by a probability distribution on S. Thus, in such cases, there is no reason to explicitly introduce lotteries on S into the society's alternative set.

The proof of Lemma 4.10 in Appendix 4.3 has made it clear that one qualitative assumption (about the groups' scaling functions) that guarantees concavity for the implicit social objective function $W(x)$ defined by (4.10) is "Each scaling function that a group may potentially have is concave." The following proposition states this observation more precisely.

Proposition 5.1

Suppose there is an election in which (i) there is a finite set of groups and (ii) there is a compact, convex set of possible locations for the candidates. $W(v)$ is concave for each profile in $\mathcal{F}^m$ if each $f \in \mathcal{F}$ is concave on S.

This proposition is generalized in Theorem 5.1. In particular, the theorem identifies a condition that is necessary and sufficient to assure concavity for the social objective function $W(x)$ defined by (4.10). As it turns out, the condition involves a property for a function that has been widely investigated elsewhere. More specifically, recall that a function $\phi(y)$ is said to be *log-concave* if and only if the composition $\log[\phi(y)]$ is defined (i.e., ϕ is a positive, real-valued function) and concave (e.g., see Klinger and Mangasarian, 1968; Roberts and Varberg, 1973; or Kallberg and Ziemba, 1981). The result itself is as follows.

Theorem 5.1

Suppose there is an election in which (i) there is a set of groups and (ii) there is a compact, convex set of possible locations for the candidates. $W(v)$ is concave for each profile in $\mathcal{F}^m$ if and only if each $f \in \mathcal{F}$ is log-concave on S.

Proposition 5.1 and Theorem 5.1 indirectly tell us that if a given $f \in \mathcal{F}$ is concave, then it is log-concave. This implication (also) follows directly from the fact that f is a positive, real-valued function and $\log(\cdot)$ is a concave and strictly increasing function on E^1_{++}; see, for instance, property (iv) in theorem 5.14, p. 254, Sydsaeter (1981). That the converse does not hold can be seen by considering (for instance) $f(x) = e^x$, which is log-concave but not concave. Indeed, it should be noted (as pointed out on pp. 390 and 397, Klinger and Mangasarian, 1968) that this reasoning applies to all positive, real-valued functions and not just to $f \in \mathcal{F}$.

5.3 Log-concavity and the candidates' objective functions

By Theorem 5.1, assuming that each $f \in \mathcal{F}$ is log-concave on S is necessary and sufficient to assure concavity for the implicit social objective function $W(v)$. By Theorem 4.2, the set of maxima for $W(v)$ is the same as the set of electoral outcomes for the electoral competition $(S, S; P\ell^1, P\ell^2)$. As a consequence, the following natural question arises: Is assuming that each $f \in \mathcal{F}$ is log-concave on S sufficient to assure that, for each c, $P\ell^c$ is concave with respect to ψ_c? The fact that assuming "each $f \in \mathcal{F}$ is log-concave on S" is not sufficient to assure that each candidate's expected plurality function is concave can be easily seen from the following simple counterexample.

EXAMPLE 5.1

Suppose that all of the assumptions in Section 4.2 are satisfied except for the assumption that for each $\theta \in \Theta$ the corresponding scaling function is concave on S. Let S be the closed interval $[-1, +1]$ in E^1. Assume that for each group $\theta \in \Theta$ the corresponding scaling function is the log-concave function $f(v \mid \theta) = e^v$. Then, by (4.5)–(4.7),

$$P\ell^1(x, y) = \left(\frac{e^x - e^y}{e^x + e^y} \right) \tag{5.2}$$

Let y be any (fixed) element of $(-1, +1]$. Taking the (ordinary) first derivative of the resulting function of the variable x gives us

$$\frac{dP\ell^1(x, y)}{dx} = \frac{(e^x + e^y) \cdot e^x - (e^x - e^y) \cdot e^x}{(e^x + e^y)^2}$$

$$= 2 \cdot \left[\frac{e^x \cdot e^y}{(e^x + e^y)^2} \right] \tag{5.3}$$

Therefore, taking the second derivative, we get

$$\frac{d^2 P\ell^1(x, y)}{dx^2} = 2 \cdot \left[\frac{(e^x + e^y)^2 \cdot e^x \cdot e^y - e^x \cdot e^y \cdot 2 \cdot (e^x + e^y) \cdot e^x}{(e^x + e^y)^4} \right]$$

$$= 2 \cdot \left\{ \left[\frac{(e^x + e^y) \cdot e^x \cdot e^y}{(e^x + e^y)^4} \right] \cdot (e^y - e^x) \right\} \tag{5.4}$$

Finally, (5.4) implies that

$$\frac{d^2 P\ell^1(x, y)}{dx^2} > 0, \qquad \forall\, x \in [-1, y) \tag{5.5}$$

Therefore, $P\ell^1(x, y)$ is not a concave function of x.

Analogous to the definition (stated in Appendix 2.2) of a payoff function $\pi(x, y)$ that is concave in x, we say that a function $\zeta(\psi_1, \psi_2)$ on $S \times S$ is log-concave in ψ_c (where $c \in \{1, 2\}$) if and only if, for each given $\psi_k \in S$ (where k is the unique element in the set $\{1, 2\} - \{c\}$), $\zeta(\psi_1, \psi_2)$ is a log-concave function of ψ_c. Following the line of inquiry raised at the beginning of this section, we ask at this point whether assuming log-concavity on S for the groups' scaling functions is sufficient to assure log-concavity for the candidates' objective functions.

Since (as Example 5.1 illustrates) assuming that each $f \in \mathcal{F}$ is log-concave on S does not rule out the possibility of a candidate's expected plurality function taking on negative values, it is immediately clear that it is also not sufficient to assure that the function $P\ell^c(\psi_1, \psi_2)$ is log-concave in ψ_c. This simple observation, however, provides an incomplete analysis of the implications (of the condition identified in Theorem 5.1) for the candidates' objective functions because it does not apply, for instance, to the expected vote function on $S \times S$,

$$EV^c(\psi_1, \psi_2) = \sum_{\theta \in \Theta} P_\theta^c(\psi_1, \psi_2) \cdot g(\theta) \tag{5.6}$$

at each $(\psi_1, \psi_2) \in S \times S$, which is an equivalent objective function for candidate c (in the sense that assuming a candidate wants to maximize his expected vote, rather than his expected plurality, does not change any of the conclusions about the equilibria in the resulting two-candidate game; see Aranson, Hinich, and Ordeshook, 1973, 1974).

In Lemmata 4.1 and 4.2, we established that assuming "each $f \in \mathcal{F}$ is concave on S" is sufficient to assure that each candidate's expected plurality function is concave in her strategy. At this stage, we address the question of whether, analogously, assuming "each $f \in \mathcal{F}$ is log-concave on S" is sufficient to assure that each candidate's expected vote function is log-concave in her strategy. The first part of the answer deals with the expected vote for a given candidate c from a given group θ; that is, with the function

$$EV_\theta^c(\psi_1, \psi_2) = P_\theta^c(\psi_1, \psi_2) \cdot g(\theta) \tag{5.7}$$

The second part of the answer deals with the expected vote for a candidate from all groups: that is, with the function $EV^c(\psi_1, \psi_2)$ defined in (5.6).

The first part is provided by the following result, which is analogous to what was established in the first part of the proof of Lemma 4.1, in the argument leading up to (A4.6).

Proposition 5.2

Suppose there is an election in which (i) there is a finite set of groups and (ii) there is a compact, convex set of possible locations for the candidates. Let $\theta \in \Theta$ and $c \in \{1, 2\}$ be given. If $f(v \mid \theta)$ is log-concave on S, then $EV_\theta^c(\psi_1, \psi_2)$ is log-concave in ψ_c.

Note that Proposition 5.2 immediately implies: If each group θ has the same scaling function $f(s \mid \theta)$, and this function is log-concave on S, then (for each candidate c) $EV^c(\psi_1, \psi_2)$ is log-concave in ψ_c (since, in this case, $EV^c(\psi_1, \psi_2) = EV_\theta^c(\psi_1, \psi_2) / g(\theta)$, $\forall \, \theta \in \Theta$). This implication can be easily illustrated using Example 5.1.

EXAMPLE 5.1 (continued)

By (5.6) and (4.7),

$$EV^1(x, y) = \left(\frac{e^x}{e^x + e^y} \right) \tag{5.8}$$

Therefore,

$$\log\{EV^1(x, y)\} = x - \log\{e^x + e^y\} \tag{5.9}$$

By (5.9) at each $y \in S$,

$$\frac{d \, \log\{EV^1(x, y)\}}{dx} = 1 - \left(\frac{e^x}{e^x + e^y} \right), \qquad \forall \, x \in S \tag{5.10}$$

Therefore, by (5.10), at each $y \in S$,

$$\frac{d^2}{dx^2} \log\{EV^1(x, y)\} = \frac{-e^x \cdot e^y}{[e^x + e^y]^2} < 0, \qquad \forall \, x \in S \qquad (5.11)$$

Therefore, $EV^1(\psi_1, \psi_2)$ is log-concave in ψ_1. By a similar argument, $EV^2(\psi_1, \psi_2)$ is log-concave in ψ_2.

In the proof of Lemma 4.1, establishing that each $P\ell_\theta^1(\psi_1, \psi_2)$ is concave in ψ_1 led directly to the lemma's conclusion that $P\ell^1(\psi_1, \psi_2)$ is concave in ψ_1 (viz., making use of the fact that a weighted sum of concave functions is itself concave). It has already been shown that an analogous result holds in Example 5.1. In addition, it is well known that a weighted sum of log-convex functions is log-convex (e.g., see theorem 13.F, p. 19, Roberts and Varberg, 1973, and the more general results about the closure properties of log-convex functions that are stated on p. 392, Klinger and Mangasarian, 1968). It is, therefore, natural to think that the result established in Proposition 5.2 might always lead to the conclusion that for each c the function $EV^c(\psi_1, \psi_2)$ is log-concave in ψ_c.

One consideration that indicates that things might not go as smoothly as in the proof of Lemma 4.1 is the fact that (as pointed out on pp. 391 and 397 and illustrated by an example on p. 397 in Klinger and Mangasarian, 1968) the sum of two log-concave functions is not necessarily concave; a simple alternative example that is closely related to Example 5.1 is provided by the fact that

$$\frac{d^2[\log\{e^x \cdot (.5) + (.5) \cdot (.5)\}]}{dx^2} = \left[\frac{e^x}{e^x + 1}\right] > 0, \qquad \forall \, x$$

implying that the weighted sum of the log-concave functions $g(x) = e^x$ and $h(x) = .5$ that is inside the curly brackets is not log-concave. This fact does not (in and of itself) rule out the possibility that the assumption "each $f \in \mathcal{F}$ is log-concave on S" is sufficient to assure that EV^c is log-concave in ψ_c since, because of the additional structure that the model has, not all (weighted) log-concave functions can turn up as one of the terms in the sum in (5.6); for instance, having $EV^c_\theta(x, y) = e^x \cdot g(\theta)$ requires $f(x \mid \theta) = [e^x / (1 - e^x)] / f(y \mid \theta)$, which is not a log-concave function. Nonetheless, it gives the right indication, as established by the following counterexample (which proves that combining log-concavity for the groups' scaling functions and the additional structure in the election model under consideration is not enough to guarantee log-concavity for a candidate's expected vote function).

EXAMPLE 5.2

Make the same assumptions as in Example 5.1 except the assumption that the scaling function for each group is e^y. Instead, assume that (i)

$\Theta = \{1, 2\}$, (ii) $f(v \mid 1) = e^v$, (iii) $f(v \mid 2) = k$ (where k is a constant), and (iv) $g(1) = g(2) = \frac{1}{2}$.
By (5.6) and (4.7),

$$EV^1(x, y) = \left(\frac{e^x}{e^x + e^y}\right) \cdot (.5) + (.5) \cdot (.5) \qquad (5.12)$$

Therefore, by (5.12),

$$\log\{EV^1(x, 0)\} = \log(.5) + \log\left(\frac{e^x}{e^x + 1} + \frac{1}{2}\right)$$

$$= \log(.5) + \log\{3 \cdot e^x + 1\} - \log\{2 \cdot e^x + 2\} \qquad (5.13)$$

Therefore, by (5.13),

$$\frac{d \log\{EV^1(x, 0)\}}{dx} = \left(\frac{3 \cdot e^x}{3 \cdot e^x + 1} - \frac{2 \cdot e^x}{2 \cdot e^x + 2}\right)$$

$$= \left[\frac{4 \cdot e^x}{6 \cdot (e^x)^2 + 8 \cdot e^x + 2}\right] \qquad (5.14)$$

Therefore, by (5.14),

$$\frac{d^2 \log\{EV^1(x, 0)\}}{dx^2} = \left\{\frac{8 \cdot e^x - 24 \cdot (e^x)^3}{[6 \cdot (e^x)^2 + 8 \cdot e^x + 2]^2}\right\} \qquad (5.15)$$

Equation (5.15) implies that, for any given $x \in S$,

$$\frac{d^2 \{\log[EV^1(x, 0)]\}}{dx^2} \gtreqless 0 \qquad (5.16)$$

if and only if

$$8 \cdot e^x - 24 \cdot (e^x)^3 \gtreqless 0 \qquad (5.17)$$

which holds if and only if

$$\sqrt{\tfrac{1}{3}} \gtreqless e^x \qquad (5.18)$$

or, equivalently,

$$\log\{\sqrt{\tfrac{1}{3}}\} \gtreqless x \qquad (5.19)$$

Therefore,

$$\frac{d^2 \log\{EV^1(x, 0)\}}{dx^2} > 0, \qquad \forall\, x \in [-1, \log\{\sqrt{\tfrac{1}{3}}\}) \qquad (5.20)$$

Therefore, by (5.20), $EV^1(\psi_1, \psi_2)$ is not log-concave in ψ_1.

5.4   Concave candidate objective functions

In what follows, we say that $P\ell^1(\psi_1, \psi_2)$ is "concave-convex" for a particular profile $[f(v \mid 1), \dots, f(v \mid m)]$ if and only if the expected plurality function for candidate 1 that corresponds to $[f(v \mid 1), \dots, f(v \mid m)]$ is (i) concave in ψ_1 and (ii) convex in ψ_2 (by the definitions stated before Lemma 2.2 in Appendix 2.2). Such a profile is, of course, one at which each candidate has a concave objective function since the definition immediately implies that (i), for any given ψ_2, candidate 1's expected plurality is a concave function of ψ_1 on S and (ii), for any given ψ_1, candidate 2's expected plurality is a concave function of ψ_2 on S.

Observe that $P\ell^1(\psi_1, \psi_2)$ being concave–convex for a particular profile, implies that if we were to expand the candidates' strategy sets to include the possibility of them choosing mixed strategies on S (i.e., with the corresponding probability distributions being defined on S), then each candidate would be able to do at least as well by choosing his strategy directly from S as he would by choosing a mixed strategy on S. Therefore, when the candidates have concave objective functions at a particular profile, even if it is reasonable to assume that they could choose mixed strategies (an assumption which, as was pointed out in footnote 14 in Chapter 1, is somewhat controversial), there is no loss from analyzing the candidates' decisions using the simpler model that results if we assume that each candidate must select one of the strategies contained in the set S.

As noted in the introduction, Lemmata 4.1 and 4.2 in Appendix 4.1 have already made it clear that one qualitative assumption about the groups' scaling functions that guarantees concavity for the candidates' objective functions is that each scaling function that a group can potentially have is concave on S. Proposition 5.3 states this observation in more precise terms.

Proposition 5.3

Suppose there is an election in which (i) there is a finite set of groups and (ii) there is a compact, convex set of possible locations for the candidates. $P\ell^1(\psi_1, \psi_2)$ is concave–convex for each profile in $\mathcal{F}^m$ if each $f \in \mathcal{F}$ is concave on S.

Example 5.1 has ruled out the possibility of log-concavity being necessary and sufficient to assure that the candidates' payoff function is concave–convex. The next theorem, therefore, identifies an alternative condition that *is* necessary and sufficient. In stating this condition, we make use of the "shifted scaling function" that results when a scaling function in $\mathcal{F}$ is "shifted" by having its maximum value added to it. This (resulting) function is denoted by ρ. To state the same thing more precisely, for any given $f(s \mid \theta) \in \mathcal{F}$, we use ρ to denote the positive, real-valued function on S that satisfies

$$\rho(v \mid \theta) = f(v \mid \theta) + \max_{s \in S} \{f(s \mid \theta)\} \qquad (5.21)$$

(at each $v \in S$). Note that – since $f \in \mathcal{F}$ implies that f is continuous on S and the set of possible locations for the candidates $S \subset E^n$, is compact – Weierstrass' (or the extreme value) theorem implies that a maximum of f on S exists and is achieved by some $a \in S$ (e.g., see theorem 5.1, Sydsaeter, 1981).

In stating the (promised) condition that assures that each candidate's payoff function is concave in her strategy, $D_v g(z)$ is used to denote the directional derivative of the C^1 function $g : E^n \to E^1$ in the direction v at the point z; that is, $D_v g(z) = \lim_{t \to \infty}([g(z + h_t \cdot v) - g(z)] / h_t)$ for each sequence $\{h_t\}$ of nonzero real numbers that converges to zero (e.g., see Apostol, 1974, p. 344; Buck, 1978, pp. 125–6; Roberts and Varberg, 1973, p. 62; or Sydsaeter, 1981, pp. 114–5).

Theorem 5.2

Suppose there is an election in which (i) there is a finite set of groups and (ii) there is a compact, convex set of possible locations for the candidates. $P\ell^1(\psi_1, \psi_2)$ is concave–convex for each profile in $\mathcal{F}^m$ if and only if each $f \in \mathcal{F}$ is such that

$$[f(x \mid \theta) - f(y \mid \theta)] \cdot \left\{ \frac{\rho(y \mid \theta)}{\rho(x \mid \theta)} \right\} \leq D_{(x-y)} f(y \mid \theta) \qquad (5.22)$$

holds for each pair $x, y \in S$.

By the well-known theorem about C^1 concave functions stated before the proof of Lemma 5.2 in Appendix 5.2, it follows that the sole difference between the assumption that a given $f \in \mathcal{F}$ is concave and the property of a real-valued, C^1 function stated in Theorem 5.2 is the presence of the ratio $\{\rho(y \mid \theta) / \rho(x \mid \theta)\}$ in the inequalities in (5.22). In the next few paragraphs, we show that it is possible to directly confirm (as Proposition 5.3 and Theorem 5.2 indirectly tell us must be the case) that if a given $f \in \mathcal{F}$ is concave on S, then those inequalities must be satisfied. That is, the ensuing argument establishes that, for any given $f \in \mathcal{F}$, the assumption "f is concave on S" is sufficient for the condition in Theorem 5.2 to hold.

Suppose that a given $f(s \mid \theta) \in \mathscr{F}$ is concave on S. Consider any particular $x, y \in S$. Since $f(s \mid \theta)$ is concave on S, the theorem about C^1 concave functions stated before the proof of Lemma 5.2 in Appendix 5.2 implies

$$f(x \mid \theta) - f(y \mid \theta) \le D_{(x-y)} f(y \mid \theta) \tag{5.23}$$

Since f is a positive, real-valued function, either (i) $f(x \mid \theta) \ge f(y \mid \theta)$ or (ii) $f(x \mid \theta) < f(y \mid \theta)$ must be true. Suppose that (i) is true. Then,

$$f(x \mid \theta) - f(y \mid \theta) \ge 0 \tag{5.24}$$

and, by (5.21) and the fact that $f(v \mid \theta) > 0, \forall \, v \in S$,

$$\frac{\rho(y \mid \theta)}{\rho(x \mid \theta)} = \frac{f(y \mid \theta) + \max_{s \in S}\{f(s \mid \theta)\}}{f(x \mid \theta) + \max_{s \in S}\{f(s \mid \theta)\}} \le 1 \tag{5.25}$$

Therefore, by (5.24) and (5.25),

$$[f(x \mid \theta) - f(y \mid \theta)] \cdot \left\{\frac{\rho(y \mid \theta)}{\rho(x \mid \theta)}\right\} \le [f(x \mid \theta) - f(y \mid \theta)] \tag{5.26}$$

Hence, by (5.23) and (5.26), we have (5.22). Suppose that (ii) is true. Then,

$$f(x \mid \theta) - f(y \mid \theta) < 0 \tag{5.27}$$

and, by (5.21) and the fact that $f(v \mid \theta) > 0, \forall \, v \in S$,

$$\frac{\rho(y \mid \theta)}{\rho(x \mid \theta)} = \frac{f(y \mid \theta) + \max_{s \in S}\{f(s \mid \theta)\}}{f(x \mid \theta) + \max_{s \in S}\{f(s \mid \theta)\}} > 1 \tag{5.28}$$

Therefore, by (5.27) and (5.28), we (once again) have (5.26). Therefore, using (5.23) and (5.26) again, we (once again) have (5.22).

Up to this point, we have been studying models in which it is assumed that each possible scaling function for the groups is C^1. As a consequence, it has not been possible to use second derivatives in deriving general results (because their existence is not assured). In the next two theorems, we replace the assumption that each possible scaling function is C^1 with the alternative assumption that each possible scaling function is C^2. With this additional assumption, it is possible (by using second derivatives) to derive very different necessary and sufficient conditions for assuring that the candidates' objective functions are concave.

To make it easy to refer to the resulting class of possible scaling functions, the notation F is used (in the ensuing analyses) to denote the set that results when the definition of $\mathscr{F}$ is altered by replacing the assumption that each possible scaling function is C^1 with the assumption that each possible scaling function is C^2. That is, stating the definition in full, F denotes a set of functions such that each $f \in F$ is a C^2 function on a set X, which has $S \subset \text{int}(X)$, such that (4.1) and (4.2) are satisfied for each $i \in \Theta$ and each $(\psi_1, \psi_2) \in S \times S$. Analogous to (5.1), let

$$F^m = \mathop{\mathsf{X}}_{\theta=1}^{m} F \tag{5.29}$$

(i.e., F^m denotes the m-fold Cartesian product of F with itself).

The following notation and definitions are useful in stating the next theorem, that is, in stating our first necessary and sufficient condition for assuring concave candidate objective functions when the possible scaling functions are C^2. To begin, we use $H[\xi(v \mid \theta)]$ to denote the Hessian of a C^2 function ξ at the point v. To conserve space, we also use the following (standard) shorthand notation for the first and second partial derivatives of a C^2 function ξ at a point, $v = y$ in its domain:

$$\xi_h(y) \equiv \left. \frac{\partial \xi(v)}{\partial v_h} \right|_{v=y} \tag{5.30}$$

for any $h \in \{1, \ldots, n\}$ and

$$\xi_{hj}(y) \equiv \left. \frac{\partial^2 \xi(v)}{\partial v_h \, \partial v_j} \right|_{v=y} \tag{5.31}$$

for any pair $h, j \in \{1, \ldots, n\}$.

Additionally, we use the following standard definition of a negative semidefinite matrix (e.g., see Chiang, 1984, pp. 320 and 381).

Definition

An $(n \times n)$ matrix $[q_{hj}]$ is negative semidefinite on a given set $Y \subseteq E^n$ if and only if

$$\sum_{h=1}^{n} \sum_{j=1}^{n} y_h \cdot q_{hj} \cdot y_j \leq 0 \tag{5.32}$$

holds at each $(y_1, \ldots, y_n) \in Y$.

Finally, we also use the following notation:

$$Z(y) \equiv \{z \in E^n : \exists \, x \in S \text{ such that } z = (x - y)\} \tag{5.33}$$

Theorem 5.3

Suppose there is an election in which (i) there is a finite set of groups and (ii) there is a compact, convex set of possible locations for the candidates. $P\ell^1(\psi_1, \psi_2)$ is concave–convex for each profile in F^m if and only if each $f \in F$ is such that, for each $v \in S$, the matrix

$$H[f(v \mid \theta)] + \left[\frac{-2 \cdot f_h(v \mid \theta) \cdot f_j(v \mid \theta)}{\rho(v \mid \theta)} \right] \tag{5.34}$$

is negative semidefinite on $Z(v)$.

From the theorem about C^2 concave functions (stated before the proof of Lemma 5.5 in Appendix 5.3) together with the definition of $Z(y)$ (stated before Theorem 5.3), it follows that the sole difference between an $f \in F$ being concave on S and its satisfying the condition that has been identified in Theorem 5.3 is the presence of additional terms in the entries of the matrix that must be negative semidefinite on $Z(v)$. Note that by (A5.54) (from the proof of Lemma 5.6) and (5.21), it follows that the second term in (5.34) is negative semidefinite. Therefore, that term provides some additional leeway for a scaling function, in the sense of allowing any particular $z'H[f(v \mid \theta)]z$ to be positive up to the value that is given by the product $z'[\{2 \cdot f_h(v \mid \theta) \cdot f_j(v \mid \theta)\} / \rho(v \mid \theta)]z$.

The following definitions are used in stating the necessary and sufficient condition for concave–convex candidate payoff functions for Theorem 5.4. The first definition is closely related to the following familiar measure of risk aversion for a utility function $U(x)$, defined on a set of possible amounts of money (which has $U'(x) > 0, \forall x$):

$$r(x) = -\frac{U''(x)}{U'(x)} \tag{5.35}$$

(due to Pratt, 1964; and Arrow, 1965, 1970). In particular, we use the following (related) concept, which is based on the directional derivative $D_y(x)$ (rather than on ordinary derivatives) and which applies to any real-valued function that (i) has a Euclidean domain and (ii) is C^1.

Definition

Let (i) $x \in A \subseteq E^\ell$, (ii) a C^1 function $\xi : A \to E^1$, and (iii) a direction $y \in E^\ell$ be given. The "relative rate of change" in ξ is

$$-r_y(x) = \begin{cases} \dfrac{D_y\xi(x)}{\xi(x)} & \text{if} \quad \xi(x) \neq 0 \\ D_y\xi(x) & \text{if} \quad \xi(x) = 0 \end{cases} \tag{5.36}$$

The familiar Arrow–Pratt measure of risk aversion stated in (5.35) is, of course, simply the negative of the special case of (5.36) that arises when ξ is a positive marginal utility function defined on a set of possible amounts of money [i.e., $\xi(x) = U'(x)$, with $U'(x) > 0$, $\forall\, x$], the particular x under consideration is a specific amount of money, and $y = 1$. Note that (as Pratt, 1984, p. 136, pointed out) when Arrow independently introduced the measure of risk aversion that bears their two names, he used the negative of (5.35). Thus, in this special case, (5.36) specifically reduces to Arrow's original measure of risk aversion.

A second definition used in the statement of Theorem 5.4 is the following.

Definition

Let $q, r \in E^1$ be given. We say that "q is bounded by r, according to its sign" if and only if

$$r \geq 0 \Rightarrow q \leq r \tag{5.37}$$

and

$$r < 0 \Rightarrow q \geq r \tag{5.38}$$

To help interpret this definition, note that q being bounded by r, according to its sign, is not the same thing as q being bounded by the absolute value of r. For instance, consider $[q_1 = -3, r_1 = +1]$ or $[q_2 = +3, r_2 = -1]$. In each case, q is bounded by r according to its sign, but the absolute value of q is not bounded by the absolute value of r.

The statement of Theorem 5.4 uses the following familiar definition (e.g., see p. 203, Hestenes, 1975).

Definition

For any given $s \in S$, a vector $y \in E^n$ is a "feasible direction" if and only if there exists a positive real number δ such that

$$(s + t \cdot y) \in S, \qquad \forall\, t \in [0, \delta] \tag{5.39}$$

The set of feasible directions at a given $v \in S$ are denoted by $T(v)$.

Finally, we turn to the theorem itself.

Theorem 5.4

Suppose there is an election in which (i) there is a finite set of groups and (ii) there is a compact, convex set of possible locations for the candidates. $P\ell^1(\psi_1, \psi_2)$ is concave–convex for every profile in F^m if and only if each $f \in F$ is such that for each

$v \in S$ and $y \in T(v)$ the relative rate of change in the directional derivative of f is bounded by twice the relative rate of change in the shifted scaling function ρ according to its sign.

Analogous to the analysis of Theorem 5.2, it is (also) possible to directly confirm that (as Proposition 5.3 and Theorem 5.4 indirectly tell us must be the case), if a scaling function $f(s \mid \theta) \in \mathscr{F}$ is concave on S, then the condition identified in Theorem 5.4 holds.

First, by the theorem for C^2 concave functions (stated before Lemma 5.5 in Appendix 5.3), $f(s \mid \theta) \in F$ is concave on S if and only if at each $v \in S$

$$\sum_{h=1}^{n}\sum_{j=1}^{n}[f_{hj}(v \mid \theta) \cdot (x_h - v_h) \cdot (x_j - v_j)] \le 0 \tag{5.40}$$

holds for each $x \in S$. By an argument similar to the proof of Lemma 5.7, this implies that $f(s \mid \theta) \in F$ is concave on S if and only if at each $v \in S$

$$\sum_{h=1}^{n}\sum_{j=1}^{n}[f_{hj}(v \mid \theta) \cdot y_h \cdot y_j] \le 0 \tag{5.41}$$

holds for each feasible direction y. Therefore, by (A5.78) from the proof of Lemma 5.7 and (5.36), $f(s \mid \theta) \in F$ is concave if and only if at each $v \in S$

$$D_y[D_y f(v \mid \theta)] \le 0 \tag{5.42}$$

holds for each feasible direction y.

Next, at the end of the proof of Lemma 5.7, for any given $v \in S$ and feasible direction y, let $\alpha_y(v)$ denote the relative rate of change in the directional derivative of f. Then, by (A5.88) from Appendix 5.4 and (5.37), it follows that $f(s \mid \theta) \in F$ is concave if and only if

$$D_y f(v \mid \theta) > 0 \Rightarrow \alpha_y(v) \le 0 \tag{5.43}$$

$$D_y f(v \mid \theta) = 0 \Rightarrow \alpha_y(v) = 0 \tag{5.44}$$

and

$$D_y f(v \mid \theta) < 0 \Rightarrow \alpha_y(v) \ge 0 \tag{5.45}$$

holds for each $v \in S$ and feasible direction y. Also (again, as at the end of the proof of Lemma 5.7), for any given $v \in S$ and feasible direction y, let $\beta_y(v) \equiv 2 \cdot$ (the relative change in the shifted scaling function ρ). By (A5.79) and (A5.89) (from Appendix 5.4), it follows that $\beta_y(v) = 2 \cdot [D_y f(v \mid \theta) / \rho(v \mid \theta)]$, for each $v \in S$ and feasible direction y. Therefore, by the fact that $\rho(s \mid \theta)$ is a positive, real-valued function, it follows that $D_y f(v \mid \theta) \gtreqless 0$ if and only if $\beta_y(v) \gtreqless 0$, for each $v \in S$ and feasible direction y. Therefore, it follows that $f(s \mid \theta) \in F$ is concave if and only if

$$\beta_y(v) \geq 0 \Rightarrow \alpha_y(v) \leq 0 \tag{5.46}$$

and

$$\beta_y(v) < 0 \Rightarrow \alpha_y(y) \geq 0 \tag{5.47}$$

hold for each $v \in S$ and feasible direction y.

Finally, for each $v \in S$ and feasible direction y, (5.46)–(5.47) imply

$$\beta_y(v) \geq 0 \Rightarrow \alpha_y(v) \leq \beta_y(v) \tag{5.48}$$

and

$$\beta_y(v) < 0 \Rightarrow \alpha_y(v) \geq \beta_y(v) \tag{5.49}$$

Therefore, using the definition of one number being bounded by another number according to its sign (stated before Theorem 5.4), we have the following: Assuming that $f(s \mid \theta) \in F$ is concave implies that for each $v \in S$ and feasible direction y the relative rate of change in the directional derivative of f is bounded by twice the relative rate of change in the shifted scaling function ρ according to its sign.

With reference to the preceding analysis, it is interesting to note that the one and only change in moving from (5.46) and (5.47) to (5.48) and (5.49) is that the zero bounds on $\alpha_y(v)$ that appear on the right-hand side of (5.46) and (5.47) are replaced with the wider bounds given by $\beta_y(v)$. This change specifically reflects the greater flexibility of the condition in Theorem 5.4 vis-à-vis the assumption "each possible scaling function is concave."

As a way of illustrating the nature of Theorem 5.4, consider the special case in which (i) X is a set of amounts of money and (ii) $f(v \mid \theta)$ is a C^2 utility function on X. Then the property identified in Theorem 5.4 can be written as, at each $x \in S$,

$$\beta_1(x) \geq 0 \Rightarrow -r(x) \leq \beta_1(x) \tag{5.50}$$

and

$$\beta_1(x) < 0 \Rightarrow -r(x) \geq \beta_1(x) \tag{5.51}$$

where r is the Arrow–Pratt measure of risk aversion, and the subscript on the β function specifies that it is being evaluated in the direction $y = 1$. Thus, in this special case, Theorem 5.4 identifies (functional) bounds on any given voter's "preference for risk" that are necessary and sufficient for the candidates' payoff functions to be concave–convex for every profile in F^m.

Among other things, the bounds in (5.50) and (5.51) have an interest-ing implication for models in which (as discussed in Section 4.5) each voter's scaling function is also his utility function. In particular, because the corresponding bounds for a concave $f(v \mid \theta) = U_\theta(x)$ are zeros, the bounds in (5.50) and (5.51) tell us that there are situations in which *no voter is risk averse but both candidates are*. In such situations, the can-didates are (arguably) not reflecting the electorate's risk preferences in an appropriate way because they are not exhibiting the electorate's unanimous view that an actuarially fair gamble is always at least as good as the expected value of that gamble.

The following examples illustrate how Theorem 5.4 can be used to identify whether including a particular C^2 function in a set of possible scaling functions can keep the candidates' objective functions from being concave. Example 5.1 has already made use of the scaling function $f(s \mid \theta) = e^s$, defined on the set $S = [-1, +1]$. This function, of course, is not concave (and, indeed, is strictly convex) on S, and hence is one to which the preceding analysis does not apply. What is more, the initial analysis of Example 5.1 (carried out in Section 5.3) has already made it clear that this function definitely can keep the candidates' objective functions from being concave. Because the answer is (therefore) al-ready known for this function, it provides us with a clear illustration of the way in which Theorem 5.4 can be used with any given C^2 function.

EXAMPLE 5.1 (continued)

Consider any $v \in S$ and feasible direction $y \in E^1_{++}$.

$$D_y f(v \mid \theta) = \left(\left. \frac{df(s \mid \theta)}{ds} \right|_{s=v} \right) \cdot y = e^v \cdot y \qquad (5.52)$$

Therefore, the relative rate of change in the directional derivative of f is

$$\alpha_y(v) = \frac{\{(d \mid ds) [e^s \cdot y]_{s=v}\} \cdot y}{e^v \cdot y} = y \qquad (5.53)$$

By (5.21) and the fact that $f(s \mid \theta) = e^s$ is increasing in s, the corre-sponding shifted scaling function on S is $\rho(s \mid \theta) = e^s + e^1$. Hence, for the given v and y, twice the relative rate of change in the shifted scaling function is

$$\beta_y(v) = 2 \cdot \frac{\{(d \mid ds) [e^s + e^1]_{s=v}\} \cdot y}{e^v + e^1} = 2 \cdot \left(\frac{e^v}{e^v + e^1} \right) \cdot y \qquad (5.54)$$

Now consider any $v \in [-1, +1)$. Since $y > 0$, (5.54) implies $\beta_y(v) > 0$. Hence, by (5.53) and (5.54) and the definition of one number being bounded by another, according to its sign (stated before Theorem 5.4), the condition derived in Theorem 5.4 is satisfied at the given v and y if and only if

$$y \le 2 \cdot \left(\frac{e^v}{e^v + e^1} \right) \cdot y \qquad (5.55)$$

Since $e^x > 0$, $\forall x$, and we have assumed that y is positive, the inequality in (5.55) is satisfied if and only if $(e^v + e^1) \le 2 \cdot e^v$, or equivalently, if and only if $e^v \ge e^1$. However, since $v \in [-1, +1)$ and e^x is increasing in x, this inequality is false. Therefore, the inequality in (5.55) is (also) false. Hence, the condition derived in Theorem 5.4 is violated at the v and y under consideration. Therefore, by Theorem 5.4, if a set F contains $f(s \mid \theta) = e^s$, then the candidates are not risk averse for every profile in F^m. Therefore, including this function in the set of possible scaling functions can keep the candidates' objective functions from being concave.

We now consider a scaling function that has not been used in the previous examples.

EXAMPLE 5.3

Let $S = [-1, +1]$ and let $f(s \mid \theta) = 2 + s^2$. As an initial observation, it is easy to see that (unlike the function we have just analyzed) this function is not log-concave on S. In particular, let $g(s) = \log\{f(s \mid \theta)\} = \log\{2 + s^2\}$. Then $dg / ds = (2 \cdot s)(2 + s^2)$. Hence,

$$\frac{d^2 g}{ds^2} = \frac{\{(2 + s^2) \cdot (2) - (2 \cdot s)(2 \cdot s)\}}{\{(2 + s^2)\}^2}$$

Therefore, $[d^2 g / ds^2 \gtreqless 0] \Leftrightarrow [4 + 2 \cdot s^2 - 4 \cdot s^2 \gtreqless 0] \Leftrightarrow [4 \gtreqless 2 \cdot s^2] \Leftrightarrow [\sqrt{2} \gtreqless s]$ Hence, since $S = [-1, +1]$, we have $[d^2 g / ds^2 > 0, \forall s \in S]$. Indeed, since $d^2 g / ds^2$ is positive on S, this analysis tells us that f is log-convex on S.

Since (for any positive, real-valued function) log-concavity is a necessary condition for concavity, the initial observation just made immediately implies that the scaling function under consideration is also not concave on S. Since f is not concave but is C^2, we (again) use Theorem 5.4 to obtain an answer to the question: "Can including this f in the set of possible scaling functions keep the candidates' objective functions from being concave?"

Consider any location $v \in (0, 1]$ and feasible direction $y \in E^1_{++}$. The directional derivative of f at v in the direction y is

$$D_y f(v \mid \theta) = \left(\left. \frac{df(s \mid \theta)}{ds} \right|_{s=v} \right) \cdot y = 2 \cdot v \cdot y > 0 \qquad (5.56)$$

Hence, the relative rate of change in the directional derivative $D_y f(v \mid \theta)$ is

$$\alpha_y(v) = \frac{\{(d/ds)[2 \cdot s \cdot y]_{s=v}\} \cdot y}{2 \cdot v \cdot y} = \frac{y}{v} > 0 \qquad (5.57)$$

From (5.21) plus the assumption that $S = [-1, +1]$ and the fact that $f(s \mid \theta)$ = $2 + s^2$ is increasing in $|s|$, it follows that the corresponding shifted scaling function on S is $\rho(s \mid \theta) = (2 + s^2) + 3$. Therefore, for the given v and y, twice the relative rate of change in the shifted scaling function is

$$\beta_y(v) = 2 \cdot \frac{\{(d/ds)[5 + s^2]_{s=v}\} \cdot y}{5 + v^2} = \frac{4 \cdot v \cdot y}{5 + v^2} > 0 \qquad (5.58)$$

From (5.57) and (5.58) and the definition of a number being bounded by a second number according to its sign (stated before Theorem 5.4), it follows that the condition derived in Theorem 5.4 is violated at the particular $v \in (0, +1]$ and positive y under consideration, if and only if

$$\frac{y}{v} \le \left(\frac{4 \cdot v \cdot y}{5 + v^2} \right) \qquad (5.59)$$

Rearranging terms and using the fact that both v and y are positive, we find that (5.59) holds if and only if $(5 + v^2) \le 4 \cdot v^2$, or equivalently, if and only if

$$\tfrac{5}{3} \le v^2 \qquad (5.60)$$

Since $v \in (0, +1]$, (5.60) is clearly false. Hence, (5.59) is also false, implying, in turn, that the condition derived in Theorem 5.4 is violated. Therefore, by Theorem 5.4, if a set F contains $f(s \mid \theta) = 2 + s^2$, then the candidates are not risk averse for every profile in F^m. Therefore, the answer to the question posed in the first paragraph in this example is (as in the last example): "Yes, including this function in the set of possible group scaling functions can keep the candidates' objective functions from being concave."

Our final example analyzes a function that (as before) is not concave on S but which, unlike the previous functions, is not a scaling function that can keep the candidates' objective functions from being concave. Before we begin the analysis of the C^2 function in Example 5.4, note that (as the statement of Theorem 5.4 makes clear) establishing this conclusion entails showing that the condition derived in Theorem 5.4 holds for each location and feasible direction, rather than (as before) simply finding a special case in which the derived condition fails to hold.

EXAMPLE 5.4

Let $S = [-1, +1]$ and $f(s \mid \theta) = \exp\{-s^2\}$. To start off, it is easy to confirm that this function is log-concave on S. In particular, let $g(s) = \log\{f(s \mid \theta)\} = \log\{\exp\{-s^2\}\} = -s^2$. The $dg/ds = -2 \cdot s$. Therefore, $d^2g/ds^2 = -2$, $\forall s \in S$. As the next step, we establish that it is (additionally) a function that is not concave on S. Taking the first derivative, we get

$$\frac{df(s \mid \theta)}{ds} = \left(-2 \cdot s \cdot e^{-s^2}\right) \tag{5.61}$$

Therefore, the second derivative is

$$\frac{d^2 f(s \mid \theta)}{ds^2} = \left(-2 \cdot e^{-s^2}\right) + \left(4 \cdot s^2 \cdot e^{-s^2}\right) \tag{5.62}$$

Therefore,

$$\frac{d^2 f(s \mid \theta)}{ds^2} \gtreqless 0 \Leftrightarrow s^2 \gtreqless \frac{1}{2} \tag{5.63}$$

Therefore, in particular,

$$\frac{d^2 f(s \mid \theta)}{ds^2} > 0, \qquad \forall s \in [-1, -\sqrt{\tfrac{1}{2}}) \cup (+\sqrt{\tfrac{1}{2}}, +1] \tag{5.64}$$

Hence, f is not concave on S; more specifically, f is concave around $s = 0$ but is not concave in its (truncated) tails. With this established, we turn to our derivation of the fact that including this f in the set of possible scaling functions cannot keep the candidates' objective functions from being concave.

Consider any $v \in S$ and feasible direction $y \in E^1$. Using (5.61), we get

$$D_y f(v \mid \theta) = \left(\frac{df(s \mid \theta)}{ds}\bigg|_{s=v}\right) \cdot y = \left(-2 \cdot v \cdot e^{-v^2}\right) \cdot y \tag{5.65}$$

Therefore, the relative rate of change in the directional derivative of f is

$$\alpha_y(v) = \begin{cases} \dfrac{\left(\left[(d/ds)\left[\left(-2 \cdot s \cdot e^{-s^2}\right) \cdot y\right]\right]_{s=v}\right) \cdot y}{\left(-2 \cdot v \cdot e^{-v^2}\right) \cdot y} = \dfrac{\left((-2 + 4 \cdot v^2) \cdot e^{-v^2}\right) \cdot y^2}{\left(-2 \cdot v \cdot e^{-v^2}\right)} \\ \qquad\qquad\qquad\qquad\qquad \text{if} \quad v \neq 0 \text{ and } y \neq 0 \\[2mm] \left(\dfrac{d}{ds}\left[\left(-2 \cdot s \cdot e^{-s^2}\right) \cdot y\right]_{s=v}\right) \cdot y = \left((-2 + 4 \cdot v^2) \cdot e^{-v^2}\right) \cdot y^2 \\ \qquad\qquad\qquad\qquad\qquad \text{if} \quad v = 0 \text{ or } y = 0 \end{cases} \tag{5.66}$$

Therefore, simplifying (5.66),

$$\alpha_y(v) = \begin{cases} \left[\left(\dfrac{1}{v} - 2 \cdot v\right) \cdot y\right] & \text{if} \quad v \neq 0 \\ -2 \cdot y^2 & \text{if} \quad v \neq 0 \end{cases} \tag{5.67}$$

Since $S = [-1, +1]$,

$$\max_{s \in S}\{e^{-s^2}\} = 1 \tag{5.68}$$

Therefore, by (5.21), the shifted scaling function on S is $\rho(s \mid \theta) = \exp\{-s^2\}$ + 1. Hence, at the given v and y, twice the relative rate of change in the shifted scaling function is

$$\beta_y(v) = 2 \cdot \frac{\left((d/ds)\left[(e^{-s^2}) + 1\right]_{s=v}\right) \cdot y}{(e^{-v^2}) + 1} = \frac{(-4 \cdot v \cdot e^{-v^2}) \cdot y}{(e^{-v^2}) + 1} \tag{5.69}$$

Case 1: $[y = 0]$. By (5.67) and (5.69), $\alpha_y(v) = 0 = \beta_y(v)$. Therefore (in this case), the relative rate of change in the directional derivative of f is bounded by twice the relative rate of change in the shifted scaling function, according to its sign.

Case 2: $[y \neq 0$ and $\beta_y(v) = 0]$. By (5.69), we must also have $v = 0$. Therefore, by (5.67), $\alpha_y(v) = -2 \cdot y^2 < 0$. Hence, $\alpha_y(v) < \beta_y(v)$. Therefore (in this case), the relative rate of change in the directional derivative of f is bounded by twice the relative rate of change in the shifted scaling function, according to its sign.

Case 3: $[y > 0$ and $\beta_y(v) > 0]$. By (5.69), we also have

$$v < 0 \tag{5.70}$$

Using (5.67) and (5.69), plus (5.70) and the assumption that $y > 0$, gives

$$\alpha_y(v) \leq \beta_y(v) \tag{5.71}$$

if and only if

$$\frac{1}{v} - 2 \cdot v \leq \left[\frac{-4 \cdot v \cdot e^{-v^2}}{(e^{-v^2}) + 1}\right] \tag{5.72}$$

Using (5.70) and the fact that $(\exp\{-v^2\} + 1) > 0$, we find that (5.72) holds if and only if

$$(e^{-v^2}) + 1 - (2 \cdot v^2 \cdot e^{-v^2}) - 2 \cdot v^2 \geq -4 \cdot v^2 \cdot (e^{-v^2}) \tag{5.73}$$

Therefore, (5.71) holds if and only if

$$(1 + 2 \cdot v^2) \cdot \left(e^{-v^2}\right) - 2 \cdot v^2 + 1 \geq 0 \tag{5.74}$$

Let χ denote the function on S that satisfies

$$\chi(s) = (1 + 2 \cdot s^2) \cdot \left(e^{-s^2}\right) - 2 \cdot s^2 + 1 \tag{5.75}$$

(at each $s \in S$). By (5.75), at $s = -1$,

$$\chi(-1) = (3 \cdot e^{-1}) - 1 \tag{5.76}$$

Because the value for e^{-1} in standard tables (where the values of e^x are rounded to four places after the decimal point) is .3679, (5.76) tells us that

$$\chi(-1) > 0 \tag{5.77}$$

Note that, by (5.75), the first derivative of χ is

$$\frac{d}{ds}\chi(s) = \left(-2 \cdot s \cdot e^{-s^2}\right) - \left(4 \cdot s^3 \cdot e^{-s^2}\right) + \left(4 \cdot s \cdot e^{-s^2}\right) - 4 \cdot s$$

$$= (2 \cdot s) \cdot \left[\left(e^{-s^2}\right) \cdot (1 - 2 \cdot s^2) - 2\right] \tag{5.78}$$

Also note that

$$\left[0 < \left(e^{-s^2}\right) < 1\right] \quad \text{and} \quad [-1 < (1 - 2 \cdot s^2) < +1], \quad \forall\, s \in [-1, 0) \tag{5.79}$$

By (5.79),

$$-1 < \left(e^{-s^2}\right) \cdot (1 - 2 \cdot s^2) < +1, \quad \forall\, s \in [-1, 0) \tag{5.80}$$

Therefore, by (5.80), at each $S \in [-1, 0)$, the right-hand side of (5.78) is the product of two negative numbers. Therefore,

$$\frac{d}{ds}\chi(s) > 0, \quad \forall\, s \in [-1, 0) \tag{5.81}$$

By the definition of S (at the beginning of the example) and (5.70), we have $v \in [-1, 0)$. Therefore, by (5.77) and (5.81), it follows that $\chi(v) > 0$. Hence, using (5.75), we have $[(1 + 2 \cdot v^2) \cdot \exp\{-v^2\} - 2 \cdot v^2 + 1] > 0$. Therefore, using the conclusion at the end of the previous paragraph, we have $\alpha_y(v) \leq \beta_y(v)$. Therefore, since $\beta_y(v) > 0$, (in this case) the relative rate of change in the directional derivative of f is bounded by twice the relative rate of change in the shifted scaling function, according to its sign.

All Remaining Cases: $[y > 0$ and $\beta_y(v) < 0]$ or $[y < 0$ and $\beta_y(v) \neq 0]$. Since $f(s \mid \theta) = \exp\{-s^2\}$ is symmetric around $s = 0$, arguments similar to those for Case 3 imply that (in these remaining cases) the relative rate of change in the directional derivative of f is bounded by twice the relative rate of change in the shifted scaling function, according to its sign.

Finally, from Theorem 5.4, it now follows that including $f(s \mid \theta) = \exp\{-s^2\}$ in the set of possible scaling functions F will not keep the candidates' objective functions from being concave for each profile in F^m.

Note

A natural question about Example 5.4 is "Does the same conclusion always hold if the domain for f is widened from $[-1, +1]$?" It is therefore worth observing that, for a sufficiently wide interval, the necessary and sufficient condition obtained in Theorem 5.3 no longer holds at every s (in particular, it then fails at each s that is far enough away from zero).

The analyses after Theorems 5.2–5.4 have made it clear that, assuming that a scaling function in F is concave implies that it satisfies the conditions derived in Theorems 5.3 and 5.4 and assuming that a scaling function in $\mathcal{F}$ is concave implies that it satisfies the condition derived in Theorem 5.2. However, we have left open the question of whether the converses hold, that is, whether (for a scaling function in F or $\mathcal{F}$, respectively) the (corresponding) derived conditions are equivalent to concavity. It is, therefore, worth observing that Example 5.4 makes it clear that (again, for a scaling function in F or $\mathcal{F}$, respectively) the (corresponding) derived condition is more general than concavity. Looked at another way, Theorem 5.4 and Example 5.4 (together) imply that the assumption (in Chapter 4) that "each scaling function is concave on S" is one of the cases (albeit, an important one) in which the candidates' objective functions are concave.

5.5   Electoral equilibria

Combining the results in the previous section with the arguments used to prove Theorem 4.1 (in Appendix 4.1) leads us immediately to the conclusion (given that the remaining assumptions in Chapter 4 are maintained) that an electoral equilibrium continues to exist if we drop the assumption that each group's scaling function is concave and replace it with either the assumption that each group's scaling function satisfies the condition obtained in Theorem 5.2 or the assumption that each group's scaling function is C^2 and satisfies either the condition obtained in Theorem 5.3 or the condition obtained in Theorem 5.4.

In stating the first of these implications more precisely, we supplement the starting assumption used in Theorems 5.1–5.4 with all of the remaining conditions in Section 4.2 except the requirement that each group's scaling function is concave. We refer to this longer list of assumptions by using the phrase that results when we add "the candidates use a C^1 binary Luce model" to the descriptive phrase that has been used so far in this chapter. Note that this is also the phrase that we get when we delete the word *concave* from the descriptive phrase used in Chapter 4 to refer to the model specified in Section 4.2. The phrase that we are using, therefore, has the virtue of emphasizing that the only difference between the model studied in Chapter 4 and the starting assumption for Corollary 5.1 is that the former assumes that each group's scaling function is concave whereas the latter does not.

The implication to which Theorem 5.2 leads is given by the following corollary.

Corollary 5.1

Suppose there is an election in which (i) there is a finite set of groups, (ii) there is a compact, convex set of possible locations for the candidates, and (iii) the candidates use a C^1 binary Luce model. If, for each $\theta \in \Theta$, $f(s \mid \theta)$ is such that (5.22) is satisfied for each pair $x, y \in S$, then an electoral equilibrium exists.

In stating the implications of Theorems 5.3 and 5.4 more precisely, we add the requirement that each group's scaling function is C^2 to those that were invoked in the starting assumption for Corollary 5.1. To refer to the resulting model, we use the phrase that we get when the descriptive phrase used in the premise of Corollary 5.1 is altered by replacing C^1 with C^2. The implication obtained with Theorem 5.3 is stated in Corollary 5.2.

Corollary 5.2

Suppose there is an election in which (i) there is a finite set of groups, (ii) there is a compact, convex set of possible locations for the candidates, and (iii) the candidates use a C^2 binary Luce model. If, for each $\theta \in \Theta$, $f(s \mid \theta)$ is such that for each $v \in S$ the matrix given in (5.31) is negative semidefinite on $Z(v)$, then an electoral equilibrium exists.

Theorem 5.4 implies the next corollary.

Corollary 5.3

Suppose there is an election in which (i) there is a finite set of groups, (ii) there is a compact, convex set of possible locations for the candidates, and (iii) the candidates use a C^2 binary Luce model. If, for each $\theta \in \Theta, f(s \mid \theta)$ is such that for each $v \in S$ and feasible direction y the relative rate of change in the directional derivative of f is bounded by twice the relative rate of change in the shifted scaling function, according to its sign, then an electoral equilibrium exists.

Theorems 5.1–5.4 enable us to identify the locations of these electoral equilibria. More specifically, they lead to the following *location theorems* for the electoral outcomes that occur under the conditions obtained in Theorems 5.1–5.4.

Theorem 5.5

Suppose there is an election in which (i) there is a finite set of groups, (ii) there is a compact, convex set of possible locations for the candidates, (iii) the candidates use a C^1 binary Luce model, and (iv) for each $\theta \in \Theta, f(s \mid \theta)$ is such that (5.22) is satisfied for each pair $x, y \in S$. Let $s \in S$ be given. Then s is an electoral outcome if and only if s maximizes W on S.

Theorem 5.6

Suppose there is an election in which (i) there is a finite set of groups, (ii) there is a compact, convex set of possible locations for the candidates, (iii) the candidates use a C^2 binary Luce model, and (iv) for each $\theta \in \Theta, f(s \mid \theta)$ is such that for each $v \in S$ the matrix in (5.31) is negative semidefinite on $Z(v)$. Let $s \in S$ be given. Then s is an electoral outcome if and only if s maximizes W on S.

Theorem 5.7

Suppose there is an election in which (i) there is a finite set of groups, (ii) there is a compact, convex set of possible locations for the candidates, (iii) the candidates use a C^2 binary Luce model, and (iv) for each $\theta \in \Theta, f(s \mid \theta)$ is such that for each $v \in S$ and feasible direction y the relative rate of change in the directional derivative of f is bounded by twice the relative rate of change in the shifted scaling function according to its sign. Let $s \in S$ be given. Then s is an electoral outcome if and only if s maximizes W on S.

Corollary 5.1 and Theorem 5.5 are, of course, generalizations of Theorems 4.1 and 4.2 (viz., generalizing those results to include all of the cases covered by the conditions obtained in Theorem 5.2). Corollaries 5.2 and 5.3 and Theorems 5.6 and 5.7, on the other hand, are analogous extensions for situations in which the groups' scaling functions are C^2 (viz., including all of the cases covered by the conditions obtained in Theorems 5.3 and 5.4).

Theorems 5.2–5.4 have identified exactly how far the assumption made about the qualitative pattern of the possible (C^1 or C^2) group-scaling functions can be pushed without losing the conclusion that each candidate's objective function is concave. Therefore, Corollaries 5.1–5.3 (in turn) have taken us as far as it is possible to go with using results about symmetric, concave–convex, two-person, zero-sum games to identify assumptions about the qualitative pattern of the possible (C^1 or C^2) group-scaling functions that assure that electoral equilibria exists.

However, it should be made clear, the alternative sufficient conditions for the existence of an electoral equilibrium provided by Corollaries 5.1–5.3 are not necessary for an electoral equilibrium to exist. This can be seen by considering Examples 5.1 and 5.2. In each example, there is at least one group that has the scaling function $f(s \mid \theta) = e^s$, a function that (as pointed out in the preceding section) violates the conditions derived in Theorems 5.2–5.4. However, there is still an electoral equilibrium in each example that occurs at $(\psi_1^*, \psi_2^*) = (+1, +1)$.

The fact that the sufficient conditions identified in Corollaries 5.1–5.3 are not also necessary for the existence of an equilibrium should not be very surprising, for two reasons. First, the saddle-point existence theorem (stated in Appendix 2.2), which has been used to obtain this book's electoral equilibrium existence results, can itself identify conditions that are sufficient, but not necessary, for the existence of a saddle-point (e.g., see the more general saddle-point existence theorem in Moulin, 1986, p. 18). Second, theorems 5.2–5.4 are concerned with assuring concavity for every profile in $\mathscr{F}^m$ or F^m (rather than with assuring concavity at a single profile).

Significantly, in establishing the concavity–convexity of $P\ell^1(\psi_1, \psi_2)$, the proofs of Theorems 5.2–5.4 concentrated on showing that for each $\theta \in \Theta$ $P\ell_\theta^1(\psi_1, \psi_2)$ is concave–convex. Then, since the expected plurality for a given candidate is the sum of the group-expected plurality functions for that candidate and since the sum of concave functions is concave, it followed that $P\ell^1(\psi_1, \psi_2)$ is concave–convex. On the other hand, establishing quasi concavity for each group's expected plurality function would not assure quasi concavity for $P\ell^1(\psi_1, \psi_2)$. As a consequence, more general saddle-point existence theorems (such as the one in Moulin, 1986, p. 18), which use quasi concavity rather than concavity could not be used in the same way. This fact, of course, heightens interest in the concave–convex games studied in this chapter.

Importantly, however, (it should also be made clear) if this chapter's convexity assumptions – the assumption that S is convex and the conditions that assure that $P\ell^1(\psi_1, \psi_2)$ is concave–convex – are dropped completely, then the existence of an equilibrium is not assured. This can be seen from the next example.

EXAMPLE 5.5

Make the assumptions in Section 4.2 except for the assumptions that (i) S is convex and (ii) for each $\theta \in \Theta$, $f(v \mid \theta)$ is concave on S. Assume that $\Theta = \{1, 2, 3\}$ and that $g(1) = g(2) = g(3) = \frac{1}{3}$. Let $S = \{s^1, s^2, s^3\} \subset E^1$, with $s^1 < s^2 < s^3$. Let the groups' scaling functions be such that

$$f(s^1 \mid 1) = 1, \qquad f(s^2 \mid 1) = 2, \qquad f(s^3 \mid 1) = 3 \tag{5.82}$$

$$f(s^1 \mid 2) = 2, \qquad f(s^2 \mid 2) = 3, \qquad f(s^3 \mid 2) = 1 \tag{5.83}$$

and

$$f(s^1 \mid 3) = 3, \qquad f(s^2 \mid 3) = 1, \qquad f(s^3 \mid 3) = 2 \tag{5.84}$$

Using (5.82)–(5.84) and (4.5)–(4.7), we get

$$P\ell^1(s^1, s^2) = \left(\frac{1-2}{1+2}\right) \cdot \left(\frac{1}{3}\right) + \left(\frac{2-3}{2+3}\right) \cdot \left(\frac{1}{3}\right) + \left(\frac{3-1}{3+1}\right) \cdot \left(\frac{1}{3}\right) = \frac{-1}{90} \tag{5.85}$$

$$P\ell^1(s^1, s^3) = \left(\frac{1-3}{1+3}\right) \cdot \left(\frac{1}{3}\right) + \left(\frac{2-1}{2+1}\right) \cdot \left(\frac{1}{3}\right) + \left(\frac{3-2}{3+2}\right) \cdot \left(\frac{1}{3}\right) = \frac{+1}{90} \tag{5.86}$$

and

$$P\ell^1(s^2, s^3) = \left(\frac{2-3}{2+3}\right) \cdot \left(\frac{1}{3}\right) + \left(\frac{3-1}{3+1}\right) \cdot \left(\frac{1}{3}\right) + \left(\frac{1-2}{1+2}\right) \cdot \left(\frac{1}{3}\right) = \frac{-1}{90} \tag{5.87}$$

Therefore, from (5.85)–(5.87) and the fact the $(S, S; P\ell^1, P\ell^2)$ is symmetric and zero-sum, it follows that the payoff matrix for candidate 1 in this game is

$$[P\ell^1(s^i, s^j)] = \begin{bmatrix} 0 & -\frac{1}{90} & +\frac{1}{90} \\ +\frac{1}{90} & 0 & -\frac{1}{90} \\ -\frac{1}{90} & +\frac{1}{90} & 0 \end{bmatrix} \tag{5.88}$$

Therefore, by (5.88),

$$\max_{s^i}\left\{\min_{s^j}\{P\ell^1(s^i, s^j)\}\right\} = \frac{-1}{90} < \frac{+1}{90} = \min_{s^j}\left\{\max_{s^i}\{P\ell^1(s^i, s^j)\}\right\} \tag{5.89}$$

Thus (e.g., see theorem 13:B*, Von Neumann and Morgenstern, 1953, p. 95), there is no saddle-point. Hence, there is no electoral equilibrium.

It is worth noting that if utility functions are introduced into Example 5.5 in either of the ways in which they were introduced into the model in Chapter 4 (viz., in the analysis carried out in the second half of Section 4.5), then, by (5.82)–(5.84) and either (4.11) or (4.12), the voter preferences in the example constitute a *Condorcet profile*. At the same time, however, we emphasize that, unlike with models in which (2.7) is satisfied, the presence of a Condorcet profile is not a sufficient condition for the absence of an electoral equilibrium (as Theorem 2.2 in Chapter 2 has already made clear).

5.6   Conclusion

This chapter has investigated the model that results when the assumption that each group's scaling function is necessarily concave is removed from the election model that was specified in Section 4.2. The primary focus has been on identifying more general assumptions that assure concavity properties for the implicit social objective function that was identified in Chapter 4 and the objective functions for the candidates. The new results have extended our knowledge about the conditions under which these functions are concave and at the same time have identified boundaries on the qualitative patterns (for the groups' scaling functions) that lead to concavity being present. In addition, we have generalized and extended Chapter 4's equilibrium existence and equilibrium location theorems all the way to these boundaries. The final example has made it clear that when an electoral equilibrium is defined as it was in Section 2.3, the election model being studied may have no equilibrium.

In light of what has been learned, it seems clear that there is reason to investigate some alternative (viz., less demanding) concepts about what constitutes an electoral equilibrium. This is done in the next chapter with alternative concepts based on the view that candidates may have less flexibility in choosing strategies than has been assumed so far in this book. The resulting analyses provide a very different perspective on (and some important further insights about) the strategies that are rational for a candidate to adopt.

Appendix 5.1: Proofs of Theorem 5.1 and Proposition 5.2

Proof of Theorem 5.1

("If")   Assume that each $f \in \mathcal{F}$ is log-concave on S. Consider any profile $[f(v \mid 1), \ldots, f(v \mid m)]$ in $\mathcal{F}^m$. By (4.10), $W(v)$ is a weighted sum of the restrictions of $\log\{f(v \mid 1)\}, \ldots, \log\{f(v \mid m)\}$ on S. In addition, by the assumption at the start of the proof and the definition of a log-concave function (stated right before Theorem 5.1), each of the functions $\log\{f(v \mid 1)\}, \ldots, \log\{f(v \mid m)\}$ is defined and concave on S. Therefore, since a weighted sum of concave functions is concave, it follows that $W(v)$ is concave. Hence, $W(v)$ is concave for each profile in $\mathcal{F}^m$.

("Only if")   Assume that $W(v)$ is concave for each profile in $\mathcal{F}^m$. Now, suppose $\exists \phi \in \mathcal{F}$ that is not log-concave on S. It will be shown that this leads to a contradiction, thereby establishing that each $f \in \mathcal{F}$ is log-concave.

First, since $\phi \in \mathcal{F}$, by (5.1) $\mathcal{F}^m$ contains at least one profile $[f(v \mid 1), \ldots, f(v \mid m)]$ which has

$$f(v \mid \theta) = \phi(v), \qquad \forall \, v \in X, \qquad \forall \, \theta \in \Theta \tag{A5.1}$$

At this profile,

$$W(v) = \sum_{\theta \in \Theta} [\log\{f(v \mid \theta)\}] \cdot g(\theta)$$

$$= \sum_{\theta \in \Theta} [\log\{\phi(v)\} \cdot g(\theta)] = \log\{\phi(v)\}, \qquad \forall \, v \in S \tag{A5.2}$$

using (4.10), then (A5.1), and then the fact that g is a discrete probability distribution.

Finally, by the supposition made at the beginning of this argument (viz., $\phi \in \mathcal{F}$ but is not log-concave on S), it follows (using the definitions of $\mathcal{F}$ and log-concavity) that $\log\{\phi(v)\}$ is not concave on S. But this implies, by (A5.2), that $W(v)$ is not concave on S at the profile in $\mathcal{F}^m$

under consideration, which contradicts the starting assumption. There-fore, each $f \in \mathscr{F}$ is log-concave on the set S.

QED

Proof of Proposition 5.2

Consider $c = 1$. By (5.7) and (4.7),

$$EV_\theta^1 (x, y) = \left[\frac{f(x \mid \theta)}{f(x \mid \theta) + f(y \mid \theta)} \right] \cdot g(\theta) \qquad (A5.3)$$

Consider any given $y^* \in S$. Since $g(\theta) > 0$, (A5.3) implies that $EV_\theta^1(x, y^*)$ is a log-concave function of x if and only if the function $H : S \to E^1$ that satisfies

$$H(x) = \frac{f(x \mid \theta)}{f(x \mid \theta) + f(y^* \mid \theta)} \qquad (A5.4)$$

(at each $x \in S$) is log-concave. Since the fact that $f(x \mid \theta) > 0, \forall x \in S$ implies that $H(x) > 0, \forall x \in S$, the definition of a log-concave function (stated right before Theorem 5.1) implies that the statement that $H(x)$ is log-concave is equivalent to the statement that $\log\{H(x)\}$ is concave. Therefore, it follows that $H(x)$ is log-concave if and only if

$$\log\{H[\alpha \cdot x + (1 - \alpha) \cdot z]\} \geq \alpha \cdot \log\{H(x)\} + (1 - \alpha) \cdot H(z) \qquad (A5.5)$$

for all $x, z \in X$ and $\alpha \in [0, 1]$.

Consider any particular $x, z \in X$ and $\alpha \in [0, 1]$. By the log-concavity of $f(x \mid \theta)$,

$$f[\alpha \cdot x + (1 - \alpha) \cdot z \mid \theta] \geq f(x \mid \theta)^\alpha \cdot f(z \mid \theta)^{1-\alpha} \qquad (A5.6)$$

Letting k denote the constant $f(y^* \mid \theta)$, we find that (A5.6) implies

$$\left[\frac{f(\alpha \cdot x + (1 - \alpha) \cdot z \mid \theta)}{f(\alpha \cdot x + (1 - \alpha) \cdot z \mid \theta) + k} \right] \geq \left[\frac{f(x \mid \theta)^\alpha \cdot f(z \mid \theta)^{1-\alpha}}{f(x \mid \theta)^\alpha \cdot f(z \mid \theta)^{1-\alpha} + k} \right] \qquad (A5.7)$$

Therefore, since

$$[f(x \mid \theta)^\alpha \cdot f(z \mid \theta)^{1-\alpha} + k] \leq [[f(x \mid \theta) + k]^\alpha \cdot [f(z \mid \theta) + k]^{1-\alpha}] \qquad (A5.8)$$

we have

150   **Concave objective functions**

$$\left[\frac{f(\alpha \cdot x + (1-\alpha) \cdot z \mid \theta)}{f(\alpha \cdot x + (1-\alpha) \cdot z \mid \theta) + k}\right] \geq \left[\frac{f(x \mid \theta)^\alpha \cdot f(z \mid \theta)^{1-\alpha}}{[f(x \mid \theta) + k]^\alpha \cdot [f(z \mid \theta) + k]^{1-\alpha}}\right]$$

$$(A5.9)$$

Therefore, since $\log(\cdot)$ is an increasing function,

$$\log\left[\frac{f(\alpha \cdot x + (1-\alpha) \cdot z \mid \theta)}{f(\alpha \cdot x + (1-\alpha) \cdot z \mid \theta) + k}\right] \geq \alpha \cdot \log\left[\frac{f(x \mid \theta)}{f(x \mid \theta) + k}\right]$$

$$+ (1-\alpha) \cdot \log\left[\frac{f(z \mid \theta)}{f(z \mid \theta) + k}\right] \quad (A5.10)$$

Hence, from (A5.10), the fact that $k = f(y^* \mid \theta)$, (A5.4), and the conclusion at the end of the preceding paragraph, it follows that $H(x)$ is log-concave. Therefore, $EV_\theta^1(x, y^*)$ is a log-concave function of x for each given $y^* \in S$. Therefore, $EV_\theta^1(\psi_1, \psi_2)$ is log-concave in ψ_1.

The fact that $EV_\theta^2(\psi_1, \psi_2)$ is log-concave in ψ_2 follows from a similar argument.

QED

Appendix 5.2: Proof of Theorem 5.2

Lemmata 5.1–5.3 are used in the proof of Theorem 5.2. In stating these lemmata, the starting assumption for Theorem 5.2 is taken as given; that is, an unstated assumption in each case is that there is an election in which (i) there is a finite set of groups and (ii) there is a compact, convex set of possible locations for the candidates.

As an extension of the earlier definition (in Appendix 2.2) of a payoff function that is concave in the strategies available to a particular player, we say that any real-valued function $\xi(v, w)$ on $S \times S$ is concave in v if and only if, for each given $w \in S$, ξ is a concave function of v on S.

Lemma 5.1

$P\ell^1(\psi_1, \psi_2)$ is concave–convex for each profile in $\mathcal{F}^m$ if and only if each $f \in \mathcal{F}$ is such that the corresponding function $\eta : S \times S \to E^1$ that satisfies

$$\eta(v, w) = \frac{f(v)}{f(v) + f(w)} \quad (A5.11)$$

at each $(v, w) \in S \times S$ is concave in v.

Proof of Lemma 5.1

("If") Assume that each $f \in \mathcal{F}$ is such that the corresponding function on $S \times S$ defined by (A5.11) is concave in v. Choose any profile $[f(v \mid 1), \ldots, f(v \mid m)]$ in $\mathcal{F}^m$. Consider any $\theta \in \Theta$ and $w \in S$. By adding $f(v \mid \theta) - f(v \mid \theta) = 0$ to the numerator on the right-hand side, we can rewrite (A4.5) as

$$h(f(v \mid \theta)) = \frac{[f(v \mid \theta) - f(w \mid \theta)] - [f(v \mid \theta) - f(v \mid \theta)]}{f(v \mid \theta) + f(w \mid \theta)}$$

$$= 2 \cdot \frac{f(v \mid \theta)}{f(v \mid \theta) + f(w \mid \theta)} - \frac{f(v \mid \theta) + f(w \mid \theta)}{f(v \mid \theta) + f(w \mid \theta)}$$

$$= 2 \cdot \frac{f(v \mid \theta)}{f(v \mid \theta) + f(w \mid \theta)} - 1 \qquad (A5.12)$$

(A5.12) implies that $h(f(v \mid \theta))$ is a positive affine transformation of $\eta_\theta(v, w) = \{f(v \mid \theta) / [f(v \mid \theta) + f(w \mid \theta)]\}$. In addition, since by (5.1), $f(v \mid \theta) \in \mathcal{F}$, the starting assumption implies that $\eta_\theta(v, w)$ is concave in v on S. Therefore, $h(f(v \mid \theta))$ is a concave function of v on S. Therefore, by the argument that starts in the line that precedes (A4.6), $P\ell^1(v, w)$ is concave in v. By a similar argument, $P\ell^2(v, w)$ is concave in w. Therefore, $P\ell^1(\psi_1, \psi_2)$ is concave–convex for every profile in $\mathcal{F}^m$.

("Only if") Assume that $P\ell^1(\psi_1, \psi_2)$ is concave–convex for every profile in $\mathcal{F}^m$. Suppose there exists $\phi \in \mathcal{F}$ such that the corresponding function η on $S \times S$ defined by (A5.11) is not concave in v. Then, for some given $w \in S$, $\eta(v, w)$ is not a concave function of v on S. Since $\phi \in \mathcal{F}$, by (5.1) $\mathcal{F}^m$ contains the profile $[f(v \mid \theta), \ldots, f(v \mid \theta)]$, which satisfies (A5.1). As noted at the beginning of the proof of Lemma 4.1, (4.5)–(4.7) imply (A4.1). Using (A5.1) and (A4.1) and using the fact that g is a discrete probability distribution, we get

$$P\ell^1(v, w) = \sum_{\theta \in \Theta} \left[\frac{\phi(v) - \phi(w)}{\phi(v) + \phi(w)} \right] \cdot g(\theta) = \frac{\phi(v) - \phi(w)}{\phi(v) + \phi(w)} \qquad (A5.13)$$

Therefore, using the same argument as in (A5.12), we get

$$P\ell^1(v, w) = 2 \cdot \frac{\phi(v)}{\phi(v) + \phi(w)} - 1 \qquad (A5.14)$$

Therefore, by (A5.14) and (A5.11),

$$P\ell^1(v, w) = 2 \cdot \eta(v, w) - 1 \qquad (A5.15)$$

Finally, since (for the given w) $\eta(v, w)$ is not a concave function of v on S, (A5.15) implies that $P\ell^1(\psi_1, \psi_2)$ is not concave in ψ_1, contradicting the starting assumption. Therefore, each $f \in \mathcal{F}$ is such that the function $\eta(v, w)$ on $S \times S$ defined by (A5.11) is concave in v.

QED

The proof of Lemma 5.2 uses the following well-known result (e.g., see theorem 5.2, p. 29, Hestenes, 1975; or theorem 5.12, p. 250, Sydsaeter, 1981).

Theorem

Let $\xi(x)$ be a C^1 function defined on a set A in E^{ℓ} and let B be a convex set in the interior of A. Then ξ is concave on B if and only if

$$\xi(x) - \xi(y) \leq D_{(x-y)}\xi(y) \tag{A5.16}$$

for each pair $x, y, z \in B$.

Lemma 5.2

Let $f \in \mathcal{F}$ be given. The corresponding function $\eta : S \times S \to E^1$ that satisfies (A5.11), at each $(v, w) \in S$, is concave in v if and only if

$$[f(x \mid \theta) - f(y \mid \theta)] \cdot \left\{ \frac{[f(y \mid \theta) + f(z \mid \theta)]}{[f(x \mid \theta) + f(z \mid \theta)]} \right\} \leq D_{(x-y)}f(y \mid \theta) \tag{A5.17}$$

holds for each triple $x, y, z \in S$.

Proof of Lemma 5.2

Let $A = X$ and $B = S$. Since $f \in \mathcal{F}$, $f(v \mid \theta)$ is a positive, real-valued, C^1 function of v on X. Therefore, from (A5.11), the corresponding function $\eta(v, w)$ that satisfies (A5.11) at each $(v, w) \in S \times S$ is a C^1 function of v on $A = X$ for each $w \in S$. By the premise for Theorem 5.2 we have $B = S$ is convex and $B = S \subseteq int(x) = int(A)$. Therefore (by the theorem stated right before this lemma), the corresponding function $\eta : S \times S \to E^1$ that satisfies (A5.11) at each $(v, w) \in S \times S$ is concave in v if and only if for each $w \in S$,

$$\eta(x, w) - \eta(y, w) \leq D_{(x-y)}\eta(y, w) \tag{A5.18}$$

holds for each pair $x, y \in S$. Therefore, from (A5.18) and (A5.11), the corresponding function $\eta : S \times S \to E^1$ that satisfies (A5.11) at each $(v, w) \in S \times S$ is concave in v if and only if

$$\frac{f(x \mid \theta)}{f(x \mid \theta) + f(z \mid \theta)} - \frac{f(y \mid \theta)}{f(y \mid \theta) + f(z \mid \theta)}$$

$$\leq \sum_{j=1}^{n} \left\{ \frac{\partial}{\partial v_j} \left[\frac{f(y \mid \theta)}{f(y \mid \theta) + f(z \mid \theta)} \right] \cdot (x_j - y_j) \right\} \qquad (A5.19)$$

holds for each triple $x, y, z \in S$. Therefore, from (A5.19), the corresponding function $\eta : S \times S \to E^1$ that satisfies (A5.11), at each $(v, w) \in S \times S$ is concave in v if and only if

$$\frac{f(x|\theta) \cdot f(y|\theta) + f(x|\theta) \cdot f(z|\theta) - f(x|\theta) \cdot f(y|\theta) - f(z|\theta) \cdot f(y|\theta)}{[f(x|\theta) + f(z|\theta)] \cdot [f(y|\theta) + f(z|\theta)]}$$

$$\leq \sum_{j=1}^{n} \left\{ \left(\frac{[\partial f(y \mid \theta) / \partial v_j] \cdot f(z \mid \theta)}{[f(y \mid \theta) + f(z \mid \theta)]^2} \right) \right\} \cdot (x_j - y_j) \qquad (A5.20)$$

holds for each triple $x, y, z \in S$. Therefore, simplifying (A5.20), the corresponding function $\eta : S \times S \to E^1$ that satisfies (A5.11) at each $(v, w) \in S \times S$ is concave in v if and only if (A5.17) holds for each triple $x, y, z \in S$.

QED

Lemma 5.3

Let $f \in \mathcal{F}$ and $x, y, z \in S$ be given. (A5.17) holds for each $z \in S$ if and only if (5.22) is satisfied.

Note

In the ensuing proof and at other points in the remaining material in these appendices, we use a (as in the text right before Theorem 5.2) to denote an element of S where f achieves its maximum on S; that is, $a \in S$ is a potential location for the candidates and is such that

$$f(a \mid \theta) = \max_{v \in S} \{ f(v \mid \theta) \} \qquad (A5.21)$$

Proof of Lemma 5.3

("Only if") Assume (A5.17) holds for each $z \in S$. Since $a \in S$, the starting assumption implies that at $z = a$,

$$[f(x \mid \theta) - f(y \mid \theta)] \cdot \left\{ \frac{[f(y \mid \theta) + f(m \mid \theta)]}{[f(x \mid \theta) + f(m \mid \theta)]} \right\}$$

$$\leq D_{(x-y)} f(y \mid \theta) \qquad (A5.22)$$

Therefore, from (A5.22), (A5.21), and (5.20), it follows that (5.21) is satisfied.

("If")   Assume that (5.21) is satisfied. Consider any $z \in S$. To begin with, by (5.21) and (5.20),

$$[f(x \mid \theta) - f(y \mid \theta)] \cdot \left\{ \frac{f(y \mid \theta) + M}{f(x \mid \theta) + M} \right\} \le D_{(x-y)} f(y \mid \theta) \quad (A5.23)$$

where

$$M = \max_{v \in S} \{f(v \mid \theta)\} \quad (A5.24)$$

In addition, since f is a positive, real-valued function either (i) $f(x \mid \theta) \ge f(y \mid \theta)$ or (ii) $f(x \mid \theta) < f(y \mid \theta)$ must be true.

Suppose that (i) is true. Then,

$$[f(x \mid \theta) - f(y \mid \theta)] \ge 0 \quad (A5.25)$$

By (A5.24) and (A5.25),

$$M \cdot [f(x \mid \theta) - f(y \mid \theta)] \ge f(z \mid \theta) \cdot [f(x \mid \theta) - f(y \mid \theta)] \quad (A5.26)$$

Therefore, rearranging the terms in (A5.26) yields

$$M \cdot f(x \mid \theta) + f(z \mid \theta) \cdot f(y \mid \theta) \ge f(z \mid \theta) \cdot f(x \mid \theta) + M \cdot f(y \mid \theta) \quad (A5.27)$$

Therefore, adding $[f(y \mid \theta) \cdot f(x \mid \theta) + M \cdot f(z \mid \theta)]$ to both sides of the inequality in (A5.27) and then rearranging terms, we get

$$f(y \mid \theta) \cdot f(x \mid \theta) + f(y \mid \theta) \cdot f(z \mid \theta) + M \cdot f(x \mid \theta) + M \cdot f(z \mid \theta)$$
$$\ge f(y \mid \theta) \cdot f(x \mid \theta) + f(y \mid \theta) \cdot M + f(z \mid \theta) \cdot f(x \mid \theta) + f(z \mid \theta) \cdot M \quad (A5.28)$$

Therefore, rearranging terms in (A5.28) yields

$$[f(y \mid \theta) + M] \cdot [f(x \mid \theta) + f(z \mid \theta)] \ge [f(y \mid \theta) + f(z \mid \theta)] \cdot [f(x \mid \theta) \cdot M] \quad (A5.29)$$

Therefore, rearranging the terms in (A5.29) and using the fact that $f(v \mid \theta) > 0, \forall v \in S$, we get

$$\left[\frac{f(y \mid \theta) + M}{f(x \mid \theta) + M} \right] \ge \left[\frac{f(y \mid \theta) + f(z \mid \theta)}{f(x \mid \theta) + f(z \mid \theta)} \right] \quad (A5.30)$$

Therefore, by (A5.30) and (A5.25),

$$[f(x \mid \theta) - f(y \mid \theta)] \cdot \left[\frac{f(y \mid \theta) + M}{f(x \mid \theta) + M} \right]$$

$$\ge [f(x \mid \theta) - f(y \mid \theta)] \cdot \left[\frac{f(y \mid \theta) + f(z \mid \theta)}{f(x \mid \theta) + f(z \mid \theta)} \right] \quad (A5.31)$$

Therefore, by (A5.31) and (A5.23),

$$[f(x \mid \theta) - f(y \mid \theta)] \cdot \left[\frac{f(y \mid \theta) + f(z \mid \theta)}{f(x \mid \theta) + f(z \mid \theta)} \right] \le D_{(x-y)}\, f(y \mid \theta) \qquad \text{(A5.32)}$$

That is, (A5.17) is satisfied at the given z.

Suppose that (ii) is true. Then,

$$[f(x \mid \theta) - f(y \mid \theta)] < 0 \qquad \text{(A5.33)}$$

Therefore, by (A5.31) and (A5.24),

$$M \cdot [f(x \mid \theta) + f(y \mid \theta)] \le f(z \mid \theta) \cdot [f(x \mid \theta) - f(y \mid \theta)] \qquad \text{(A5.34)}$$

Therefore, with an argument similar to the one used to go from (A5.26) to (A5.30) (with $\le$ replacing $\ge$), we obtain

$$\left[\frac{f(y \mid \theta) + M}{f(x \mid \theta) + M} \right] \le \left[\frac{f(y \mid \theta) + f(z \mid \theta)}{f(x \mid \theta) + f(z \mid \theta)} \right] \qquad \text{(A5.35)}$$

Therefore, by (A5.35) and (A5.33), we (once again) have (A5.31). Therefore, (once again) using (A5.31) and (A5.23), we know that (A5.17) (once again) holds for the given z.

Hence, (A5.18) holds for each $z \in S$.

QED

Proof Theorem 5.2

("Only if") Assume that $P\ell^1(\psi^1, \psi^2)$ is concave–convex for all possible profiles in $\mathcal{F}^m$. Then, by Lemma 5.1, each $f \in \mathcal{F}$ is such that the corresponding function $\eta : S \times S \to E^1$ that satisfies (A5.11) at each $(v, w) \in S \times S$ is concave in v. Therefore, by Lemma 5.2, each $f \in \mathcal{F}$ is such that (A5.18) holds for each triple $x, y, z \in S$. Therefore, each $f \in \mathcal{F}$ is such that for each given pair $x, y \in S$, (A5.18) holds for each $z \in S$. Therefore, by Lemma 5.3, each $f \in \mathcal{F}$ is such that (5.22) holds for each pair $x, y \in S$.

("If") Assume that each $f \in \mathcal{F}$ is such that (5.22) holds for each pair $x, y \in S$. Then, by Lemma 5.3, each $f \in \mathcal{F}$ is such that for each given pair $x, y \in S$, (A5.18) holds for each $z \in S$. Therefore, each $f \in \mathcal{F}$ is such that (A5.18) holds for each triple $x, y, z \in S$. Therefore, by Lemma 5.2, each $f \in \mathcal{F}$ is such that the corresponding function $\eta : S \times S \to E^1$ that satisfies (A5.11) at each $(v, w) \in S \times S$ is concave in v. Therefore, by Lemma 5.1, $P\ell^1(\psi^1, \psi^2)$ is concave–convex for every possible profile in $\mathcal{F}^m$.

QED

Appendix 5.3: Proofs of Theorems 5.3 and 5.4

Lemmata 5.4–5.6 are used in the proof of Theorem 5.3. As with Lemmata 5.1–5.3, an unstated assumption in each case is that there is an election in which (i) there is a finite set of groups and (ii) there is a compact, convex set of possible locations for the candidates.

Lemma 5.4

$P\ell^1(\psi^1, \psi^2)$ is concave–convex for every profile in $\mathcal{F}^m$ if and only if each $f \in \mathcal{F}$ is such that the corresponding function $\eta : S \times S \to E^1$ that satisfies (A5.11), at each $(v, w) \in S \times S$ is concave in v.

Proof of Lemma 5.4

This proof is similar to that of Lemma 5.1, with F replacing $\mathcal{F}$.

QED

The proof of Lemma 5.5 uses the following well-known theorem (e.g., see theorem 5.4, p. 32, Hestenes, 1975).

Theorem

Let $\xi(x)$ be a C^2 function defined on a set A in E^ℓ and let B be a convex set in the interior of A. Then ξ is concave on B if and only if, at each $y \in S$,

$$\sum_{h=1}^{n}\sum_{j=1}^{n}\{\xi_{hj}(y) \cdot (x_h - y_h) \cdot (x_j - y_j)\} \le 0 \qquad (A5.36)$$

holds of each $x \in S$.

We now turn to the lemma itself.

Lemma 5.5

Let $f(s \mid \theta) \in F$ be given. The corresponding function $\eta : S \times S \to E^1$ that satisfies (A5.11) at each $(v, w) \in S \times S$ is concave in v if and only if for each $(v, w) \in S \times S$, the matrix

$$G(v, w) \equiv [[f(v \mid \theta) + f(w \mid \theta)] \cdot f_{hj}(v \mid \theta) - 2 \cdot f_h(v \mid \theta) \cdot f_j(v \mid \theta)]$$
$$(A5.37)$$

is negative semidefinite on $Z(v)$.

Proof of Lemma 5.5

By definition, the corresponding function $\eta : S \times S \to E^1$ that satisfies (A5.11) at each $(v, w) \in S \times S$ is concave in v if and only if for each given $w \in S$, $\eta(v, w)$ is a concave function of v on S. Consider any given $w \in S$. Let $w(v)$ be the function on S that satisfies

$$w(v) = \eta(v, w) \tag{A5.38}$$

By an argument similar to that used (at the beginning of the proof of Lemma 5.2) to establish that the theorem that precedes Lemma 5.2 applies to the corresponding $\eta(v, w)$ when $f \in \mathcal{F}$, it follows that the theorem that precedes this lemma applies to the corresponding $\eta(v, w)$ when $f \in F$. Therefore, the corresponding function $w(v) = \eta(v, w)$ is a concave function of v on S if and only if at each $v \in S$,

$$\sum_{h=1}^{n}\sum_{j=1}^{n}\{w_{hj}(v) \cdot (x_h - v_h) \cdot (x_j - v_j)\} \leq 0 \tag{A5.39}$$

holds for each $x \in S$: that is – using (A5.39) and the notation defined before this lemma – if and only if at each $v \in S$,

$$\sum_{h=1}^{n}\sum_{j=1}^{n}\{z_h \cdot w_{hj}(v) \cdot z_k\} \leq 0 \tag{A5.40}$$

holds at each $z \in Z(v)$. Therefore, by the definition that precedes this lemma, $w(v)$ is a concave function of v on S if and only if at each $v \in S$ the matrix $[w_{hj}(v)]$ is negative semidefinite on $Z(v)$.

Consider any particular $v \in S$. By an argument similar to that used in (A4.27), for each $h \in \{1, \ldots, n\}$,

$$w_h(v) = \left[\frac{f_h(v \mid \theta) \cdot f(w \mid \theta)}{(f(v \mid \theta) + f(w \mid \theta))^2} \right] \tag{A5.41}$$

Therefore, using (A5.41), for each pair $h, j \in \{1, \ldots, n\}$, we get

$$w_{hj}(v) = \left[\frac{(f(v \mid \theta) + f(w \mid \theta))^2 \cdot f_{hj}(v \mid \theta) \cdot f(w \mid \theta)}{(f(v \mid \theta) + f(w \mid \theta))^4} \right.$$
$$\left. - \frac{f_h(v \mid \theta) \cdot f(w \mid \theta) \cdot 2 \cdot [f(v \mid \theta) + f(w \mid \theta)] \cdot f_j(v \mid \theta)}{(f(v \mid \theta) + f(w \mid \theta))^4} \right] \tag{A5.42}$$

Therefore, by (A5.42), for each pair $h, j \in \{1, \ldots, n\}$,

$$w_{hj}(v) = \alpha(v) \cdot \{[f(v \mid \theta) + f(w \mid \theta)] \cdot f_{hj}(v \mid \theta) - 2 \cdot f_h(v \mid \theta) \cdot f_j(v \mid \theta)\} \tag{A5.43}$$

where

$$\alpha(v) = \frac{[f(v \mid \theta) + f(w \mid \theta)] \cdot f(w \mid \theta)}{(f(v \mid \theta) + f(w \mid \theta))^4} \qquad (\text{A}5.44)$$

The fact that $f(v \mid \theta) > 0$, $\forall v \in S$, implies that $\alpha(v) > 0$, $\forall v \in S$. Therefore, by (A5.43) and the definition given before the lemma, the matrix $[w_{hj}(v)]$ is negative semidefinite on $Z(v)$ if and only if

$$\sum_{h=1}^{n}\sum_{j=1}^{n}(z_h \cdot \{[f(v \mid \theta) + f(w \mid \theta)] \cdot f_{hj}(v \mid \theta) - 2 \cdot f_h(v \mid \theta) \cdot f_j(v \mid \theta)\} \cdot z_j \leq 0$$

$$(\text{A}5.45)$$

for each $(z_1, \dots, z_n) \in Z(v)$. Therefore, by (A5.37) and the definition given before the lemma, the matrix $[w_{hj}(v)]$ is negative semidefinite on $Z(v)$ if and only if the matrix $G(v, w)$ is negative semidefinite on $Z(v)$.

Hence, by the conclusions of the two preceding paragraphs, together with (A5.38), for any given $w \in S$ the corresponding function $w(v) = \eta(v, w)$ is a concave function of v on S if and only if for each $v \in S$ the matrix $G(v, w)$ is negative semidefinite on $Z(v)$. Therefore, by the observation stated in the first sentence in this proof, $\eta(v, w)$ is concave in v if and only if for each $(v, w) \in S \times S$ the matrix $G(v, w)$ is negative semidefinite on $Z(v)$.

QED

Lemma 5.6

Let $f \in F$ and $v \in S$ be given. The matrix $G(v, w)$ is negative semidefinite on $Z(v)$ for each $w \in S$ if and only if the matrix in (5.31) is negative semidefinite on $Z(v)$.

Proof of Lemma 5.6

("Only if")   Assume that the matrix $G(v, w)$ is negative semidefinite on $Z(v)$ for each $w \in S$. Then (since $a \in S$), by setting $w = a$, we immediately see that the matrix $G(v, a)$ is negative semidefinite on $Z(v)$. Multiplying $G(v, a)$ by $1 / [f(v \mid \theta) + f(w \mid \theta)]$, and then rewriting the resulting expression in the notation used in (5.31), we find that the matrix given in (5.31) is negative semidefinite on $Z(v)$.

("If")   Assume that the matrix given in (5.31) is negative semidefinite on $Z(v)$. Then, by reversing the argument used in the last sentence in the previous paragraph, we immediately find that $G(v, a)$ is negative semidefinite on $Z(v)$.

Consider any particular $w \in S$ and $z \in Z(v)$. Since z is an $(n \times 1)$ vector, the product

$$z'[f_{hj}(v \mid \theta)]z = \sum_{h=1}^{n}\sum_{j=1}^{n}[z_h \cdot f_{hj}(v \mid \theta) \cdot z_j] \tag{A5.46}$$

is a real number. Therefore, either (i) $z'[f_{hj}(v \mid \theta)]z \le 0$ or (ii) $z'[f_{hj}(v \mid \theta)]z > 0$.

Suppose that (i) is true. Since $f(x \mid \theta) > 0, \forall\, x \in S$, it follows that $\{f(v \mid \theta) + f(w \mid \theta)\} > 0$. Therefore, since (i) is true,

$$z'[\{f(v \mid \theta) + f(w \mid \theta)\} \cdot f_{hj}(v \mid \theta)]z = \{f(v \mid \theta) + f(w \mid \theta)\} \cdot z'[f_{hj}(v \mid \theta)]z \le 0 \tag{A5.47}$$

In addition,

$$z'[f_h(v \mid \theta) \cdot f_j(v \mid \theta)]z = z'[f_h(v \mid \theta)] \cdot [f_j(v \mid \theta)]'z \tag{A5.48}$$

where $[f_h(v \mid \theta)]$ is $(n \times 1)$ and (hence) $[f_j(v \mid \theta)]'$ is $(1 \times n)$. Therefore, by (A5.48),

$$z'[f_h(v \mid \theta) \cdot f_j(v \mid \theta)]z = \left\{ \sum_{h=1}^{n}[f_h(v \mid \theta) \cdot z_h] \right\} \cdot \left\{ \sum_{j=1}^{n}[f_j(v \mid \theta) \cdot z_j] \right\} \ge 0 \tag{A5.49}$$

Therefore, by (A5.47) and (A5.49),

$$z'[\{f(v \mid \theta) + f(w \mid \theta)\} \cdot f_{hj}(v \mid \theta) - 2 \cdot f_h(v \mid \theta) \cdot f_j(v \mid \theta)]z$$
$$= z'[\{f(v \mid \theta) + f(w \mid \theta)\} \cdot f_{hj}(v \mid \theta)]z - 2 \cdot z'[f_h(v \mid \theta) \cdot f_j(v \mid \theta)]z \le 0 \tag{A5.50}$$

at any z where (i) is true.

Suppose that (ii) is true. Since f achieves its maximum at $a \in S$,

$$f(a \mid \theta) \ge f(w \mid \theta) \tag{A5.51}$$

Therefore, by (A5.51),

$$f(v \mid \theta) + f(a \mid \theta) \ge f(v \mid \theta) + f(w \mid \theta) \tag{A5.52}$$

Therefore, using (A5.52), since (ii) is true,

$$\{f(v \mid \theta) + f(a \mid \theta)\} \cdot z'[f_{hj}(v \mid \theta)]z \ge \{f(v \mid \theta) + f(w \mid \theta)\} \cdot z'[f_{hj}(v \mid \theta)]z \tag{A5.53}$$

Therefore, by (A5.53),

$$z'[\{f(v \mid \theta) + f(a \mid \theta)\} \cdot f_{hj}(v \mid \theta)]z \ge z'[\{f(v \mid \theta) + f(w \mid \theta)\} \cdot f_{hj}(v \mid \theta)]z \tag{A5.54}$$

Therefore, by (A5.54),

$$z'[\{f(v \mid \theta) + f(a \mid \theta)\} \cdot f_{hj}(v \mid \theta)]z + z'[-2 \cdot f_h(v \mid \theta) \cdot f_j(v \mid \theta)]z$$
$$\geq z'[\{f(v \mid \theta) + f(w \mid \theta) \cdot f_{hj}(v \mid \theta)]z + z'[-2 \cdot f_h(v \mid \theta) \cdot f_j(v \mid \theta)]z$$
$$\text{(A5.55)}$$

Therefore, by (A5.55),

$$z'[\{f(v \mid \theta) + f(a \mid \theta)\} \cdot f_{hj}(v \mid \theta) - 2 \cdot f_h(v \mid \theta) \cdot f_j(v \mid \theta)]z$$
$$\geq z'[\{f(v \mid \theta) + f(w \mid \theta)\} \cdot f_{hj}(v \mid \theta) - 2 \cdot f_h(v \mid \theta) \cdot f_j(v \mid \theta)]z$$
$$\text{(A5.56)}$$

By the starting assumption, that $G(x, a)$ is negative semidefinite on $Z(v)$, and by (A5.37),

$$z'[\{f(v \mid \theta) + f(a \mid \theta)\} \cdot f_{hj}(v \mid \theta) - 2 \cdot f_h(v \mid \theta) \cdot f_j(v \mid \theta)]z \leq 0 \qquad \text{(A5.57)}$$

Therefore, by (A5.56) and (A5.57),

$$z'[\{f(v \mid \theta) + f(w \mid \theta)\} \cdot f_{hj}(v \mid \theta) - 2 \cdot f_h(v \mid \theta) \cdot f_j(v \mid \theta)]z \leq 0 \qquad \text{(A5.58)}$$

also holds at any z where (ii) is true.

Finally, using (A5.37), since (A5.58) holds for each $w \in S$ and $z \in Z(v)$, we have

$$z'G(v, w) \leq 0, \qquad \forall z \in Z(v) \qquad \text{(A5.59)}$$

for each $w \in S$. Therefore, by the definition given before Lemma 5.5, the matrix $G(v, w)$ is negative semidefinite on $Z(v)$ for each $w \in S$.

QED

Proof of Theorem 5.3

("Only if") Assume that $P\ell^1(\psi_1, \psi_2)$ is concave–convex for each profile in F^m. Then, by Lemma 5.4, each $f \in F$ is such that the corresponding function $\eta : S \times S \to E^1$ that satisfies (A5.11) at each $(v, w) \in S \times S$, is concave in v. Therefore, by Lemma 5.5, each $f \in F$ is such that, for each $(v, w) \in S \times S$, the matrix $G(v, w)$ defined in (A5.37) is negative semidefinite on $Z(v)$. Therefore, by Lemma 5.6, each $f \in F$ is such that, for each $v \in S$, the matrix given in (5.31) is negative semidefinite on $Z(v)$.

("If") Assume that each $f \in F$ is such that for each $v \in S$ the matrix in (5.31) is negative semidefinite on $Z(v)$. Then, by Lemma 5.6, each $f \in F$ is such that for each $(v, w) \in S \times S$ the matrix $G(v,w)$ is negative semidefinite on $Z(v)$. Therefore, by Lemma 5.5, each $f \in F$ is such that the corresponding function $\eta : S \times S \to E^1$ that satisfies (A5.11) at each $(v, w) \in S \times S$ is concave in v. Therefore, by Lemma 5.4, $P\ell^1(\psi_1, \psi_2)$ is concave–convex for every profile in F^m.

QED

Note

Lemma 5.4 (stated near the beginning of this appendix) and Lemma 5.1 (stated near the beginning of Appendix 5.2) tell us that this chapter's analysis of the candidates' payoff functions provides characterizations of "G_s-concavity" (as defined by Avriel and Zang, 1974) with $G_s(y) = y / [y + f(s \mid \theta)]$ for each $s \in S$. That is starting with a model of elections in which the candidates use a binary Luce model, answering the question "What conditions are necessary and sufficient to assure that the candidates' payoff functions are concave–convex?" has led us to theorems that characterize the assumption that $G_s(f(v \mid \theta))$ is concave for each $s \in S$.

Because G and f are both differentiable, Theorem 3.6 in Avriel and Zang (1974, p. 28) immediately tells us that the kind of concavity we are characterizing implies pseudoconcavity. This (of course), in turn, tells us that the kind of concavity we are characterizing implies semi strict quasi concavity and quasi concavity (e.g., see Diewert, Avriel, and Zang, 1981, p. 407). It is also easy to show that there exist strongly pseudoconcave functions that violate the conditions derived here: for instance, $f(x \mid \theta) = \exp\{x\}$ on $X \subseteq E^1$. Thus (again drawing on the results in Diewert et al., 1981), it follows that none of these kinds of concavity imply the kind of concavity that has been characterized in Theorems 5.2 and 5.3.

The proof of Theorem 5.4 uses Lemmata 5.7 and 5.8. An unstated premise for each of these lemmata is that there is an election in which (i) there is a finite set of groups and (ii) there is a compact, convex set of possible locations for the candidates. The statements of the lemmata use the notation for the set of feasible directions at v, that is, $T(v)$, which was introduced right before Theorem 5.4.

Lemma 5.7

Let $f \in F$ and $v \in S$ be given. The matrix in (5.34) is negative semidefinite on $Z(v)$ if and only if the matrix $G(v, a)$ is negative semidefinite on $T(v)$.

Proof of Lemma 5.7

("Only if")   Assume that the matrix in (5.34) is negative semidefinite on $Z(v)$. Translating this assumption into the notation used in (A5.37), we find that $G(v, a)$ is negative semidefinite on $Z(v)$. Consider any

$y \in T(v)$. From the definition of a feasible direction (stated right before Theorem 5.4), it follows that there exists a positive, real number δ such that

$$(v + t \cdot y) \in S, \qquad \forall\, t \in [0, \delta] \tag{A5.60}$$

The vector $x = v + \delta \cdot y$ (for instance) is also such that

$$\delta \cdot y = v - x = v - (v + \delta \cdot y) \tag{A5.61}$$

Therefore, by (A5.60), (A5.61), and the definition of $Z(v)$ (stated right before Theorem 5.3), it follows that

$$\delta \cdot y \in Z(v) \tag{A5.62}$$

Because $G(v, a)$ is negative semidefinite on $Z(v)$, (A5.62) implies (by the definition of negative semidefiniteness on a given set, stated before Theorem 5.3) that

$$[\delta \cdot y]' G(v, a)[\delta \cdot y] \le 0 \tag{A5.63}$$

Therefore, by (A5.63),

$$\delta^2 \cdot y' G(v, a)y \le 0 \tag{A5.64}$$

Therefore, using (A5.64) and the fact that δ is a positive real number, we have

$$y' G(v, a)y \le 0 \tag{A5.65}$$

Since (A5.65) holds for each feasible direction y at v, it follows (directly from the definition of negative semidefiniteness on a given set) that $G(v, a)$ is negative semidefinite on $T(v)$.

("If")   Assume that $G(v, a)$ is negative semidefinite on $T(v)$. Consider any $z \in Z(v)$. By the definition of $Z(v)$, there exists $x \in S$ such that

$$z = x - v \tag{A5.66}$$

(A5.66) implies

$$v + t \cdot z = v + t \cdot (x - v) = t \cdot x + (1 - t) \cdot v, \qquad \forall\, t \in [0, 1] \tag{A5.67}$$

Since S is convex and $x, v \in S$, (A5.67) implies

$$v + t \cdot z \in S, \qquad \forall\, t \in [0, 1] \tag{A5.68}$$

Therefore (with $\delta = 1$ in the definition of a feasible direction), it follows that z is a feasible direction. Because this holds for each $z \in Z(v)$, it follows (from the starting assumption) that the matrix $G(v, a)$ is negative semidefinite on the set $Z(v)$. Therefore, translating this conclusion into the notation that was used in (5.34), we find that the matrix in (5.34) is negative semidefinite on $T(v)$.

QED

Lemma 5.8

Let $f \in F$ and $v \in S$ be given. The matrix $G(v, a)$ is negative semidefinite on $T(v)$ if and only if for each $y \in T(v)$ the relative rate of change in the directional derivative of f is bounded by twice the relative rate of change in the shifted scaling function ρ according to its sign.

Proof of Lemma 5.8

By the definition of negative semidefiniteness on a given set, the matrix $G(v, a)$ is negative semidefinite on $T(v)$ if and only if for each $y \in T(v)$,

$$y' \, G(v, a)y \leq 0 \tag{A5.69}$$

Therefore, from (A5.69) and (A5.37), $G(v, a)$ is negative semidefinite on $T(v)$ if and only if for each $y \in T(v)$,

$$y'[\{f(v \mid \theta) + f(a \mid \theta)\} \cdot f_{hj}(v \mid \theta) - 2 \cdot f_h(v, \theta) \cdot f_j(v, \theta)]y \leq 0 \tag{A5.70}$$

Therefore, from (A5.70), $G(v, a)$ is negative semidefinite on $T(v)$ if and only if for each $y \in T(v)$,

$$\{f(v \mid \theta) + f(a \mid \theta)\} \cdot y'[f_{hj}(v \mid \theta)]y - 2 \cdot y'[f_h(v \mid \theta) \cdot f_j(v \mid \theta)] \leq 0 \tag{A5.71}$$

By definition, the directional derivative of f satisfies

$$D_y f(v \mid \theta) = \sum_{h=1}^{n} \left(\frac{\partial}{\partial s_h} f(v \mid \theta) \cdot y_h \right) = \sum_{h=1}^{n} (f_h(v \mid \theta) \cdot y_h) \tag{A5.72}$$

Applying the definition of a directional derivative again, we get

$$D_y D_y f(v \mid \theta) = \sum_{j=1}^{n} \left(\frac{\partial}{\partial s_j} \left(\sum_{h=1}^{n} \{f_h(v \mid \theta) \cdot y_h\} \right) \cdot y_j \right) = \sum_{j=1}^{n} \sum_{h=1}^{n} (f_{hj}(v \mid \theta) \cdot y_h \cdot y_j) \tag{A5.73}$$

Rewriting (A5.73) in matrix form, we have

$$D_y(D_y f(v \mid \theta)) = y'[f_{hj}(v \mid \theta)]y \tag{A5.74}$$

In addition,

$$y'[f_h(v \mid \theta) \cdot f_j(v \mid \theta)] y = y'[f_h(v \mid \theta)] [f_j(v \mid \theta)] y$$

$$= \left\{ \sum_{h=1}^{n} (f_h(v \mid \theta) \cdot y_h) \right\} \cdot \left\{ \sum_{j=1}^{n} (f_j(v \mid \theta) \cdot y_j) \right\} \qquad (A5.75)$$

Therefore, by (A5.75) and (A5.72),

$$y'[f_h(v \mid \theta) \cdot f_j(v \mid \theta)] y = (D_y f(v \mid \theta))^2 \qquad (A5.76)$$

Therefore, by (A5.76), (A5.74), and the conclusion at the end of the preceding paragraph, it follows that $G(v, a)$ is negative semidefinite on $T(v)$ if and only if for each $y \in T(v)$,

$$\{f(v \mid \theta) + f(a \mid \theta)\} \cdot D_y(D_y f(v \mid \theta)) - 2 \cdot (D_y f(v \mid \theta))^2 \le 0 \qquad (A5.77)$$

or, equivalently, if and only if for each $y \in T(v)$,

$$\{f(v \mid \theta) + f(a \mid \theta)\} \cdot D_y(D_y f(v \mid \theta)) \le 2 \cdot (D_y f(v \mid \theta))^2 \qquad (A5.78)$$

Using (5.21) and the fact that $f(a \mid \theta)$ is a constant, we get

$$D_y \rho(v \mid \theta) = D_y [f(v \mid \theta) + f(a \mid \theta)] = D_y f(v \mid \theta) \qquad (A5.79)$$

Therefore, from (A5.79) and the conclusion at the end of the preceding paragraph, it follows that $G(v, a)$ is negative semidefinite on $T(v)$ if and only if

$$\rho(v \mid \theta) \cdot D_y(D_y f(v \mid \theta)) \le 2 \cdot D_y \rho(v \mid \theta) \cdot D_y f(v \mid \theta) \qquad (A5.80)$$

for each $y \in T(v)$. Therefore, by (A5.80) plus (5.21) and the fact that $f(s \mid \theta) > 0$, $\forall s \in S$, it follows that $G(v, a)$ is negative semidefinite on $T(v)$ if and only if, for each $y \in T(v)$,

$$D_y f(v \mid \theta) > 0 \Rightarrow \frac{D_y(D_y f(v \mid \theta))}{D_y f(v \mid \theta)} \le 2 \cdot \left(\frac{D_y \rho(v \mid \theta)}{\rho(v \mid \theta)} \right) \qquad (A5.81)$$

$$D_y f(v \mid \theta) = 0 \Rightarrow D_y(D_y f(v \mid \theta)) \le 0 \qquad (A5.82)$$

and

$$D_y f(v \mid \theta) < 0 \Rightarrow \frac{D_y(D_y f(v \mid \theta))}{D_y f(v \mid \theta)} \ge 2 \cdot \left(\frac{D_y \rho(v \mid \theta)}{\rho(v \mid \theta)} \right) \qquad (A5.83)$$

Using (A5.79) (again) plus (5.21) and the fact that $f(s \mid \theta) > 0$, $\forall s \in S$, we get

$$D_y f(v \mid \theta) \gtreqless 0 \Leftrightarrow 2 \cdot \frac{D_y \rho(v \mid \theta)}{\rho(v \mid \theta)} \gtreqless 0 \qquad (A5.84)$$

Hence, by (A5.84) and (A5.81)–(A5.83), it follows that $G(v, a)$ is negative semidefinite on $Z(v)$ if and only if for each $y \in T(v)$,

$$2 \cdot \frac{D_y \rho(v \mid \theta)}{\rho(v \mid \theta)} > 0 \Rightarrow \frac{D_y(D_y f(v \mid \theta))}{D_y f(v \mid \theta)} \le 2 \cdot \left(\frac{D_y \rho(v \mid \theta)}{\rho(v \mid \theta)} \right) \qquad (A5.85)$$

$$2 \cdot \frac{D_y\rho(v \mid \theta)}{\rho(v \mid \theta)} = 0 \Rightarrow D_y(D_y f(v \mid \theta)) \leq 2 \cdot \left(\frac{D_y\rho(v \mid \theta)}{\rho(v \mid \theta)} \right) \qquad \text{(A5.86)}$$

and

$$2 \cdot \frac{D_y\rho(v \mid \theta)}{\rho(v \mid \theta)} < 0 \Rightarrow \frac{D_y(D_y f(v \mid \theta))}{D_y f(v \mid \theta)} \geq 2 \cdot \left(\frac{D_y\rho\ (v \mid \theta)}{\rho(v \mid \theta)} \right) \qquad \text{(A5.87)}$$

Finally, for any $y \in T(v)$, let $\alpha_y(v)$ denote the relative rate of change in the directional derivative of f and let $\beta_y(v)$ denote twice the relative change in the shifted scaling function ρ. From the definition of the relative rate of change stated before Theorem 5.4 and, in the case of $\beta_y(v)$, (5.21) and the fact that $f(s \mid \theta) > 0$, $\forall\, s \in S$, it follows that

$$\alpha_y(v) = \begin{cases} \dfrac{D_y(D_y f(v \mid \theta))}{D_y f(v \mid \theta)} & \text{if} \quad D_y f(v \mid \theta) \neq 0 \\[2ex] D_y(D_y f(v \mid \theta)) & \text{if} \quad D_y f(v \mid \theta) = 0 \end{cases} \qquad \text{(A5.88)}$$

and

$$\beta_y(v) = 2 \cdot \left(\frac{D_y\rho(v \mid \theta)}{\rho(v \mid \theta)} \right) \qquad \text{(A5.89)}$$

By (A5.85), (5.21), and the fact that $f(s \mid \theta) > 0$, $\forall\, s \in S$,

$$D_y f(v \mid \theta) \gtreqless 0 \Leftrightarrow 2 \cdot \left(\frac{D_y\rho(v \mid \theta)}{\rho(v \mid \theta)} \right) \gtreqless 0 \qquad \text{(A5.90)}$$

for each $y \in T(v)$. Therefore, using (A5.88)–(A5.90), we can write (A5.85)–(A5.87) more simply as

$$\beta_y(v) > 0 \Rightarrow \alpha_y(v) \leq \beta_y(v) \qquad \text{(A5.91)}$$

$$\beta_y(v) = 0 \Rightarrow \alpha_y(v) \leq \beta_y(v) \qquad \text{(A5.92)}$$

and

$$\beta_y(v) < 0 \Rightarrow \alpha_y(v) \geq \beta_y(v) \qquad \text{(A5.93)}$$

Therefore, from the definition of one number being bounded by another number according to its sign (stated before Theorem 5.4) and from (A5.91)–(A5.93), it follows that $G(v, a)$ is negative semidefinite on $T(v)$ if and only if for each $y \in T(v)$ the relative rate of change in the directional derivative of f is bounded by twice the relative rate of change in the shifted scaling function ρ according to its sign.

QED

Proof of Theorem 5.4

("Only if") Assume that $P\ell^1(\psi_1, \psi_2)$ is concave–convex for each profile in F^m. Then, by Theorem 5.3 each $f \in F$ is such that for each $v \in S$ the matrix given in (5.31) is negative semidefinite on $Z(v)$. Therefore, by Lemma 5.7, each $f \in F$ is such that for each $v \in S$ the matrix $G(v, a)$ is negative semidefinite on $T(v)$. Therefore, by Lemma 5.7, each $f \in F$ is such that for each $v \in S$ and $y \in T(v)$ the relative rate of change in the directional derivative of f is bounded by twice the relative rate of change in the shifted scaling function ρ according to its sign.

("If")   Assume that each $f \in F$ is such that for each $v \in S$ and $y \in T(v)$ the relative rate of change in the directional derivative of f is bounded by twice the relative rate of change in the shifted scaling function ρ according to its sign. Then, by Lemma 5.8, the matrix $G(v, a)$ is negative semidefinite on $T(v)$. Therefore, by Lemma 5.7, the matrix in (5.31) is negative semidefinite on $Z(v)$. Therefore, by Theorem 5.3, $P\ell^1(\psi_1, \psi_2)$ is concave–convex for every profile in F^m.

QED

Note

In the proofs of Theorems 5.1–5.4, Section 4.2's assumption that S is compact was used only to establish that the shifted scaling functions are well defined (by, more specifically, being used to assure that each scaling function achieves a maximum is S). Therefore, it should be clear, the conclusions of Theorems 5.1 and 5.2 continue to hold if the assumption that S is compact is dropped, and the conclusions in Theorems 5.3 and 5.4 continue to hold if this assumption is replaced by the (less demanding) assumption that each scaling function achieves a maximum in S. In addition, note that if (as an alternative) it is assumed that S is open, then the proofs of Theorems 5.3 and 5.4 can be simplified by working with "negative semidefiniteness" throughout, instead of with "negative semidefiniteness on $Z(v)$." Importantly, however, the assumption that S is compact has been used in Chapters 2–4 and is of crucial importance when Theorems 5.2–5.4 are applied (in the first part of Section 5.5) to obtain extensions of Theorem 4.1. What is more, the assumption that S is compact is used again in Chapter 6. Therefore, to have the analyses in Sections 5.2–5.5 match more closely the analyses in the rest of this book, the assumption that S is compact has been retained.

Note

In stating and proving Theorems 5.1–5.4, we assumed that, though the profile $[f(s \mid 1), \ldots, f(s \mid m)]$ may vary, the distribution g on θ is fixed. An alternative approach would have been to allow both the profile $[f(s\,|\,1),\ldots,f(s\,|\,m)]$ and the distribution g to vary (within the set of distributions that satisfy the assumptions about g made in Section 4.2). This approach, it should be made clear, would have led to the same basic results as have been obtained. Indeed, the only differences would have been that (i) the statements of the results would have been a little more complicated, in that the phrase "for every profile in $\mathcal{F}^m$ (or F^m)" would have always been replaced by "for every profile in $\mathcal{F}^m$ (or F^m) and $g \in \mathcal{G}$," with $\mathcal{G}$ being suitably defined; and (ii) the proofs would have been a bit longer. Similarly, the analysis could have been made more complicated by allowing S to vary over a suitable collection of possible sets of candidate locations (as with a choice function for a society or an individual; e.g., see Arrow, 1951, 1959, 1963). Again, this would not have changed any of the basic results but would have made the statements of the results and the proofs more complicated. Because the approach that has been taken has captured the same insights as would have been obtained with these alternative formulations, it seemed more sensible to take g and S as given and simply to point out (in this format) that results similar to those in the text could also be derived with these alternative and more complicated formulations.

Appendix 5.4: Proofs of Theorems 5.5–5.7

The proof of Theorem 5.5 uses the following lemma. The first sentence in the theorem is an unstated assumption for this lemma.

Lemma 5.9

Let $f(s\,|\,\theta) \in \mathcal{F}$ be given. If (5.22) holds for each pair $x, y \in S$, then $f(s\,|\,\theta)$ is log-concave.

Proof of Lemma 5.9

Assume that (5.22) holds for each pair $x, y \in S$. By property 2.22 (B) in Klinger and Mangasarian (1968, p. 395), $f(s\,|\,\theta)$ is log-concave on S if and only if

$$D_{(x-y)}f(y\,|\,\theta) \geq f(y\,|\,\theta) \cdot [\log\{f(x\,|\,\theta)\} - \log\{f(y\,|\,\theta)\}], \qquad \forall\, x, y \in S$$
$$(A5.94)$$

Therefore (combining this fact with the starting assumption), the conclusion of the lemma follows if we can show that

$$[f(x \mid \theta) - f(y \mid \theta)] \cdot \frac{f(y \mid \theta) + f(a \mid \theta)}{f(x \mid \theta) + f(a \mid \theta)}$$

$$\geq f(y \mid \theta) \cdot [\log\{f(x \mid \theta)\} - \log\{f(y \mid \theta)\}], \qquad \forall\, x, y \in S \quad \text{(A5.95)}$$

When $f(x \mid \theta) = f(y \mid \theta)$, (A5.95) becomes $0 \geq 0$. Therefore, (A5.95) is immediately satisfied in this case. We now show that (A5.95) also holds for each case in which $f(x \mid \theta) \neq f(y \mid \theta)$.

Consider any particular $y \in S$. The expression on the left-hand side of (A5.95) can be thought of as the composition of (i) the function $\alpha : E_{++}^1 \to E^1$ that satisfies

$$\alpha(v) = [v - f(y \mid \theta)] \cdot \left(\frac{f(y \mid \theta) + f(a \mid \theta)}{v + f(a \mid \theta)} \right) \quad \text{(A5.96)}$$

at each $v \in E_{++}^1$ and (ii) $f(x \mid \theta)$. The expression on the right-hand side of (A5.96) can be thought of as the composition of (i) the function $\beta : E_{++}^1 \to E^1$ that satisfies

$$\beta(v) = f(y \mid \theta) \cdot [\log\{v\} - \log\{f(y \mid \theta)\}] \quad \text{(A5.97)}$$

at each $v \in E_{++}^1$ and (ii) $f(x \mid \theta)$.

From (A5.96), it follows that α is C^1 and

$$\frac{d\alpha(v)}{dv} = \frac{f(y \mid \theta) + f(a \mid \theta)}{[v + f(a \mid \theta)]} + [v - f(y \mid \theta)] \cdot \left(\frac{-[f(y \mid \theta) + f(a \mid \theta)]}{[v + f(a \mid \theta)]^2} \right)$$

$$\text{(A5.98)}$$

at each $v \in E_{++}^1$. From (A5.97), it follows that β is C^1 and

$$\frac{d\beta(v)}{dv} = f(y \mid \theta) \cdot \left(\frac{1}{v} \right) \quad \text{(A5.99)}$$

at each $v \in E_{++}^1$. Consider any particular $v \in E_{++}^1$. By (A5.98) and (A5.99),

$$\frac{d\alpha(v)}{dv} \gtreqless \frac{d\beta(v)}{dv} \quad \text{(A5.100)}$$

holds if and only if

$$\frac{f(y \mid \theta) + f(a \mid \theta)}{[v + f(a \mid \theta)]} - \frac{v \cdot f(y \mid \theta) + v \cdot f(a \mid \theta)}{[v + f(a \mid \theta)]^2}$$

$$+ \frac{[f(y \mid \theta)]^2 + f(y \mid \theta) \cdot f(a \mid \theta)}{[v + f(a \mid \theta)]^2} \gtreqless \left(\frac{f(y \mid \theta)}{v} \right) \quad \text{(A5.101)}$$

Therefore, multiplying both sides of (A5.101) by $[v + f(a \mid \theta)]^2 \cdot v > 0$, we see that (A5.100) holds if and only if

$$\{[v + f(a \mid \theta)] \cdot v \cdot [f(y \mid \theta) + f(a \mid \theta)]\} - \{v \cdot [v \cdot f(y \mid \theta)] + v \cdot f(a \mid \theta)]\}$$
$$+ \{v \cdot [(f(y \mid \theta))]^2 + f(y \mid \theta) \cdot f(a \mid \theta)]\} \gtreqless \{(v + f(a \mid \theta))^2 \cdot f(y \mid \theta)\} \tag{A5.102}$$

Therefore, by multiplying the terms in (A5.102), we see that (A5.100) holds if and only if

$$[v^2 \cdot f(y \mid \theta) + v \cdot f(a \mid \theta) \cdot f(y \mid \theta) + v^2 \cdot f(a \mid \theta) + v \cdot (f(a \mid \theta))^2$$
$$- v^2 \cdot f(y \mid \theta) - v^2 \cdot f(a \mid \theta) + v \cdot (f(y \mid \theta))^2 + v \cdot f(y \mid \theta) \cdot f(a \mid \theta)]$$
$$\gtreqless [v^2 \cdot f(y \mid \theta) + 2 \cdot v \cdot f(a \mid \theta) \cdot f(y \mid \theta) + (f(a \mid \theta))^2 \cdot f(y \mid \theta)] \tag{A5.103}$$

Therefore, combining terms in (A5.103), we know that (A5.100) holds if and only if

$$v \cdot [f(a \mid \theta)]^2 + v \cdot [f(y \mid \theta)]^2 - v^2 \cdot f(y \mid \theta) - [f(a \mid \theta)]^2 \cdot f(y \mid \theta) \gtreqless 0 \tag{A5.104}$$

Therefore, by (A5.104), we have (A5.100) if and only if

$$[v - f(y \mid \theta)] \cdot ([f(a \mid \theta)]^2 - v \cdot f(y \mid \theta)) \gtreqless 0 \tag{A5.105}$$

Consider any v in the range of $f(s \mid \theta)$ that is not equal to $f(y \mid \theta)$. Because a is an element of S, where f achieves its maximum (on S), any such v must satisfy

$$f(a \mid \theta) \geq v > f(y \mid \theta) \tag{A5.106}$$

or

$$f(a \mid \theta) \geq f(y \mid \theta) > v \tag{A5.107}$$

Suppose that (A5.106) is satisfied. Then, from the fact that $f(y \mid \theta) > 0$, it follows that $[f(a \mid \theta)]^2 \geq v^2 > v \cdot f(y \mid \theta)$. Therefore,

$$([f(a \mid \theta)]^2 - v \cdot f(y \mid \theta)) > 0 \tag{A5.108}$$

Alternatively, suppose that (A5.107) is satisfied. Then, from the fact that $v > 0$, it follows that $[f(a \mid \theta)]^2 \geq [f(y \mid \theta)]^2 > v \cdot f(y \mid \theta)$. Therefore, once again, (A5.108) holds. Hence, (A5.108) holds for each $v \neq f(y \mid \theta)$ in the range of $f(s \mid \theta)$. Finally, using this conclusion and the result established at the end of the preceding paragraph, we find that, for each v in the range of $f(s \mid \theta)$,

$$\frac{d\alpha(v)}{dv} \gtreqless \frac{d\beta(v)}{dv} \Leftrightarrow v \gtreqless f(y \mid \theta) \tag{A5.109}$$

We now show that (A5.95) holds for any $x \in S$ where $f(x \mid \theta) > f(y \mid \theta)$. $\alpha(v)$ and $\beta(v)$ are C^1. Therefore, by the second fundamental theorem fo integral calculus.

$$\int_{f(y|\theta)}^{f(x|\theta)} \left(\frac{d\alpha(v)}{dv} \right) dv = \alpha[f(x \mid \theta)] - \alpha[f(y \mid \theta)] \tag{A5.110}$$

and

$$\int_{f(y|\theta)}^{f(x|\theta)} \left(\frac{d\beta(v)}{dv} \right) dv = \beta[f(x \mid \theta)] - \beta[f(y \mid \theta)] \tag{A5.111}$$

(e.g., see Apostol, 1974, pp. 162–3; Buck, 1978, p. 182; Sydsaeter, 1981, p. 167; and Chiang, 1984, p. 447). By (A5.96),

$$\alpha[f(y \mid \theta)] = 0 = \beta[f(y \mid \theta)] \tag{A5.112}$$

Using (A5.109), (A5.99), and the fact that $f(y \mid \theta) > 0$, we have

$$\frac{d\alpha(v)}{dv} > \frac{d\beta(v)}{dv} > 0, \qquad \forall \, v \in [f(y|\theta), f(x|\theta)] \tag{A5.113}$$

Therefore, by (A5.110)–(A5.113),

$$\alpha[f(x \mid \theta)] = \int_{f(y|\theta)}^{f(x|\theta)} \left(\frac{d\alpha(v)}{dv} \right) dv > \int_{f(y|\theta)}^{f(x|\theta)} \left(\frac{d\beta(v)}{dv} \right) dv = \beta[f(x \mid \theta)] \tag{A5.114}$$

Therefore, using (A5.114), (A5.96), and (A5.97), we have (A5.95) for each $x \in S$ where $f(x \mid \theta) > f(y \mid \theta)$.

Finally, consider any $x \in S$ where $f(x \mid \theta) < f(y \mid \theta)$. Using the fact that $\alpha(v)$ and $\beta(v)$ are C^1 and the second fundamental theorem of integral calculus again, we obtain

$$\int_{f(x|\theta)}^{f(y|\theta)} \left(\frac{d\alpha(v)}{dv} \right) dv = \alpha[f(y \mid \theta)] - \alpha[f(x \mid \theta)] \tag{A5.115}$$

and

$$\int_{f(x|\theta)}^{f(y|\theta)} \left(\frac{d\beta(v)}{dv} \right) dv = \beta[f(y \mid \theta)] - \beta[f(x \mid \theta)] \tag{A5.116}$$

Using (A5.109), (A5.98), and the fact that $f(s \mid \theta) > 0$, $\forall s \in S$, we have

$$\frac{d\beta(v)}{dv} > \frac{d\alpha(v)}{dv} > 0, \qquad \forall \, v \in [f(x \mid \theta), f(y \mid \theta)) \tag{A5.117}$$

By (A5.96), we (once again) have (A5.112). Therefore, using (A5.115)–(A5.117) and (A5.112), we obtain

$$-\beta[f(x \mid \theta)] = \int_{f(x\mid\theta)}^{f(y\mid\theta)} \left(\frac{d\beta(v)}{dv} \right) dv > \int_{f(x\mid\theta)}^{f(y\mid\theta)} \left(\frac{d\alpha(v)}{dv} \right) dv = -\alpha[f(x \mid \theta)]$$

(A5.118)

Therefore, by (A5.118),

$$\alpha[f(x \mid \theta)] > \beta[f(x \mid \theta)] \tag{A5.119}$$

Therefore, using (A5.119), (A5.96), and (A5.97), we have (A5.95) for each $x \in S$ where $f(x \mid \theta) < f(y \mid \theta)$.

QED

Note

The continued analysis of Example 5.1 in Section 5.4 has already established that the converse of Lemma 5.9 does not hold as a general result. Therefore (also from the observations in the last paragraph in Section 5.4), the conditions derived in Theorems 5.2–5.4 are "between" concavity and log-concavity. That is, (i) for C^1 functions, [f is concave] $\Rightarrow$ [f satisfies the condition derived in Theorem 5.2] $\Rightarrow$ [f is log-concave], but the converses of these two implications do not hold; (ii) for C^2 functions, [f is concave] $\Rightarrow$ [f satisfies the condition derived in Theorems 5.3 and 5.4] $\Rightarrow$ [f is log-concave], but the converses of these two implications do not hold.

Proof of Theorem 5.5

By Lemma 5.5 and Theorem 5.1, it follows that $W(v)$ is concave. By Theorem 5.2, $P\ell^1(\psi_1, \psi_2)$ is concave–convex. As a consequence, Theorem 5.5 follows from an argument analogous to the one that was used to prove Theorem 4.2.

QED

Proof of Theorem 5.6

The premise implies that, for each $\theta \in \Theta$, (5.22) holds for each pair $x, y \in S$. As a consequence, this theorem follows from an argument similar to the proof of Theorem 5.5.

QED

Proof of Theorem 5.7

This proof is similar to that of Theorem 5.6.

QED

CHAPTER 6

Directional, stationary, and global electoral equilibria

The election model in this chapter generalizes that of the preceding chapter in two important ways: (i) This model allows much greater flexibility in the specification of the number of groups in the electorate and the distribution of voters across groups, and (ii) the set of possible locations for the candidates is not assumed to be convex. Significantly, (as in Chapter 5) the remaining convexity assumptions used in the equilibrium existence results in Theorem 4.1 and Corollaries 5.1–5.3 are again treated as possible special cases for the model. These and the remaining features of this more general model are identified in precise terms in Section 6.1.

Because the convexity assumptions used to obtain the equilibrium existence results in Chapters 4 and 5 are not required in this chapter, it immediately follows that there need not be an electoral equilibrium (as defined in Section 2.3), as Example 5.5 (in Section 5.5) made clear. In this chapter, therefore, we study some alternative concepts of what constitutes an electoral equilibrium that are weaker (i.e., less demanding) than the concept used so far. The specific feature of the earlier concept that is relaxed is the assumption that the candidates are free to choose any location in the set S. Relaxing this feature may be desirable in a particular context for reasons that have been discussed in the literature (e.g., see Kramer and Klevorick, 1974, pp. 540–1; Kats and Nitzan, 1976; and/or Matthews, 1979, pp. 142–3). As a consequence, various public-choice scholars have developed and analyzed models in which each of the candidates and/or the society as a whole considers only directions of motion away from a given point or considers only alternatives in a small neighborhood of a given point. The best-known results on majority rule when the social alternatives are directions away from a given point have been developed in Plott (1967), Sloss (1973, sects. IV and VI), Schofield (1978a,b, 1980, 1983a,b, 1984a,b, 1985, 1986, 1989), Matthews (1979, 1980, 1982), Cohen and Matthews (1980), and Coughlin and Nitzan (1981b). The best-known work on majority rule when the social alternatives are restricted to a small neighborhood of a given point has been carried out in Klevorick and Kramer (1973), Kramer and Klevorick

172

(1974), and Schofield (1978a,b, 1980, 1983a,b, 1984a,b, 1985, 1986, 1989), Coughlin and Nitzan (1981b), and Feldman and Lee (1988). Matthews (1979), Coughlin and Nitzan (1981b), and Feldman and Lee (1988), in particular, have analyzed explicit models of elections. The remaining analyses have been of models of direct democracy or committees. Importantly, however, as Mueller (1979, p. 98) has put it: "While many of the results in these literatures have been described . . . in the context of a model of direct democracy or committees . . . many of the problems and results . . . carry over almost directly into the representative democracy area." In particular, this is true because if voting is "deterministic" – it satisfies (2.7) – then, quoting Black (1958, p. 1) "an election is a species of committee."

As the preceding paragraph indicates, the key difference between the concept of an electoral equilibrium used in Chapters 2–5 and the alternative notions of an electoral equilibrium that are studied in this chapter is the fact that up to this point it has consistently been assumed that candidates are able to choose any location in S, whereas here we consider the implications of candidates with considerably less mobility. As a consequence, Section 6.2 relabels the electoral competitions, electoral equilibria, and electoral outcomes that have been studied as "global" electoral competitions, equilibria, and outcomes. This relabling has the merit of making it easier to distinguish the approach that has been used exclusively so far from the two alternative approaches that are now used, while emphasizing the distinguishing feature of the electoral equilibria that have been studied in the earlier chapters.

The first alternative approach to defining an electoral equilibrium is developed in Section 6.3. This approach is to study candidates' decisions "on the margin" rather than from a "global" point of view. Section 6.3 provides reasons for wanting to study two-candidate games in which only directions away from the status quo can be chosen and also provides precise definitions of the directional games and directional equilibria studied here. The results at the end of the section establish that there is a directional electoral equilibrium (in "marginal strategies") at every possible location for the candidates and characterize the nature of these equilibria.

A directional electoral equilibrium can be such that (in it) each candidate chooses a direction of motion away from the starting location, leading to a change in the underlying status quo. Such a situation is an equilibrium (in the usual game-theoretic sense) in the directional game between the candidates (in that it is a saddle-point for the game). At the same time, however, it does not match the alternative notion of an equilibrium as a state of rest (or "no change") for the status quo.

Therefore, we also develop a second alternative approach (in Section 6.4), addressing the question of whether there is a location where neither candidate has an incentive to move away, and implying that, if this location is the status quo, the status quo does not change. The results in the section characterize the nature of such stationary electoral equilibria and establish that stationary electoral equilibria necessarily exist in the model being studied – in sharp contrast with the general nonexistence results on stationary voting equilibria that have been established for the models studied in Plott (1967), Sloss (1973, pp. 27–30), Schofield (1978a,b, 1983a,b, 1984a,b, 1985, 1986, 1989), Matthews (1979, 1980, 1982), and Cohen and Matthews (1980).

The relation between the results in Sections 6.3 and 6.4 and the results about stationary equilibria with majority rule that have been derived by Plott et al. are discussed in Section 6.4. The relation between the results in Section 6.4 and some of the results derived in Chapters 4 and 5 are also (briefly) discussed at the end of the section. Section 6.5 then uses the theorems of Section 6.4 about stationary electoral equilibria to obtain some further results about global electoral equilibria. Section 6.6 provides some illustrative examples. The final section contains concluding remarks.

6.1   The more general model

In the model analyzed in Chapter 5 (which, of course, contains all of the models in the earlier chapters as special cases), it was assumed that there is a finite number of groups in the electorate. This, of course, immediately implied that the distribution of voters across groups is a discrete distribution. In this chapter, it is assumed that there is an index set Θ for the groups in the electorate, without requiring this set to be finite or to satisfy any other restrictions. This, of course, still allows the possibility that (as in Chapter 5) $\Theta = \{1, \ldots, m\}$ but also allows many other possibilities. This chapter's assumption about the distribution of voters across the various groups in the electorate is simply that there is a probability measure space (Θ, Σ, μ) in which, for each measurable set $Z \in \Sigma$, the number $\mu(Z)$ assigned by the measure μ is the proportion of the total electorate with indices in Z. This includes, as a special case, the assumption that the candidates' beliefs about the distribution of voters across groups can be summarized by a discrete probability distribution on a finite set of integers (as in Chapter 5). It also includes, more generally, the assumption that the candidates' beliefs about the distribution can be summarized by a probability density function on a subset of a Euclidean space (e.g., as in Coughlin and Nitzan, 1981b). In addition, this chapter's assumption about the distribution of voters across groups also includes a large number of other possibilities.

As the second modification of the model analyzed in Chapter 5, it is not assumed that S is necessarily convex. Rather, instead of assuming that S is nonempty, compact, convex, and contained in the interior of $X \subseteq E^n$, we simply assume that S is nonempty, compact, and contained in the interior of $X \subseteq E^n$.

To keep things clear, note that (as in Chapter 5) the only assumption made about the groups' "scaling functions" is that, for each $\theta \in \Theta$, there exists a C^1 positive, real-valued function $f(x \mid \theta)$ on X which is such that, for each $c \in \{1, 2\}$ and $(\psi_1, \psi_2) \in S \times S$, (4.7) is satisfied. This, of course, implies that (i) it is not being assumed that each group's scaling function is concave on S (unlike in Chapter 4), and (ii) it is not being assumed that each group's scaling function satisfies one of the conditions derived in Theorems 5.2–5.4 (unlike in Corollaries 5.1–5.3). Thus, from this observation and the assumption in the preceding paragraph, it follows that we are not requiring any of the convexity assumptions included in the sufficient conditions for the existence of an electoral equilibrium that were identified in Theorem 4.1 and Corollaries 5.1–5.3.

In line with this more general assumption about the candidates' beliefs about the distribution of voters across groups, the following regularity assumptions are made on the groups scaling functions and their partial derivatives. First, at each $x \in X$, $f(x \mid \theta)$ is a measurable function of θ with respect to (Θ, Σ, μ); second, $f(x \mid \theta)$ and $\partial f(x \mid \theta) / \partial x_h$ $(h = 1, \ldots, n)$ are bounded functions of (x, θ) on $X \times \Theta$, with the lower bound on $f(x \mid \theta)$ being positive.

In reference to the first regularity assumption, note that this assumption and the assumption that at each $\theta \in \Theta$ the function $f(x \mid \theta)$ is C^1 in x (together) imply that, for any open set $\boldsymbol{S}$ such that $S \subset \boldsymbol{S} \subseteq \text{int}(X)$, each $\partial f(x \mid \theta) / \partial x_h$ is a measurable function of θ at each $x \in \boldsymbol{S}$. The fact that this is true is easily seen from the following standard argument. Choose any $h \in \{1, \ldots n\}$. Consider any $x = (x_1, \ldots, x_n) \in \boldsymbol{S}$. Since $x \in \boldsymbol{S} \subseteq \text{int}(X)$, there exists an infinite sequence of real numbers $\{t_\ell\}$ (with $t_\ell \neq 0, \forall \ell$) such that (i) $\{t_\ell\}$ converges to 0 and (ii) $(x_h + t_\ell) \in X, \forall \ell$. Let

$$\phi_\ell(\theta) = \frac{f((x_1, \ldots, x_h + t_\ell, \ldots, x_n) \mid \theta) - f((x_1, \ldots, x_h, \ldots, x_n) \mid \theta)}{t_\ell}$$

Since (by the first regularity assumption) $f(x \mid \theta)$ is a measurable function of θ at each $x \in X$, both $f((x_1, \ldots, x_h + t_\ell, \ldots, x_n) \mid \theta)$ and $f((x_1, \ldots, x_h, \ldots, x_n) \mid \theta)$ are measurable functions of θ. In addition, by definition, $t_\ell \neq 0$. Therefore (e.g., by lemma 2.6, p. 9, Bartle, 1966), $\phi_\ell(\theta)$ is a measurable function of θ. Now, consider any particular θ. From the definition of $\phi_\ell(\theta)$ together with the definition of a partial derivative, the fact that $f(x \mid \theta)$ is C^1 at x implies that $\lim \phi_\ell(\theta) = \partial f(x \mid \theta) / \partial x_h$. Therefore, $\{\phi_\ell(\theta)\}$ converges to $\partial f(x \mid \theta) / \partial x_h$ on Θ. Therefore (e.g., by corollary 2.1, p. 12, Bartle, 1966), $\partial f(x \mid \theta) / \partial x_h$ is a measurable function of θ. Hence, $\partial f(x \mid \theta) / \partial x_h$ is a measurable function of θ at each $x \in S$.

In reference to the second regulatory assumption, note that assuming that a function with two variables, such as $f(x \mid \theta)$, is a bounded function of these two variables goes beyond the assumption that it is bounded when either variable is held constant. This is easily seen by considering the function $\text{Min}\{1/y_1, 1/y_2\}$ on $Y_1 \times Y_2 = (0, 1) \times (0, 1)$, which is bounded when either y_1 or y_2 is held constant but unbounded as a function of (y_1, y_2). Also note (because, in Chapters 4 and 5, $g(\theta)$ was a discrete probability distribution on the set $\{1, \ldots, m\}$ and each $f(x \mid \theta)$ is a positive, real-valued, C^1 function of x) that the two regularity conditions listed earlier are implicitly satisfied in Chapters 4 and 5.

Chapter 4's definition of expected plurality for a given candidate c from a given group θ at a particular pair of candidate strategies, see (4.2), applies here as well. However, because of the more general assumption about the candidates' beliefs about the distribution of voters across groups that has been made here, the definition of a candidate's overall expected plurality that was used in Chapters 2–5, see (2.4) and (4.6), is no longer appropriate. Rather, again normalizing so that the total expected vote from all of the voters is one, the expected plurality for a given candidate c at a particular pair of candidate strategies $(\psi_1, \psi_2) \in S \times S$ is now

$$Pe^c(\psi_1, \psi_2) = \int_\Theta Pe^c_\theta(\psi_1, \psi_2) \cdot d\mu(\theta) \tag{6.1}$$

if the integral in (6.1) exists. Note that (6.1) reduces to (2.4) and (4.6) under the assumptions in Chapters 2 and 4, respectively.

Analogous to what was done in Chapter 5, the phrase "there is an election in which (i) there is a compact set of possible locations for the candidates and (ii) the candidates use a C^1 binary Luce model" is used to refer to the model that results when the modifications just discussed are made in the assumptions listed in Section 4.2. This terminology serves, in particular, to emphasize the ways in which the resulting model generalizes the models that were studied in Chapters 4 and 5.

Before proceeding with an analysis of the decisions that rational candidates make in the resulting model, an important question that has to be resolved is whether the integral in (6.1) exists for each $c \in \{1, 2\}$ at each $(\psi_1, \psi_2) \in S \times S$; otherwise, the electoral competition specified by

(2.5) is not defined. The answer to this question is given by the following proposition (proven in Appendix 6.1).

Proposition 6.1

Suppose there is an election in which (i) there is a compact set of possible locations for the candidates and (ii) the candidates use a C^1 binary Luce model. Then the integral in (6.1) exists for each $c \in \{1, 2\}$ at each $(\psi_1, \psi_2) \in S \times S$.

Because every other assumption in Section 4.2 is retained in exactly the form in which it was stated in that section, the model here is a straightforward generalization of the model studied in Chapter 5. As a consequence, there is no need to write a list of the assumptions for the model that is analyzed here (e.g., as was done in Section 4.2, when moving from the model analyzed in Sections 2.3–2.6 and in Chapter 3 to the model being specified in Chapter 4). Instead, we turn directly to a discussion of the candidate decisions that are analyzed in this chapter.

6.2   Global electoral competitions and global outcomes

In this chapter, the approach that has been used so far when specifying what an electoral equilibrium is, given by (2.6), is supplemented by two alternative approaches to specifying this concept, both of which are based on the notion of the candidates making their choices "on the margin." Therefore, it is important for us to be able to distinguish the previously used concept of an electoral equilibrium from the alternatives that are now considered. In the game specified by (2.5), each candidate is free to choose any location in S and therefore, in an equilibrium, selects a location that is a global maximum for his objective function $P\ell^c$ when his opponent's location is taken as fixed; see (2.6). Because this game has this feature, it is called, from now on, the *global electoral competition* for the candidates, and correspondingly, any pair of locations $(\psi_1^*, \psi_2^*) \in S \times S$ that satisfies (2.6) is (hereafter) called a *global electoral equilibrium*.

Because the model specified in Chapter 4 is a special case of the model in this chapter, it immediately follows that the existence of a unique global electoral equilibrium is, again, not assured. Therefore, it also would be inappropriate to talk about "the location of the electoral equilibrium." At the same time, however, the two properties identified in Propositions 4.1 and 4.2 also show up in the more general model being analyzed in this chapter. Stated precisely, using the definitions given in Section 4.3, with the term *global electoral outcome* replacing the term *electoral outcome*, these two properties are the following.

Proposition 6.2

Suppose there is an election in which (i) there is a compact set of possible locations for the candidates and (ii) the candidates use a C^1 binary Luce model. Then $E_1 = E_2$.

Proposition 6.3

Suppose there is an election in which (i) there is a compact set of possible locations for the candidates and (ii) the candidates use a C^1 binary Luce model. Let $s \in S$ be given. s is a global electoral outcome if and only if $(s, s) \in S \times S$ is a global electoral equilibrium.

6.3   Directional games and directional electoral equilibria

Proposition 6.3 makes it clear that an interest in global electoral equilibria leads directly to an interest in pairs of candidate strategies in which each candidate uses the same strategy. In particular, it implies that, when appropriate convexity assumptions (such as those in Chapter 4 or those identified in Theorems 5.2–5.4) are satisfied, the study of such *convergent equilibria* can (in turn) be reduced to the question of whether there is a feasible direction away from the common strategy that would lead to an alternative strategy that would make one of the candidates better off – in the sense that, when the strategy of one candidate is taken to be the strategy that is initially their common strategy and the strategy of the other is taken to be this alternative, the candidate who uses the alternative strategy has a higher expected plurality than when both of them use the same strategy. That is, the study of convergent global electoral equilibria can be reduced to the question of whether either candidate can get a higher payoff on the margin, in the sense of being able to choose a direction away from the common strategy, which has a positive marginal payoff (i.e., a positive directional derivative). Therefore, even if we are interested solely in global electoral equilibria, we are led to the study of pairs of strategies in which each candidate uses the same strategy and the question of what direction will give a particular candidate his greatest marginal payoff, because – to sum up the observations just made – when appropriate convexity assumptions are made, such marginal analyses are equivalent to analyses of the candidates' decisions from a global point of view.

In addition, such marginal decisions are also of interest when each candidate (or the society) is restricted to choosing solely among alternative *directions of change* (i.e., directions of motion away from the status quo). Such social-choice situations are of interest for a number of reasons. For example, the expense of acquiring information may restrict candidates to learning about voter behavior only near the status quo. Alternatively, institutional restrictions may rule out large changes. In such settings, the society always has a current state (or status quo). As a consequence, the marginal analyses of candidates decisions just described are also clearly relevant in any situation in which the candidates can, at most, marginally vary their positions from the status quo and the status quo is associated with a candidate if he does not choose a direction that varies his position away from it.

Of primary interest in the two contexts described is a directional game between the two candidates at a given location, more specifically, a game in which (i) the possible directions in which a candidate can move her position away from the given location together with the choice of "no change" define the (common) strategy set for the candidates, and (ii) the marginal changes in expected plurality for the two candidates that result from simultaneous variations in positions define their respective payoffs. So that we can rigorously analyze such situations, the description provided is now supplemented with a precise specification of the directional game for the candidates.

Let ψ denote a given location (i.e., a given element of S). Stated in general terms, a *directional strategy* at ψ is a vector that either specifies no change from ψ or specifies a direction away from ψ. Stated precisely, t is a directional strategy at ψ if and only if either $t = 0 \in E^n$ or t is a sequential tangent (or tangent) vector of S in E^n at the point ψ and t has unit length. That is, a directional strategy at ψ is either the zero vector in E^n or is a vector h in the unit sphere in E^n for which there exists a sequence $\{x_q\}$ of points in S and a sequence of positive numbers $\{t_q\}$ such that

$$\lim_{q \to \infty} \frac{x_q - x_o}{t_q} = h \qquad \text{and} \qquad \lim_{q \to \infty} t_q = 0 \qquad (6.2)$$

(e.g., see Hestenes, 1975, p. 204).

The common strategy set $T(\psi)$ for the two candidates in the directional game at a given location is taken to be the set of all directional strategies at that location. That is, $T(\psi)$ is the set that consists of all of the vectors with unit length that are in the tangent space of S at ψ

together with $O \in E^n$. This definition implies that if ψ is in the interior of S, then

$$T(\psi) = \{O\} \cup \{t \in E^n : [\|t\| = 1] \,\&$$
$$[\exists \, \lambda_1 > 0 \text{ such that } \psi + \lambda \cdot t \in S, \, \forall \, \lambda \in (0, \lambda_1)]\}$$

We note that, for $\psi \in \text{int}(S)$, this is equivalent to saying that $T(\psi)$ is simply the zero vector together with the unit sphere in E^n. If ψ is on the boundary of S, and S is convex, or even just weakly locally convex at ψ (e.g., as defined in Valentine, 1964, pp. 48–9), then $T(\psi)$ is the union of $\{O\}$ and the closure of the set $\{t \in E^n : [\|t\| = 1] \,\& \, [\exists \, \lambda_1 > 0 \text{ such that } \psi + \lambda \cdot t \in S, \, \forall \, \lambda \in (0, \lambda_1)]\}$ (e.g., see Hestenes, 1975, p. 209). Indeed, it is only for cases in which ψ is on the boundary of S, and S fails to been weakly locally convex at ψ that it is not possible to write $T(\psi)$ in this form and the definition given in (6.2) must be directly applied. In what follows, $u \in T(\psi)$ and $v \in T(\psi)$ denote directional strategies selected by candidates 1 and 2, respectively.

The payoff for a candidate at a given pair of directional strategies $(u, v) \in T(\psi) \times T(\psi)$ is taken to be his marginal expected plurality in the direction $(u, v) \in E^{2 \cdot n}$, evaluated at the pair $(\psi, \psi) \in S \times S$. That is, in more precise terms, the payoff function for candidate c in the directional game at a given location ψ is the directional derivative of the function $P\ell_e^c(\psi_1, \psi_2)$ in the direction (u, v) at $\psi_1 = \psi_2 = \psi$, where, as in Appendix 6.1, $P\ell_e^c(\psi_1, \psi_2)$ is the function on $X \times X$ that satisfies (6.1) at each $(\psi_1, \psi_2) \in X \times X$. Thus, the candidate's directional payoff is the net effect on his expected plurality of the simultaneous variations u and v.

The payoff function for candidate 1 in the directional game at a given location ψ is denoted by $P(u, v)$. The following result makes it possible for us to write $P(u, v)$ in a convenient way.

Proposition 6.4

Suppose there is an election in which (i) there is a compact set of possible locations for the candidates and (ii) the candidates use a C^1 binary Luce model. Then $P\ell_e^1(\psi_1, \psi_2)$ is C^1 on $S \times S$.

More specifically, this result directly implies that the directional derivative of $P\ell_e^1(\psi_1, \psi_2)$ in the direction (u, v) equals the inner product of the gradient of $P\ell_e^1(\psi_1, \psi_2)$ with this direction (e.g., see theorems 12.11 and 12.15, Apostol, 1974). Therefore,

$$P(u, v) = D_{(u,v)} P\ell_e^1(\psi_1, \psi_2)$$

$$= \sum_{h=1}^{n} \left[\frac{\partial P\ell_e^1(\psi_1, \psi_2)}{\partial \psi_{1h}} \cdot u_h \right] + \sum_{h=1}^{n} \left[\frac{\partial P\ell_e^1(\psi_1, \psi_2)}{\partial \psi_{2h}} \cdot v_h \right] \qquad (6.3)$$

at $\psi_1 = \psi_2 = \psi$. From the definition of a directional derivative, together with the fact that, by (A6.3), $P\ell_e^1(\psi_1, \psi_2) = -P\ell_e^2(\psi_1, \psi_2)$, $\forall (\psi_1, \psi_2) \in X \times X$, it follows that, for any given location $\psi \in S$ and direction $(u, v) \in T(\psi) \times T(\psi)$, the directional payoff for candidate 2 equals $-P(u, v)$. Hence, we also know that the directional electoral competition at any given location ψ is zero-sum.

It should be made clear that three considerations lead to the function $P\ell_e^c(\psi_1, \psi_2)$ on $X \times X$ being used in the definition of a candidate's directional payoffs, rather than the function $P\ell^c(\psi_1, \psi_2)$ on $S \times S$. The first consideration is the fact that, at a given location $\psi \in S$, a tangent vector w may "lie outside of S" in the sense that $\psi + k \cdot w \notin S$, $\forall k > 0$, resulting in $D_{(u,v)} P\ell^1(\psi_1, \psi_2)$ not being defined when $\psi_1 = \psi_2 = \psi$ and either u or v equals w. For example, suppose that S is either the nonconvex unit circle $\{(x, y) \in E^2 : x^2 + y^2 = 1\}$ or the convex unit disk $\{(x, y) \in E^2 : x^2 + y^2 \leq 1\}$. Consider the boundary point $\psi = (1, 0)$. In each case, $(0, 1)$ is one of the unit tangent vectors at ψ; and $\psi + k \cdot (0, 1) = (1, k) \notin S$, $\forall k > 0$. Therefore, $D_{((0,1),(0,0))} P\ell^1(\psi_1, \psi_2)$, for instance, is not defined at $\psi_1 = \psi_2 = \psi$. The second consideration is the fact that (by Lemma 6.7 in Appendix 6.3), for any given location $\psi \in S$, the directional derivative $D_{(u,v)} P\ell_e^c(\psi_1, \psi_2)$ is defined for each pair $(u, v) \in T(\psi) \times T(\psi)$ at $\psi_1 = \psi_2 = \psi$. The third consideration is the fact that because $P\ell_e^c$ is an extension of $P\ell^c$ onto $X \times X$, the function $D_{(u,v)} P\ell_e^c(\psi_1, \psi_2)$ at $\psi_1 = \psi_2 = \psi$ is an extension of the function $D_{(u,v)} P\ell^c(\psi_1, \psi_2)$ at $\psi_1 = \psi_2 = \psi$ onto the entire set $T(\psi) \times T(\psi)$; and, importantly, it is the most natural definition of marginal expected plurality for the cases in which $D_{(u,v)} P\ell^c(\psi_1, \psi_2)$ is not defined.

In line with the definition of the candidates' payoff functions just given, at any given location ψ a pair of directional strategies $(u^*, v^*) \in T(\psi) \times T(\psi)$ is a *directional electoral equilibrium* (in pure strategies) if and only if

$$P(u, v^*) \leq P(u^*, v^*) \leq P(u^*, v), \qquad \forall u, v \in T(\psi) \qquad (6.4)$$

We can now characterize the directional electoral equilibria that occur at a given location ψ.

Theorem 6.1

Suppose there is an election in which (i) there is a compact set of possible locations for the candidates and (ii) the candidates use a C^1 binary Luce model. Let $\psi \in S$ be given. $(w^*, z^*) \in T(\psi) \times T(\psi)$ is a directional electoral equilibrium at the location ψ if and only if

$$D_{(w^*,0)}P\ell_e^1(\psi_1, \psi_2) = \max_{u \in T(\psi)} D_{(u,0)}P\ell_e^1(\psi_1, \psi_2) \tag{6.5}$$

and

$$D_{(0,z^*)}P\ell_e^1(\psi_1, \psi_2) = \max_{v \in T(\psi)} D_{(0,v)}P\ell_e^1(\psi_1, \psi_2) \tag{6.6}$$

at $\psi_1 = \psi_2 = \psi$.

Stated informally, Theorem 6.1 says that the direction(s) chosen in a two-candidate competition with directional strategies is (are) the same as the direction(s) that would be chosen by a challenger with directional strategies who is opposing a fixed incumbent. Theorem 6.1, in turn, implies Theorem 6.2.

Theorem 6.2

Suppose there is an election in which (i) there is a compact set of possible locations for the candidates and (ii) the candidates use a C^1 binary Luce model. Then there exists a directional electoral equilibrium at every location in S.

In addition, (6.3) also implies that these equilibria are always dominant strategy equilibria.

6.4   Stationary electoral equilibria and the social log-scaling function

At any given location the definition of a directional electoral equilibrium leaves open the possibility that each directional equilibrium is one in which the candidates choose to move away from their starting location. That is, when the candidates assess the marginal expected pluralities available for the directions in which they might move, each one may find an incentive to shift away from the given location. When this is the case, the candidates clearly would not remain at the location for very long if they found themselves there. Such a location, therefore, lacks the persistence or staying power that an equilibrium location (as opposed to an equilibrium pair of directions at a location) should have.

The remaining possibility is that at a given location neither candidate has an incentive to make a marginal change in his location. It is clear that this remaining possibility is the appropriate definition of an *equilibrium location* whenever both candidates start out at a status quo and have only directional strategies available (as discussed in the previous section). In addition, it is clear that when the candidates have a wider set of options (such as a local neighborhood of the status quo or the set of all possible locations), this condition is necessary for a location to be considered an equilibrium location. Because this is analogous to thinking about a stationary point for a real-valued function, a location that has this alternative property is called a *stationary electoral equilibrium.* Stated precisely, there is a stationary electoral equilibrium at a location ψ if and only if the zero vector in $E^{2 \cdot n}$ is a directional electoral equilibrium at ψ. Rephrased in informal terms, this definition says that if, at a given location, there is a directional electoral equilibrium in which both candidates choose to remain at the given location, then the candidates are in a stationary equilibrium (in which both of their locations remain stationary).

It is also possible to adopt the marginal perspective just used when thinking in terms of a social objective function. From this perspective, if a society is concerned solely with the marginal changes in a given social objective function $g_e : X \to E^1$ that result from variations from a given location $\psi \in S$, then the society will not vary ψ (i.e., it chooses "no change") if and only if

$$D_u g_e(\psi) \le 0, \qquad \forall\, u \in T(\psi) \tag{6.7}$$

Accordingly, we refer to any such point in the set of possible locations for the candidates as a *stationary outcome* for the social objective function $g : S \to E^1$, where g is the restriction of g_e to S. The next theorem uses this concept to characterize the locations at which stationary electoral equilibria occur.

Theorem 6.3

Suppose there is an election in which (i) there is a compact set of possible locations for the candidates and (ii) the candidates use a C^1 binary Luce model. Let $\psi \in S$ be given. There is a stationary electoral equilibrium at ψ if and only if ψ is a stationary outcome for the social objective function $W : S \to E^1$, which is the restriction of

$$W_e(x) = \int_\Theta \log(f(x \mid \theta))\, d\mu(\theta) \tag{6.8}$$

to the set S.

Stated informally, Theorem 6.3 says that candidates who are evaluating their payoffs on the margin at a given location have "no change" as an optimal strategy if and only if "no change" is found to be optimal for the society when a marginal evaluation is carried out at the given location using the social objective function specified by (6.8). This says that (6.8), which generalizes (4.10), can be thought of as being an implicit social objective function for stationary electoral equilibria, analogous to the interpretation of (4.10) in Section 4.5. Because the function W_e given by (6.8) takes an average of the logs of the groups' scaling functions across the society, the social-objective function $W : S \to E^1$, which is the restriction of W_e to the set S, is called (in what follows) the *social log-scaling function*. Theorem 6.3, in turn, implies Theorem 6.4.

Theorem 6.4

Suppose there is an election in which (i) there is a compact set of possible locations for the candidates and (ii) the candidates use a C^1 binary Luce model. There exists some location $\psi \in S$ at which there is a stationary electoral equilibrium.

Plott (1967), Sloss (1973, pp. 27–30), Schofield (1978a,b, 1980, 1983a,b, 1984a,b, 1985, 1986, 1989), Matthews (1979, 1980, 1982), and Cohen and Matthews (1980) have studied what happens under majority rule when there is a status quo and the social choice is either the status quo or a direction of motion away from the status quo (as in the directional games at status quo discussed in Section 6.3). In those studies, it has been assumed that voters' choices are determined by the preferences on the possible locations in the society's policy space (analogous to the assumption about the candidates' expectations about voters' choices studied in Section 2.3). Their results have established that in this context there is almost always an equilibrium direction (or equilibrium directions) of change at each possible status quo, analogous to the result in Theorem 6.2. At the same time, their results have established that in this context a stationary equilibrium "would be an almost nonexistent phenomenon" (Plott, 1967, p. 795) and that "even if [the conditions that lead to the existence of a stationary equilibrium] were, by some amazing chance, to be satisfied, it would still be true that even a slight change in *one* voter's preferences would disrupt the equilibrium, because it would upset the necessary pairing of voters" (Riker, 1982a, p. 15). Importantly, Theorem 6.4 (on the other hand) contains exactly the opposite conclusions. First, it explicitly states that in the model specified in Section 6.1 there is always at least one status quo in which there is a stationary equilibrium. Second, it directly implies that, if there is a change in a voter's preferences (which leaves us within the model), the most that will happen is that there be a change in the location(s) that has (have) a stationary equilibrium.

In light of the substantial difference between Theorem 6.4 and earlier results for stationary equilibria, it seems useful to discuss how it and the characterization in Theorem 6.3 have been obtained. The next paragraph, therefore, provides an informal discussion of the proofs of Theorems 6.3 and 6.4 that are in Appendix 6.3.

Our first observation is that the basic approach is very similar to those used in obtaining the existence and location theorems for global equilibria in the earlier chapters. Starting with Theorem 6.3, the characterization of the stationary equilibria is obtained by deriving necessary and sufficient conditions for each candidate to have a stationary strategy and then showing that these conditions are also necessary and sufficient for a location to be a stationary point for the social log-scaling function. Theorem 6.2 makes it possible for the conditions for a stationary equilibrium to be obtained by focusing on the stationary points for a candidate when her rival's position is fixed. The analysis of the equilibria then reduces to the question: Is there an underlying function that has the same partial derivatives (with respect to x) as we obtain from $P\ell^1(x, y)$ at $x = y$, as y is varied? "Integrating up" from these partials leads to the social log-scaling function, thus giving this function its central role in Theorem 6.3. Because it is possible to integrate up to a specific underlying function, the question of existence is reduced to the question of whether the underlying function has a stationary point. Since S is compact and the underlying function is continuous, the answer to this question is affirmative, thereby establishing Theorem 6.4.

Finally, we turn briefly to the relation between Theorems 6.3 and 6.4 and the results that have been established in Chapters 4 and 5. Two important observations are that Theorem 6.4 is a generalization of Theorem 4.1 and Corollary 5.1 and that Theorem 6.3 is a generalization of Theorem 4.2. The fact that this is true is an immediate implication of the following two general observations. First, the model analyzed here contains the models that were analyzed in Chapters 4 and 5 as special cases. Second, because of the differentiation assumptions in Section 4.2 (and retained in Chapter 5 and in this chapter), the set of global electoral equilibria is by necessity a subset of the set of stationary electoral equilibria. Interestingly, however, the important connection that these general observations reveal is actually only part of the full link between Theorems 6.3 and 6.4 on the one hand and Theorems 4.1 and 4.2 and Corollary 5.1 on the other. More specifically, the link between these results is even stronger than these general observations suggest because the convexity assumptions used in Chapter 4 and in Corollary 5.1 are sufficient (in the presence of the other assumptions in Chapter 5) to assure that the set of stationary electoral equilibria is exactly the same as the set of global equilibria. The fact that this is so can most easily be seen by reviewing the main results in Appendix 4.3 that were proven on the way to establishing Theorem 4.2.

6.5   Concave objective functions and global electoral equilibria

The theorems that have been obtained so far in this chapter have not involved the earlier chapters' assumptions of a convex S and scaling function properties that assure a concave–convex $P\ell^1$. The convexity properties assumed in the earlier chapters were valuable in the analyses in those chapters primarily because they assure that a stationary point for a particular objective function is a global maximum for that function. However, our sole concern in this chapter has been with stationary equilibria. Therefore, only what happens to $P\ell^1$ "close" to a particular ψ has been important.

Now, we bring in convexity assumptions and use them to obtain further results about global electoral equilibria. Chapter 5's theorems about concave (implicit) social objective functions and concave–convex candidate payoff functions and their implications for the existence of global electoral equilibria are generalized to the model that is being analyzed in this chapter. After this is done, we follow up on Section 6.3's discussion of the relation between global and directional electoral equilibria. More specifically, the results in the first part of Section 6.3 are then combined with Section 6.4's theorem about the locations of stationary electoral equilibria (viz., Theorem 6.3) to obtain two final results about the locations of global electoral equilibria.

The following terminology and notation enable us to state precisely and succinctly this chapter's generalizations of Chapter 5's results about concave social and candidate objective functions and their implications about the existence of global electoral equilibria. (i) Analogous to the approach used in Chapter 5, the part of this chapter's model that does not involve any specific assumptions about the nature of the groups' scaling functions is separated from the part of the model that does make these assumptions. More specifically, the assumptions in this model other than the assumptions about the nature of the groups' scaling functions is referred to by using the phrase "there is an election in which there is a compact set of possible locations for the candidates." Thus, using this phrase specifically invokes this chapter's versions of the assumptions in Section 4.2 up through (and including) the specification of the candidates' objectives (i.e., the versions that result after the modifications stated in Section 6.1 are made). When the word *convex* is included after the word *compact*, the earlier assumption that S is convex (used throughout Chapters 2–5) is also being made. (ii) Because μ is taken as given, the distribution of scaling functions in the electorate is fully specified by a function that assigns a scaling function $f(x \mid \theta) \in \mathcal{F}$, or $f(x \mid \theta) \in F$, to each $\theta \in \Theta$. $\mathcal{F}^{\mu}$, or F^{μ}, is used to denote the set of all functions from Θ into $\mathcal{F}$, or F, that satisfies the two regularity assumptions in Section 6.1. (iii) The term *profile in $\mathcal{F}^{\mu}$*, or F^{μ}, is refers to a function in $\mathcal{F}^{\mu}$, or F^{μ}.

This new terminology and notation makes it easy to state the following result about the social log-scaling function, which generalizes Theorem 5.1.

Theorem 6.5

Suppose there is an election in which there is a compact set of possible locations for the candidates. The social log-likelihood function is concave for each profile in $\mathcal{F}^{\mu}$ if and only if each $f \in \mathcal{F}$ is log-concave on S.

With the new terminology and notation and the terminology and notation used in Chapter 5, it is also easy to state the following generalizations of Theorems 5.2–5.4.

Theorem 6.6

Suppose there is an election in which there is a compact, convex set of possible locations for the candidates. $P\ell^{1}(\psi_1, \psi_2)$ is concave–convex for each profile in $\mathcal{F}^{\mu}$ if and only if each $f \in \mathcal{F}$ is such that

$$[f(x \mid \theta) - f(y \mid \theta)] \cdot \left(\frac{\rho(y \mid \theta)}{\rho(x \mid \theta)}\right) \leq D_{(x-y)} f(y \mid \theta) \qquad (6.9)$$

holds for each pair $x, y \in S$.

Theorem 6.7

Suppose there is an election in which there is a compact, convex set of possible locations for the candidates. $P\ell^{1}(\psi_1, \psi_2)$ is concave–convex for each profile in $\mathcal{F}^\mu$ if and only if each $f \in F$ is such that for each $v \in S$ the matrix

$$H(f(v \mid \theta)) + \left[\frac{-2 \cdot f_h(v \mid \theta) \cdot f_j(v \mid \theta)}{\rho(v \mid \theta)} \right] \tag{6.10}$$

is negative semidefinite on $Z(v)$.

Theorem 6.8

Suppose there is an election in which there is a compact, convex set of possible locations for the candidates. $P\ell^1(\psi_1, \psi_2)$ is concave–convex for each profile in F^μ if and only if each $f \in F$ is such that for any given $v \in S$ and feasible direction y the relative rate of change in the directional derivative of f is bounded by twice the relative rate of change in the shifted scaling function ρ according to its sign.

Theorems 6.6–6.8 provide generalizations of Corollaries 5.1–5.3. In line with the approach in Chapter 5, the phrase that results when "the candidates use a C^1 binary Luce model" is added to the phrase in the starting assumption for Theorems 6.6–6.8 is used to refer to the special case of the model specified in Section 6.1 in which S is convex.

Corollary 6.1

Suppose there is an election in which (i) there is a compact, convex set of possible locations for the candidates and (ii) the candidates use a C^1 binary Luce model. *If*, for each $\theta \in \Theta$, $f(s \mid \theta)$ is such that (6.9) is satisfied for each pair in S, *then* a global electoral equilibrium exists.

The next two results are concerned with the variation on the starting assumption in Corollary 6.1 that is obtained when each scaling function is assumed to be C^2. In line with the approach in Chapter 5, this variation is referred to by the phrase that results when we analogously alter the phrase used in Corollary 5.1's starting assumption by replacing C^1 with C^2.

Corollary 6.2

Suppose there is election in which (i) there is a compact, convex set of possible locations and (ii) the candidates use a C^2 binary

Luce model. *If,* for each $\theta \in \Theta, f(s \mid \theta)$ is such that, for each $v \in S$, the matrix in (6.10) is negative semidefinite, *then* a global electoral equilibrium exists.

Corollary 6.3

Suppose there is an election in which (i) there is a compact, convex set of possible locations for the candidates and (ii) the candidates' use a C^2 binary Luce model. *If,* for each $\theta \in \Theta, f(s \mid \theta)$ is such that for each $v \in S$ and each feasible direction y the relative rate of change in the directional derivative of f is bounded by twice the relative rate of change in the shifted scaling function according to its sign, *then* a global electoral equilibrium exists.

These three results follow (as with Corollaries 5.1–5.3) from combining the preceding theorems with the well-known saddle-point existence theorem stated in Appendix 2.2. Noted (as with Corollaries 5.1–5.3) that the assumption that S is convex in the premises of these corollaries plays a role both in invoking the preceding theorems and in invoking the saddle-point existence theorem used in this book.

Theorems 6.6–6.8 also provide (in combination with Theorem 6.3) the basis for identifying the locations of the global electoral equilibria that exist under the sufficient conditions identified in Corollaries 6.1–6.3. In particular, they lead to the following theorems.

Theorem 6.9

Suppose there is an election in which (i) there is a compact, convex set of possible locations for the candidates, (ii) the candidates use a C^1 binary Luce model, and (iii) for each $\theta \in \Theta$, $f(s \mid \theta)$ is such that (6.9) is satisfied for each pair in S. Let $s \in S$ be given. Then s is a global electoral outcome if and only if s maximizes the social log-scaling function W on S.

Theorem 6.10

Suppose there is an election in which (i) there is a compact, convex set of possible locations for the candidates, (ii) the candidates use a C^2 binary Luce model, and (iii) for each $\theta \in \Theta$, $f(s \mid \theta)$ is such that for each $v \in S$ the matrix in (6.10) is negative semidefinite. Let $s \in S$ be given. Then s is a global electoral equilibrium if and only if s maximizes the social log-scaling function W on S.

Theorem 6.11

Suppose there is an election in which (i) there is a compact, convex set of possible locations for the candidates, (ii) the candidates use a C^1 binary Luce model, and (iii) for each $\theta \in \Theta$, $f(s \mid \theta)$ is such that for any given $v \in S$ and feasible direction y the relative rate of change in the directional derivative of f is bounded by twice the relative rate of change in the shifted scaling function ρ according to its sign. Let $s \in S$ be given. Then s is a global electoral outcome if and only if s maximizes the social log-scaling function W on S.

Note that Theorem 6.9 generalizes Theorem 4.2, and that Theorems 6.10 and 6.11 provide further extensions for the case in which the groups' scaling functions are assumed to be C^2.

6.6   Some examples

Because this chapter's existence and location theorems generalize and extend those of the preceding chapters, it is possible to initially illustrate some of the results obtained here by drawing on the examples in Chapters 3 and 4. The first thing that should be noted is that those earlier examples satisfy the premises of Theorems 6.1–6.4. Therefore (by Theorems 6.3 and 6.4, in particular), we know that, in each of the examples in Chapters 3 and 4, (i) there is at least one location where there is a stationary electoral equilibrium, and (ii) the locations with stationary equilibria are the stationary outcomes for the (corresponding) social log-likelihood functions. A second noteworthy aspect of the earlier examples is that, in each case, the social log-likelihood function is the (Benthamite or Nash) social objective function that was used to find the global electoral outcome. A third feature of those examples that should be noted is that, because of their convexity properties, the observations made at the end of Section 6.4 apply to them. As a result, we can readily identify the locations where there are stationary equilibria. In particular, those observations tell us that the locations where there are stationary electoral equilibria are precisely those that have already been shown to be the global electoral outcomes.

The straightforward conclusions of the preceding paragraph serve to emphasize the link between the existence and location results for global equilibria obtained in Chapters 2–4 and the existence and location results for stationary equilibria obtained in this chapter. More specifically, they illustrate the fact that this chapter's existence and location theorems for stationary electoral equilibria reduce to the existence and location theorems for global electoral equilibria in Chapters 3 and 4 when the assumptions in those chapters are made. Significantly, the election models studied in Chapters 3 and 4 are also special cases of the premises of Corollaries 6.1–6.3 and Theorems 6.9–6.11. Therefore, the examples in Chapters 3 and 4 also illustrate the properties obtained in those results.

Because, importantly, Theorems 6.1–6.4 do not use the convexity assumptions in the previous chapters (and which are, therefore, satisfied by the examples in Chapters 3 and 4), it is useful to consider some examples in which S is not assumed to be convex and/or not all of the groups' scaling functions satisfy the conditions for concave–convex candidate payoff functions derived in this book. One such example was considered at the end of Chapter 5 (viz., Example 5.5). The earlier analysis of that example revealed that it does not have a global electoral equilibrium. However, it is easy to see that in the example (which satisfies the premise of Theorems 6.1–6.4) each feasible location is both a location where there is a stationary electoral equilibrium and a stationary outcome for the social log-likelihood function, because $T(s^k) = \{O\}$ at each feasible location.

As the preceding observations make clear, Example 5.5 provides another illustration of the fact that this chapter's results about stationary equilibria generalize the book's global existence and location results. In particular, the conclusion stated at the end of the preceding paragraph provides one illustration of the type of conclusion that Theorems 6.3–6.4 enable us to obtain about election models that are covered by the premise for those theorems but are not covered by the book's results about global equilibria. Example 5.5 is, however, a somewhat extreme special case of Theorems 6.1–6.4, since the candidates and the society have no feasible directions away from the locations from which they might potentially start. As a consequence, we also consider some examples in which the absence of change does not result solely from the total absence of feasible directions of change.

The next example to be analyzed is one in which (in line with the goal stated at the end of the preceding paragraph) feasible directions of change are available at every possible starting location. The example additionally illustrates how the book's results about stationary equilibria can be applied to situations covered by the premise for Theorems 6.1–6.4 but are not covered by the premises for the book's results about global equilibria. In line with this second goal, the scaling functions for the first two groups are ones that have already been shown (viz., in the earlier analyses of Examples 5.1 and 5.2) to violate the conditions for concave–convex candidate payoffs derived in this book.

EXAMPLE 6.1

Suppose there is an election in which (i) $S = [-1, +1]$ and (ii) the candidates use a C^1 binary Luce model. Assume that $N = \{1, 2, 3\}$, $g(1) = g(2) = g(3) = \frac{1}{3}$, and

$$f(s \mid 1) = e^s \tag{6.11}$$

$$f(s \mid 2) = 2 + s^2 \tag{6.12}$$

$$f(s \mid 3) = 3 - s \tag{6.13}$$

Theorem 6.3 immediately tells us that there exists at least one location where there is a stationary electoral equilibrium. In what follows, we use Theorem 6.4 to identify the location(s) where this is the case.

The social log-scaling function for this example is

$$W_1(s) = [s + \log(2 + s^2) + \log(3 - s)] \cdot \frac{1}{3} \tag{6.14}$$

Taking the first derivative of W_1, we get

$$\frac{dW_1(s)}{ds} = \left[1 + \frac{2 \cdot s}{2 + s^2} - \frac{1}{3 - s} \right] \cdot \frac{1}{3} \tag{6.15}$$

Therefore, $dW_1(s) / ds \gtreqless 0 \Leftrightarrow [6 - 2 \cdot s + 3 \cdot s^2 - s^3 + 6 \cdot s - 2 \cdot s^2 - 2 - s^2] \gtreqless 0$. Therefore, letting

$$\phi_1(s) \equiv -s^3 + 4 \cdot s + 4 \tag{6.16}$$

yields

$$\frac{dW_1(s)}{ds} \gtreqless 0 \Leftrightarrow \phi_1(s) \gtreqless 0 \tag{6.17}$$

By (6.16), $\phi_1(-1) = +1$ and $d\phi_1(s) / ds = -3 \cdot s^2 + 4 > 0$, $\forall s \in [-1, +1]$. Hence, $\phi_1(s) > 0$, $\forall s \in [-1, +1]$. Therefore, by (6.17), $dW_1(s) / ds > 0$, $\forall s \in [-1, +1]$. Therefore, there is a unique stationary outcome for W_1, the point $s = +1$. Therefore, $s = +1$ is the one and only location where there is a stationary electoral equilibrium.

Because the premise for Theorems 6.3 and 6.4 does not require S to be convex, it is also of some interest to consider the special cases of

Example 6.1 that we get when we replace $S = [-1, +1]$ with a compact subset that is not convex. As it turns out, since we already know that (6.15) is positive at each $s \in [-1, +1]$, such cases are also easy to analyze. In particular, this property of Example 6.1 tells us that the social log-likelihood function in any such special case has a stationary outcome at the right endpoint of each segment in S. Therefore, in each such case, those endpoints constitute the set of locations at which there is a stationary electoral equilibrium. For instance, if the set of potential starting locations for the candidates is $[-1.0, -0.5] \cup [+0.5, +1.0]$, then there is a stationary electoral equilibrium at $s = +1$ (as in Example 6.1) and also at $s = -0.5$, but none at the remaining locations.

As in the discussion of Example 5.5, it is also useful to think about the variations on these examples that result from assuming (as in Section 4.5) that the voters have utility functions that satisfy (4.11) or (4.12), and assuming that the candidates use a deterministic voting model, that is, they assume (2.7) instead of using a binary Luce model. In the resulting examples, the single-peaked preferences of the voters make it easy for us to see that we get the same conclusions about the locations that do (respectively, do not) have stationary equilibria. Indeed, in the analogous variation of Example 5.5, the same thing happens, that is, the conclusion about whether a given location has a stationary equilibrium is the same with both (2.7) and the binary Luce model.

The observations in the preceding paragraph illustrate the fact that the conclusions that we reach about stationary equilibria in probabilistic and deterministic voting models can coincide, although the book's earlier analyses of global equilibria have made it clear that this is the exception rather than the rule. In light of this, it is also be useful to consider at least one example in which those conclusions do not coincide. The next example accomplishes this goal.

It should also be noted that in all of the examples we have considered that fall outside of the premises for the book's results about global equilibria but within the premise for its results about stationary equilibria, all the locations with stationary equilibria have been boundary points (of the set of feasible locations). The following example also illustrates that this characteristic of those examples is not a general property.

EXAMPLE 6.2

Suppose there is an election in which (i) $S = [0.1, 0.9]$ and (ii) the candidates use a C^1 binary Luce model. Assume that $N = \{1, 2, 3\}$, $g(1) = g(2) = g(3) = \frac{1}{3}$, and

$$f(s \mid 1) = e^s \qquad (6.18)$$

$$f(s \mid 2) = 1 - s \qquad (6.19)$$

$$f(s \mid 3) = s^2 - 2 \cdot s + 2 \qquad (6.20)$$

This example satisfies the premise of Theorem 6.3. Therefore, as with Example 6.1, that theorem immediately tells us that there is at least one location where there is a stationary equilibrium. Also as with Example 6.1, Theorem 6.4 is used to identify the location(s) at which there is a stationary electoral equilibrium. For purposes of comparison, it is useful first to think about the corresponding examples in which (i) the voters have utility functions that satisfy (4.11) or (4.12) and (ii) it is alternatively assumed that the candidates use a deterministic voting model. As with Example 6.1, the voters have single-peaked preferences. Therefore, it is easy to see that once again there is a unique location with a stationary equilibrium in those alternative examples. This time around, that location is $\psi = .1$.

The social log-scaling function for this example is

$$W_2(s) = [s + \log(1 - s) + \log(s^2 - 2 \cdot s + 2)] \cdot \tfrac{1}{3} \qquad (6.21)$$

By (6.21),

$$\frac{dW_2(s)}{ds} = \left[1 + \frac{-1}{1 - s} + \frac{2 \cdot s + 2}{s^2 - 2 \cdot s + 2} \right] \cdot \frac{1}{3} \qquad (6.22)$$

Therefore $dW(s)/ds \gtreqless 0 \Leftrightarrow [(s^2 - 2 \cdot s + 2 - s^3 + 2 \cdot s^2 - 2 \cdot s) + (-s^2 + 2 \cdot s - 2) + (2 \cdot s - 2 \cdot s^2 + 2 - 2 \cdot s)] \gtreqless 0$. Therefore, from

$$\phi_2(s) \equiv -s^3 - 2 \cdot s + 2 \qquad (6.23)$$

it follows that

$$\frac{dW_1(s)}{ds} \gtreqless 0 \Leftrightarrow \phi_2(s) \gtreqless 0 \qquad (6.24)$$

By (6.23), $\phi_2(.1) = +1.799$. Therefore, by (6.24), $\psi = .1$ is not a stationary outcome for W_2. Hence, by Theorem 6.4, there is no stationary electoral equilibrium at $\psi = .1$ (unlike in the corresponding deterministic examples that were discussed earlier). By (6.23), $\phi(.9) = -.529$. Therefore, using (6.24) and Theorem 6.4 again, we find there is also no stationary equilibrium at the other boundary point for S. Thus, unlike in the previous examples that satisfy the premise for Theorems 6.1–6.4 but not the premises for the book's global equilibrium results, the location(s) with stationary equilibria must be in the interior of S.

By (6.4) and the conclusion at the end of the preceding paragraph, it follows that there is a stationary equilibrium at a given $s \in S$ if and only if that location is a root of the algebraic equation of the third degree $\phi_2(s) = 0$. The discriminant for that equation is $4 \cdot (2)^3 + 27 \cdot (-2)^2 > 0$ (see Sydsaeter, 1981, p. 54). Therefore, $\phi_2(s) = 0$ has one real and two complex roots (see Sydsaeter, 1981, p. 54). This tells us that there is a unique location at which there is a stationary electoral equilibrium. From the Cardano formula (see Sydsaeter, 1981, p. 54), it follows that (rounding off to the second decimal place) that location is approximately .77.

Thus far, in considering examples that fall outside of the premises for the book's results about global equilibria but within the premise for its results about stationary equilibria, either all of the locations with stationary equilibria have been boundary points or there has been a unique location with a stationary equilibrium. In addition, in those examples, we have encountered multiple locations with stationary equilibria only for cases in which S is not convex. The following example illustrates the fact that neither of these patterns is a general property.

EXAMPLE 6.3

Suppose there is an election in which (i) $S = [1.0, 3.0]$ and (ii) the candidates use a C^1 binary Luce model. Assume that $N = \{1, 2, 3\}$, $g(1) = g(2) = g(3) = \frac{1}{3}$, and

$$f(s \mid 1) = s \tag{6.25}$$

$$f(s \mid 2) = 1 \tag{6.26}$$

$$f(s \mid 3) = \frac{3}{2} \cdot s^2 - \frac{13}{2} \cdot s + 8 \tag{6.27}$$

This time around, the social log-scaling function is

$$W_3(s) = \{\log(s) + 0 + \log[\frac{3}{2} \cdot s^2 - \frac{13}{2} \cdot s + 8]\} \cdot \frac{1}{3} \tag{6.28}$$

Using (6.28), we get

$$\frac{dW_3(s)}{ds} = \left[\frac{1}{s} + \frac{3 \cdot s - \frac{13}{2}}{\frac{3}{2} \cdot s^2 - \frac{13}{2} \cdot s + 8}\right] \cdot \frac{1}{3} \tag{6.29}$$

Therefore, $dW_3(s) / ds \gtreqless 0 \Leftrightarrow [\frac{3}{2} \cdot s^2 - \frac{13}{2} \cdot s + 8 + 3 \cdot s^2 - \frac{13}{2} \cdot s] \gtreqless 0$. Therefore, letting

$$\phi_3(s) \equiv \frac{9}{2} \cdot s^2 - 13 \cdot s + 8 \tag{6.30}$$

we obtain

$$\frac{dW_3(s)}{ds} \gtreqless 0 \Leftrightarrow \phi_3(s) \gtreqless 0 \qquad\qquad (6.31)$$

By (6.30), $\phi_3(1) = -\frac{1}{2}$ and $\phi_3(3) = +\frac{19}{2}$. Therefore, by Theorem 6.4, there are stationary equilibria at both $\psi = 1$ and $\psi = 3$. There is, of course, also a stationary equilibrium at any real root of $\phi_3(s) = 0$ that is in S. Using the quadratic formula reveals that the roots of $\phi_3(s) = 0$ are 2 and $\frac{8}{9}$. Therefore, $\{1, 2, 3\}$ is the complete set of locations at which there is a stationary electoral equilibrium.

This example has two boundary locations and one interior location (at a local minimum for W) where there are stationary equilibria. There is, however, nothing special about this pattern. For instance, if we alternatively assume that $S = [0.5, 3.0]$, then there are two boundary locations and two interior locations (one at a local maximum for W and one at a local minimum for W) where there is a stationary electoral equilibrium. If we alternatively assume that $S = [0.5, 2.5] \cup [2.6, 3.0]$, then the same four locations and $\psi = 2.5$ all have stationary equilibria.

Example 6.3 can also be used to illustrate one other aspect of stationary equilibria. Directly analyzing the election reveals that there is a unique global electoral equilibrium at $(\psi_1^*, \psi_2^*) = (3, 3)$. The unique global equilibrium strategy ($\psi = 3$) is, of course, also a location where there is a stationary electoral equilibrium. In addition, even though such a strategy exists, the set of global equilibrium strategies is a proper subset of the set of locations with stationary equilibria. This final observation is worth noting because it contrasts with one of the observations made in the opening paragraphs in this section (viz., the fact that, in each of the examples discussed there, a global equilibrium exists and the set of global equilibria is the same as the set of locations with stationary equilibria).

6.7   Conclusion

This chapter started off by generalizing the model studied in Chapter 5 by (i) including the possibility that the candidates use a distribution with an infinite set of groups (rather than a discrete distribution, defined on a finite set of groups) and by (ii) relaxing the preceding chapters' assumption that the set of locations for the candidates is necessarily convex. A distinction was then made between the global concept of an electoral equilibrium used in Chapters 2–5 and the notion of an equilibrium on the margin, which is at the heart of the analysis in this chapter. The idea of candidates simultaneously making their decisions on the margin was rigorously formulated as a directional game. The saddle-points for the resulting two-candidate, zero-sum, directional games were characterized and their existence established. Attention was then focused on directional electoral equilibria in which neither candidate wants to vary the location. The locations where such stationary equilibria occur were also characterized and their existence established. Special attention was then paid to the significant fact that the theorem that establishes the existence in this chapter's probabilistic voting model of locations where stationary electoral equilibria exist is in sharp contrast with the important prior results in the public choice literature that have established the general nonexistence of stationary equilibria in multi-dimensional, deterministic voting models. In Section 6.5, the book's earlier results about concave social and candidate objective functions and the conditions under which global electoral equilibria exist were generalized for the election model that was developed in this chapter. These new results were then used, to generalize and extend the book's earlier existence and location results for global electoral equilibria. The examples in Section 6.6 illustrated some of the main results in the chapter.

This chapter's theorems have provided global existence and location results for a significant subset of the class of elections in which (i) there is a compact set of possible locations for the candidates and (ii) the candidates use a C^1 binary Luce model. Its theorems have also established that there are locations with stationary equilibria in all of the remaining elections in that class and have characterized those locations. In addition, the analysis has shown that the set of global electoral outcomes is always contained in the set of locations with stationary equilibria. Therefore, this chapter's analysis of locations with stationary equilibria and global outcomes has expanded the equilibrium analyses that were carried out in the earlier chapters. Significantly, the results in this chapter have also established that these locations and outcomes exhibit the same important characteristic that we saw in the earlier chapters: The strategic decisions that candidates make maximize (globally or, at least, on the margin) an implicit social objective function.

Appendix 6.1: Proofs of Propositions 6.1–6.4

For each $c \in \{1, 2\}$, let $P\ell_e^c(\psi_1, \psi_2)$ denote the function on $X \times X$ that satisfies (6.1) at each $(\psi_1, \psi_2) \in X \times X$. Proposition 6.1 is a special case of the following result about the functions $P\ell_e^1(\psi_1, \psi_2)$ and $P\ell_e^2(\psi_1, \psi_2)$ (where it is implicitly assumed that the premise in Proposition 6.1 is satisfied).

Lemma 6.1

At each $(\psi_1, \psi_2) \in X \times X$, both $P\ell_e^1(\psi_1, \psi_2)$ and $P\ell_e^2(\psi_1, \psi_2)$ exist.

Proof of Lemma 6.1

Consider $c = 1$ and any $(\psi_1, \psi_2) \in X \times X$. To begin with, for any individual in a given group θ, (4.5) and (4.7) imply that

$$P\ell_\theta^1(\psi_1, \psi_2) = 2 \cdot \frac{f(\psi_1 \mid \theta)}{f(\psi_1 \mid \theta) + f(\psi_2 \mid \theta)} - \frac{f(\psi_2 \mid \theta)}{f(\psi_1 \mid \theta) + f(\psi_2 \mid \theta)} \quad \text{(A6.1)}$$

Adding $f(\psi_1 \mid \theta) / [f(\psi_1 \mid \theta) + f(\psi_2 \mid \theta)]$ to the first term and $-f(\psi_1 \mid \theta) / [f(\psi_1 \mid \theta) + f(\psi_2 \mid \theta)]$ to the second term on the right-hand side of (A6.1) and then simplifying gives

$$P\ell_\theta^1(\psi_1, \psi_2) = 2 \cdot \frac{f(\psi_1 \mid \theta)}{f(\psi_1 \mid \theta) + f(\psi_2 \mid \theta)} - 1 \quad \text{(A6.2)}$$

Therefore, the expected plurality for candidate 1 from the entire population of voters is the integral

$$P\ell_e^1(\psi_1, \psi_2) = \int_\Theta P\ell_\theta^1(\psi_1, \psi_2) \cdot d\mu(\theta)$$

$$= \int_\Theta \left\{ 2 \cdot \frac{f(\psi_1 \mid \theta)}{f(\psi_1 \mid \theta) + f(\psi_2 \mid \theta)} - 1 \right\} d\mu(\theta) \quad \text{(A6.3)}$$

Since $f(x \mid \theta)$ is a measurable function of θ for any given $x \in X$, $[f(x \mid \theta) + f(y \mid \theta)]$ is measurable for any given $x, y \in X$. In addition, $f(x \mid \theta) > 0$ for every $x \in X$ and $\theta \in \Theta$. Therefore, for each $\kappa > 0$,

$$\left\{ \theta \in \Theta : \frac{1}{f(x \mid \theta) + f(y \mid \theta)} < \kappa \right\} = \left\{ \theta \in \Theta : f(x \mid \theta) + f(y \mid \theta) > \frac{1}{\kappa} \right\}$$

$$\text{(A6.4)}$$

is a measurable set. Furthermore,

$$\left\{ \theta \in \Theta : \frac{1}{f(x \mid \theta) + f(y \mid \theta)} < \kappa \right\} = \phi \quad \text{(A6.5)}$$

for each $\kappa \leq 0$. Hence, $1 / [f(x \mid \theta) + f(y \mid \theta)]$ and, in turn, $P\ell_\theta^1(\psi_1, \psi_2)$ are measurable functions of θ.

Additionally, for each $\theta \in \Theta$, both $P_\theta^1(\psi_1, \psi_2)$ and $P_\theta^2(\psi_1, \psi_2)$ are bounded above by $+1$ and bounded below by θ (since they are probabilities). Hence, by (4.5), $P\ell_\theta^1(\psi_1, \psi_2)$ is bounded above by $+1$ and bounded below by -1. Therefore,

$$\int_\Theta (-1)\, d\mu(\theta) \le \int_\Theta P\ell_\theta^1(\psi_1, \psi_2)\, d\mu(\theta) \le \int_\Theta (+1)\, d\mu(\theta) \qquad (A6.6)$$

Therefore, since μ is a probability measure,

$$-\infty < -1 \le \int_\Theta P\ell_\theta^1(\psi_1, \psi_2)\, d\mu(\theta) \le +1 < +\infty \qquad (A6.7)$$

Therefore, the integral

$$P\ell_e^1(\psi_1, \psi_2) = \int_\Theta P\ell_\theta^1(\psi_1, \psi_2)\, d\mu(\theta) \qquad (A6.8)$$

exists.

The existence of $P\ell_e^2(\psi_1, \psi_2)$ at each $(\psi_1, \psi_2) \in X \times X$ follows from a similar argument.

QED

Proof of Proposition 6.2

The proof follows from arguments analogous to those used to prove Proposition 4.1 in Appendix 4.2.

QED

Proof of Proposition 6.3

The proof follows from arguments analogous to those used to prove Proposition 4.2 in Appendix 4.2.

QED

The remainder of this appendix is devoted to establishing Proposition 6.4. Before turning to the logical arguments, recall that (as pointed out right before the proof of Lemma 4.6 in Appendix 4.3) a function is C^1 on a compact set S if and only if it is C^1 at each point in an open set that contains S. Because of the nature of this definition, in the proof of Proposition 6.4 we consider (as in the proof of Lemma 4.6) an open superset of S that is contained in the interior of X, for instance, any set that is obtained as the union

$$\bigcup_{s \in S} O(s) \qquad (A6.9)$$

of open sets which satisfy $s \in O(S) \subseteq \text{int}(X)$, $\forall\, s \in S$. Because we are using $T(\psi)$ in this chapter to denote the strategy sets for the candidates at a given location ψ, to avoid confusion we use $\boldsymbol{S}$ to denote an open set that is such that $S \subset \boldsymbol{S} \subseteq \text{int}(X)$, rather than the notation T that was used in the proof of Lemma 4.6.

The following lemma is used in the proof of Proposition 6.4. In stating it, we take the premise of that proposition as given.

Lemma 6.2

Let S be any open set such that $S \subset \boldsymbol{S} \subseteq \text{int}(X)$. At each $(\psi_1, \psi_2) \in \boldsymbol{S} \times \boldsymbol{S}$, the partial derivatives of $P\ell_e^1(\psi_1, \psi_2)$ exist and satisfy

$$\frac{\partial P\ell_e^1(\psi_1', \psi_2')}{\partial \psi_{1h}} = 2 \cdot \int_\Theta \frac{f(\psi_2' \mid \theta) \cdot [\partial f(\psi_1' \mid \theta) / \partial \psi_{1h}]}{[f(\psi_1' \mid \theta) + f(\psi_2' \mid \theta)]^2} \, d\mu(\theta),$$

$$h = 1, \ldots, n \tag{A6.10}$$

and

$$\frac{\partial P\ell_e^2(\psi_1', \psi_2')}{\partial \psi_{2h}} = 2 \cdot \int_\Theta \frac{f(\psi_2' \mid \theta) \cdot [\partial f(\psi_2' \mid \theta) / \partial \psi_{2h}]}{[f(\psi_1' \mid \theta) + f(\psi_2' \mid \theta)]^2} \, d\mu(\theta),$$

$$h = 1, \ldots, n \tag{A6.11}$$

In proving Lemma 6.2 we use the following well-known result, which is given, for instance, as corollary 6.9 in Bartle (1966, p. 46).

Theorem

Suppose that for some $t_0 \in [\alpha, \beta]$, the function $\phi \to k(\phi, t_0)$ is integrable with respect to a measure space (Φ, Ξ, v), that $\partial k / \partial t$ exists on $\Phi \times [a, b]$, and that there exists a function $b(\phi)$ that is integrable with respect to (Φ, Ξ, v) and such that

$$\left| \frac{\partial k(\phi, t)}{\partial t} \right| \leq b(\phi) \tag{A6.12}$$

Then the function

$$K(t) = \int_\Phi k(\phi, t) \, dv(\phi) \tag{A6.13}$$

is differentiable on $[\alpha, \beta]$ and

$$\frac{dK(t)}{dt} = \frac{d}{dt} \left\{ \int_\Phi k(\phi, t) \, dv(\phi) \right\} = \int_\Phi \frac{\partial k(\phi, t)}{\partial t} \, dv(\phi) \tag{A6.14}$$

Proof of Lemma 6.2

Choose any $(\psi_1', \psi_2') \in \boldsymbol{S} \times \boldsymbol{S}$. Consider $c = 1$ and any particular $h \in \{1, \ldots, n\}$. In establishing that the partial of $P\ell_e^1$ (with respect to ψ_{1h})

exists at (ψ_1', ψ_2') and satisfies (A6.9), we have only to concern ourselves with points that differ from (ψ_1', ψ_2') (at most) in its $(1h)$th
component. To make things easier, we let

$$x_j' = \psi_{1j}', \qquad \forall\, j \in \{1, \dots, n\} - \{h\} \tag{A6.15}$$

and use x' to denote a point in $\boldsymbol{S}$ that satisfies (A6.15). For the argument
that follows, it is useful to note that, by (A6.3), at any given (x, ψ_2')

$$P\ell_e^1(x', \psi_2') = \int_\Theta r(\theta, x_h')\, d\mu(\theta) \tag{A6.16}$$

where

$$r(\theta, x_h) = 2 \cdot \frac{f((x_1', \dots, x_{h-1}', x_h, x_{h+1}', \dots, x_n') \mid \theta)}{f((x_1', \dots, x_{h-1}', x_h, x_{h+1}', \dots, x_n') \mid \theta) + f(\psi_2' \mid \theta)} - 1 \tag{A6.17}$$

Let ϕ be the variable θ. Let t be the variable x_h. Let $(\Phi, \Xi, \nu) = (\Theta, \Sigma, \mu)$.
Let $k(\phi, t) = r(\theta, x_h)$. By an argument similar to that used in (A4.27) in
Appendix 4.3, we have

$$\frac{\partial}{\partial x_h}\left\{2 \cdot \frac{f(x \mid \theta)}{f(x \mid \theta) + f(\psi_2' \mid \theta)} - 1\right\} = \frac{2 \cdot f(\psi_2' \mid \theta) \cdot [\partial f(x \mid \theta)/\partial x_h]}{[f(x \mid \theta) + f(\psi_2' \mid \theta)]^2} \tag{A6.18}$$

In addition, by the second regulatory assumption in Section 6.1, $f(x \mid \theta)$
and $\partial f(x \mid \theta)/\partial x_h$ are bounded functions of (x, θ) on $X \times \Theta$, with the
lower bound on $f(x \mid \theta)$ being positive. Now, since $\boldsymbol{S}$ is contained in
the interior of X, there exist $\alpha, \beta \in E^1$ such that $\{x \in X : [\alpha < x_h < \beta]$
and $[x_j = x_j', \forall\, j \neq h]\} \subset \mathrm{int}(X)$. Consider any such α, β. By what has
already been established in this paragraph, $\partial k(\phi, t)/\partial t = \partial r(\theta, x_h)/\partial x_h$
is a bounded function of $(\phi, t) = (\theta, x_h$ on $\Phi \times [\alpha, \beta] = \Theta \times [\alpha, \beta]$. That is,
$b \in E^1$ such that

$$\left|\frac{\partial k(\phi, t)}{\partial t}\right| \leq b, \qquad \forall (\phi, t) \in \Phi \times [\alpha, \beta] \tag{A6.19}$$

Let $b(\phi) = b, \forall\, \phi \in \Phi$. By (A6.19), $b(\phi)$ satisfies (A6.12). In addition, since
(Θ, Σ, μ), and hence (Φ, Ξ, ν) is a probability space, $b(\phi)$ is also integrable with respect to (Φ, Ξ, ν). Finally, by what has already been established in the proof of Lemma 6.1, $k(\phi, t)$ is integrable with respect
to (Φ, Ξ, ν) at each $t \in [\alpha, \beta]$. Therefore, the premise of the theorem
that immediately precedes this proof is satisfied. That theorem, therefore, directly implies that (for the particular Φ, k, ϕ, t, and ν under
consideration, (A6.13) is differentiable on $[\alpha, \beta]$ and (A6.14) holds.

Therefore, substituting this chapter's notation into those equations, we find that (A6.16) is a differentiable function of x_h on $[\alpha, \beta]$ and

$$\frac{\partial P\ell_e^1(\psi_1', \psi_2')}{\partial x_h} = \int_\theta \frac{\partial r(\theta, x_h')}{\partial x_h} d\mu(\theta) \qquad (A6.20)$$

Therefore, using (A6.17) and (A6.18) to rewrite (A6.20), we find that the partial of $P\ell_e^1$ (with respect to ψ_{1h}) exists at (ψ_1', ψ_2') and satisfies (A6.10).

By a similar argument, for $c = 2$ and any particular $h \in \{1, \dots, n\}$, the partial of $P\ell_e^1$ (with respect to ψ_{2h}) exists and satisfies (A6.11).

QED

The proof of Proposition 6.4 also involves the following well-known result, which follows directly from the Lebesgue dominated convergence theorem, as stated, for instance, in Bartle, 1966, p. 44.

Theorem

Let $\{\xi_t\}$ be an infinite sequence of functions, integrable with respect to a given measure space (Φ, Ξ, ν), that converge to a real-valued function ξ that is integrable with respect to the same measure space. *If* there exists a function g that is integrable with respect to (Φ, Ξ, ν) such that $|\xi_t(\phi)| \leq g(\phi)$, $\forall \phi$, $\forall t$, *then*

$$\int_\Phi \xi(\phi) \cdot d\nu(\phi) = \lim_{t \to \infty} \int_\Phi \xi_t(\phi) \, d\nu(\phi) \qquad (A6.21)$$

Proof of Proposition 6.4

Let $\boldsymbol{S}$ be any open set such that $S \subset \boldsymbol{S} \subseteq \text{int}(X)$. It immediately follows that $\boldsymbol{S} \times \boldsymbol{S}$ is an open set that contains the compact set $S \times S$. Lemma 6.2 has established that at each $(\psi_1', \psi_2') \in \boldsymbol{S} \times \boldsymbol{S}$ the partial derivatives of $P\ell_e^1(\psi_1, \psi_2)$ exist and satisfy (A6.11) and (A6.12). Therefore, showing that each of the partial derivatives in (A6.11) and (A6.12) are continuous on $\boldsymbol{S} \times \boldsymbol{S}$ will establish this proposition.

Recall that, by definition, a function $\chi : \boldsymbol{S} \to E^1$ is continuous on $\boldsymbol{S}$ if and only if it is continuous at each $x^* \in \boldsymbol{S}$; that is, it is such that at any given $x^* \in \boldsymbol{S}$ for each infinite sequence $\{x'\}$ in $\boldsymbol{S}$ that converges to x^*, the corresponding sequence $\{\chi(x')\}$ converges to $\chi(x^*)$. Consider $c = 1$ and any given $h \in \{1, \dots, n\}$. Consider any particular $(\psi_1^*, \psi_2^*) \in \boldsymbol{S} \times \boldsymbol{S}$. Now choose any infinite sequence $\{(\psi_1', \psi_2')\}$ in S that converges to (ψ_1^*, ψ_2^*). As in the proof of Lemma 6.2, let

$$(\Phi, \Xi, \nu) = (\Theta, \Sigma, \mu) \tag{A6.22}$$

For each t, let ξ_t be the function on $\Phi = \Theta$ that satisfies

$$\xi_t(\phi) = \frac{f(\psi_2^t | \phi) \cdot [\partial f(\psi_1^t | \phi) / \partial \psi_{1h}]}{[f(\psi_1^t | \phi) + f(\psi_2^t | \phi)]^2} \tag{A6.23}$$

at each $\phi \in \Phi$.

Since $(\psi_1^t, \psi_2^t) \in \boldsymbol{S} \times \boldsymbol{S}$, $\forall\, t$, it follows, by (A6.23) and the logic used in the proof of Lemma 6.2, that $\{\xi_t\}$ is a sequence of functions that are integrable with respect to (Φ, Ξ, ν). Consider any particular $\phi \in \Phi$. Since $f(x | \phi)$ is C^1 and positive, real-valued on X, it follows that

$$\lim_{t \to \infty} f(\psi_1^t | \phi) = f(\psi_1^* | \phi) > 0 \tag{A6.24}$$

$$\lim_{t \to \infty} f(\psi_2^t | \phi) = f(\psi_2^* | \phi) > 0 \tag{A6.25}$$

$$\lim_{t \to \infty} \frac{\partial f(\psi_1^t | \phi)}{\partial \psi_{1h}} = \frac{\partial f(\psi_1^* | \phi)}{\partial \psi_{1h}} \tag{A6.26}$$

Therefore, using (A6.24)–(A6.26), we obtain

$$\lim_{t \to \infty} \left\{ \frac{f(\psi_2^t | \phi) \cdot [\partial f(\psi_1^t | \phi) / \partial \phi_{1h}]}{[f(\psi_1^t | \phi) + f(\psi_2^t | \phi)]^2} \right\}$$

$$= \frac{\lim_{t \to \infty} \{f(\psi_2^t | \phi) \cdot [\partial f(\psi_1^t | \phi) / \partial \psi_{1h}]\}}{\lim_{t \to \infty} \{[f(\psi_1^t | \phi) + f(\psi_2^t | \phi)]^2\}}$$

$$= \frac{\lim_{t \to \infty} [f(\psi_2^t | \phi) \cdot \lim_{t \to \infty} [\partial f(\psi_1^t | \phi) / \partial \psi_{1h}]}{\{\lim_{t \to \infty} [f(\psi_1^t | \phi) + f(\psi_2^t | \phi)]\}^2}$$

$$= \frac{f(\psi_2^* | \phi) \cdot [\partial f(\psi_1^* | \phi) / \partial \psi_{1h}]}{[f(\psi_1^* | \phi) + f(\psi_2^* | \phi)]^2} \tag{A6.27}$$

(e.g., see theorem 12, p. 44, Buck, 1978).

Now, let ξ be the function on Φ that satisfies

$$\xi(\phi) = \frac{f(\psi_2^* | \phi) \cdot [\partial f(\psi_1^* | \phi) / \partial \psi_{1h}]}{[f(\psi_1^* | \phi) + f(\psi_2^* | \phi)]^2} \tag{A6.28}$$

at each $\phi \in \Phi$. From (A6.28) and the fact that f is a C^1 positive, real-valued function on X, it follows that ξ is real-valued. In addition, since $(\psi_1^*, \psi_2^*) \in \boldsymbol{S} \times \boldsymbol{S}$, (A6.28) and the logic used in the proof of Lemma 6.2

lead to the conclusion that ξ is integrable with respect to (Φ, Ξ, ν). Therefore, from (A6.23), (A6.27), and (A6.28), $\{\xi_t\}$ is a sequence of functions, integrable with respect to the given measure space (Φ, Ξ, ν), that converge to a real-valued function that is integrable with respect to the same measure space.

By the second regularity assumption in Section 6.1, there exist $u_f, \ell_f, u_p, \ell_p \in E^1$ such that

$$0 < \ell_f < f(x \mid \theta) < u_f, \qquad \forall x \in X, \forall \theta \in \Theta \tag{A6.29}$$

$$\ell_p < \frac{\partial f(x \mid \theta)}{\partial x_h} < u_p, \qquad \forall x \in X, \forall \theta \in \Theta \tag{A6.30}$$

We separately consider the following possible cases: (i) $0 \le \ell_p$, (ii) $\ell_p < 0 < u_p$, and (iii) $u_p \le 0$. Suppose (i) holds. Using (A6.29) and (A6.30), we immediately have

$$0 < \frac{f(\psi_2 \mid \phi) \cdot [\partial f(\psi_1 \mid \phi) / \partial \psi_{1h}]}{[f(\psi_1 \mid \phi) + f(\psi_2 \mid \phi)]^2}, \qquad \forall ((\psi_1, \psi_2), \theta)) \in X^2 \times \Theta \tag{A6.31}$$

By (A6.29),

$$\log\{f(\psi_2 \mid \theta)\} < \log\{u_f\}, \qquad \forall (\psi_2, \theta) \in X \times \Theta \tag{A6.32}$$

By (i) and (A6.30),

$$\log\left\{\frac{\partial f(\psi_1 \mid \theta)}{\partial \psi_{1h}}\right\} < \log\{u_p\}, \qquad \forall (\psi_1, \theta) \in X \times \Theta \tag{A6.33}$$

By (A6.32) and (A6.33)

$$\log\{f(\psi_2 \mid \theta)\} + \log\left\{\frac{\partial f(\psi_1 \mid \theta)}{\partial \psi_{1h}}\right\} < \log\{u_f\} + \log\{u_p\},$$

$$\forall ((\psi_1, \psi_2), \theta) \in X^2 \times \Theta \tag{A6.34}$$

Therefore, using (A6.34), we get

$$\log\left\{f(\psi_2 \mid \theta) \cdot \frac{\partial f(\psi_1 \mid \theta)}{\partial \psi_{1h}}\right\} < \log\{u_f \cdot u_p\}, \qquad \forall ((\psi_1, \psi_2), \theta) \in X^2 \times \Theta \tag{A6.35}$$

By (A6.29),

$$2 \cdot \log\{f(\psi_1 \mid \theta) + f(\psi_2 \mid \theta)\} > 2 \cdot \log\{2 \cdot \ell_f\}, \qquad \forall ((\psi_1, \psi_2), \theta) \in X^2 \times \Theta \tag{A6.36}$$

Therefore, using (A6.35) and (A6.36), we get

$$\log\left\{ f(\psi_2 \mid \theta) \cdot \frac{\partial f(\psi_1 \mid \theta)}{\partial \psi_{1h}} \right\} - 2 \cdot \log\{ f(\psi_1 \mid \theta) + f(\psi_2 \mid \theta)\}$$

$$< \log\{ u_f \cdot u_p\} - 2 \cdot \log\{2 \cdot \ell_f\}, \qquad \forall ((\psi_1, \psi_2), \theta) \in X^2 \times \Theta \qquad \text{(A6.37)}$$

Therefore, by (A6.37),

$$\frac{f(\psi_2 \mid \theta) \cdot [\partial f(\psi_1 \mid \theta) / \partial \psi_{1h}]}{[f(\psi_1 \mid \theta) + f(\psi_2 \mid \theta)]^2} < \frac{u_f \cdot u_p}{4 \cdot \ell_f^2}, \qquad \forall ((\psi_1, \psi_2), \theta) \in X^2 \times \Theta$$

$$\text{(A6.38)}$$

Therefore, by (A6.31) and (A6.38), if (i) holds, then $h((\psi_1, \psi_2), \theta) = \{[f(\psi_2 \mid \theta) \cdot \partial f(\psi_1 \mid \theta) / \partial \psi_{1h}] / [f(\psi_1 \mid \theta) + f(\psi_2 \mid \theta)]^2\}$ is a bounded function of $((\psi_1, \psi_2), \theta)$ on $X^2 \times \Theta$.

Suppose (ii) holds (i.e., $\ell_p < 0 < \ell_u$). For each $((\psi_1, \psi_2), \theta) \in X^2 \times \Theta$ where $\partial f(\psi_1 \mid \theta) / \partial \psi_{1h} > 0$, the argument leading to (A6.38) applies once again. In each remaining case (using the fact that f is a positive, real-valued function), we get

$$\frac{f(\psi_2 \mid \theta) \cdot [\partial f(\psi_1 \mid \theta) / \partial \psi_{1h}]}{[f(\psi_1 \mid \theta) + f(\psi_2 \mid \theta)]^2} \leq 0 \qquad \text{(A6.39)}$$

In addition, by (ii) and (A6.29),

$$\frac{u_f \cdot u_p}{4 \cdot \ell_f^2} > 0 \qquad \text{(A6.40)}$$

Therefore, by (A6.39) and (A6.40), the inequality in (A6.38) also holds at each $((\psi_1, \psi_2), \theta) \in X^2 \times \Theta$ where $\partial f(\psi_1 \mid \theta) / \partial \psi_{1h} \leq 0$. Therefore, if (ii) holds, then (A6.38) (once again) holds. The next step is to obtain a lower bound. Consider any $((\psi_1, \psi_2), \theta) \in X^2 \times \Theta$ where $\partial f(\psi_1 \mid \theta) / \partial \psi_{1h} < 0$. Then, by (ii) and (A6.30),

$$\log\left\{ -\frac{\partial f(\psi_1 \mid \theta)}{\partial f_{1h}} \right\} < \log\{-\ell_p\} \qquad \text{(A6.41)}$$

As in case (i), we can use the fact that (A6.29) implies (A6.32). Using (A6.32) together with (A6.41) gives

$$\log\{ f(\psi_2 \mid \theta)\} + \log\left\{ -\frac{\partial f(\psi_1 \mid \theta)}{\partial \psi_{1h}} \right\} < \log\{u_f\} + \log\{-\ell_p\} \qquad \text{(A6.42)}$$

Therefore, by (A6.42),

$$\log\left\{-f(\psi_2\mid\theta)\cdot\frac{\partial f(\psi_1\mid\theta)}{\partial\psi_{1h}}\right\} < \log\{-u_f\cdot\ell_p\} \tag{A6.43}$$

Also as in case (i), we can use the fact that (A6.29) implies (A6.36). Using (A6.36) together with (A6.43) gives

$$\log\left\{-f(\psi_2\mid\theta)\cdot\frac{\partial f(\psi_1\mid\theta)}{\partial\psi_{1h}}\right\} - 2\cdot\log\{f(\psi_1\mid\theta)+f(\psi_2\mid\theta)\}$$

$$< \log\{-u_f\cdot\ell_p\} - 2\cdot\log\{2\cdot\ell_p\} \tag{A6.44}$$

Therefore, by (A6.44),

$$\frac{-f(\psi_2\mid\theta)\cdot[\partial f(\psi_1\mid\theta)/\partial\psi_{1h}]}{[f(\psi_1\mid\theta)+f(\psi_2\mid\theta)]^2} < \frac{-u_f\cdot u_p}{4\cdot\ell_f^2} \tag{A6.45}$$

Therefore, by (A6.45)

$$\frac{u_f\cdot u_p}{4\cdot\ell_f^2} < \frac{f(\psi_2\mid\theta)\cdot[\partial f(\psi_1\mid\theta)/\partial\psi_{1h}]}{[f(\psi_1\mid\theta)+f(\psi_2\mid\theta)]^2} \tag{A6.46}$$

Now consider any $[(\psi_1,\psi_2,\theta] \in X^2\times\Theta$ where $\partial f(\psi_1\mid\theta)/\partial\psi_{1h}\geq 0$. Using the fact that $f(x\mid\theta)$ is a positive, real-valued function, we obtain

$$\frac{f(\psi_2\mid\theta)\cdot[\partial f(\psi_1\mid\theta)/\partial\psi_{1h}]}{[f(\psi_1\mid\theta)+f(\psi_2\mid\theta)]^2} \geq 0 \tag{A6.47}$$

In addition, from (ii) and (A6.29),

$$\frac{u_f\cdot u_p}{4\cdot\ell_f^2} < 0 \tag{A6.48}$$

Therefore, by (A6.47) and (A6.48), (A6.46) once again holds. Hence, $[u_f\cdot\ell_p]/[4\cdot\ell_f^2]$ is a lower bound. Summing up, we have established that if (ii) holds, then $\{f(\psi_2\mid\theta)\cdot[\partial f(\psi_1\mid\theta)/\partial\psi_{1h}]\}/\{[f(\psi_1\mid\theta)]^2\}$ is a bounded function of $((\psi_1,\psi_2),\theta)$ on $X^2\times\Theta$.

Suppose (iii) holds (i.e., $u_p\leq 0$). Using (A6.29) and (A6.30), we immediately have

$$\frac{f(\psi_2\mid\theta)\cdot[\partial f(\psi_1\mid\theta)/\partial\psi_{1h}]}{[f(\psi_1\mid\theta)+f(\psi_2\mid\theta)]^2} \leq 0 \qquad \forall((\psi_1,\psi_2),\theta)\in X^2\times\Theta \tag{A6.49}$$

From (iii) and (A6.29), it follows that $\ell_p < 0$. As a consequence, the argument establishing a lower bound for case (ii) applies again. Therefore, if (iii) holds, then $h((\psi_1,\psi_2),\theta) = \{f(\psi_2\mid\theta)\cdot[\partial f(\psi_1\mid\theta)/\partial f_{1h}]\}/\{[f(\psi_1\mid\theta)+f(\psi_2\mid\theta)]^2\}$ is a bounded function of $((\psi_1,\psi_2),\theta)$ on $X^2\times\Theta$.

By the conclusions established at the ends of the three preceding paragraphs, $h((\psi_1, \psi_2), \theta) = \{f(\psi_2 \mid \theta) \cdot [\partial f(\psi_1 \mid \theta) / \partial f_{1h}]\} / \{[f(\psi_1 \mid \theta) + f(\psi_2 \mid \theta)]^2\}$ is a bounded function of $((\psi_1, \psi_2), \theta)$ on $X^2 \times \Theta$. Let b_ℓ and b_u denote lower and upper bounds, respectively. Let g denote the function on Φ that satisfies $g(\phi) = \max\{|b_\ell|, |b_u|\}$, $\forall\, \phi \in \Phi$. Since $g(\phi)$ is a constant function and $u = \mu$ is a probability measure, $g(\phi)$ is integrable with respect to (Φ, Ξ, v). In addition, by using (A6.23) and the definition of g,

$$|\xi_t(\phi)| = \left| \frac{f(\psi_2' \mid \theta) \cdot [\partial f(\psi_1' \mid \phi) / \partial \psi_{1h}]}{[f(\psi_1' \mid \theta) + f(\psi_2' \mid \theta)]^2} \right| \leq \max\{|b_\ell|, |b_u| = g(\phi), \qquad \forall\, \phi, \forall\, t$$

(A6.50)

Therefore, also using the conclusion established at the end of the paragraph that contains (A6.28), we obtain the premise of the well-known result stated right before this proof is satisfied. Therefore, substituting from (A6.22), (A6.23), and (A6.28) into (A6.21) gives

$$\lim_{t \to \infty} \int_\Theta \left\{ \frac{f(\psi_2' \mid \theta) \cdot [\partial f(\psi_1' \mid \phi) / \partial \psi_{1h}]}{[f(\psi_1' \mid \theta) + f(\psi_2' \mid \theta)]^2} \right\} d\mu(\theta)$$

$$= \int_\Theta \left\{ \frac{f(\psi_2' \mid \theta) \cdot [\partial f(\psi_1' \mid \phi) / \partial \psi_{1h}]}{[f(\psi_1' \mid \theta) + f(\psi_2' \mid \theta)]^2} \right\} d\mu(\theta) \qquad \text{(A6.51)}$$

Therefore, each of the partial derivatives in (A6.11) is continuous at every $(\psi_1^*, \psi_2^*) \in S \times S$. By a similar argument, each of the partial derivatives in (A6.12) is also continuous at every $(\psi_1^*, \psi_2^*) \in S \times S$. Therefore (referring back to the end of the first paragraph in this proof), we find that the proposition holds.

QED

Appendix 6.2: Proofs of Theorems 6.1 and 6.2

Proof of Theorem 6.1

By (A6.3), $P\ell_e^1(x, y) = -P\ell_e^1(y, x)$, $\forall\, x, y \in X$. Therefore, (6.3) implies $P(w, z)$, $\forall\, w, z \in T(\psi)$. In other words, the candidates' directional game is symmetric and zero-sum. Consequently, $(w^*, z^*) \in T(\psi) \times T(\psi)$ is a directional electoral equilibrium if and only if both (w^*, w^*) and (z^*, z^*) are also directional electoral equilibria. Additionally, (6.3), (6.4), and the symmetry of the directional game between the candidates imply that (w^*, w^*) is a directional electoral equilibrium at ψ if and only if

$$D_{(u,w^*)} P\ell_e^1(\psi, \psi) \le D_{(w^*,w^*)} P\ell_e^1(\psi, \psi) = 0 \qquad (A6.52)$$

for every $u \in T(\psi)$.

By (6.3), (A6.52) is equivalent to

$$\sum_{h=1}^{n} \left\{ \frac{\partial P\ell_e^1(\psi, \psi)}{\partial \psi_{1h}} \right\} \cdot u_h + \sum_{h=1}^{n} \left\{ \frac{\partial P\ell_e^1(\psi, \psi)}{\partial \psi_{2h}} \right\} \cdot w_h^* \le 0 \qquad (A6.53)$$

for every $u \in T(\psi)$.

Now, the fact that $P\ell_e^1(x, y) = -P\ell_e^1(y, x), \forall\, x, y \in X$ implies

$$\frac{\partial P\ell_e^1(\psi, \psi)}{\partial \psi_{2h}} = -\frac{\partial P\ell_e^1(\psi, \psi)}{\partial \psi_{1h}} \qquad (A6.54)$$

Therefore, (A6.53) is equivalent to

$$\sum_{h=1}^{n} \left\{ \frac{\partial P\ell_e^1(\psi, \psi)}{\partial \psi_{1h}} \right\} \cdot u_h - \sum_{h=1}^{n} \left\{ \frac{\partial P\ell_e^1(\psi, \psi)}{\partial \psi_{2h}} \right\} \cdot w_h^* \le 0 \qquad (A6.55)$$

for every $u \in T(\psi)$.

Finally, (A6.55) is equivalent to

$$D_{(u,0)} P\ell_e^1(\psi, \psi) \le D_{(w^*,0)} P\ell_e^1(\psi, \psi) \qquad (A6.56)$$

for each $u \in T(\psi)$.

By a similar argument, (z^*, z^*) is a directional electoral equilibrium at ψ if and only if

$$D_{(0,v)} P\ell_e^1(\psi, \psi) \le D_{(0, z^*)} P\ell_e^1(\psi, \psi) \qquad (A6.57)$$

for each $v \in T(\psi)$.

Hence, the theorem follows.

$$\text{QED}$$

Proof of Theorem 6.2

At any $\psi \in S$,

$$D_{(u,0)} P\ell_e^1(x, \psi)\big|_{x=\psi} = \sum_{h=1}^{n} \left\{ \frac{\partial P\ell_e^1(x, \psi)}{\partial x_{1h}} \bigg|_{x=\psi} \right\} \cdot u_h \qquad (A6.58)$$

Therefore, $D_{(u,0)} P\ell_e^1(x, \psi)\big|_{x=\psi}$ is linear as a function if the vector $u \in E^n$.

By lemma 4.2, p. 206, Hestenes (1975), the tangent space of S at ψ is closed. Therefore, the intersection of the unit sphere in E^n (which is compact) and the tangent space of S at ψ is compact. Therefore, since S is the union of the resulting compact set with the zero vector in E^n, it follows that $T(\psi)$ is compact.

Combining the linearity of $D_{(u,0)}P\ell_e^1(x, \psi)|_{x=\psi}$ (as a function of u) with the compactness of $T(\psi)$, we find that $D_{(u,0)}P\ell_e^1(x, \psi)|_{x=\psi}$ achieves a maximum over this set. Denote this vector by w^*.

By a similar argument, there also exists a z^* that solves

$$\min_{v \in T(\psi)} D_{(0,v)}P\ell_e^1(\psi_1, \psi_2) \tag{A6.59}$$

at $\psi_1 = \psi_2 = \psi$.

Finally, by Theorem 6.1, $(w^*, z^*) \in T(\psi) \times T(\psi)$ is a directional electoral equilibrium at ψ.

QED

Appendix 6.3: Proofs of Theorems 6.3 and 6.4

The following lemma is used in the proofs of Theorems 6.3 and 6.4. In stating them, we assume as an unstated premise an election in which (i) there is a compact set of possible locations for the candidates and (ii) the candidates use a C^1 binary Luce model for the voters' selection probabilities.

Lemma 6.3

At each $x \in X$, the integral given by (6.8) exists.

Proof of Lemma 6.3

Consider any $x \in X$. First, since each $f(x \mid \theta)$ is a positive, real-valued function, $\log[f(x \mid \theta)]$ is defined for every $\theta \in \Theta$. Second, since $f(x \mid \theta)$ is a bounded function of θ whose lower bound is strictly positive (see Section 6.1), $\log[f(x \mid \theta)]$ is a bounded function of θ. Let b_u and b_ℓ denote the upper and lower bounds, respectively.

By the definition of the natural logarithm, for each $k \in E^1$,

$$\{\theta \in \Theta : \log[f(x \mid \theta)] > k\} = \{\theta \in \Theta : f(x \mid \theta) > e^k\} \tag{A6.60}$$

Since $f(x \mid \theta)$ is a measurable function of θ, for each $k \in E^1$, the set $\{\theta \in \Theta : f(x \mid \theta) > e^k\}$ is a measurable set. Therefore, by (A6.60), for each $k \in E^1$, the set $\{\theta \in \Theta : \log[f(x \mid \theta)] > k\}$ is a measurable set. Therefore, $\log[f(x \mid \theta)]$ is a measurable function of θ. Therefore (also using what was proven in the first paragraph in this proof), we have

$$\int_\Theta b_\ell\, d\mu(\theta) \le \int_\Theta \log[f(x\,|\,\theta)]\, d\mu(\theta) \le \int_\Theta b_u\, d\mu(\theta) \qquad (A6.61)$$

Therefore, since μ is a probability measure and $b_\ell, b_u \in E^1$,

$$-\infty < b_\ell \le \int_\Theta \log[f(x\,|\,\theta)]\, d\mu(\theta) \le b_u < +\infty \qquad (A6.62)$$

Consequently, the integral given by (6.8) exists.

QED

We now let $W_e(x)$ denote the function on X that satisfies (6.8) at each $x \in X$.

Lemma 6.4

Let S be any open set such that $S \subset \mathcal{L} \subseteq \text{int}(X)$. At each $x \in S$, the partial derivatives of $W_e(x)$ exist and satisfy

$$\frac{\partial W_e(x')}{\partial x_h} = \int_\Theta \frac{\partial f(x'\,|\,\theta)/\partial x_h}{f(x'\,|\,\theta)}\, d\mu(\theta), \qquad h = 1,\ldots,n \qquad (A6.63)$$

Proof of Lemma 6.4

Consider any $x \in S$ and $h \in \{1,\ldots,n\}$. Let ϕ be the variable θ and let t be the variable x_h. Also let $(\phi, \Xi, \nu) = (\Theta, \Sigma, \mu)$ and let $k(\phi, t) = r(\theta, x_h) = \log[f(x'_1,\ldots,x'_{h-1},x_h,x'_{h+1},\ldots,x'_n)\,|\,\theta)]$.

Since $f(x\,|\,\theta)$ is C^1 on X, $\log(y)$ is C^1 at each $y > 0$, and $f(x\,|\,\theta) > 0$ at each $(\theta, x) \in \Theta \times X$, it follows that, at each $x \in X$, $\partial \log[f(x\,|\,\theta)]/\partial x_h$ exists and satisfies

$$\frac{\partial \log[f(x\,|\,\theta)]}{\partial x_h} = \frac{\partial f(x\,|\,\theta)/\partial x_h}{f(x\,|\,\theta)} \qquad (A6.64)$$

(e.g., see theorem 12.7, Apostol, 1974, p. 352).

By the assumptions in Section 6.1, $f(x\,|\,\theta)$ and $\partial f(x\,|\,\theta)/\partial x_h$ are bounded, real-valued functions of (x, θ) on $X \times \Theta$ with the lower bound on $f(x\,|\,\theta)$ being strictly positive. Therefore, by (A6.64), $\partial \log[f(x\,|\,\theta)]/\partial x_h$ is a bounded, real-valued function of (x, θ) on $X \times \Theta$. Since S is contained in the interior of X, there exist real numbers α, β such that $\{x \in X : [\alpha < x_h < \beta] \text{ and } [x_j - x_j, \forall j \ne h]\} \subset \text{int}(X)$. Consider any such α, β. By what has been established in this paragraph, $\partial k(\phi, t)/\partial t = \partial \log[f((x'_1,\ldots,x'_{h-1},x_h,x'_{h+1},\ldots,x'_n)\,|\,\theta)]/\partial x_h$ is a bounded, real-valued function of $(\phi, t) = (\theta, x_h)$ on $\phi \times [\alpha, \beta] = \Phi \times [\alpha, \beta]$. That is $\exists b \in E^1$ such that

$$\frac{\partial k(\phi, t)}{\partial t} \le b, \qquad \forall (\phi, t) \in \Phi \times [\alpha, \beta] \qquad (A6.65)$$

Let $b(\phi) = b, \forall \phi \in \Phi$. Since (Θ, Σ, μ), and hence also (Φ, Ξ, ν), is a probability measure space, $b(\phi)$ is integrable with respect to (Φ, Ξ, ν). By (A6.65), $b(\phi)$ also satisfies (A6.12). Finally, by what has been established in the proof of Lemma 6.2, $k(\phi, t)$ is integrable with respect to (Φ, Ξ, ν) at each $t \in [\alpha, \beta]$. Therefore, the premise of the theorem stated immediately before the proof of Lemma 6.2 is satisfied. That theorem, therefore, directly implies that

$$K(t) = \int_\Phi k(\phi, t) \, d\nu(\phi) \tag{A6.66}$$

is differentiable on $[\alpha, \beta]$ and

$$\frac{dK(t)}{dt} = \int_\Phi \frac{\partial k(\phi, t)}{\partial t} \, d\nu(\phi) \tag{A6.67}$$

Therefore, substituting in the notation from the model and evaluating the functions involved at $t = x_h$, we find that $\partial W_e(x) / \partial x_h$ exists at $x = x'$ and satisfies

$$\frac{\partial W_e(x')}{\partial x_h} = \int_\Theta \frac{\partial \log[f(x' \mid \theta)]}{\partial x_h} \, d\mu(\theta) \tag{A6.68}$$

Therefore, by (A6.68) and (A6.64),

$$\frac{\partial W_e(x')}{\partial x_h} = \int_\Theta \frac{\partial f(x' \mid \theta) / \partial x_h}{f(x' \mid \theta)} \, d\mu(\theta) \tag{A6.69}$$

QED

For any given $\psi \in S$, we let $P\ell_e^1(x, \psi)$ and $P\ell_e^2(\psi, x)$ denote the corresponding functions on X that satisfy (6.1) at each $x \in X$.

Lemma 6.5

Let $\psi \in S$ be given. Let S be any open set such that $S \subset \mathcal{L} \subseteq \text{int}(X)$. At each $x \in S$, the partial derivatives of $P\ell_e^1(x, \psi)$ and $P\ell_e^2(\psi, x)$ exist and satisfy

$$\frac{\partial P\ell_e^1(x, \psi)}{\partial x_h} = \frac{\partial P\ell_e^2(\psi, x)}{\partial x_h}$$

$$= 2 \cdot \int_\Theta \frac{f(\psi \mid \theta) \cdot [\partial f(x \mid \theta) / \partial x_h]}{[f(x \mid \theta) + f(\psi \mid \theta)]^2} \, d\mu(\theta),$$

$$h = 1, \ldots, n \tag{A6.70}$$

Proof of Lemma 6.5

This proof follows directly from Lemma 6.2.

QED

Lemma 6.6

$W_e(x)$ is C^1 on S.

Proof of Lemma 6.6

Let S be any open set such that $S \subset \mathcal{A} \subseteq \text{int}(X)$. Lemma 6.4 has already established that at each $x \in S$ the partial derivatives of $W_e(x)$ exist and satisfy (A6.63). Therefore, showing that the partial derivatives given by (A6.63) are continuous on S will establish this lemma.

Consider any particular $h \in \{1, \ldots, n\}$ and $x^* \in S$. Choose any infinite sequence $\{x'\}$ in S that converges to x^*. As in Appendix 6.1, let

$$(\Phi, \Xi, v) \equiv (\Theta, \Sigma, \mu) \tag{A6.71}$$

for each t, and let ξ_t be the function on $\Phi = \Theta$, which satisfies

$$\xi_t(\phi) = \frac{\partial f(x' \mid \phi) / \partial x_h}{f(x' \mid \phi)} \tag{A6.72}$$

at each $\phi \in \Phi$.

Since $x' \in S$, $\forall t$, it follows, by (A6.72) and the same logic as in the proof of Lemma 6.2, that $\{\xi_t\}$ is a sequence of functions that are integrable with respect to (Φ, Ξ, v). Consider any particular $\phi \in \Phi$. Since $f(x \mid \theta)$ is C^1 in x, both $\partial f(x \mid \phi) / \partial x_h$ and $f(x \mid \theta)$ are continuous in x. Therefore, since $\{x'\}$ converges to x^*,

$$\lim_{t \to \infty} \left[\frac{\partial f(x' \mid \phi)}{\partial x_h} \right] = \frac{\partial f(x^* \mid \theta)}{\partial x_h} \tag{A6.73}$$

and, also using the fact that $f(x \mid \theta)$ is a positive, real-valued function,

$$\lim_{t \to \infty} [f(x' \mid \phi)] = f(x^* \mid \phi) > 0 \tag{A6.74}$$

Therefore, by (A6.73) and (A6.74),

$$\lim_{t \to \infty} \left[\frac{\partial f(x' \mid \phi) / \partial x_h}{f(x' \mid \phi)} \right] = \frac{\lim_{t \to \infty}[f(x' \mid \phi) / \partial x_h]}{\lim_{t \to \infty}[f(x' \mid \phi)]} = \frac{\partial f(x^* \mid \phi) / \partial x_h}{f(x^* \mid \phi)}$$

(A6.75)

(e.g., see theorem 12, p. 44, Buck, 1978).

Now, let ξ be the function on Φ that satisfies

$$\xi(\phi) = \frac{\partial f(x^* \mid \phi) / \partial x_h}{f(x^* \mid \phi)} \tag{A6.76}$$

at each $\phi \in \Phi$. By (A6.76) and the fact that f is a C^1, positive, real-valued function on X, it follows that ξ is real-valued. In addition, by (A6.76) and the logic used in the proof of Lemma 6.2, it follows that ξ is integrable with respect to (Φ, Ξ, ν). Therefore, by (A6.72), (A6.75), and (A6.76), $\{\xi_t\}$ is a sequence of functions, integrable with respect to the given measure space (Φ, Ξ, ν), that converge to a real-valued function that is integrable with respect to the same measure space.

From the second regularity assumption in Section 6.1 and arguments similar to those used to establish the boundedness of $h((\psi_1, \psi_2), \theta) = \{f(\psi_2 \mid \theta) \cdot [\partial f(\psi_1 \mid \theta) / \partial \psi_{1h}]\} / \{[f(\psi_1 \mid \theta) + f(\psi_2 \mid \theta)]^2\}$ (in the proof of Proposition 6.4), it follows that $[\partial f(x \mid \theta) / \partial x_h] / f(x \mid \theta)$ is a bounded function of (x, θ) on $X \times \Theta$. Let b_ℓ and b_u denote lower and upper bounds, respectively. Let g denote the function on Φ that satisfies $g(\phi) = \max\{|b_\ell|, |b_u|\}$, $\forall \phi \in \Phi$. Since g is a constant function and $\nu = \mu$ is a probability measure, g is integrable with respect to (Φ, Ξ, ν). In addition, by construction, $|\xi_t(\phi)| \le g(\phi)$, $\forall \phi$, $\forall t$. Therefore (also using the conclusion at the end of the preceding paragraph), the premise of the well-known result stated right before the proof of Proposition 6.4 is satisfied. Therefore, substituting from (A6.71), (A6.72), and (A6.76) into (A6.21) gives

$$\lim_{t \to \infty} \int_\Theta \frac{\partial f(x^t \mid \theta) / \partial x_h}{f(x^t \mid \theta)} \, d\mu(\theta) = \int_\Theta \frac{\partial f(x^* \mid \theta) / \partial x_h}{f(x^* \mid \theta)} \, d\mu(\theta) \tag{A6.77}$$

Finally, since (A6.77) holds for each choice of $h \in \{1, \ldots, n\}$ and $x^* \in \mathcal{L}$ and any sequence $\{x^t\}$ that converges to x^*, the partial derivatives given by (A6.63) are continuous on $\mathcal{L}$. Therefore, $W_e(x)$ is C^1 on S.

QED

Lemma 6.7

Let $\psi \in S$ be given. $P\ell_e^1(x, \psi)$ and $P\ell_e^2(\psi, x)$ are C^1 in x on S.

Proof of Lemma 6.7

This proof follows directly from Proposition 6.4.

QED

Proof of Theorem 6.3

By the definition of a stationary electoral equilibrium (see Section 6.4), there is a stationary electoral equilibrium at ψ if and only if the zero vector in E^{2n} is a directional electoral equilibrium at ψ. Therefore, from (6.3) and the definition of a directional electoral equilibrium (see Section 6.5), there is a stationary electoral equilibrium at ψ if and only if

$$D_{(u,0)}P\ell_e^1(\psi_1, \psi_2) \leq D_{(0,0)}P\ell_e^1(\psi_1, \psi_2) \leq D_{(0,v)}P\ell_e^1(\psi_1, \psi_2),$$
$$\forall\, u, v \in T(\psi) \tag{A6.78}$$

at $\psi_1 = \psi_2 = \psi$. Therefore, from (A6.78) and the definition of a directional derivative, there is a stationary electoral equilibrium at ψ if and only if

$$D_u P\ell_e^1(x, \psi) \leq 0 \leq D_v P\ell_e^1(\psi, x), \qquad \forall\, u, v \in T(\psi) \tag{A6.79}$$

at $x = \psi$.

By Lemma 6.7, $P\ell_e^1(x, \psi)$ and $P\ell_e^2(\psi, x)$ are C^1 in x on S. In the proof of Theorem 6.1 in Appendix 6.2, it was noted that $P\ell_e^1(w, z) = -P\ell_e^2(z, w)$, $\forall\, w, z \in X$. This, in turn, implies that $\partial\{P\ell_e^1(\psi, x)\}/\partial x_h = -\partial\{P\ell_e^2(\psi, x)\}/\partial x_h$, $\forall\, h \in \{1, \ldots, n\}$. Therefore, $P\ell_e^1(\psi, x) = -P\ell_e^2(\psi, x)$ is also C^1 in x on S. Therefore, it follows that the directional derivative $D_u P\ell_e^1(x, \psi)|_{x=\psi}$ equals the inner product of $\nabla_x P\ell_e^1(x, \psi)|_{x=\psi}$ with u and that (similarly) the directional derivative $D_v P\ell_e^1(\psi, x)|_{x=\psi}$ equals the inner product of $\nabla_x P\ell_e^1(x, \psi)|_{x=\psi}$ with v (e.g., see theorems 12.11 and 12.15, Apostol, 1974). Therefore, using the conclusion at the end of the preceding paragraph, we find a stationary electoral equilibrium at the location ψ if and only if

$$\sum_{h=1}^{n}\left\{\frac{\partial}{\partial x_h} P\ell_e^1(x, \psi)\right\} \cdot u_h \leq 0 \leq \sum_{h=1}^{n}\left\{\frac{\partial}{\partial x_h} P\ell_e^2(\psi, x)\right\} \cdot v_h,$$
$$\forall\, u, v \in T(\psi) \tag{A6.80}$$

at $x = \psi$. Therefore [from (A6.80) plus, once again, the fact that $P\ell_e^1(w, z) = -P\ell_e^2(z, w)$, $\forall\, w, z \in X$ implies that $\partial\{P\ell_e^1(x, \psi)\}/\partial x_h = -\partial\{P\ell_e^2(\psi, x)\}/\partial x_h$, $\forall\, h \in \{1, \ldots, n\}$], it follows that there is a stationary electoral equilibrium at ψ if and only if

$$\sum_{h=1}^{n}\left\{\frac{\partial}{\partial x_h} P\ell_e^1(x, \psi)\right\} \cdot u_h \leq 0 \leq \sum_{h=1}^{n}-\left\{\frac{\partial}{\partial x_h} P\ell_e^2(\psi, x)\right\} \cdot v_h,$$
$$\forall\, u, v \in T(\psi) \tag{A6.81}$$

at $x = \psi$. Therefore, by (A6.81) and Lemma 6.2, there is a stationary electoral equilibrium at ψ if and only if

$$\sum_{h=1}^{n}\left\{2 \cdot \int_{\Theta}\left[\frac{f(\psi \mid \theta) \cdot \partial f(x \mid \theta) / \partial x_h}{(f(x \mid \theta) + f(\psi \mid \theta))^2}\right] d\mu(\theta)\right\} \cdot u_h \leq 0,$$

$$\forall u \in T(\psi) \qquad \text{(A6.82)}$$

at $x = \psi$. Therefore, substituting $x = \psi$ into (A6.82) and then using an argument analogous to that carried out in (A4.35), we find a stationary electoral equilibrium at ψ if and only if

$$\sum_{h=1}^{n}\left\{\int_{\Theta}\left[\frac{\partial f(x \mid \theta) / \partial x_h|_{x=\psi}}{2 \cdot f(\psi \mid \theta)}\right] d\mu(\theta)\right\} \cdot u_h \leq 0, \qquad \forall u \in T(\psi) \qquad \text{(A6.83)}$$

Therefore, by (A6.83) we find a stationary electoral equilibrium at ψ if and only if

$$\sum_{h=1}^{n}\left\{\int_{\Theta}\left[\frac{\partial f(x \mid \theta) / \partial x_h|_{x=\psi}}{f(\psi \mid \theta)}\right] d\mu(\theta)\right\} \cdot u_h \leq 0, \qquad \forall u \in T(\psi) \qquad \text{(A6.84)}$$

By Lemma 6.6, $W_e(x)$ is C^1 on S. Therefore, it follows that

$$D_u W_e(\psi) = \sum_{h=1}^{n}\left\{\frac{\partial}{\partial x_h} W_e(x)\bigg|_{x=\psi}\right\} \cdot u_h, \qquad \forall u \in T(\psi) \qquad \text{(A6.85)}$$

(e.g., see theorems 12.11 and 12.5, Apostol, 1974). Therefore, by (A6.85) and Lemma 6.4,

$$D_u W_e(\psi) = \sum_{h=1}^{n}\left\{\int_{\Theta}\frac{\partial f(x \mid \theta) / \partial x_h|_{x=\psi}}{f(\psi \mid \theta)} d\mu(\theta)\right\} \cdot u_h \leq 0,$$

$$\forall u \in T(\psi) \qquad \text{(A6.86)}$$

Therefore, using (A6.86) and the conclusion at the end of the preceding paragraph, we find a stationary electoral equilibrium at ψ if and only if

$$D_u W_e(\psi) \leq 0, \qquad \forall u \in T(\psi) \qquad \text{(A6.87)}$$

Therefore, by the definition of a stationary outcome (see Section 6.4), there is a stationary electoral equilibrium at ψ if and only if ψ is a stationary outcome for the social objective function $W : S \to E^1$ that satisfies (6.8) at each $x \in S$.

QED

The proof of Theorem 6.4 uses the following well-known result (e.g., see theorem 6.1, p. 214, Hestenes, 1975).

Theorem

Suppose that $Y \subseteq Z \subseteq E^n$ and that $g : Z \to E^1$ is C^1 on Y. If $x \in Y$ is a local maximum point of g on the set Y, then

$$D_h g(x) \leq 0 \qquad\qquad (A6.88)$$

holds for each vector h in the tangent space of Y at x.

Proof of Theorem 6.4

By Lemma 6.6, $W_e(x)$ is C^1 on S. Therefore, $W_e(x)$ is continuous on S. Therefore, since S (the set of possible locations for the candidates) is compact, Weierstrass' (or the extreme value) theorem implies that there exists $\psi^* \in S$ where $W_e(x)$ achieves its maximum on S (e.g., see theorem 5.1, Sydsaeter, 1981). Since ψ^* maximizes W_e on S, ψ^* is (also) a local maximum point of $W_e(x)$ on S. Therefore, since $W_e(x)$ is C^1 on S, the theorem stated right before this proof implies that (6.7) is satisfied at ψ^*. Therefore (by the definitions in Section 6.4), ψ^* is a stationary outcome for the social log-scaling function W. Therefore, by Theorem 6.3, there is a stationary electoral outcome at ψ^*. Therefore, since ψ^* is an element of S, there exists a location in S at which there is an electoral equilibrium.

QED

Appendix 6.4: Proofs of Theorems 6.5–6.11

Proof of Theorem 6.5

This theorem follows from arguments similar to those that were used in Appendix 5.1 to prove Theorem 5.1.

QED

Proof of Theorem 6.6

This theorem follows from arguments similar to those that we used in Appendix 5.2 to prove Theorem 5.2.

QED

Proof of Theorem 6.7

This theorem follows from arguments similar to those that were used in Appendix 5.3 to prove Theorem 5.3.

QED

Proof of Theorem 6.8

This theorem follows from arguments similar to those that were used in Appendix 5.3 to prove Theorem 5.4.

QED

Note

The reason why the assumption that S is convex has been included in the premises of Theorems 6.6–6.8 is because the well-known theorems that were applied in the proofs of Theorems 5.2–5.4 are used here as well.

The proof of Theorem 6.9 uses the following well-known result (e.g., see theorem 6.2, p. 215, Hestenes, 1975).

Theorem

Suppose that $Y \subseteq Z \subseteq E^t$ (where Y is convex) and that $g: Z \to E^1$ is C^1 and concave on Y. Then $x \in Y$ is a global maximum point of g on Y if and only if

$$D_h g(x) \le 0 \tag{A6.89}$$

holds for each tangent vector h of Y at x.

Proof of Theorem 6.9

By Proposition 6.3, $s \in S$ is a global electoral outcome if and only if (s, s) is a global electoral equilibrium. By definition, (s, s) is a global electoral equilibrium if and only if

$$P\ell^1(\psi_1, s) \le P\ell^1(s, s) \le P\ell^1(s, \psi_2), \qquad \forall\, \psi_1, \psi_2 \in S \tag{A6.90}$$

Since $P\ell^1_e$ is an extension of $P\ell^1$, this implies that (s, s) is an electoral equilibrium if and only if both

$$P\ell^1_e(s, s) \ge P\ell^1_e(\psi_1, s), \qquad \forall\, \psi_1 \in S \tag{A6.91}$$

and

$$P\ell_e^1(s, s) \le P\ell_e^1(s, \psi_2), \qquad \forall\, \psi_2 \in S \tag{A6.92}$$

are satisfied. In the proof of Theorem 6.1 (in Appendix 6.2), it was noted that

$$P\ell_e^1(w, z) = -P\ell_e^1(z, w), \qquad \forall\, w, z \in S \tag{A6.93}$$

Therefore, by (A6.93), the inequalities in (A6.92) are satisfied if and only if

$$-P\ell_e^1(s. s) \le -P\ell_e^1(\psi, s), \qquad \forall\, \psi \in S \tag{A6.94}$$

Therefore, since (A6.94) is also equivalent to (A6.91), it follows that (s, s) is a global electoral equilibrium if and only if (A6.91) is satisfied. Hence, (s, s) is a global electoral equilibrium if and only if x maximizes $P\ell_e^1(\psi_1, s)$ (as a function of ψ_1) on S.

By Theorem 6.5 the premise of this theorem implies that $P\ell_e^1(\psi_1, s)$ is a concave function of ψ_1 on S. By Lemma 6.5, the theorem's premise also implies that $P\ell_e^1(\psi_1, s)$ is a C^1 function of ψ_1 on S. What is more, the premise also explicitly assumes that S is convex. Therefore, by the well-known theorem stated right before this proof, s is a global maximum point of $P\ell_e^1(\psi_1, s)$ (as a function of ψ_1) on S if and only if

$$D_u P\ell_e^1(\psi_1, s) \le 0, \qquad \forall\, u \in T(x) \tag{A6.95}$$

at $\psi_1 = s$. Therefore (from the conclusion at the end of the preceding paragraph), (s, s) is a global electoral equilibrium if and only if (A6.63) is satisfied at $\psi_1 = s$. Therefore, from (A6.95) and the definition of a directional derivative, (s, s) is a global electoral equilibrium if and only if

$$D_{(u,0)} P\ell_e^1(\psi_1, \psi_2) \le 0, \qquad \forall\, u \in T(x) \tag{A6.96}$$

at $\psi_1 = \psi_2 = s$. Therefore, from (A6.96) and (6.3), (s, s) is a global electoral equilibrium if and only if, at the location s,

$$P(u, 0) \le 0, \qquad \forall\, u \in T(s) \tag{A6.97}$$

By (6.3), at the location s,

$$P(0, v) = 0 + \sum_{h=1}^{n} \left\{ \frac{\partial}{\partial \psi_{2h}} P\ell_e^1(\psi_1, \psi_2) \right\} v_h \tag{A6.98}$$

at $\psi_1 = \psi_2 = s$. By (A6.93), it follows that

$$\frac{\partial}{\partial \psi_{2h}} P\ell_e^1(\psi_1, \psi_2) = -\frac{\partial}{\partial \psi_{1h}} P\ell_e^1(\psi_1, \psi_2), \qquad h = 1, \ldots, n \tag{A6.99}$$

at $\psi_1 = \psi_2 = s \in S$. Therefore, from (A6.98), (A6.99), and (6.3), it follows that, for each $v \in T(s)$,

$$P(0, v) = -\sum_{h=1}^{n}\left\{\frac{\partial}{\partial\psi_{1h}}\, P\ell_e^1(\psi_1, \psi_2)\right\} v_h = -P(v, 0) \qquad \text{(A6.100)}$$

at $\psi_1 = \psi_2 = s$. Therefore, from the conclusion at the end of the preceding paragraph, (s, s) is a global electoral equilibrium if and only if, at the location s, both (A6.97) and

$$P(0, v) = -P(v, 0) \geq 0, \qquad \forall\, v \in T(s) \qquad \text{(A6.101)}$$

are satisfied.

By (6.3),

$$P(0, 0) = 0 \qquad \text{(A6.102)}$$

Therefore, by (A6.70) and the conclusion at the end of the preceding paragraph, (s, s) is a global electoral equilibrium if and only if

$$P(u, 0) \leq P(0, 0) \leq P(0, v), \qquad \forall\, u, v \in T(x) \qquad \text{(A6.103)}$$

Therefore, from the definition of a stationary electoral equilibrium (see Section 6.4), (s, s) is a global electoral equilibrium if and only if s is a stationary electoral equilibrium. Therefore, by Theorem 6.3, (s, s) is a global electoral equilibrium if and only if s is a stationary outcome for the social log-scaling function W. Using Lemma 5.9 in Appendix 5.4 and the definition of W, we find that W is concave. Therefore, once again by the theorem stated right before this proof, (s, s) is a global electoral equilibrium if and only if s maximizes the social log-scaling function W on S.

QED

Proof of Theorem 6.10

This proof is similar to that of Theorem 6.9.

QED

Proof of Theorem 6.11

This proof is similar to that of Theorem 6.9.

QED

CHAPTER 7

Epilogue

My objective here is to step back from the detailed analyses in Chapters 2–6 and provide a useful perspective on what was accomplished. Specifically, I discuss the broad significance of the results that have been established, focusing on (i) the existence of political equilibria, (ii) the maximization of implicit social welfare functions by these equilibria, (iii) normative interpretations of the implicit social welfare maxima, and (iv) this book's potential for providing the basis for future applications of election models.

7.1 Political equilibria

Stigler (1975, pp. 138–9; 1983, pp. 262–4), Peltzman (1976, 1980), Becker (1983, 1985), and scholars who have applied their models of the public sector, such as Roberts (1984, 1985) and Godek (1985, 1986), have had faith that political equilibria exist. They have therefore simply assumed that a political equilibrium exists, even though, in their analyses, they have neither referred to any existing models nor specified any new models from which this important assumption can be derived.

The election models with abstentions that have been developed by Hinich, Ordeshook, and others (discussed in Section 1.5) are multi-dimensional models in which equilibrium existence results have previously been derived. The role that abstentions played in the derivation of existence results for these models was described by Hinich et al. (1972) as follows: "We show ... that if citizens abstain in a prescribed manner, an electoral equilibrium exists. ... Thus, abstentions yield a majority choice" (p. 145). The idea of relying solely on these results as the basis for studying political equilibria has, however, been objected to on the grounds that "such an equilibrium would presumably fail to exist whenever compulsory voting laws or the salience of the election resulted in high voter turnout" (Kramer, 1977a, p. 696). In line with this, Mueller (1989a) has recently described the abstentions-based equilibrium results as follows: "Equilibria appeared to emerge as a sort of accidental consequence of some voters refusing to vote" (p. 125).

Importantly, this book's multidimensional election models, which do not involve abstentions, also lead to the conclusion that political equilibria exist. Thus, when this book's equilibrium existence results are taken together with the earlier equilibrium existence results for election models with abstentions, they establish that the existence of a political equilibrium can be derived from a multidimensional election model whether or not one assumes that abstentions will occur. Thus, the equilibrium existence results in this book and the complementary existence results that have been derived for models with abstentions together provide a logical foundation for the Stigler–Peltzman–Becker view that political equilibria exist.

7.2 Implicit social welfare functions

Atkinson (1987) described one of Buchanan's "key contributions" (p. 5) as follows:

> He contrasted two opposing views of the state. According to one, "the state is considered as a single decision-making unit acting for society as a whole" [Buchanan (1949)]; the state subsumes all individual interests and aims to maximise social welfare. According to the other, "the state is represented as the sum of its individual members acting in a collective capacity" [Buchanan (1949)]. The government represents only the collective will of individuals and "cannot be assumed to maximise anything." Buchanan's own view is that it is the second of these representations that is relevant to democratic societies. (p. 6)

Atkinson added that this description "reads like a manifesto for [Buchanan's] entire life" (p. 6).

A number of other scholars have also expressed or exemplified one of the important components of Buchanan's manifesto: namely, the position that political decisions should be analyzed with "individualistic" models (i.e., models in which the collective choices that emerge are the end result of the separate decisions of the individuals in the model, e.g., see Buchanan, 1987a,b). Prominent early examples include Wicksell (1896), Arrow (1950, 1951, 1963), Downs (1957a,b), Black (1958), Coase (1960), and Olson (1965). However, Buchanan's manifesto goes beyond this position in that it also asserts that the view that the government can be considered to be maximizing something is separate and opposed to the position that political decisions should be analyzed with individualistic models.

In the election models in this book "the state is represented as the sum of its individual members acting in a collective capacity." That is, these are individualistic models. Significantly, however, the collective choices that emerge from this book's election models are exactly the same as those that would be made if it were possible for the state to act as a single decision-making unit that is maximizing something.

In particular, it has been shown here that the collective choices are *as if* the state is maximizing a social welfare function that subsumes all individual interests (in the sense that it is made up of and responds positively to all of the individuals' scaling functions). Therefore, under the particular assumptions that have been considered in this book, the individualistic approach has led to what Buchanan asserted is a "separate and opposing theor[y] of the state" (1949, p. 496): namely, the view that the state can be "considered as a single decision-making unit for society as a whole . . . [which] maximizes some conceptually quantifiable magnitude" (Buchanan, 1949, p. 496).

To keep the interpretation of these observations clear, I emphasize that I am *not* concluding that the state is a separate entity that intentionally maximizes an objective function. The important distinction between this position and my conclusion that the collective choices are *as if* the state is a single decision maker is emphasized by the following observations. First, I have assumed throughout that each of the competing candidates simply wants to maximize her expected plurality. As a consequence, there is no conscious sense on the part of the political candidates that a social welfare maximum will emerge from the political process. Nonetheless, the strategies that the candidates choose turn out to be strategies that implicitly maximize a social welfare function.

The upshot of the these observations is that the book's welfare maximization results do not support the position that Buchanan's manifesto should be accepted as a basic tenet of public-choice theory. Instead, they suggest that (under at least some circumstances) it is more appropriate for us to adopt a view that is closer to Olson's (1982, sect. 3.V; 1986) position that a political party in a two-party system tends to be an "encompassing organization."

7.3   Normative interpretations

Samuelson's influential "enlargement and development of [Bergson's (1938)] important work" (p. 219) made it clear that a social welfare function is simply "a function of all of the economic magnitudes of a system which is supposed to characterize some ethical belief" and "we only require that the belief be such as to admit of an unequivocal answer as to whether one configuration of the economic system is 'better' or 'worse' than any other or 'indifferent' and that these relationships are transitive" (p. 221). Arrow (1951, 1963, 1973a, pp. 228–30) subsequently established that, for a reasonable set of normative axioms, there may very well be no satisfactory way of assigning social welfare functions to societies. In addition, later work on axiomatic social-choice theory has made it clear that when possibility theorems are established with weaker axioms the best social welfare function will depend on the particular set of axioms used (e.g., see Arrow, 1977a,b). Thus, although I have established (in the models studied) that holding an election leads to the implicit maximization of a social welfare function, it would be inappropriate either to assert that the function that is implicitly maximized is "the best of all possible social welfare functions" or even to assert that there *is* a best of all possible social welfare functions, without specifying explicit normative criteria. Put another way, it has been established that the candidates implicitly maximize a specific social welfare function, but this result does not imply that their strategies are best according to an absolute or universally accepted ethical belief about what is good for society.

One implication of this observation is that the conclusions discussed in Section 7.2 should not be taken to be Panglossian (i.e., they do not reduce to the view that whatever results from an election is, by its nature, the best of all possible results). In particular, this implication follows because once the particular social welfare function that is implicitly maximized is identified, it may be considered inappropriate by someone who has normative beliefs that lead to a different social welfare function or lead to the conclusion that there is no acceptable social welfare function. Thus, for instance, on reading the welfare maximization result in Corollary 4.5, anyone who is not a utilitarian would conclude that the elections covered by that corollary are not leading to the best of all possible outcomes and would, therefore, have reason to object to elections being used to make social choices in such societies. At the same time, of course, anyone who does approve of the social welfare function that is implicitly maximized by the political candidates in a particular setting should be happy about the results of holding elections. Thus, to recapitulate, the welfare maximization results in this book make it possible for us to assess the desirability of electoral outcomes from a normative point of view; and this assessment may be either favorable or unfavorable, depending on which normative criteria are brought to bear.

7.4 Potential for applications

In most applications of results from individualistic models of elections, the authors have included assumptions that get the set of policies under consideration to be unidimensional. Some examples of this approach are income redistribution being collapsed into one dimension (e.g., Stigler, 1970; Meltzer and Richard, 1981, 1983), taxation being treated as a unidimensional issue (e.g., Romer, 1975, 1977; Roberts, 1977; Snyder and Kramer, 1988), social security being reduced to a single dimension (e.g., Browning, 1975; Sjoblom, 1985; Boadway and Wildasin, 1989), government debt and deficits being analyzed with bond sales as the sole policy variable (e.g., Cukierman and Meltzer, 1989), and a government's choice among projects being viewed as a unidimensional matter (e.g., Glazer, 1989).

The results that I have derived here, however, have shown that there are circumstances in which it is legitimate to analyze policies in their *natural multidimensional settings* instead of artificially constraining them to one dimension. The results in this book have already been used in this way in: (i) analyses of income redistribution in its natural multidimensional setting (in Chapter 3 and Coughlin, 1986b, and in Wittman, 1989a, 1989b), (ii) Hettich and Winer's (1988) analysis of taxation in its natural multidimensional setting, (iii) Lott and Reed's (1989) analysis of whether politicians will shirk on carrying out (multidimensional) campaign promises that they've made, and (iv) Magee, Brock, and Young's (1989) analysis of tariff policies.

Importantly, my results have also identified circumstances in which political equilibria can be found *by solving a maximization problem*. Thus, the methods that can be used to find these equilibria are familiar to economists and others (see, for instance, Samuelson, 1971). At the same time, the results derived here have made it clear that elections don't lead to the maximization of "any old social welfare function" that an analyst may want to specify. Rather, the particular social welfare function that will implicitly be maximized depends on the specific assumptions made about the election model. Interestingly, though, in important cases, the maximization problem has turned out to be a very familiar one – such as maximizing a Nash social-welfare function or a Benthamite-social welfare function.

In closing this section, I want to emphasize that the theorems derived in this volume have the potential for use in many further applications. More specifically, they have opened up the possibility of more widespread and realistic analyses of equilibrium public policies that can be expected in economies with elections. This potential is particularly great because, through what has been established here, scholars who want to work with assumptions about political decisions that they know are consistent with what can be derived from individualistic election models have now been set free from the unidimensional "jail" to which earlier analyses of deterministic election models had confined them.

7.5   Summing up

There are four primary reasons why the analyses in the preceding chapters are valuable. (i) The book's equilibrium existence results match the important empirical observation that political decisions in democratic nations tend to be stable. Borrowing the phrasing used in the quote from Romer and Rosenthal (1984) in Section 1.4, the research on voting models in this book has focused on aspects of the political process that "solve" the instability problem. (ii) Under the assumptions that have been studied here, the candidates end up maximizing an implicit social welfare function. (iii) Because the analyses identify the implicit social welfare functions being maximized, they make it possible for the outcomes from elections to be assessed directly from a normative point of view. (iv) The theory in this book provides a logical basis for analyses of government decisions that are not constrained to one dimension.

References

Abrams, R., 1980. *Foundations of Political Analysis: An Introduction to the Theory of Collective Choice.* New York: Columbia University Press.

Aldrich, J., 1983a. "A Spatial Model with Party Activists," *Public Choice*, 41, 63–100.

Aldrich, J., 1983b. "Response to Comments by Melvin J. Hinich," *Public Choice*, 41, 103–5.

Aldrich, J., 1983c. "A Downsian Spatial Model with Party Activism," *American Political Science Review*, 77, 974–90.

Aldrich, J., and M. McGinnis, 1989. "A Model of Party Constraints on Optimal Candidate Positions," *Mathematical and Computer Modelling*, 12, 437–50.

Alesina, A., and H. Rosenthal, 1989. "Partisan Cycles in Cogressional Elections and the Macroeconomy," *American Political Science Review*, 83, 373–98.

Amemiya, T., 1981. "Qualitative Response Models: A Survey," *Journal of Economic Literature*, 19, 483–536.

Apostol, T., 1974. *Mathematical Analysis*, 2nd ed. Reading: Addison-Wesley.

Aranson, P., 1981. *American Government: Strategy and Choice.* Cambridge: Winthrop.

Aranson, P., M. Hinich, and P. Ordeshook, 1973. "Campaign Strategies for Alternative Election Systems: Candidate Objectives as Intervening Variables," in *Mathematical Approaches to Politics* (H. Alker et al., Eds.), pp. 193–229. Amsterdam: Elsevier.

Aranson, P., M. Hinich, and P. Ordeshook, 1974. "Election Goals and Strategies: Equivalent and Nonequivalent Candidate Objectives," *American Political Science Review*, 68, 135–52.

Aranson, P., and P. Ordeshook, 1972. "Spatial Strategies for Sequential Elections," in *Probability Models of Collective Decision-Making* (R. Niemi and H. Weisberg, Eds.), pp. 298–331. Columbus: Merrill.

Aranson, P., and P. Ordeshook, 1981. "Regulation, Redistribution, and Public Choice," *Public Choice*, 37, 69–100.

Arrow, K., 1950. "A Difficulty in the Concept of Social Welfare," *Journal of Political Economy*, 58, 328–46.

Arrow, K., 1951, 1963 (2nd ed.). *Social Choice and Individual Values.* New York: Wiley.

Arrow, K., 1952. "Le Principe de Rationalité dans les Decisions Collectives," *Economie Appliquée*, 5, 469–84.

Arrow, K., 1959. "Rational Choice Functions and Orderings," *Economica*, 26, 121–7.

227

Arrow, K., 1965. *Aspects of the Theory of Risk-Bearing*. Helsinki: Yrjo Jahnsson Foundation.

Arrow, K., 1967. "Values and Collective Decision Making," in *Philosophy, Politics and Society, Third Series* (P. Laslett and W. G. Runciman, Eds.), pp. 215–32. Oxford: Blackwell.

Arrow, K., 1969. "Tullock and an Existence Theorem," *Public Choice*, 6, 105–11.

Arrow, K., 1970. *Essays in the Theory of Risk Bearing*. Chicago: Markham.

Arrow, K., 1973a. "General Economic Equilibrium: Purpose, Analytic Techniques, Collective Choice," in *Les Prix Nobel en 1972*, pp. 209–31. Stockholm: Nobel Foundation.

Arrow, K., 1973b. "Formal Theories of Social Welfare," in *Dictionary of the History of Ideas*, Vol. 4 (P. Wiener, Ed.), pp. 276–84. New York: Scribner.

Arrow, K., 1977a. "Extended Sympathy and the Possibility of Social Choice," *American Economic Review, Papers and Proceedings*, 67, 219–25.

Arrow, K., 1977b. "Current Developments in the Theory of Social Choice," *Social Research*, 44, 607–22.

Arrow, K. 1979. "The Tradeoff Between Growth and Equity," in *Theory for Economic Efficiency* (H. Greenfield et al., Eds.), Cambridge: MIT Press.

Arrow, K., 1981. "Optimal and Voluntary Income Distribution," in *Economic Welfare and the Economics of Soviet Socialism* (S. Rosefielde, Ed.), pp. 267–88. Cambridge University Press.

Arrow, K., 1987. "Arrow's Theorem," in *The New Palgrave: A Dictionary of Economics*, Vol. 1 (J. Eatwell et al., Eds.), pp. 124–6. London: Macmillan.

Arrow, K., 1990. "Foreword," in *Advances in the Spatial Theory of Voting* (J. Enelow and M. Hinich, Eds.), pp. ix–xi. Cambridge University Press.

Arrow, K., and H. Raynaud, 1986. *Social Choice and Multicriterion Decision-Making*. Cambridge: MIT Press.

Atkinson, A., 1987. "James M. Buchanan's Contributions to Economics," *Scandinavian Journal of Economics*, 89, 5–15.

Austen-Smith, D., 1981. "Party Policy and Campaign Costs in a Multi-Constituency Model of Electoral Competition," *Public Choice*, 37, 389–402.

Austen-Smith, D., 1983. "The Spatial Theory of Electoral Competition: Instability, Institutions, and Information," *Environment and Planning C: Government and Policy*, 1, 439–59.

Austen-Smith, D., 1984a. "Two-Party Competition with Many Constituencies," *Mathematical Social Sciences*, 7, 177–98.

Austen-Smith, D., 1984b. "Comment on the Ledyard Paper," *Public Choice*, 44, 43–7.

Austen-Smith, D., 1986. "Legislative Coalitions and Electoral Equilibria," *Public Choice*, 50, 185–210.

Austen-Smith, D., 1987. "Parties, Districts and the Spatial Theory of Elections," *Social Choice and Welfare*, 4, 9–23.

Austen-Smith, D., 1989. "Sincere Voting in Models of Legislative Elections," *Social Choice and Welfare*, 6, 287–99.

Austen-Smith, D., and J. Banks, 1988. "Elections, Coalitions and Legislative Outcomes," *American Political Science Review*, 82, 405–22.

Austen-Smith, D., and J. Banks, 1989. "Electoral Accountability and Incumbency," in *Models of Strategic Choice in Politics* (P. Ordeshook, Ed.), pp. 121–48. Ann Arbor: University of Michigan Press.

Austen-Smith, D., and W. Riker, 1987. "Asymmetric Information and the Coherence of Legislation," *American Political Science Review*, 81, 897–918.

Avriel, M., W. E. Diewert, S. Schaible, and W. Ziemba, 1981. "Introduction to Concave and Generalized Concave Functions," in *Generalized Concavity in Optimization and Economics* (S. Schaible and W. Ziemba, Eds.), pp. 21–50. New York: Academic Press.

Avriel, M., and I. Zang, 1974. "Generalized Convex Functions with Applications to Nonlinear Programming," in *Mathematical Programs for Activity Analysis* (P. Van Moeseke, Ed.), pp. 23–33. Amsterdam: North-Holland:

Baron, D., and J. Ferejohn, 1987. "Bargaining and Agenda Formation in Legislatures," *American Economic Review, Papers and Proceedings*, 77, 303–9.

Barr, J., and O. Davis, 1966. "An Elementary Political and Economic Theory of the Expenditures of Local Governments," *Southern Economic Journal*, 33, 149–65.

Bartle, R. 1966. *The Elements of Integration*. New York: Wiley.

Becker, G. S., 1983. "A Theory of Competition Among Pressure Groups for Political Influence," *Quarterly Journal of Economics*, 98, 371–400.

Becker, G. S., 1985. "Public Policies, Pressure Groups, and Dead Weight Costs," *Journal of Public Economics*, 28, 329–47.

Becker, G. M., M. DeGroot, and J. Marschak, 1963. "Stochastic Models of Choice Behavior," *Behavioral Science*, 8, 41–55.

Bell, C., 1978. "What Happens When Majority Rule Breaks Down?" *Public Choice*, 33, 121–6.

Bell, C., 1981. "A Random Voting Graph Almost Surely Has a Hamiltonian Cycle When the Number of Alternatives Is Large," *Econometrica*, 6, 1597–1603.

Berg, S., 1988. "Voting Paradox," in *Encyclopedia of Statistical Sciences*, Vol. 9 (S. Kotz and N. Johnson, Eds.), pp. 507–9. New York: Wiley.

Bergson, A., 1938. "A Reformulation of Certain Aspects of Welfare Economics," *Quarterly Journal of Economics*, 52, 314–44.

Bernhardt, M., and D. Ingberman, 1985. "Candidate Reputations and the 'Incumbency Effect'," *Journal of Public Economics*, 27, 47–67.

Bernoulli, D., 1954, "Exposition of a New Theory on the Measurement of Risk" (translated by L. Sommer), *Econometrica*, 22, 23–36; translation of "Specimen Theoriae Novae de Mensura Sortis," *Commentarii Academiae Scientiarum Imperiales Petropolitanae*, 5 (1738), pp. 175–92.

Black, D., 1948. "On the Rationale of Group Decision-Making," *Journal of Political Economy*, 56, 23–34.

Black, D., 1958. *The Theory of Committees and Elections*. Cambridge University Press.

Black, D., and R. Newing, 1951. *Committee Decisions with Complementary Valuation*. London: William Hodge.

Blair, D., 1979. "On Variable Majority Rule and Kramer's Dynamic Competitive Process," *Review of Economic Studies*, 46, 667–73.

Block, H. D., and J. Marschak, 1960. "Random Orderings and Stochastic Theories of Responses," in *Contributions to Probability and Statistics* (I. Olkin et al., Eds.), pp. 97–132. Stanford: Stanford University Press.

Blumel, W., R. Pethig, and O. von dem Hagen, 1986. "The Theory of Public Goods: A Survey of Recent Issues," *Journal of Institutional and Theoretical Economics*, 142, 241–309.

Boadway, R., and D. Wildasin, 1989. "A Median Voter Model of Social Security," International *Economic Review*, 30, 307–28.

Borooah, V., and F. Van der Ploeg, 1983. *Political Aspects of the Economy*, Cambridge University Press.

Bowden, R., 1987. "Repeated Sampling in the Presence of Publication Effects," *Journal of the American Statistical Association*, 82, 476–84.

Bowden, R., 1989. *Statistical Games and Human Affairs*. Cambridge University Press.

Bradley, R., 1976. "Science, Statistics, and Paired Comparisons," *Biometrics*, 32, 213–32.

Bradley, R., and M. Terry, 1952. "Rank Analysis of Incomplete Block Designs. I. The Method of Paired Comparisons," *Biometrika*, 39, 324–45.

Brams, S., 1975. *Game Theory and Politics*. London: Macmillan.

Brams, S., 1978. *The Presidential Election Game*, New Haven: Yale University Press.

Brams, S., 1985. *Rational Politics: Decisions, Games, and Strategies*. Washington, D.C.: Congressional Quarterly Press.

Brams, S., and M. Davis, 1973. "Models of Resource Allocation in Presidential Campaigning: Implications for Democratic Representation," in *Annals of the New York Academy of Sciences*, 219, 105–23.

Brams, S., and M. Davis, 1974. "The 3/2's Rule in Presidential Campaigning," *American Political Science Review*, 68, 113–34.

Brams, S., and M. Davis, 1982. "Optimal Resource Allocation in Presidential Primaries," *Mathematical Social Sciences*, 3, 373–88.

Brams, S., and P. Straffin, 1982. "The Entry Problem in a Political Race," in *Political Equilibrium* (P. Ordeshook and K. Shepsle, Eds.), pp. 181–95. Kluwer-Nijhoff.

Browning, E., 1975. "Why the Social Insurance Budget is Too Large in a Democratic Society," *Economic Inquiry*, 13, 373–88.

Buchanan, J., 1949. "The Pure Theory of Government Finance," *Journal of Political Economy*, 57, 496–505.

Buchanan, J., 1987a. "Constitutional Economics," in *The New Palgrave: A Dictionary of Economics*, Vol. 1 (J. Eatwell et al., Eds.), pp. 587–8. London: Macmillan.

Buchanan, J., 1987b. "The Constitution of Economic Policy," in *Les Prix Nobel en 1986*, pp. 334–43. Stockholm: Nobel Foundation.

Buck, R. C., 1978. *Advanced Calculus*, 3rd ed. New York: McGraw-Hill.

Calvert, R., 1985. "Robustness of the Multidimensional Voting Model: Candidate Motivations, Uncertainty and Convergence," *American Journal of Political Science*, 29, 69–95.

Calvert, R., 1986. *Models of Imperfect Information in Politics*, Vol. 6 of *Fundamentals of Pure and Applied Economics* (J. Lesourne and H. Sonnenchein, Eds.). Chur: Harwood Academic Publishers.

Calvert, R., 1987. "Reputation and Legislative Leadership," *Public Choice*, 55, 81–120.

Caplin, A., and B. Nalebuff, 1988. "On 64% Majority Rule," *Econometrica*, 56, 787–814.

Caplin, A., and B. Nalebuff, 1991 "Aggregation and Social Choice: A Mean Voter Theorem," *Econometrica*, 59, 1–23.

Chiang, A., 1984. *Fundamental Methods of Mathematical Economics*, 3rd ed. New York: McGraw-Hill.

Chichilnisky, G., 1982. "Structural Instability of Decisive Majority Rules," *Journal of Mathematical Economics*, 9, 207–21.

Chichilnisky, G., and G. Heal, 1983. "Necessary and Sufficient Conditions for a Resolution of the Social Choice Paradox," *Journal of Economic Theory*, 31, 68–87.

Coase, R., 1960. "The Problem of Social Cost," *Journal of Law and Economics*, 3, 1–44.

Cohen, L., 1979. "Cyclic Sets in Multidimensional Voting Models," *Journal of Economic Theory*, 20, 1–12.

Cohen, L., and S. Matthews, 1980. "Constrained Plott Equilibria and Global Cycling Sets," *Review of Economic Studies*, 46, 975–86.

Colantoni, C., T. Levesque, and P. Ordeshook, 1975. "Rejoinder to 'Comment' by S. J. Brams and M. D. Davis," *American Political Science Review*, 69, 157–61.

Coleman, J., 1971. "Internal Processes Governing Party Positions in Elections," *Public Choice*, 11, 35–60.

Coleman, J., 1972. "The Positions of Political Parties in Elections," in *Probability Models of Collective Decision-Making* (R. Niemi and H. Weisberg, Eds.), pp. 332–57. Columbus: Merrill.

Coleman, J., 1973. *The Mathematics of Collective Action*. London: Heinemann.

Collier, K., R. McKelvey, P. Ordeshook, and K. Williams, 1987. "Retrospective Voting: An Experimental Study," *Public Choice*, 53, 101–30.

Collier, K., P. Ordeshook, and K. Williams, 1989. "The Rationally Uninformed Electorate: Some Experimental Evidence," *Public Choice*, 60, 3–29.

Comaner, W., 1976. "The Median Voter Rule and the Theory of Political Choice," *Journal of Public Economics*, 5, 169–78.

Coughlin, P. 1976. "Incomplete Information, Noisy Signals, and Uncertainty-Averse Voting in Political Elections: A Note," *Public Choice*, 28, 13–116.

Coughlin, P., 1977. "A Mathematical Model of Elections with Sequences of

Decisions and Incomplete Information," in *Proceedings of the First International Conference on Mathematical Modeling*, Vol. 2 (X. Avula, Ed.), pp. 701–10. Rolla: University of Missouri.

Coughlin, P., 1979. "Nonlinear Optimization and Equilibria in Policy Formation Games with Random Voting," in *Applied Nonlinear Analysis* (V. Lakshmikantham, Ed.), pp. 519–27. New York: Academic Press.

Coughlin, P., 1980. "Optimal Voting Under Uncertainty in Mathematical Models of Electoral Competition," in *Proceedings of the First World Conference on Mathematics at the Service of Man*, Vol. 2 (A. Ballester et al., Eds.), pp. 17–37. Barcelona: Universidad Politechnica.

Coughlin, P., 1981. "Necessary and Sufficient Conditions for δ-relative Majority Voting Equilibria," *Econometrica*, 49, 1223–4.

Coughlin, P., 1982. "Pareto Optimality of Policy Proposals with Probabilistic Voting," *Public Choice*, 39, 427–33.

Coughlin, P., 1983. "Social Utility Functions for Strategic Decisions in Probabilistic Voting Models," *Mathematical Social Sciences*, 4, 275–93.

Coughlin, P., 1984a. "Expectations About Voter Choices: A Comment," *Public Choice*, 44, 49–59.

Coughlin, P., 1984b. "Unidimensional Median Voter Results in Probabilistic Voting Models," *Economics Letters*, 14, 9–15.

Coughlin, P., 1984c. "Davis-Hinich Conditions and Median Outcomes in Probabilistic Voting Models," *Journal of Economic Theory*, 34, 1–12.

Coughlin, P., 1985. "Directional Nash Behavior in Probabilistic Voting Models," in *Modeling and Simulation*, 16 (W. Vogt and M. Mickle, Eds.), pp. 1121–7. Research Triangle Park: Instrument Society of America.

Coughlin, P., 1986a. "Special Majority Rules and the Existence of Voting Equilibria," *Social Choice and Welfare*, 3, 31–5.

Coughlin, P., 1986b. "Elections and Income Redistribution," *Public Choice*, 50, 27–91.

Coughlin, P., 1986c. "Reply to Ledyard's Comment," *Public Choice*, 50, 101–3.

Coughlin, P., 1986d. "Reply to Slutsky's Comment," *Public Choice*, 50, 131–3.

Coughlin, P., 1986e. "Probabilistic Voting Models," in *Encyclopedia of Statistical Sciences*, Vol. 7 (S. Kotz and N. Johnson, Eds.), pp. 204–10. New York: Wiley.

Coughlin, P., 1988. "Single-Peakedness and Median Voters," in *Encyclopedia of Statistical Sciences*, Vol. 8 (S. Kotz and N. Johnson, Eds.), pp. 491–5. New York: Wiley.

Coughlin, P., 1990a. "Candidate Uncertainty and Electoral Equilibria," in *Advances in the Spatial Theory of Voting* (J. Enelow and M. Hinich, Eds.), pp. 145–66. Cambridge University Press.

Coughlin, P., 1990b. "Majority Rule and Election Models," *Journal of Economic Surveys*, 4, 157–88.

Coughlin, P., 1990c. "Pairwise Equilibria in Probabilistic Voting Models," *European Journal of Political Economy*, 6, 99–106.

Coughlin, P., 1991. "Balanced-Budget Redistribution As the Outcome of Political Competition: A Comment," *Public Choice*, 70, 239–43.

Coughlin, P., and M. Hinich, 1984. "Necessary and Sufficient Conditions for Single-Peakedness in Public Economic Models," *Journal of Public Economics*, 25, 161–79.

Coughlin, P., and E. Howe, 1989. "Policies Over Time and Pareto Optimality," *Social Choice and Welfare*, 6, 259–73.

Coughlin, P., and K. Lin, 1981. "Continuity Properties of Majority Rule with Intermediate Preferences," *Mathematical Social Sciences*, 1, 289–96.

Coughlin, P., D. Mueller, and P. Murrell, 1990a. "A Model of Electoral Competition with Interest Groups," *Economics Letters*, 32, 307–11.

Coughlin, P., D. Mueller, and P. Murrell, 1990b. "Electoral Politics, Interest Groups, and the Size of Government," *Economic Inquiry* 28, 682–705.

Coughlin, P., and S. Nitzan, 1981a. "Electoral Outcomes with Probabilistic Voting and Nash Social Welfare Maxima," *Journal of Public Economics*, 15, 113–22.

Coughlin, P., and S. Nitzan, 1981b, "Directional and Local Electoral Equilibria with Probabilistic Voting," *Journal of Economic Theory*, 24, 226–40.

Coughlin, P., and T. Palfrey, 1985. "Pareto Optimality in Spatial Voting Models," *Social Choice and Welfare*, 1, 307–19.

Cox, G., 1984a. "Non-Collegial Simple Games and the Nowhere Denseness of the Set of Preference Profiles Having a Core," *Social Choice and Welfare*, 1, 159–64.

Cox, G., 1984b. "An Expected-Utility Model of Electoral Competition," *Quality and Quantity*, 18, 337–49.

Cox, G., 1984c. "Electoral Equilibrium in Double Member Districts," *Public Choice*, 44, 443–51.

Cox, G., 1984d. "Strategic Electoral Choice in Multi-Member Districts," *American Journal of Political Science*, 28, 722–38.

Cox, G., 1985. "Electoral Equilibrium Under Approval Voting," *American Journal of Political Science*, 29, 112–18.

Cox, G., 1987. "Electoral Equilibrium Under Alternative Voting Institutions," *American Journal of Political Science*, 31, 82–108.

Cox, G., 1989. "Undominated Candidate Strategies Under Alternative Voting Rules," *Mathematical and Computer Modelling*, 12, 451–9.

Cox, G., 1990. "Multicandidate Spatial Competition," in *Advances in the Spatial Theory of Voting* (J. Enelow and M. Hinich, Eds.), pp. 179–98. Cambridge University Press.

Cukierman, A., and A. Meltzer, 1989. "A Political Theory of Government Debt and Deficits in a Neo-Ricardian Framework," *American Economic Review*, 79, 713–32.

d'Aspremont, C., 1985. "Axioms for Social Welfare Orderings," in *Social Goals and Social Organization* (L. Hurwicz et al., Eds.), pp. 19–76. Cambridge University Press.

Davis, O., M. DeGroot, and M. Hinich, 1972. "Social Preference Orderings and Majority Rule," *Econometrica*, 40, 147–57.

Davis, O., and G. H. Haines, Jr., 1966. "A Political Approach to a Theory of Public Expenditures: The Case of Municipalities," *National Tax Journal*, 19, 259–75.

Davis, O., and M. Hinich, 1966. "A Mathematical Model of Policy Formation in a Democratic Society," in *Mathematical Applications in Political Science, II* (J. Bernd, Ed.), pp. 175–208. Dallas: Southern Methodist University Press.

Davis, O., and M. Hinich, 1967. "Some Results Related to a Mathematical Model of Policy Formation in a Democratic Society," in *Mathematical Applications in Political Science, III* (J. Bernd, Ed.), pp. 14–38. Charlottesville: University Press of Virginia.

Davis, O., and M. Hinich, 1968. "On the Power and Importance of the Mean Preference in a Mathematical Model of Democratic Choice," *Public Choice*, 5, 59–72.

Davis, O., and M. Hinich, 1971. "Some Extentions to a Mathematical Model of Democratic Choice," in *Social Choice* (B. Lieberman, Ed.), pp. 323–47. New York: Gordon and Breach.

Davis, O., and M. Hinich, 1972. "Spatial Competition under Constrained Choice," in *Probability Models of Collective Decision Making* (R. Niemi and H. Weisberg, Eds.), pp. 358–77. Columbus: Merrill.

Davis, O., M. Hinich, and P. Ordeshook, 1970. "An Expository Development of a Mathematical Model of Policy Formation in a Democratic Society," *American Political Science Review*, 64, 426–48.

de Condorcet, M., 1785. *Essai sur l'Application de l'Analyse à la Probabilité des Décisions Rendues à la Pluralité de Voix*. Paris.

Debreu, G., 1959. *Theory of Value*. New York: Wiley.

Debreu, G., 1960. "Review of R. D. Luce, *Individual Choice Behavior*," *American Economic Review*, 50, 186–8.

Denzau, A., and A. Kats, 1977. "Expected Plurality Voting Equilibrium and Social Choice Functions," *Review of Economics Studies*, 44, 227–33.

Denzau, A., A. Kats, and S. Slutsky, 1985. "Multi-Agent Equilibria with Market Share and Ranking Objectives," *Social Choice and Welfare*, 2, 95–117.

Denzau, A., and R. Mackay, 1981. "Structure Induced Equilibrium and Perfect Foresight Expectations," *American Journal of Political Science*, 25, 762–79.

Denzau, A., and R. Mackay, 1983. "Gatekeeping and the Monopoly Power of Committees," *American Journal of Political Science*, 27, 740–61.

Denzau, A., and R. Parks, 1975. "The Continuity of Majority Rule Equilibrium," *Econometrica*, 43, 853–66.

Denzau, A., and R. Parks, 1983. "Existence of Voting-Market Equilibria," *Journal of Economic Theory*, 30, 243–65.

de Palma, A., G. Hong, and J. F. Thisse, 1990. "Equilibria in Multi-Party Competition Under Uncertainty," *Social Choice and Welfare* 7, 247–59.

Diewert, W., M. Avriel, and I. Zang, 1981. "Nine Kinds of Quasi-concavity and Concavity," *Journal of Economic Theory*, 25, 397–420.

Downs, A., 1957a. "An Economic Theory of Political Action in a Democracy," *Journal of Political Economy*, 65, 135–50.

Downs, A., 1957b. *An Economic Theory of Democracy*. New York: Harper and Row.

Eaton, B., and R. Lipsey, 1975. "The Principle of Minimum Differentiation

Reconsidered: Some New Developments in the Theory of Spatial Competition," *Review of Economic Studies*, 42, 27–49.

Enelow, J., 1990. "An Expanded Approach to Analyzing Policy-Minded Candidates," working paper, University of Texas at Austin.

Enelow, J., and M. Hinich, 1981. "A New Approach to Voter Uncertainty in the Downsian Spatial Model," *American Journal of Political Science*, 25, 483–93.

Enelow, J., and M. Hinich, 1982a. "Ideology, Issues and the Spatial Theory of Elections," *American Political Science Review*, 76, 493–501.

Enelow, J., and M. Hinich, 1982b. "Non-Spatial Candidate Characteristics and Electoral Competition," *Journal of Politics*, 44, 115–30.

Enelow, J., and M. Hinich, 1983a, "On Plott's Pairwise Symmetry Condition for Majority Rule Equilibrium," *Public Choice*, 40, 317–21.

Enelow, J., and M. Hinich, 1983b. "Voting One Issue at a Time: The Question of Voter Forecasts," *American Political Science Review*, 77, 435–45.

Enelow, J. and M. Hinich, 1983c. "Voter Expectations in Multi-Stage Voting Systems: An Equilibrium Result," *American Journal of Political Science*, 27, pp. 820–7.

Enelow, J., and M. Hinich, 1984a. *The Spatial Theory of Voting*. Cambridge University Press.

Enelow, J., and M. Hinich, 1984b. "Probabilistic Voting and the Importance of Centrist Ideologies in Democratic Elections," *Journal of Politics*, 46, 459–78.

Enelow, J., and M. Hinich, 1989a. "The Location of American Presidential Candidates: An Empirical Test of a New Spatial Model of Elections," *Mathematical and Computer Modelling*, 12, 461–70.

Enelow, J., and M. Hinich, 1989b. "A General Probabilistic Spatial Theory of Elections," *Public Choice*, 61, 101–13.

Enelow, J., and M. Hinich, 1990. "The Theory of Predictive Mappings," in *Advances in the Spatial Theory of Voting* (J. Enelow and M. Hinich, Eds.), pp. 167–78. Cambridge University Press.

Fair, R., 1978. "The Effect of Economic Events on Votes for President," *Review of Economics and Statistics*, 60, 159–73.

Feld, S., B. Grofman, and N. Miller, 1988. "Centripetal Forces in Spatial Voting: On the Size of the Yolk," *Public Choice*, 59, 37–50.

Feldman, A., 1980. *Welfare Economics and Social Choice Theory*. Higham: Martinus Nijhoff.

Feldman, A., 1987. "Welfare Economics," in *The New Palgrave: A Dictionary of Economics*, Vol. 4 (J. Eatwell et al., Eds.), pp. 889–94. London: Macmillan.

Feldman, A., and K. Lee, 1988. "Existence of Electoral Equilibria with Probabilistic Voting," *Journal of Public Economics*, 35, 205–27.

Fenno, R., 1973. *Congressmen in Committees*. Boston: Little, Brown.

Ferejohn, J., 1986. "Incumbent Performance and Electoral Control," *Public Choice*, 50 5–25.

Ferejohn, J., and D. Grether, 1974. "On a Class of Rational Social Decision Procedures," *Journal of Economic Theory*, 8, 471–82.

Ferejohn, J., and E. Packel, 1983. "Continuous Social Decision Procedures," *Mathematical Social Sciences*, 6, 65–73.

Fiorina, M., 1974. *Representatives, Roll Calls, and Constituencies*. Lexington: Lexington Books.

Fiorina, M., 1981. *Retrospective Voting in American National Elections*. New Haven: Yale University Press.

Fishburn, P., 1972. "Lotteries and Social Choices," *Journal of Economic Theory*, 5, 189–207.

Fishburn, P., 1973. *The Theory of Social Choice*. Princeton: Princeton University Press.

Fishburn, P., 1983. "Dimensions of Election Procedures: Analyses and Comparisons," *Theory and Decision*, 15, 371–97.

Fishburn, P., 1987. *Interprofile Conditions and Impossibility*, Vol. 18 of *Fundamentals of Pure and Applied Economics* (J. Lesourne and H. Sonnenschein, Eds.). Chur: Harwood Academic Publishers.

Fishburn, P., and W. Gehrlein, 1977. "Towards a Theory of Elections with Probabilistic Preferences," *Econometrica*, 45, 1907–24.

Frey, B., 1988. *Modern Political Economy*. Oxford: Martin Robertson.

Frohlich, N., and J. Oppenheimer, 1978. *Modern Political Economy*. Englewood Cliffs: Prentice-Hall.

Gehrlein, W., 1983. "Condorcet's Paradox," *Theory and Decision*, 15, 161–97.

Ginsburgh, V., P. Pestieau, and J. F. Thisse, 1987. "A Spatial Model of Party Competition with Electoral and Ideological Objectives," in *Spatial Analysis and Location-Allocation Models*, pp. 101–17. (A. Ghosh and G. Rushton, Eds.), New York: Van Nostrand Reinhold.

Glazer, A., 1989. "Politics and the Choice of Durability," *American Economic Review*, 79, 1207–13.

Glazer, A., B. Grofman, and G. Owen, 1989. "A Model of Candidate Convergence Under Uncertainty About Voter Preferences," *Mathematical and Computer Modeling*, 12, 471–8.

Godek, P., 1985. "Industry Structure and Redistribution through Trade Restrictions," *Journal of Law and Economics*, 28, 687–703.

Godek, P., 1986. "The Politically Optimal Tariff: Levels of Trade Restrictions Across Developed Countries," *Economic Inquiry*, 24, 587–93.

Grandmont, J. M., 1978. "Intermediate Preferences and the Majority Rule," *Econometrica*, 46, 317–30.

Greenberg, J., 1979. "Consistent Majority Rules Over Compact Sets of Alternatives," *Econometrica*, 47, 627–36.

Greenberg, J., and K. Shepsle, 1987. "The Effect of Electoral Rewards in Multiparty Competition with Entry," *American Political Science Review*, 81, 525–37.

Greenberg, J., and S. Weber, 1985a, "Consistent δ-relative Majority Equilibria," *Econometrica*, 53, 463–4.

Greenberg, J., and S. Weber, 1985b. "Multiparty Equilibria under Proportional Representation," *American Political Science Review*, 79, 693–703.

Hansson, I., and C. Stuart, 1984. "Voting Competitions with Interested Politicians: Platforms Do Not Converge to the Preferences of the Median Voter," *Public Choice*, 44, 431–41.

Harrington, J., in press. "The Power of the Proposal Maker in a Model of Endogenous Agenda Formation," *Public Choice*.

Hestenes, M., 1975. *Optimization Theory*. New York: Wiley.

Hettich, W., and S. Winer, 1988. "Economic and Political Foundations of Tax Structure," *American Economic Review*, 78, 701–12.

Hinich, M., 1977. "Equilibrium in Spatial Voting: The Median Voter Result Is an Artifact," *Journal of Economic Theory*, 16, 208–19.

Hinich, M., 1978, 'The Mean versus the Median in Spatial Voting Games," in *Game Theory and Political Science* (P. Ordeshook, Ed.), pp. 357–74. New York: New York University Press.

Hinich, M., 1983. "Comment on the Aldrich Paper," *Public Choice*, 41, 101–2.

Hinich, M., J. Ledyard, and P. Ordeshook, 1972. "Nonvoting and the Existence of Equilibrium Under Majority Rule," *Journal of Economic Theory*, 4, 144–53.

Hinich, M., J. Ledyard, and P. Ordeshook, 1973. "A Theory of Electoral Equilibrium: A Spatial Analysis Based on the Theory of Games," *Journal of Politics*, 35, 154–93.

Hinich, M., and P. Ordeshook, 1969. "Abstentions and Equilibrium in the Electoral Process," *Public Choice*, 7, 81–106.

Hinich, M., and P. Ordeshook, 1970. "Plurality Maximization vs. Vote Maximization: A Spatial Analysis with Variable Participation," *American Political Science Review*, 64, 772–91.

Hinich, M., and P. Ordeshook, 1971. "Social Welfare and Electoral Competition in Democratic Societies," *Public Choice*, 11, 73–87.

Hinich, M., and W. Pollard, 1981. "A New Approach to the Spatial Theory of Electoral Competition," *American Journal of Political Science*, 25, 323–41.

Hotelling, H., 1929. "Stability in Competition," *Economic Journal*, 39, 41–57.

Hoyer, R., and L. Mayer, 1975. "Social Preference Orderings Under Majority Rule," *Econometrica*, 43, 803–6.

Inada, K., 1964. " A Note on the Simple Majority Decision Rule," *Econometrica*, 32, 525–31.

Inada, K., 1969. "The Simple Majority Decision Rule," *Econometrica*, 37, 490–506.

Ingberman, D., 1985. "Running Aginst the Status Quo: Institutions for Direct Democracy Referenda and Allocations Over Time," *Public Choice*, 46, 19–43.

Ingberman, D., 1989. "Reputational Dynamics in Spatial Competition," *Mathematical and Computer Modelling*, 12, 479–96.

Ingberman, D., and R. Inman, 1988. "The Political Economy of Fiscal Policy," in *Surveys in Public Sector Economics* (P. Hare, Ed.), pp. 105–60. Oxford: Basil Blackwell.

Inman, R., 1987. "Markets, Governments and the 'New' Political Economy," in *Handbook of Public Economics*, Vol. II (A. Auerbach and M. Feldstein, Eds.), pp. 647–777. Amsterdam: North-Holland.

Intriligator, M., 1979. "Income Redistribution: A Probabilistic Approach," *American Economic Review*, 69, 97–105.

Kadane, J., 1972. "On Division of the Question," *Public Choice*, 13, 47–54.

Kakutani, S., 1941. "A Generalization of Brouwer's Fixed-point Theorem," *Duke Mathematical Journal*, 8, 457–9.

Kallberg, J., and W. Ziemba, 1981. "Generalized Concave Functions in Stochastic Programming and Portfolio Theory," in *Generalized Concavity in Optimization and Economics* (S. Schaible and W. Ziemba, Eds.), pp. 719–67. New York: Academic Press.

Kaneko, M., and K. Nakamura, 1979. "The Nash Social Welfare Function," *Econometrica*, 47, 423–35.

Kats, A., and S. Nitzan, 1976. "Global and Local Equilibrium in Majority Voting," *Public Choice*, 26, 105–6.

Kelly, J., 1978, *Arrow Impossibility Theorems*. New York: Academic Press.

Kelly, J., 1988. *Social Choice Theory*. Berlin: Springer-Verlag.

Kingdon, J., 1966. *Candidates for Office: Beliefs and Strategies*. New York: Random House.

Klevorick, A., and G. Kramer, 1973. "Social Choice on Pollution Management: The Genossenschaften," *Journal of Public Economics*, 2, 101–46.

Klinger, A., and O. L. Mangasarian, 1968. "Logarithmic Convexity and Geometric Programming," *Journal of Mathematical Analysis and Applications*, 24, 388–408.

Kotz, S., and N. Johnson, 1982. "Bradley-Terry Models," in *Encyclopedia of Statistical Sciences*, Vol. 1 (S. Kotz and N. Johnson, Eds.), pp. 313–14. New York: Wiley.

Kramer, G., 1966. "A Decision-Theoretic Analysis of a Problem in Political Campaigning," in *Mathematical Applications in Political Science, II* (J. Bernd, Ed.), pp. 137–60. Dallas: Southern Methodist University Press.

Kramer, G., 1971. "Short-term Fluctuation in U.S. Voting Behavior, 1896–1964," *American Political Science Review*, 65, 131–43.

Kramer, G., 1973. "On a Class of Equilibrium Conditions for Majority Rule," *Econometrica*, 41, 285–97.

Kramer, G., 1977a. "Theories of Political Processes," in *Frontiers of Quantitative Economics, III* (M. Intriligator, Ed.), pp. 685–702. Amsterdam: North-Holland.

Kramer, G., 1977b. "A Dynamical Model of Political Equilibrium," *Journal of Economic Theory*, 15, 310–34.

Kramer, G., 1978a. "Existence of Electoral Equilibria," in *Game Theory and Political Science* (P. Ordeshook, Ed.), pp. 371–89. New York: New York University Press.

Kramer, G., 1978b. "Robustness of the Median Voter Result," *Journal of Economic Theory*, 19, 565–7.

Kramer, G., and J. Hertzberg, 1975. "Formal Theory," in *Handbook of Political Science*, Vol. 7 (F. Greenstein and N. Polsby, Eds.), pp. 351–403. Reading: Addison-Wesley.

Kramer, G., and A. Klevorick, 1974. "Existence of a 'Local Cooperative Equilibrium' in a Class of Voting Games," *Review of Economic Studies*, 41, 539–47.

Kreps, D., and R. Wilson, 1982. "Reputation and Imperfect Information," *Journal of Economic Theory*, 27, 253–79.

Laffont, J., 1988. *Fundamentals of Public Economics*. Cambridge: MIT Press.

Lake, M., 1979. "A New Campaign Resource Allocation Model," in *Applied Game Theory* (S. Brams et al., Eds.), pp. 118–32. Wurzburg: Physica-Verlag.

Ledyard, J., 1981. "The Paradox of Voting and Candidate Competition: A General Equilibrium Analysis," in *Essays in Contemporary Fields of Economics* (G. Horwich and J. Quirk, Eds.), pp. 54–80. West Lafayette: Purdue University Press.

Ledyard, J., 1984. "The Pure Theory of Large Two-Candidate Elections," *Public Choice*, 44, 7–41.

Ledyard, J., 1986. "Elections and Reputations: A Comment on the Papers of Coughlin and Ferejohn," *Public Choice*, 50, 93–103.

Ledyard, J., 1989. "Information Aggregation in Two-Candidate Elections," in *Models of Strategic Choice in Politics* (P. Ordeshook, Ed.), pp. 7–30. Ann Arbor: University of Michigan Press.

Lindbeck, A., 1985. "Redistribution Policy and the Expansion of the Public Sector," *Journal of Public Economics*, 28, 309–28.

Lindbeck, A., and J. Weibull, 1987. "Balanced-Budget Redistribution As the Outcome of Political Competition," *Public Choice*, 52, 273–97.

Lindbeck A., and J. Weibull, 1990. "Political Equilibrium in Representative Democracy," working paper, Stockholm University.

Lockwood, B., 1984. "Social Choice, Interpersonal Comparability and Welfare Economics," in *Mathematical Methods in Economics* (F. van der Ploeg, Ed.), pp. 371–400. New York: Wiley.

Lott, J., and W. R. Reed, 1989. "Shirking and Sorting in a Political Market with Finite-Lived Politicians," *Public Choice*, 61, 75–96.

Luce, R. D., 1959. *Individual Choice Behavior*. New York: Wiley.

Luce, R. D., 1977 "The Choice Axiom After Twenty Years," *Journal of Mathematical Psychology*, 15, 215–33.

Luce, R. D., and H. Raiffa, 1957. *Games and Decisions*. New York: Wiley.

Luce, R. D., and P. Suppes, 1965. "Preference, Utility and Subjective Probability," in *Handbook of Mathematical Psychology*, Vol. 3 (R. D. Luce et al., Eds.), pp. 249–410. New York: Wiley.

Luenberger D., 1969. *Optimization by Vector Space Methods*. New York: Wiley.

Magee, S., W. Brock, and L. Young, 1989. *Black Hole Tariffs and Endogenous Policy Theory*. Cambridge University Press.

Marschak, J., 1960. "Binary-Choice Constraints and Random Utility Indicators," in *Mathematical Methods in the Social Sciences* (K. Arrow et al., Eds.), pp. 312–29. Stanford: Stanford University Press.

Matthews, S., 1979. "A Simple Direction Model of Electoral Competition," *Public Choice*, 34, 142–56.

Matthews, S., 1980. "Pairwise Symmetry Conditions for Voting Equilibria," *International Journal of Game Theory*, 9, 141–56.

Matthews, S., 1982. "Local Simple Games in Public Choice Mechanisms," *International Economic Review*, 23, 623–45.

Matthews, S., 1989. "Veto Threats: Rhetoric in a Bargaining Game," *Quarterly Journal of Economics*, 114, 347–69.

Mayston, D., 1974. *The Idea of Social Choice*. London: Macmillan.

McFadden, D., 1974. "Conditional Logit Analysis of Qualitative Choice Behavior," in *Frontiers of Econometrics* (P. Zarembka, Ed.), pp. 105–42. New York: Academic Press.

McFadden, D., 1976. "Quantal Choice Analysis: A Survey," *Annals of Economic and Social Measurement*, 5, 363–90.

McFadden, D., 1978. "Modeling the Choice of Residential Location," in *Spatial Interaction Theory and Residential Location* (A. Karlquist et al., Eds.), pp. 75–96. Amsterdam: North-Holland.

McFadden, D., 1981. "Econometric Models of Probabilistic Choice," in *Structural Analysis of Discrete Data* (C. Manski and D. McFadden, Eds.), pp. 198–272. Cambridge: MIT Press.

McFadden, D., 1982. "Qualitative Response Models," in *Advances in Econometrics* (W. Hildenbrand, Ed.), pp. 1–37. Cambridge: Cambridge University Press.

McGuire, C. B., and R. Radner, 1986. "Preface to the Second Edition," in *Decision and Organization*, 2nd ed. (C. B. McGuire and R. Radner, Eds.), pp. vii–xxiv. Minneapolis: University of Minnesota Press.

McKelvey, R., 1975. "Policy Related Voting and Electoral Equilibria," *Econometrica*, 43, 815–44.

McKelvey, R., 1976. "Intransitivities in Multidimensional Voting Models and Some Implications for Agenda Control," *Journal of Economic Theory*, 12, 472–82.

McKelvey, R., 1979. "General Conditions for Global Intransitivities in Formal Voting Models," *Econometrica*, 47, 1085–112.

McKelvey, R., 1980. "Ambiguity in Spatial Models of Policy Formation," *Public Choice*, 35, 385–402.

McKelvey, R., 1986. "Covering, Dominance, and Institution Free Properties of Social Choice," *American Journal of Political Science*, 30, 283–314.

McKelvey, R., and P. Ordeshook, 1976. "Symmetric Spatial Games Without Majority Rule Equilibria," *American Political Science Review*, 70, 1172–84.

McKelvey, R., and P. Ordeshook, 1984. "Rational Expectations in Elections: Some Experimental Results Based on a Multidimensional Model," *Public Choice*, 44, 61–102.

McKelvey, R., and P. Ordeshook, 1985a. "Elections with Limited Information: A Fulfilled Expectations Model Using Contemporaneous Poll and Endorsement Data as Information Sources," *Journal of Economic Theory*, 36, 55–85.

McKelvey, R., and P. Ordeshook, 1985b. "Sequential Elections with Limited Information," *American Journal of Political Science*, 29, 480–512.

McKelvey, R., and P. Ordeshook, 1986. "Sequential Elections with Limited Information," *Social Choice and Welfare*, 3, 199–211.

McKelvey, R., and P. Ordeshook, 1987. "Elections with Limited Information: A Multidimensional Model," *Mathematical Social Sciences*, 14, 77–99.

McKelvey, R., and P. Ordeshook, 1990. "A Decade of Experimental Research on Spatial Models of Elections and Committees," in *Advances in the Spatial Theory of Voting* (J. Enelow and M. Hinich, Eds.), pp. 99–144. Cambridge University Press.

McKelvey, R., P. Ordeshook, and P. Ungar, 1980. "Conditions for Voting Equilibria in Continuous Voter Distributions," *SIAM Journal of Applied Mathematics*, 39, 161–8.

McKelvey, R., and J. Richelson, 1974. "Cycles of Risk," *Public Choice*, 18, 41–66.

McKelvey, R., and N. Schofield, 1986. "Structural Instability of the Core," *Journal of Mathematical Economics*, 15, 179–98.

McKelvey, R., and N. Schofield, 1987. "Generalized Symmetry Conditions at a Core Point," *Econometrica*, 55, 923–33.

McKelvey, R., and R. Wendell, 1976. "Voting Equilibria in Multidimensional Choice Spaces," *Mathematics of Operations Research*, 1, 144–58.

Meltzer, A., and S. Richard, 1981. "A Rational Theory of the Size of Government," *Journal of Political Economy*, 89, 914–27.

Meltzer, A., and S. Richard, 1983. "Tests of a Rational Theory of the Size of Government," *Public Choice*, 41, 403–18.

Milgrom, P., and J. Roberts, 1982. "Predation, Reputation and Entry Deterrence," *Journal of Economic Theory*, 27, 280–312.

Miller, N., 1987. "Voting," in *The New Palgrave: A Dictionary of Economics*, Vol. 4 (J. Eatwell et al., Eds.), pp. 826–30. London: Macmillan.

Mitchell, D., 1987. "Candidate Behavior under Mixed Motives," *Social Choice and Welfare*, 4, 153–60.

Morton, R., 1987. "A Group Majority Voting Model of Public Good Provision," *Social Choice and Welfare*, 4, 117–31.

Moulin, H., 1982. *Game Theory for the Social Sciences* (2nd ed. 1986). New York: New York University Press.

Moulin, H., 1983. *The Strategy of Social Choice*. Amsterdam: North-Holland.

Moulin, H., 1988. *Axioms for Cooperative Decision Making*. Cambridge University Press.

Mueller, D., 1976. "Public Choice: A Survey," *Journal of Economic Literature*, 14, 395–433.

Mueller, D., 1979. *Public Choice*. Cambridge University Press.

Mueller, D., 1982. "Redistribution, Growth, and Political Stability," *American Economic Review, Papers and Proceedings*, 72, 155–9.

Mueller, D., 1983. "The Political Economy of Growth and Redistribution," in *The Political Economy of Growth* (D. Mueller, Ed.), pp. 261–76. New Haven: Yale University Press.

Mueller, D., 1986. "Rational Egoism Versus Adaptive Egoism as a Fundamental Postulate for a Descriptive Theory of Human Behavior," *Public Choice*, 51, 3–23.

Mueller, D., 1989a. *Public Choice, II*. Cambridge University Press.

Mueller, D., 1989b. "Probabilistic Majority Rule," *Kyklos*, 42, 151–70.

Mueller, D., 1990. "Representative Government and Probabilistic Majority Rule," working paper, University of Maryland at College Park.

Mueller, D., and P. Murrell, 1985. "Interest Groups and the Political Economy of Government Size," in *Public Expenditure and Government Growth* (F. Forte and A. Peacock, Eds.), pp. 13–36. Oxford: Basil Blackwell.

Mueller, D., and G. Von Furstenberg, 1971. "The Pareto Optimal Approach to Income Redistribution: A Fiscal Application," *American Economic Review*, 61, 628–37.

Myerson, R., and R. Weber, 1990. "A Theory of Voting Equilibria," working paper, Northwestern University.

Nakamura, K., 1979. "The Vetoers in a Simple Game with Ordinal Preference," *International Journal of Game Theory*, 8, 55–61.

Oates, W., 1985. "The Public Sector in Economics: An Analytical Chameleon," in *Public Sector and Political Economy Today* (H. Hanusch et al., Eds.), pp. 45–58. New York: Gustav, Fischer Verlag.

Olson, M., 1965. *The Logic of Collective Action*. Cambridge: Harvard University Press.

Olson, M., 1982. *The Rise and Decline of Nations: Economic Growth, Stagflation, and Social Rigidities*. New Haven: Yale University Press.

Olson, M., 1986, "A Theory of the Incentives Facing Political Organizations: Neo-Corporatism and the Hegemonic State," *International Political Science Review*, 7, 165–89.

Ordeshook, P., 1970. "Extensions to a Model of the Electoral Process and Implications for the Theory of Responsible Parties," *Midwest Journal of Political Science*, 14, 43–70.

Ordeshook, P., 1971. "Pareto Optimality and Electoral Competition," *American Political Science Review*, 65, 1141–5.

Ordeshook, P., 1976. "The Spatial Theory of Elections: A Review and a Critique," in *Party Identification and Beyond* (I. Brudge et al., Eds.), pp. 285–313. New York: Wiley.

Ordeshook, P., 1986. *Game Theory and Political Theory*. Cambridge University Press.

Ordeshook, P., 1987. "Public Opinion Polls and Democratic Processes: A Comment," *Journal of the American Statistical Association*, 82, 486–91.

Ostrom, E., 1986. "An Agenda for the Study of Institutions," *Public Choice*, 48, 3–23.

Ostrom, E., and V. Ostrom, 1971. "Public Choice: A Different Approach to the Study of Public Administration," *Public Administration Review*, 31, 203–16.

Owen, G., 1982. *Game Theory*, 2nd ed. New York: Academic Press.

Palfrey, T., 1984. "Spatial Equilibrium with Entry," *Review of Economic Studies*, 51, 139–56.

Pattanaik, P., 1978. "A Note on Democratic Decision and the Existence of Choice Sets," *Review of Economic Studies*, 35, 1–9.

Pattanaik, P., 1970a. "Sufficient Conditions for the Existence of a Choice Set Under Majority Rule," *Econometrica*, 38, 165–70.

Pattanaik, P., 1970b. "On Social Choice with Quasitransitive Individual Preferences," *Journal of Economic Theory*, 2, 267–75.

Pattanaik, P., 1971. *Voting and Collective Choice*. Cambridge University Press.

Pattanaik, P., and M. Sengupta, 1974. "Conditions for Transitive and Quasi-Transitive Majority Decisions," *Economica*, 44, 414–23.

Peltzman, S., 1976. "Toward a More General Theory of Regulation," *Journal of Law and Economics*, 59, 211–40.

Peltzman, S., 1980. "The Growth of Government," *Journal of Law and Economics*, 23, 209–87.

Peltzman, S., 1987. "Economic Conditions and Gubernatorial Elections," *American Economic Review, Papers and Proceedings*, 77, 293–7.

Plott, C., 1967. "A Notion of Equilibrium and Its Possibility Under Majority Rule," *American Economic Review*, 57, 787–806.

Plott, C., 1971. "Recent Results in the Theory of Voting," in *Frontiers of Quantitative Economics, I* (M. Intriligator, Ed.), pp. 109–27. Amsterdam: North-Holland.

Plott, C., 1976. "Axiomatic Social Choice Theory: An Overview and Interpretation," *American Journal of Political Science*, 20, 511–96.

Pratt, J., 1964. "Risk Aversion in the Small and in the Large," *Econometrica*, 32, 122–36.

Reed, W. R., 1990. "Retrospective Versus Prospective Voting," working paper, Texas A&M University.

Riker, W., 1962. *The Theory of Political Coalitions*. New Haven: Yale University Press.

Riker, W., 1982a. "Implications from the Disequilibrium of Majority Rule for the Study of Institutions," in *Political Equilibrium* (P. Ordeshook and K. Shepsle, Eds.), pp. 3–24. Boston: Kluwer-Nijhoff.

Riker, W., 1982b. *Liberalism Against Populism: A Confrontation Between the Theory of Democracy and the Theory of Social Choice*. New York: Freeman.

Riker, W., 1986. *The Art of Political Manipulation*. New Haven: Yale University Press.

Riker, W., 1990. "Heresthetic and Rhetoric in the Spatial Model," in *Advances in the Spatial Theory of Voting* (J. Enelow and M. Hinich, Eds.), pp. 46–65. Cambridge University Press.

Riker, W., and P. Ordeshook, 1973. *An Introduction to Positive Political Theory*. Englewood Cliffs: Prentice-Hall.

Roberts, A., and D. Varberg, 1973. *Convex Functions*. New York: Academic Press.

Roberts, F., 1979. *Measurement Theory*, Vol. 7 in the *Encyclopedia of Mathematics and its Applications* (G. Rota, Ed.), Reading: Addison-Wesley.

Roberts, K., 1977. "Voting Over Income Tax Schedules," *Journal of Public Economics*, 8, 329–40.

Roberts, R., 1984. "A Positive Model of Private Charity and Public Transfers," *Journal of Political Economy*, 92, 136–48.

Roberts, R., 1985. "A Taxonomy of Public Provision," *Public Choice*, 47, 267–303.

Romer, T., 1975. "Individual Welfare, Majority Voting and the Properties of a Linear Income Tax," *Journal of Public Economics*, 4, 163–85.

Romer, T., 1977. "Majority Voting on Tax Parameters: Some Further Results," *Journal of Public Economics*, 7, 127–33.

Romer, T., and H. Rosenthal, 1978. "Political Resource Allocation, Controlled Agenda and the Status Quo," *Public Choice*, 33, 27–44.

Romer, T., and H. Rosenthal, 1979. "Bureaucrats Versus Voters: On the Political Economy of Resource Allocation by Direct Democracy," *Quarterly Journal of Economics*, 93, 563–87.

Romer, T., and H. Rosenthal, 1984. "Voting Models and Empirical Evidence," *American Scientist*, 72, 465–73.

Rosenthal, H., 1990. "The Setter Model," in *Advances in the Spatial Theory of Voting* (J. Enelow and M. Hinich, Eds.), pp. 199–234. Cambridge University Press.

Rubenstein, A., 1979. "A Note About the 'Nowhere Denseness' of Societies Having an Equilibrium Under Majority Rule," *Econometrica*, 47, 511–14.

Samuelson, L., 1984. "Electoral Equilibria with Restricted Strategies," *Public Choice*, 43, 307–27.

Samuelson, L., 1985. "On the Independence from Irrelevant Alternatives in Probabilistic Choice Models," *Journal of Economic Theory*, 35, 376–89.

Samuelson, P., 1947. *Foundations of Economic Analysis*. Cambridge: Harvard University Press.

Samuelson, P., 1971. "Maximum Principles in Analytical Economics," in *Les Prix Nobel en 1970*, pp. 273–88. Stockholm: Nobel Foundation.

Schofield, N., 1978a. "Instability of Simple Dynamic Games," *Review of Economic Studies*, 45, 575–94.

Schofield, N., 1978b. "The Theory of Dynamic Games," in *Game Theory and Political Science* (P. Ordeshook, Ed.), pp. 113–64. New York: New York University Press.

Schofield, N., 1980, "Generic Properties of Simple Bergson-Samuelson Welfare Functions," *Journal of Mathematical Economics*, 7, 175–92.

Schofield, N., 1983a. "Generic Instability of Majority Rule," *Review of Economic Studies*, 50, 695–705.

Schofield, N., 1983b. "Equilibria in Simple Dynamic Games," in *Social Choice and Welfare* (P. Pattanaik and M. Salles, Eds.), pp. 269–84. Amsterdam: North-Holland.

Schofield, N., 1984a. "Classification Theorem for Smooth Social Choice on a Manifold," *Social Choice and Welfare*, 1, 187–210.

Schofield, N., 1984b. "Social Equilibrium and Cycles on Compact Sets," *Journal of Economic Theory*, 33, 59–71.

Schofield, N., 1985. *Social Choice and Democracy*. Berlin: Springer-Verlag.

Schofield, N., 1986. "Existence of a 'Structurally Stable' Equilibrium for a Non-Collegial Voting Rule," *Public Choice*, 51, 267–84.

Schofield, N., 1989. "Smooth Social Choice," *Mathematical and Computer Modelling*, 12, 417–35.

Schwartz, T., 1986. *The Logic of Collective Choice.* New York: Columbia University Press.

Selten, R., 1971. "Anwendungen der Spieltheorie auf die Politische Wissenschaft," in *Politik und Wissenschaft* (H. Maier et al., Eds.), pp. 287–320. Munich: Beck.

Sen, A., 1966. "A Possibility Theorem on Majority Decisions," *Econometrica,* 34, 491–9.

Sen, A., 1969a. "Quasi-Transitivity, Rational Choice and Collective Decisions," *Review of Economic Studies,* 36, 381–93.

Sen, A., 1969b. "Planners' Preferences: Optimality, Distribution and Social Welfare," in *Public Economics* (J. Margolis and H. Guitton, Eds.), pp. 201–21. London: Macmillan.

Sen, A., 1970. *Collective Choice and Social Welfare.* San Francisco: Holden-Dav

Sen, A., 1973. *On Economic Inequality.* Oxford: Clarendon.

Sen, A., 1974. "Rawls versus Bentham: An Axiomatic Examination of the Pure Redistribution Problem," *Theory and Decision,* 4, 301–10.

Sen, A., 1977a. "Social Choice Theory: A Re-examination," *Econometrica,* 45, 53–89.

Sen, A., 1977b. "On Weights and Measures: Informational Constraints in Social Welfare Analysis," *Econometrica,* 45, 1539–72.

Sen, A., 1986. "Social Choice Theory," in *Handbook of Mathematical Economics,* Vol. III (K. Arrow and M. Intriligator, Eds.), pp. 1073–1181. New York: North-Holland.

Sen, A., 1987. "Social Choice," in *The New Palgrave: A Dictionary of Economics,* Vol. 4 (J. Eatwell et al., Eds.), pp. 382–93. London: Macmillan.

Sen, A., and P. Pattanaik, 1969. "Necessary and Sufficient Conditions for Rational Choice Under Majority Decision," *Journal of Economic Theory,* 1, 178–202.

Shepsle, K., 1970. "A Note on Zeckhauser's 'Majority Rule with Lotteries on Alternatives': The Case of the Paradox of Voting," *Quarterly Journal of Economics,* 84, 705–9.

Shepsle, K., 1972a. "Parties, Voters, and the Risk Environment: A Mathematical Treatment of Electoral Competition Under Uncertainty," in *Probability Models of Collective Decision Making* (R. Niemi and H. Weisberg, Eds.), pp. 273–97. Columbus: Merrill.

Shepsle, K., 1972b. "The Strategy of Ambiguity: Uncertainty and Electoral Competition," *American Political Science Review,* 66, 555–68.

Shepsle, K., 1972c. "The Paradox of Voting and Uncertainty," in *Probability Models of Collective Decision Making* (R. Niemi and H. Weisberg, Eds.), pp. 252–70. Columbus: Merrill.

Shepsle, K., 1974. "Theories of Collective Choice," in *Political Science Annual,* Vol. 5 (C. Cotter, Ed.), pp. 1–87. Indianapolis: Bobbs-Merrill.

Shepsle, K., 1979a. "The Role of Institutional Structure in the Creation of Policy Equilibrium," in *Public Policy and Public Choice* (D. Rae and T. Eismeier, Eds.), pp. 249–81. London: Sage.

Shepsle, K., 1979b. "Institutional Arrangements and Equilibrium in Multidimensional Models," *American Journal of Political Science*, 23, 27–59.

Shepsle, K., 1986a. "Institutional Equilibrium and Equilibrium Institutions," in *Political Science: The Science of Politics* (H. Weisberg, Ed.), pp. 51–81. New York: Agathon Press.

Shepsle, K., 1986b. "The Positive Theory of Legislative Institutions: An Enrichment of Social Choice and Spatial Models," *Public Choice*, 50, 135–78.

Shepsle, K., and R. Cohen, 1990. "Multiparty Competition, Entry, and Entry Deterrence in Spatial Models of Elections," in *Advances in the Spatial Theory of Voting* (J. Enelow and M. Hinich, Eds.), pp. 12–45. Cambridge University Press.

Shepsle, K., and B. Weingast, 1981a. "Political Preferences for the Pork Barrel: A Generalization," *American Journal of Political Science*, 25, 96–112.

Shepsle, K., and B. Weingast, 1981b. "Structure-induced Equilibrium and Legislative Choice," *Public Choice*, 36, 221–37.

Shepsle, K., and B. Weingast, 1984. "Political Solutions to Market Problems," *American Political Science Review*, 78, 417–34.

Shepsle, K., and B. Weingast, 1987. "The Institutional Foundations of Committee Power," *American Political Science Review*, 81, 85–104.

Shubik, M., 1968. "A Two Party System, General Equilibrium, and the Voters' Paradox," *Zeitschrift fur National-Okonomie*, 28, 341–54.

Shubik, M., 1971. "Voting or a Price System in a Competitive Market Structure," *American Political Science Review*, 65, 1141–5.

Shubik, M., 1984. *A Game-Theoretic Approach to Political Economy*. Cambridge: MIT Press.

Sjoblom, K., 1985. "Voting for Social Security," *Public Choice*, 45, 533–44.

Sloss, J., 1973. "Stable Outcomes in Majority Voting Games," *Public Choice*, 15, 19–48.

Slutsky, S., 1977. "A Voting Model for the Allocation of Public Goods: Existence of an Equilibrium," *Journal of Economic Theory*, 14, 299–325.

Slutsky, S., 1979. "Equilibrium Under α-Majority Voting," *Econometrica*, 47, 1113–25.

Slutsky, S., 1986. "Elections with Incomplete Information: Comments on the Papers of Coughlin and Ferejohn," *Public Choice*, 50, 105–29.

Smithies, A., 1941. "Optimum Location in Spatial Competition," *Journal of Political Economy*, 49, 423–39.

Snyder, J., 1989. "Election Goals and the Allocation of Campaign Resources," *Econometrica*, 57, 637–60.

Snyder, J., 1990. "Resource Allocation in Multiparty Elections," *American Journal of Political Science*, 34, 59–73.

Snyder, J., and G. Kramer, 1988. "Fairness, Self-Interest, and the Politics of the Progressive Income Tax," *Journal of Public Economics*, 36, 197–230.

Stigler, G., 1970. "Director's Law of Public Income Redistribution," *Journal of Law and Economics*, 13, 1–10.

Stigler, G., 1972. "Economic Competition and Political Competition," *Public Choice*, 8, 91–106.

Stigler, G., 1973. "General Economic Conditions and National Elections," *American Economic Review, Papers and Proceedings*, 63, 160–7.

Stigler, G., 1975. *The Citizen and the State*. Chicago: University of Chicago Press.

Stigler, G., 1983. "The Process and Progress of Economics," in *Les Prix Nobel en 1982*, pp. 253–66. Stockholm: Nobel Foundation.

Storcken, T., 1987. "Some Social Choice Problems," in *Surveys in Game Theory and Related Topics* (H. Peters and O. Vrieze, Eds.), pp. 307–30. Amsterdam: Centre for Mathematics and Computer Science.

Strauss, D., 1985. "Luce's Choice Axiom and Generalizations," in *Encyclopedia of Statistical Sciences*, Vol. 5 (S. Kotz and N. Johnson, Eds.), pp. 167–70. New York: Wiley.

Strnad, J., 1985. "The Structure of Continuous-Valued Neutral Monotonic Social Functions," *Social Choice and Welfare*, 2, 181–95.

Sydsaeter, K., 1981. *Topics in Mathematical Analysis for Economists*. New York: Academic Press.

Taylor, M., 1971. "Review Article: Mathematical Political Theory," *British Journal of Political Science*, 1, 339–82.

Taylor, M., 1975. "The Theory of Collective Choice," in *Handbook of Political Science*, Vol. 3 (F. Greenstein and N. Polsby, Eds.), pp. 413–81. Reading: Addison-Wesley.

Tullock, G., 1967a. "The General Irrelevance of the General Impossibility Theorem," *Quarterly Journal of Economics*, 81, 256–70.

Tullock, G., 1967b. *Toward a Mathematics of Politics*. Ann Arbor: University of Michigan Press.

Tullock, G., 1971. "The Charity of the Uncharitable," *Western Economic Journal*, 9, 379–92.

Tullock, G., 1981a. "Why So Much Stability?," *Public Choice*, 37, 189–202.

Tullock, G., 1981b. "The Rhetoric and Reality of Redistribution," *Southern Economic Journal*, 47, 895–907.

Tullock, G., 1983. *Economics of Income Redistribution*. Boston: Kluwer-Nijhoff.

Valentine, F., 1964. *Convex Sets*. New York: McGraw-Hill.

van den Doel, H., 1979. *Democracy and Welfare Economics*. Cambridge University Press.

Von Neumann, J., and O. Morgenstern, 1944, 1947 (2nd ed.), 1953 (3rd ed.). *The Theory of Games and Economic Behavior*. Princeton: Princeton University Press.

Von Weizsacker, C., 1972. "Kenneth Arrow's Contribution to Economics," *Swedish Journal of Economics*, 74, 488–502.

Ward, B., 1961. "Majority Rule and Allocation," *Journal of Conflict Resolution*, 5, 379–89.

Ward, B., 1965. "Majority Voting and Alternative Forms of Public Enterprise," in *The Public Economy of Urban Community* (J. Margolis, Ed.), pp. 112–26. Baltimore: Johns Hopkins University Press.

Weingast, B., 1989. "Floor Behavior in Congress: Committee Power Under the Open Rule," *American Political Science Review*, 83, 795–815.

Weingast, B., and M. Moran, 1983. "Bureaucratic Discretion or Congressional

Control? Reguiatory Policymaking by the Federal Trade Commission," *Journal of Political Economy*, 91, 765–800.

Weingast, B., K. Shepsle, and C. Johnsen, 1981. "The Political Economy of Benefits and Costs: A Neoclassical Approach to Distributive Politics," *Journal of Political Economy*, 89, 642–65.

Weintraub, E. R., 1982. *Mathematics for Economists*. Cambridge University Press.

Wendell, R., and S. Thorson, 1974. "Some Generalizations of Social Decisions Under Majority Rule," *Econometrica*, 42, 893–912.

Wicksell, K., 1896. "A New Principle of Just Taxation," *Finanztheoretische Untersuchungen*, Jena.

Wittman, D., 1973. "Parties as Utility Maximizers," *American Political Science Review*, 66, 490–5.

Wittman, D., 1975. "Political Decision Making," in *Economics of Public Choice* (R. Leiter and G. Sirkin, Eds.), pp. 29–48. New York: Cyrco Press.

Wittman, D., 1977. "Candidates with Policy Preferences: A Dynamic Model," *Journal of Economic Theory*, 14, 180–9.

Wittman, D., 1983. "Candidate Motivation: A Synthesis of Alternative Theories," *American Political Science Review*, 77, 142–57.

Wittman, D., 1984. "Multicandidate Equilibria," *Public Choice*, 43, 287–91.

Wittman, D., 1987. "Elections with N Voters, M Candidates and K Issues," in *The Logic of Multiparty Systems* (M. Holler, Ed.), pp. 129–34. Dordrecht: Martinus Nijoff.

Wittman, D., 1989a. "Pressure Group Size and the Politics of Income Redistribution," *Social Choice and Welfare*, 6, 275–86.

Wittman, D., 1989b. "Why Democracies Produce Efficient Outcomes," *Journal of Political Economy*, 99, 1395–424.

Wittman, D., 1990. "Spatial Strategies When Candidates Have Policy Preferences," in *Advances in the Spatial Theory of Voting* (J. Enelow and M. Hinich, Eds.), pp. 66–98. Cambridge University Press.

Zeckhauser, R., 1969. "Majority Rule with Lotteries on Alternatives," *Quarterly Journal of Economics*, 83, 696–703.

Index

For EU product safety concerns, contact us at Calle de José Abascal, 56–1°,
28003 Madrid, Spain or eugpsr@cambridge.org.

www.ingramcontent.com/pod-product-compliance
Ingram Content Group UK Ltd.
Pitfield, Milton Keynes, MK11 3LW, UK
UKHW010038140625
459647UK00012BA/1456